KT-469-508

CAMBRIDGE STUDIES IN AMERICAN LITERATURE
AND CULTURE

Editor

Eric Sundquist, University of California, Los Angeles

Founding Editor

Albert Gelpi, Stanford University

Advisory Board

Nina Baym, University of Illinois, Urbana–Champaign
Sacvan Bercovitch, Harvard University
Albert Gelpi, Stanford University
Myra Jehlen, Rutgers University
Carolyn Porter, University of California, Berkeley
Robert Stepto, Yale University
Tony Tanner, King's College, Cambridge University

WRITING AMERICA BLACK

RACE RHETORIC IN THE PUBLIC SPHERE

C. K. DORESKI

CAMBRIDGE
UNIVERSITY PRESS

PUBLISHED BY THE PRESS SYNDICATE OF THE UNIVERSITY OF CAMBRIDGE
The Pitt Building, Trumpington Street, Cambridge CB2 1RP, United Kingdom

CAMBRIDGE UNIVERSITY PRESS
The Edinburgh Building, Cambridge CB2 2RU, UK   http://www.cup.cam.ac.uk
40 West 20th Street, New York, NY 10011-4211, USA   http://www.cup.org
10 Stamford Road, Oakleigh, Melbourne 3166, Australia

© C. K. Doreski 1998

First published 1998

Printed in the United States of America

Typeface New Baskerville 10.5/13 pt.   *System* Quark XPress™ [CS]

*A catalog record for this book is available from
the British Library*

Library of Congress Cataloging-in-Publication Data

Doreski, Carole
Writing America Black : race rhetoric in the public sphere / C.K. Doreski
p.   cm. – (Cambridge studies in American literature and culture)
ISBN 0-521-56415-8 (hb). – ISBN 0-521-56462-X (pb)
1. American literature – Afro-American authors – History and criticism. 2.
Rhetoric – Political aspects – United States. 3. English language – United
States – Rhetoric. 4. Rhetoric – Social aspects – United States. 5. Afro-Americans – Com-
munication. 6. Afro-American press. I. Title. II. Series.
PS153.N5D597   1998
813.9'896073 – dc2   198–3701
                                    CIP

ISBN 0 521 56415 8 hardback
0 521 56462 x paperback

Page 301 constitutes a continuation of the copyright page.

WRITING AMERICA BLACK

Race Rhetoric in the Public Sphere

Writing
ed lite
histori
reveals
Rich in
interes
Americ

C. K.
(1993
and lit
zenshi
under
for the

In memory of my father –
and for Bill

White man, hear me! History, as nearly no one seems to know, is not merely something to be read. And it does not refer merely, or even principally, to the past. On the contrary, the great force of history comes from the fact that we carry it within us, are unconsciously controlled by it in many ways, and history is literally *present* in all that we do. It could scarcely be otherwise, since it is to history that we owe our frames of reference, our identities, and our aspirations. And it is with great pain and terror that one begins to realize this. In great pain and terror one begins to assess the history which has placed one where one is and formed one's point of view. In great pain and terror because, therefore, one enters into battle with that historical creation, Oneself, and attempts to recreate oneself according to a principle more humane and more liberating; one begins the attempt to achieve a level of personal maturity and freedom which robs history of its tyrannical power, and also changes history.

But, obviously, I am speaking as an historical creation which has had bitterly to contest its history, to wrestle with it, and finally accept it in order to bring myself out of it.

—James Baldwin, "White Man's Guilt"
(*Ebony*, August 1965)

CONTENTS

PREFACE

Negro weeklies make no pretense at being newspapers in the strict sense of the term. They have a more important mission than the dissemination of mere news. . . . They are race papers. They are organs of propaganda. Their chief business is to stimulate thought among Negroes about the things that vitally concern them.

> – James Weldon Johnson, "Do You Read Negro Papers?"
> (*New York Age*, October 22, 1914)

Writing America Black resurveys Walter Lippmann's "American Century of public opinion" from the perspective of African Americans committed to what W. E. B. Du Bois called "the real needs of the people,"[1] the actualization of democracy, and the authentication of the historical record. Americanism for these native sons and daughters meant a destabilizing, institutionally enforced signification subject to revision or erasure in the black independent press. Paradoxically, in the spirit of Thomas Jefferson's revolutionary conception of "the people as the only censors" and Walt Whitman's concern that "a true poem" be as realistic as "the daily newspaper," writers for the black press assumed that the "true principles" of government were located in the public sphere – and that community news, with its unrestrained airing of dissensus, was instrumental in the construction of authentic race narratives.[2]

As Houston Baker explains in "Critical Memory and the Black Public Sphere" (1994: 13–14):

Black Americans arrived on New World shores precisely as *property* belonging to the bourgeoisie. They were strategically and rigorously prevented from acquiring literacy. And they were defined by Thomas Jefferson and his compeers among America's Founding Fathers, as devoid of even a germ in their minds that might be mistaken for reason. Historically, therefore, nothing might seem less realistic, attractive or believable to black Americans than the notion of a black public sphere. Unless, of course, such a notion was meant to symbolize a strangely distorting chiasma [*sic*]: a separate and inverted opposite of a historically imagined white rationality in action. . . .

Yet, it is exactly because black Americans have so aptly read this flip side that they are attracted to a historically imagined "better time" of reason. They are drawn to the possibilities of structurally and affectively transforming the founding notion of the bourgeois public sphere into an expressive and empowering self-fashioning.

Fully rational human beings with abundant cultural resources, black Americans have always situated their unique forms of expressive publicity in a complex set of relationships to other forms of American publicity (meaning here, paradoxically enough, the sense of publicity as authority).

Such intertextualities reweave America's national narrative.

Because black national representation both mediates and is mediated by the nation as a whole, I begin at a moment of constitutional crisis when renewed affirmation of African-American citizenship was necessitated by the erosive contingencies of *Plessy v. Ferguson* (1896). This study explores the sites of several such definitional crises for the black America that located community and national identity in a public sphere employing what Houston Baker identifies as the "twin rhetorics of *nostalgia* and *critical memory*." These rhetorics combine a "purposive construction of a past filled with golden virtues, golden men, and sterling events" with the "cumulative, collective maintenance of a record that draws into relationship significant instants of time past and the always uprooted homelessness of now" (1994: 7).[3] *Writing America Black* investigates the ways in which these representational encounters between imagined communities (what T. S. Eliot identified as the "fluctuating circle of loyalties between the centre of the family and the local community, and the periphery of humanity entire" [1934, 21]) construct not simply the news of the day but history and literature as well. The allegorical capacities of history invest news with a nationalizing force. Consequently, representational practices reflect the centrality not marginality of African-American experience as they recast past events in the predication of a fully realized citizenship. Aware of, though ultimately indifferent to, the "pastness of the past" that Eliot found central to the concept of "tradition," *Writing America Black* responds to the literal presence of the history James Baldwin made the contestatory grounds of his essay for *Ebony* magazine, "White Man's Guilt" (1965). "The combativeness with which individuals and institutions decide what is tradition and what is not, what relevant and what not," which Edward Said finds essential in formulating tradition, aptly defines the contentious self-fashioning of the black independent press (1993: 4).

In whatever form – genealogical traces, news events, histories, memorializations – African-American history and tradition as concepts grew ex nihilo. Contending with what Orlando Patterson has termed the "social death of slavery," black Americans learned the importance of a legitimate social identity accomplished through the authority of naming and its associated control over the resultant genealogical and historical record. Because of the perpetually reconstructive (and therefore often adversarial) nature of their project, these witnesses relied upon collective memory and ephemeral media to a greater extent than did mainstream historians.

In the twentieth century, African-American historians (a category intended to embrace writers engaged in the construction of a viable historical record) endeavored to fill in the blanks left by white historians. They seemed to respond to Ezra Pound's modernist recollection – "And even I can remember / A day when the historians left blanks in their writings, / I mean for things they didn't know" ("Canto 13"). The Poundian historical project, however, not only presumed the existence of a master text, but also assumed authority over those "blanks in their writings." Such confidence and largesse were impossible for black Americans constructing their family, racial, and cultural histories. For them, history entailed a coinspiriting world of document and creation where the discourses of what we conventionally label "news," "history," and "literature" coalesce into an African-American narrative of history and nation that became what Baldwin called in "White Man's Guilt" a "disagreeable mirror" (410). It also involved the destabilizing presence of memory.

For more than a decade, cultural historians, led by Pierre Nora, have seriously investigated the role of memory in the historical process. Nora's concept of "lieux de mémoire" is instructive here; as he explains, sites of memory exist "where memory crystallizes and secretes itself at a particular moment, a turning point where consciousness of a break with the past is bound up with the sense that memory has been torn – but torn in such a way as to pose the problem of the embodiment of memory in certain sites where a sense of historical continuity persists" (1989: 7). Nora's suggestive mobilization of memory has prompted scholars to seriously consider it as an agent in the formation of history, tradition, and national identity. The Geneviève Fabre and Robert O'Meally anthology, *History and Memory in African-American Culture* (1994), and Michael Kammen's *Mystic Chords of Memory: The Transformation of Tradition in American Culture* (1991) are two of the most impressive products of this approach. Such transnational scholarship has inspired the terms of my investigation – history, narrative, commemoration – and provided its means of periodization.

Writing America Black reconstructs the racial memory of the twentieth century from the perspective of African-American writers committed to deconstructing the received national narrative (Americanization institutionally enforced by church, school, military, and other such agencies of socialization) in order to build a more perfect historical record. Though examples of this subtextual insubordination may be found throughout the century, they are dramatically foregrounded in what James Baldwin has characterized as "time[s] of stress . . . dangerous situation[s]" for the "great, vast, shining Republic" (1985a: 24). And so my study of black linguistic claims to the public sphere organizes itself around the nation's wars, foreign and domestic, hoping to capture what Elaine Scarry has called "the making and unmaking of the world." Wars, as Scarry notes, produce a referential instability, a "juxtaposition of injured bodies and unanchored issues," that is subsequently expressed in a "vocabulary of cost" and a "vocabulary of injury" (1985: chap. 2). The traumata of such moments are at least ideologically relieved by the liberating effect they have upon cycles of national identification, confirming Langston Hughes's conclusion that "a nation is never so alert and alive as when it is a nation at war" (1958: 498).

Wars in the twentieth century, "the first century of world wars,"[4] from the Spanish-American War to Vietnam, have occasioned some of the most profound articulations of Americanism, national purpose, and historical identity from the African-American community. War's "fundamental role in stimulating, defining, justifying, periodizing, and eventually filtering American memories and traditions," as Michael Kammen explains (1991: 13), has a poignant significance for those suffering erasure from those very definitions, justifications, and periodizations. Because of the very referential instability that threatens established national narratives or historical scenarios, counterdiscourses form, enabling, in Michel Foucault's terms, an oppressed minority "to speak on its own behalf" (1978–88: 1.101). Even at the oppositional extreme of a subnational construction like black nationalism, the textual field cleared by these lapses in national coherence discloses a fervent belief in constitutional rights and declarations of independence.

The internal and domestic complement of war is riot, and such moments of civil disturbance and (in the words of the Kerner Commission Report) "socially-directed violence" contribute to the structural organization of the study. I retain the contested term "riot" rather than its representational translations, "rebellion" or "insurrection," because of the word's broadly referential value (in the language of the report-writing official as well as the artist appropriating and destabilizing the concept) and its etymological weight. Riot as public disturbance conveys the meaning at risk for Charles Johnson's official study of the 1919 riot, *The Negro in Chicago* (1922), as well as Gwendolyn Brooks's redactive vision in "Riot": "Because the 'Negroes' were coming down the street" (1969: 470). Since we are unable to rest in the memory time that Sterling Brown identifies in "An Old Woman Remembers" as a time when "there wasn't any riot any more" (1989: 89), we must retain the strident misprision implicit in the word.

Moreover, this study seeks to enlarge the discussion of the literary and journalistic constructions of modernism and African-American history even as it squarely situates these marginal works in the ongoing assessment of modernism's central preoccupation with history and its relationship to poetics. Through rhetorical assessment of a representative selection of individual weeklies and magazines, analysis of moments of historical significance, and consideration of this century's dialectic of race liberalism, the study prepares the reader for the appropriation and aestheticization of the newsworthy and historical in the writings of authors as diverse as Gwendolyn Brooks, Sam

Cornish, Alice Walker, and Jay Wright. Notably absent from this book is sustained attention to either the Harlem Renaissance or the civil rights movement of the 1950s. Although the literature and journalism of these culturally intense periods inspired this study (and would find its method congenial), they have been extraordinarily well served by such recent critical studies as James DeJongh's *Vicious Modernism: Black Harlem and the Literary Imagination* (1990), George Hutchinson's *The Harlem Renaissance in Black and White* (1995), and Melissa Walker's *Down from the Mountaintop: Black Women's Novels in the Wake of the Civil Rights Movement, 1966–1989* (1991). I have turned to less cohesive moments, when the news challenged America's racial communities to redefine the nature of news and literature.

The first half of the book explores the formation of a racially charged national identity, investigating the ways in which regional periodical literature served as primary agents of Americanization; the second half of *Writing America Black* investigates media traces in writers who moved beyond the dominant but failed national and cultural explorations to a black nationalistic structure within a Pan-African perspective.

This study does not simply make a case for intertextual readings of African-American ephemeral media and literature. It seeks as well to enlarge the notion of discourse to move beyond the dialogic relationship between master and counterdiscourses, not only accepting the truism that history shapes literature but admitting the possibility that literature informs the national historical narratives. As Kammen concludes in *Mystic Chords of Memory*: "Public memory, which contains a slowly shifting configuration of traditions, is ideologically important because it shapes a nation's ethos and sense of identity. That explains, at least in part, why memory is always selective and is so often contested" (1991: 13). Fraudulent healing of national wounds through amnesiac commemorations encourages aggressive reopenings of the American text, such as Langston Hughes's "Let America Be America Again," Melvin Tolson's "Rendezvous with America," and Amiri Baraka's "It's Nation Time," all of which challenge received historical verities and deny the closure imposed by these ceremonial displays.

Part 1, "History, Citizenship, and the American Way," examines some key journalistic constructions of these abstractions from 1900 to 1950. Until the end of the Second World War, "America" served as a referential, and often ideal, construct for the vast majority of

African-American writers. Most commonly, "America" in the black
press involved a challenge to the nation to live up to its promises
through affirmation of its founding principles. Borrowing rhetoric
freely from a host of "methods of Americanization" texts (targeted at
the foreign born), writers located their American-ness in their nativity; they were *native* sons born into the language. So essential was the
concept of rights linked to nativity that Robert Abbott noted as a key
tenet to his founding *Defender* platform: "Government schools open
to all American citizens in preference to foreigners." Under the guise
of freedom, most such exercises were aimed at socialization. In 1922,
Robert Park, white University of Chicago sociologist and one-time
secretary to Booker T. Washington, justified such nationalizing efforts
as agency-regulated "social activity intended to extend among the
people of the United States the knowledge of their government and
the obligations to it" (Park 1925: vii). The public sphere, as Jürgen
Habermas and Benedict Anderson independently suggest, as a means
of communication found its ideal mode of transmission in the newspaper, for it "provided the technical means for 're-presenting' the
kind of imagined community that is the nation" (Anderson 1983: 25).
Whether at Boston's *Colored American Magazine* or Chicago's *Defender*
and *Negro Digest*, journalism encouraged the collective production of
a social text of race and nation, liberating editors and authors from
the philanthropic bonds of liberalism.

"Race Progress and Exemplary Biography" (Chapter 1) explores
Pauline Hopkins's cultivation of an audience for revisionist race history at Boston's *Colored American Magazine*. Transcending the journal's
bourgeois arts context by writing for "those who never read history
or biography," she hoped that, within the imitative, commodified culture of the magazine, an intellectual construction of race history
could thrive. She wrote in the certainty that her biographical texts
would inform her fiction and social notes, even as they were informed
by the larger textual whole. This chapter investigates the significant
role played by biography in shaping this century's race history
through public lives and critiques the inherited rhetoric of New England's transcendental liberalism.

"Reading Riot" (Chapter 2) draws upon four sources – Robert S.
Abbott's *Chicago Defender* editorials, Carl Sandburg's stories for the
Chicago *Daily News* (with their pamphlet introduction by Walter Lipp-
mann), the Chicago Federation of Labor's broadsides in its *New*

Majority, and Charles S. Johnson's scholarly race advocacy in *The Negro in Chicago* (Chicago Commission on Race Relations [CCRR 1922]) – to consider the rhetorical implications of these separate linguistic communities as they construct complementary and competing historical records of the post–Great War riot in Chicago. The war had become the very calculus of democracy, spawning an array of First Amendment activity. It was a time when, as Robert Kerlin noted in his introduction to *The Voice of the Negro 1919*, "the Negro seem[ed] to have discovered his fourth estate, to have realized the extraordinary power of the press" (1920: ix). Each of these responses to the city's race crisis exposed alternative agendas in their dialogues with sociologically definable constituencies too complex to speak with a single voice. Within this rhetorical chorus, the race solidarity of the *Defender* and the white liberal agency of the *Daily News* inscribe the most sharply defined constituencies of the riot.

"Rendezvous with Modernism, Fascism – and Democracy" (Chapter 3) reads Melvin B. Tolson's first collection of poetry, *Rendezvous with America*, in the light of his editorial "Caviar and Cabbage" column in the *Washington Tribune*, examining his aesthetic and political digression from nationalism to Pan-Africanism during the Second World War, a war that for black America began with the Italo-Ethiopian War. Because the Marxist communitarianism and esoteric spiritualism of Tolson's modernism derive in part from a reaction to Euromodernism and, in particular, to Ezra Pound's politicized aesthetic, his "Caviar and Cabbage" columns serve as crucial intertexts to his evolving theories of democracy, leadership, and the state. Though journalistic in expediency, the columns share a lyrical and historical ambition to place the New Negro "in *his* America" through participatory discourse in the public sphere and circumspect analysis of citizenship in a time of global war and fading empire. What begins as a disquisition into the very "matrix of America," celebratory in its historical fervor and epic in scope, turns into the challenge of "America?." His once epic "magnificent cosmorama," when considered in relation to nativist epics by Carl Sandburg and Archibald MacLeish, turns into a subversive and dissembling question for the Black America of Tolson's *Rendezvous*, abandoning what he called in the Gurdjieff-inspired, race-transcending "The Man Inside" the "common ground, in transfiguring light, / Where man inside is neither black nor white" (1944: 25).

"If I Were a Negro" (Chapter 4) continues the analysis of liberal forces shaping race news and historiography in a consideration of John Johnson's feature column for his first periodical venture, *Negro Digest*. Like the transcendentalist rhetoric incorporated into the Hopkins sketches in the *Colored American Magazine* and the admonitions scripted into the Sandburg and Lippmann accounts of the Chicago riot, "If I Were a Negro" assumes the authority of white liberalism. High-minded and earnest, these white authors attempted a dance of elision and masquerade, familiar to Pauline Hopkins and Robert Abbott, while retaining the privilege of agency for social change. And yet, when read in the racialized context of *Negro Digest*, the familiar rhetorical consolation of liberalism performs a paradoxical role. Rather than assuring white America's "goodness," "If I Were a Negro" confirms Theodor Adorno's suspicions that "goodness itself is a deformation of the good" (1951: 94).

Part 2, "Decomposing Unities, Deconstructing National Narratives," moves beyond the contestatory Americanism of the first half of the century to the disjunctive counternarratives of the second. The Vietnam War, waves of political assassination and riot, and the constitutional crisis of Watergate provided the chaotic subtext for the Bicentennial that in itself seemed a theatrical extension of the cold war. "The cold war," as Donald Pease reminds us, "structured two grand modernist narratives – Russian Marxism and Americanist liberalism – in a relation of opposition" (1997: 14). The threatened collapse of constitutional democracy and the apparent futility of civil rights predicated upon a civil society surprised few in an African-American community that, though aspiring to the "utopian ideals of modernity – the ideas of basic rights, liberty, equality, democracy, solidarity, and justice" (Cohen and Arato 1992: xii), was advancing toward a subnationally constructed, culturally intense communitarian ethos.

Focusing upon the years 1968–76, this section acknowledges the relative failure of the black press to sustain the optimism of earlier political, definitional tensions and turns to aesthetic, textual appropriations of the historical present. Hoyt Fuller's conversion of the bourgeois *Negro Digest* into the revolutionary *Black World* represents a rare instance of an editor's power to channel rhetorical *dis*integration into a new aesthetic. Televisual and feminist challenges to such textual constructs jeopardize the national narrative as well. Nationalism here is at once local and global, as the black community seeks its definitional anchor outside of a received text. Gwendolyn Brooks and Sam Cornish, working within a black urban sphere fighting for its very survival, initiate a communitarian nationalism and a genealogical historical record; Alice Walker and Jay Wright, signifying upon the impoverishment of the Bicentennial – its Enlightenment antecedents as well as its performative display – root historical awareness in the rural and ancient realms of ceremony and orality.

"Reportage as Redemption" (Chapter 5) explores Gwendolyn Brooks's *In the Mecca* as a reading of the disintegration of American civil society through the ruins of a residential apartment building on Chicago's South Side. The Mecca Building, itself twice-mediated through articles in *Life* and *Harper's*, signified for Brooks a social and economic as well as textual failure of white representations of black America. Read as lived – from the inside out – by its black inhabitants, the Mecca was subjectively a home; viewed as reported – from the outside in – by white dailies, planning commissions, and reporters, it was objectively a slum. Such competing textualities foregrounded for Brooks the oppositional realities of official renderings of her life in Chicago, declared by the U.S. Commission on Civil Rights in 1959 to be "the most residentially segregated large city in the nation" (quoted in Hampton and Fayer 1995: 298). Reports on civil unrest (in language remembered and found to be as good for a riot in 1968 as it was in 1919 or 1943), planning commission "master" plans, and mainstream journalistic accountings of her neighborhood constructed the "official" discourse that inspired the counterdiscourse of (and would serve as the intertext to) *In the Mecca*. Comprised of two sections – In the Mecca and After Mecca – the volume is both a retrospective and a prophetic accounting of an aesthetic evolution and community revolution that entails Brooks's cooptation and insistent intertextualizing of the "master's" ideas of order. Sequences of recognition, deployment, and dismissal typify her response to Western objectifications of religion, art, and law, as she moves to embrace a subjectifyingly redemptive force that will convert the ruins of the Mecca into a place of "Construction."

"Kinship as History" (Chapter 6) reconsiders the contribution of African-American ancestral narratives to the news of black history. Because kinship rituals and imbedded genealogies serve as surrogate historical texts, *Generations* (1971) reports historically as well as poetically. Consideration of Sam Cornish's decision, in the heat of the

Black Arts Movement, to publish with the liberal Beacon Press contributes to this study's ongoing discussion of liberal agency and the black community, perhaps illuminating Cornish's subsequent omission from scholarly amendments of the Black Arts Movement (most recently, his exclusion from *The Norton Anthology of African-American Literature* and Michael Harper's *Every Shut Eye Ain't Asleep*). The instability of Cornish's literary reputation serves to illustrate the simultaneous perils of repression and recovery in literary history.

"Nation-ness as Consciousness" (Chapter 7) contemplates Alice Walker's systematic deconstruction of history, personal and national. As the protagonist slips her narrative restraints, so does the novel abandon other received, totalizing narratives. Television must be countered because it insinuates an obstructive focus that frames, edits, and normalizes with its fraudulent narrative certainty. Black nationalism must be rescripted because, in its present form, it offers an inherited, violent patriarchal rhetoric that perpetuates the worst of the "master's" script. *Meridian* occasions peripheral discussions of television's corruption of the national narrative, liberalism's persistent innocence, and patriarchal privilege.

"History as Storytelling" (Chapter 8) examines what Homi Bhabha identifies as "the postcolonial passage through modernity" (1994: 253). In the words of Bhabha's paradigm, "the past [is] projective," and Jay Wright uses a similarly insistent historicism and atavistic cosmology to empower the chronotropic aesthetic of *Soothsayers and Omens*. Walter Benjamin's insight that stories are human history illuminates the potential grandeur and spectacular remove of Wright's poetic, in which he invents a simultaneous historical field in which language, culture, and nation are subsumed by the *telling* of the tale of the tribe. In his reinvention of time, space, and narrative (dependent upon his aestheticization of Dogon cosmology as incompletely apprehended by French anthropologist Marcel Griaule), Wright formulates a historical consciousness independent of nation and narration, retrieving anew the possibilities of history's literal presence.

Writing America Black presents more than a case for intertextual readings of African-American mass media and literature; it reveals that narrative is the basis of individual and community conceptions of national identity. The innocence and affirmation with which African-American journalists during the first decades of the century participated in efforts toward Americanization inform the sophistication and disaffection of subsequent black nationalist writers. The contingency of citizenship for black America quickens the pulse of justice in these writings that complement the nation's dominant narrative.

In lieu of the ideal though impossible goal of comprehensiveness, *Writing America Black* relies upon representative case studies from which to generalize about the structures and intentions of African-American historical narratives, and should encourage further investigation into the language of social identity and citizenship. Its theoretical and practical framework for reading, moving beyond the truism that history shapes literature, seeks ultimately to demonstrate how literature informs the national narratives that compose history. Works as distinctive as Spike Lee's *Jungle Fever* (1991), Deborah McDowell's *Leaving Pipe Shop* (1996), and LeAlan Jones and Lloyd Newman's *Our America* (1997) attest to the ongoing role of community journalism in the formulation and transmission of ideas of race and nation and culture. Unlike the novel, which isolates its world for close examination, or television, which as Alice Walker feared becomes the "repository of memory," weekly newspapers and magazines ("pulps" and "slicks") retain the collaborative spontaneity of a unifying textual field that becomes the literature that stays news.

C.K.D.
Peterborough, NH
July 4, 1997

ACKNOWLEDGMENTS

Writing America Black owes its very existence to A. Walton Litz, who made possible my early work on Elizabeth Bishop and Gwendolyn Brooks, and to Sam Bass Warner, who introduced me to the drama of the American city; their sense of engagement, proportion, and passion remains a source of inspiration. The study has matured through the ongoing assistance of participants in two National Endowment for the Humanities Summer Seminars: Eric Sundquist's "The Problem of Race in Afro-American Literature, 1850–1930," held at the University of California at Berkeley in 1990, and Donald Pease's "Slavery, Reconstruction, and the U.S. Civil Imagination, 1845–1900," held at Dartmouth College in 1994. Veterans of those seminars have become friends and colleagues. In particular, I thank Joseph Alvarez, John C. Gruesser, Judith Lockyer, A. L. Nielsen, and Lawrence Rodgers for their comments and encouragement over the years. Ultimately my greatest debt is to Anne Bradford Warner who, during that Berkeley summer long ago, suggested that I look to my peers.

This study has a long history. Over the years, many people have been generous with their time, opinions, and resources: Ira Sandperl and Joan Baez of the Institute for the Study of Nonviolence introduced me to the social texts of A. J. Muste, Frantz Fanon, Gandhi, Bayard Rustin, A. Philip Randolph, and Martin Luther King, Jr. – even as they brought the civil rights movement into my life. Ethelyne Ward insisted that justice was a literary matter; Frank Teti contended that, in an ad hoc society, it was the province of political theory and religion. Mary Kay Norseng familiarized me with the writings of Gunnar and Alva Myrdal on the subject of American race relations. Jon Woodson transformed my understanding of Melvin B. Tolson, supplementing my research with materials from the Moorland-Spingarn Research Center of Howard University, and presented to me the complex world of Tolson's Gurdji-effian mysticism. Patricia Hills taught the drama of black America's great migrations through the paintings of Jacob Lawrence. Kathleen Pfeiffer secured essential ephemera from the Beinecke Rare Book and Manuscript Library, Yale University. Jay and Lois Wright contributed out-of-print poetry – and pointed encouragement. Sam Cornish, with his bottomless library and particularized memory, transformed nostalgia for the energy of the Black Arts Movement into experience of its literal presence. I hope that their instruction, counsel, and contributions have kept me from foundering in the seas of near history.

Writing America Black exists because of the timely and repeated intervention of the National Endowment for the Humanities. NEH Summer Seminars at the University of California at Berkeley and Dartmouth College provided the time to research the journalistic ephemera, inspired the theoretical frame of my investigation, and, most importantly, gave me time to think. Composed during the obscure hours between extended commutes to distant and temporary classrooms, the final manuscript was assembled during the early months of an NEH Fellowship for Independent Scholars (its project a direct consequence of this study). The National Endowment's authorization of scholarship during this period of independence from employment has made it possible to imagine the peer approval essential to the success of future research.

Eric J. Sundquist has nourished this investigation with a belief that was both material and spiritual. His repeated and timely encouragement countered the despair that often threatened to consume this project. His commitment to a democratic union of scholars continues to underwrite veterans of his seminars. Donald E. Pease, with unstinting generosity, not only made the theoretical riches of the School of Criticism and Theory available to his NEH participants but continues to inspire and facilitate my work in progress. I thank both of them for honoring the potential of the NEH seminar to turn summer holidays into scholarly salvation.

By happy coincidence, Cambridge University Press continued my association with Professor Sundquist and returned T. Susan Chang to my immediate circle. Her critical intelligence and boundless enthusiasm, well known to me from our original association at Oxford University Press, sustained the development of the manuscript for Cambridge.

She remains a vital collaborator. Anne Sanow and her gracious staff at Cambridge have made the final stages of this project a pleasure.

Conferences of the Modern Language Association, the American Literature Association, the Society for Narrative Literature, the American Studies Association, and the Northeast Modern Language Association enlarged the audience for my work in progress. I thank John C. Gruesser, A. L. Nielsen, Wilfred Samuels, Michael Coyle, and Donald Pease for these opportunities. Several chapters were vastly improved by the critical responses of Henry Louis Gates, Jr., Shelley Fisher Fishkin, Charles Banner-Haley, Claudia Tate, Deborah McDowell, Maryemma Graham, Nellie McKay, Mary Helen Washington, and Donald Pease. Early versions of some chapters have appeared in *Scribners Modern American Authors*, *Contemporary Literature*, *African American Literature*, *Prospects*, and *CLA Journal*; thanks to Lea Baechler, A. Walton Litz, Thomas Schaub, Joe Weixlmann, and Jack Salzman for their editorial wisdom and encouragement.

I should like to thank the librarians and staff at many institutions for promptly answering inquiries and locating material: Widener Library, Harvard University; Baker Library, Dartmouth College; Mugar Library, Boston University; Bancroft Library, University of California at Berkeley; URL, University of California at Los Angeles; Moorland-Spingarn Research Center at Howard University, Washington, D.C.; the Manuscript Division of the Library of Congress. And, in particular, I am grateful to Mary Marks, Toni and Sandy Weller at Daniel Webster College, and the reference staff of Mason Library at Keene State College for stretching the boundaries (and perhaps policies) of interlibrary loan to accommodate this research. And, finally, my appreciation to Anna, Bob, George, Jeff, Kim, Maude, and Willard of the Toadstool Bookstore in Peterborough, New Hampshire, for handling an inordinate number of special orders with customary zeal and humor.

Nowhere has the enduring vitality of the black press been more in evidence than in my classrooms. From introductory writing courses to senior and graduate seminars, students have relived the complex dramas of *Jet* magazine's coverage of Emmett Till's death, Robert Abbott's *Defender* editorials, and Gwendolyn Brooks's *Negro Digest* essays. Many individuals brought the ardor and wisdom of experience to our discussions: memorably, Denise Simpson of Emmanuel College; Natalie Wilson, Elisa Manor, and Brian Keith Fulton of the John

ACKNOWLEDGMENTS

F. Kennedy School of Government at Harvard University; Tracee
Plowell of Daniel Webster College; Melissa Roach and Thanese Miller
of Boston University all converted the classroom into a passionate
forum for citizenship and justice.

The stresses of a compromised academic life are many; the toll
taken on one's family undesirable. No one has understood the vicissi-
tudes of my career better than William Doreski. He has shared
research, writing, and revision – often to the detriment of his own
work. His encouraging echoes of Joan Didion – "the thing is finally
yours to make – and there is a point in doing it" – made the critical
difference.

PART ONE

HISTORY, CITIZENSHIP, AND THE AMERICAN WAY

Herein lie buried many things which if read with patience may show the strange meaning of being black here in the dawning of the Twentieth Century.
– W. E. B. Du Bois, *The Souls of Black Folk* (1903a)

We must . . . remember that . . . the local community must always be the most permanent, and that the concept of the nation is by no means fixed and invariable. It is, so to speak, only one fluctuating circle of loyalties between the centre of the family and the local community, and the periphery of humanity entire. . . . It is only a law of nature, that local patriotism, when it represents a distinct tradition and culture, takes precedence over a more abstract national patriotism.
– T. S. Eliot, *After Strange Gods* (1934)

1

RACE PROGRESS AND EXEMPLARY BIOGRAPHY

PAULINE HOPKINS AT THE
COLORED AMERICAN MAGAZINE

We know that there are able publications already in the field,
but the pang that has set our active world a-borning is the
knowledge that the colored man has lost the rights already
won because he was persuaded and then bullied into lying
down and ceasing his fight for civil liberty. . . .
> – "Editorial and Publishers Announcements"
> *New Era Magazine* 1 (February 1916): 60

We are sparing neither time nor money to make this Magazine the most authentic historian of the race's progress.
> – "Editorial and Publishers Announcements"
> *New Era Magazine* 1 (March 1916): 124

More than a decade after her severance from Boston's *Colored American Magazine* (*CAM*), Pauline Hopkins retained a politically charged
philosophy of African-American arts and letters, as evidenced by her
pronouncements heralding the publication of *New Era Magazine*. Colleagues from the *Colored American* might have been surprised by the
stridency of her call to action, but none would have been shocked by
its militancy or insistence upon community-based, collective action.

By the time of this final acknowledgment of the collaborative nature
and resultant power of the periodical press, Hopkins had resolved the
earlier problematic issue of the relationship between the public self
and history. For black America the periodical press could not afford to
be ephemeral; it had consciously to shape and nurture its nascent history. In her culminating effacement of self as historian, Hopkins ceded
authority to the magazine and, by extension, to the African-American

periodical press at large. The move from author of individual significance (a concern of her transcendentalist forebears) to author as a
community force serving a larger historical project began for Hopkins
during her formative years as editor of the *Colored American Magazine*.

Throughout her tenure at the *Colored American* (1900–4), Hopkins
acknowledged her obligation not simply to cultivate but to create an
audience for her revisionist race history. She assumed the authority
of race historian and mediated between the issues of race and gender to incite a readership to pride and action (on the race and gender split, see Stansell 1992). Even the *Colored American*'s title page
claimed agency and responsibility by appealing to that segment of the
population whom Du Bois would soon call the "Talented Tenth"
(Meier 1988: 207–47; Bruce 1989: esp. chap. 5). This monthly (not
unlike such nineteenth-century bourgeois cousins as the *Atlantic
Monthly* and *Putnam's Monthly*) schooled its readers in arts and man-
ners, hoping to provide that facade of success expected in the emerging middle class. But it also advanced a political and cultural agenda
in its challenge to the status quo and its commitment to the discovery
and conservation of African-American history. The shadow of compromised citizenship cast by *Plessy v. Ferguson* necessitated an urgent
commitment to the recovery and perpetuation of race history.

Hopkins transcended the journal's arts context by writing for
"those who never read history or biography."[1] She hoped that,
through the imitative commodified culture of the magazine, ideas of
the marketplace could become a marketplace of ideas. Visually sharing qualities associated with weekly newspapers in advertisements for
products ranging from Frederick Douglass watches to cosmetics, the
Colored American offered a product-intense, textual world in which
even biography and history might become marketable commodities.
Thoroughly attuned to the intertextual power of the emulative
matrix of the press, Hopkins knew that her historical portraits could
gain power when read through the animated and often competing
texts of each issue. She wrote in the certainty that her biographical
texts would inform her fiction and social notes, even as they were
informed by the larger textual whole. In this way, she wrote in that
grander nineteenth-century tradition identified by Edmund Wilson
as one in which "criticism . . . was closely allied to history and novel
writing, and was also the vehicle for all sorts of ideas about the purpose and destiny of human life in general" (1969: 122–3).

Although Hopkins the novelist has recently earned deserved attention, Hopkins the biographer has attracted only passing interest. And, curiously, despite a commitment from scholars to African-American autobiography that includes the restoration of "the black slave's narrative to its complex status as history and as literature" (Davis and Gates 1985: iii), the significant role of biography as a means of shaping race history through public lives has received comparatively little attention.[2] Intertextual reading of Hopkins's historical counternarratives (fictional and biographical) in the *Colored American* suggests how she constructs history and challenges conventional generic distinctions by conflating discourses of history, biography, fictional narrative, race, and gender in order to shape a rhetorical self to counter the absence of a reliable race history.[3]

The validation of Hopkins as an authentic historian through her role as biographer demands exploration of her reliance on and divergence from the New England regional tradition of biography as the spiritually or ideologically informed presentation of exemplary lives. Comfortable with the tradition she seeks to challenge, she advances the cultural and racial history of slavery into present-tense instruction applicable to this era of imperiled citizenship. In so doing, her biographies and fictions find authentication through life stories that derive their significance from the ability to inspire in the individual reader what Emerson calls the "unattained but attainable self" (1841: 239). Her Emersonian emphasis that "all history is . . . but biography"[4] stems from the belief that in order to translate, as William Andrews says, "word into act" (1986: 71) readers must sense the historical possibilities of daily life. Hopkins's belief that history is firmly embedded in individual narratives would seem to accord with Hayden White's definition of narrative as "a solution of how to translate *knowing* into *telling*, the problem of fashioning human experience into a form assimilable to structures of meaning that are generally human rather than culture-specific" (1981: 1; Goody 1991). But while such "fashioning" into universals might have some appeal to a fiction writer in search of a broad audience, such grandiose universalizing would be anathema to Hopkins as race historian.

Far more ambitious than the familiar quest for totalizing fictions (whether we call them fiction or history), her portraits, like Emerson's, share the didactic ends of that distant rhetorical ancestor from the Puritan great migration: exemplary biography.[5] Sacvan Bercovitch, in discussing exemplary biography and its "organizing metaphors," argues that this kind of biography "transmutes history itself into a drama of the soul" (1975: 8). Not unlike the Cotton Mather of *Magnalia Christi Americana* – who saw "*Biography*, provoking the *whole World*, with vertuous Objects of Emulation" (1702: 89) – Hopkins sought a biographical form that would incarnate history; and not unlike the W. E. B. Du Bois of *The Souls of Black Folk*, who was aware that "the powers of single black men flash here and there like falling stars, and die sometimes before the world has rightly gauged their brightness" (1903a: 365), she pursued a history that would secure and preserve the significance of these exemplary Americans. Her preoccupation with the translation of representative lives into authentic history begins with two series of biographical sketches written for the *Colored American*. Appearing monthly from November 1900 to January 1903, "Famous Men of the Negro Race" and "Famous Women of the Negro Race" constitute her own experiments in historiography and biography in harnessing this once sacred impulse for secular service. Attending to the spirit of this world, she composes history from exemplary lives in the hope of (in Deborah McDowell's words) "elevat[ing] the image of the entire race" (1990: 95).

The formulaic inheritance of the representative biographical sketch, which denies the literary or historical uniqueness of these lives, reiterates and extends the grander, antebellum historical context of slavery so that it may inform the citizenship crisis of the day.[6] Like Lydia Maria Child, whose *Freedmen's Book* (1865) had isolated "the power of character over circumstances" as the core didactic purpose of such insistent representative lives, Hopkins transformed race icons into players in a history requiring authentication through participation (Child 1865: 218).[7] She translated the familiar lives of Toussaint-Louverture, Frederick Douglass, Sojourner Truth, and Harriet Tubman into participatory, exemplary texts, and in so doing relaxed into the conventions of the established genre and the obligations of essential biography, wherein the life described becomes an extended allegory (on social versus essential biography, see Bercovitch 1975: 149). Her challenges to this rhetorical inheritance would include figures about whom Hopkins felt ambivalent (e.g., Booker T. Washington), less famous and more local personages better served by a social biography (wherein the life is but a microcosm of its historical context of great events), and professional women whom she saw as embodiments of a community rather than as individual heroes. The personalized flexible organization of these sketches allows Hopkins to accommodate the aesthetic dimension of emplotment (employing vignette and dialogue to animate the life) as well as the cognitive historical obligation to argument (exposing the greater moral imperatives of history).[8] Drawing upon what Hazel Carby has called "an idealized concept of her New England past" (1987: 121), Hopkins sought to enlighten and inspirit readers to a kindred abolitionist fervor by using social and cultural exemplars to nullify competing racist ideologies. But, unlike her transcendentalist models, she sought not to privilege the individual but rather to celebrate an evolving sense of historical integrity and community. This chapter explores Hopkins's move from the inherited rhetoric of the representative biographical sketch to a culturally defined, intertextually enriched vision of the way in which all history *is* biography.

Committed to the "wonderful deeds and brilliant achievements which have been accomplished by men of color throughout the world," "Famous Men of the Negro Race" declares its historical project by delineating an audience "denied its history and distinguished only as the former slave[s] of the country" (*CAM* advertisement, November 1900).[9] This project is one of recovery as well as commemoration, and offers the "truth" that will give African Americans "the history of a patriot, a brave soldier, the defender of the country from foreign invaders, and God fearing producer of the nation's wealth" (*CAM*, November 1900). The role call of local heroes insists upon emulative public life and active citizenship as a prerequisite to mentorship as well as historical significance.

While ostensibly "preserving the fascinating individual personality of each man," Hopkins subverts the unique in favor of the cumulative contribution to a public genealogy and restorative kinship in order to invent history. Reading real events (i.e., the strict chronology of the men's lives) as paradigms for the larger cultural narrative, Hopkins, like any post-Hegelian historian, accepts her role as interlocutor, using anecdote (see Fineman 1989) and narrative emphasis to lend structure to lives and events as she mediates between the individual heroic soul and the grander racial and cultural tapestry.

Of the dozen portraits composing "Famous Negro Men," three representative men constitute the larger cultural matrix and inheritance of the series: Toussaint-Louverture, Frederick Douglass, and Booker T. Washington. These exemplary cultural heroes invest the series as a whole with a vaguely Emersonian stature, while the less defined and more local exemplary lives derive their historical coherence and resonance within the larger context of these three historically centered, slavery-defined cultural heroes. Readers familiar with Emerson's *Representative Men* (1850) and Child's *The Freedmen's Book* would see these lives as obligatory cultural markers as well as history. Appearing individually in the *Colored American*, these lives predicate a revisionary sense of how the representative biography might embody the political agenda of the magazine itself. The force of the collective cultural sweep – from the distant and unrecorded (other than by the enemy) trials of Toussaint-Louverture, to the meticulously historicized and self-fashioned lives of Douglass, and the contemporary and self-chronicled life of Washington – approximates Hopkins's personal commitment to the relationship of life's detritus to the embracing context of history. Each biography challenges her to exploit the exchange context of the magazine without sacrificing the integrity of her fashioned lives.

With "Toussaint L'Overture" (*CAM*, November 1900, 9–24),[10] Hopkins grounds her enterprise in a history of slave revolt while acknowledging the Emersonian rhetorical tradition she both inherits and modifies. A prefatory note displaces the expected invocation and announces a larger contextualizing project. The despoilment of a garden paradise mirrors the destruction of its inhabitants, as Hopkins reinvents the competing histories of old and new worlds in terms of the history of her race. She expands the power of descent discourse to include the recovery of Haiti's proper history.

Ever mindful of historical resonances, Hopkins displaces historical claims and certainties by calling attention to their arbitrary and transient natures. Authenticating historical documentation supplants received historical fact in a chain of calling and renaming, which loosely anchors the evidence of position or place. In order to emphasize the link between native servitude and American slavery, Hopkins resorts to fictional strategies and the literary, Christian discourse of the garden. Hispaniola becomes an Edenic place of temperate climate, "always laden with fruit and covered with flowers." To capture the precolonial and prelapsarian state of this virginal place, a place literally without commodities, she describes it as a land in which

"Gold, silver, and copper mines abound," although such metals have no exchange value there. The garden as trope yields to an accelerated Genesis tale of fall and expulsion in which African slaves replace the aborigines, who had been "driven into a cruel and barbarous servitude by the Spanish adventurers." Slavery quickly turns into a "many-headed monster," which not only casts the race into servitude but confuses the racial line: "from the mingling of the whites and blacks the mulattoes had sprung." From this island issues what Hopkins calls the "voice of history . . . the point of interest for all Negroes" (Hopkins 1900–1: 10). The embodiment of that voice is Toussaint Louverture.

Signifying upon Emerson's *Representative Men*, Hopkins extends her characterization to include the implications for race history as she envisions Toussaint as "Napoleon's black shadow," a man "who made and unmade kings and formed governments anew." She exhorts her readers to accept that "races should be judged by the great men they produce, and by the average value of the masses" (1900–1: 11) and then supplies a historical narrative that constructs a Haitian perspective on the revolution. Throughout this new history, readers engage in alternative readings of race biography and history: "Such was the beginning of a revolt that ought to have a world-wide fame. It stands without a parallel in history, – the successful uprising of slaves against their masters, and the final establishment of their independence" (14). The authorial "ought" intensifies Hopkins's claim to revisionary history. The effacement of what should have been "world-wide fame" prompts her reconstruction project. Yet as the collective history of the island is recalled, it "seems merged in the exploits of one man, L'Overture" (14). Securing the relationship between the collective "uprising of slaves" and the individual "exploits of one man," Hopkins at once privileges the hero while suspending his deeds in a collective matrix. This larger cultural impress enables a historical narrative to blossom from the life of a "Negro [who] left hardly a line for history to feed upon" (14).

In the absence of autobiographical witness, Hopkins, suspicious of the "reluctant testimony of [Toussaint's] enemies," resorts to narration to depict this Senegalese "Negro of unmixed blood" (15). She acknowledges his slave origins while stressing his literacy and classical training, thus bridging origins and circumstance for contemporary readers. In a sharp role reversal, Hopkins's heroic slave assumes mastery "at the head of the newly freed, leading them from victory to victory for France under Bonaparte" (15). He, conforming to what Claudia Tate has labeled the "gender conservatism" of the era (1992: 161), assumes the lineaments of regal patriarch, and "under his paternal administration, laws, morals, religion, education, and industry were in full force, while commerce and agriculture flourished" (Hopkins 1900–1: 17).

A dialogic interface of history and biography, kindred to that of her openly historical fictions, draws authenticity from its intertextual relationship with excerpts from journals and letters of Toussaint's "enemies." Anxious for readers to appreciate the significance of this representative man, Hopkins plots the arc of his career parallel to that of his bête noire, Napoleon. The ideological rivalry inscribed in the figures of Toussaint and Napoleon corresponds to Emerson's own sketch of Napoleon. When at last it becomes evident that Napoleon is determined to crush the spirit of liberty in the blacks of St. Domingo, Toussaint evolves into the intrepid leader who obeys to the letter the stern mandates of war.

In an unexpected inversion of the slave narrative, death rather than birth is "shrouded in mystery" (23). Under Napoleon's hand, Toussaint dies off the record, at least in Hopkins's hagiography. Hopkins, willing to compensate for that historical silence, interjects: "We know not the exact manner of his taking off, but that he was cruelly murdered *there is no doubt*" (23; emphasis added). Clearly under the sway of Thomas Carlyle's and William Wordsworth's romantic projections of the hero when she insists upon Toussaint's "grandeur of a great moral heroism" (19), Hopkins nonetheless relies upon a rhetoric of disengagement with her European models as she pinpoints that hero's fatal flaw: "the ruin of Toussaint was due in great measure to his loyalty to France and his filial feeling for Bonaparte" (16).

Hopkins's depiction both recovers a lost historical perspective and sustains an essential biography, placing Toussaint and Haiti in a historical continuum of race history for African Americans. Effecting closure with a historical sweep from Thermopylae to Fort Wagner, Hopkins as visionary historian sanctifies the record through an act of Pan-African revelation: "History recorded these deeds, and they shall be known; God intends it so! Therefore the history of the Island of St. Domingo is interesting to the Negroes of the United States; brothers in blood, though speaking different languages, we should clasp our hands in friendship when we look back upon our past" (24). Toussaint draws significance from the embracing Pan-African vision of Hopkins's newly constructed historical record, insisting as it does upon a shared history as well as a common destiny.

Unlike the unwritten history of Toussaint Louverture, Frederick Douglass's thrice-chronicled life challenged Hopkins to sculpt received narratives, lending biographical contours to a dauntingly familiar autobiography (*CAM*, December 1900, 121–32). Challenged with making the mythically familiar new, Hopkins expands Douglass's shifting frameworks of the ideal (especially in his *Narrative*), searching for historical and cultural referents in her biography aimed at a contemporary audience of marginally enfranchised citizens. Here she transforms the autobiographical, "I-centered" slave narrative into a mediated biography available to the new African-American citizen by sharing not only great deeds but the potential of a larger collective force, the "citizen" always moving toward that constituent whole of "citizenry." The broader sense of race obligation as well as history suggests the influence of Du Bois's 1897 articulation of "the real meaning of Race" (815).[11] Within this lingering Emersonian context, Hopkins imagines (in Du Bois's words) that representative men "were but epitomized expressions" (817) of a race of great men and great women drawn together by the civilizing force of culture (Moses 1989: esp. chap. 5).

Hopkins, relying upon the familiarity of Douglass's own "lives," draws his autobiographically constructed past(s) into the readers' present. Douglass's Emersonian auto-American-biography (Bercovitch 1975: esp. chap. 5) contextualizes a social biography of urgency and purpose as his life becomes an exemplum for African Americans in general. The historical resonances of slavery, bondage, and freedom echo throughout the naming rituals familiar to readers of slave narratives. Genealogy and history coalesce in Hopkins's Pan-African speculation that "in the veins of this man ran the best blood of old Maryland families mingled with the noble blood of African princes." Drawing readers anew into the drama of Douglass's narrative, Hopkins transforms a capsule history of chattel slavery into a contemporary narrative of citizenship: "Later in the evening *our invited friend* from New Bedford, *the fugitive slave* (*Frederick Douglass*), came to the platform" (1900–1: 123; emphasis added). This associative series of competing social designations prompts a complex chain of reader response: The phrase "Our invited" invests the friend with a larger society and an assumption of equality; "the" as definite article intensifies the internal conflict (i.e., a "slave" reacting to the very condition of slavery by becoming a "fugitive") in both designation and legal category; and "(Frederick Douglass)," embedded as it is in parentheses, signals both a construct (Douglass creating his own selfhood) and a public identity – albeit delivered sotto voce.

While honoring the features of Douglass's own lives, Hopkins subverts her inherited text and redirects readers to trample, what Emerson calls in *Representative Men*, "any fence of personality" that keeps them from self-discovery and action (1850: 631). Successive waves of biography and history fabricate the news of the day as figures and events recapitulate the past while predicating the future. The epilogue returns readers emphatically to the anxieties of the hour, redesignating slavery from fact to metaphor to metonym. Slavery persists in the lynch laws, race murders, and the convict-lease system: "To-day we have again the rise of slave-power, for the old spirit is not dead" (Hopkins 1900–1: 128). Douglass's autobiographical selves, in Hopkins's biography, coalesce into "an example of possibilities which may be within the reach of many young men of the rising generation" (132).

Unlike Child's sketches of Toussaint and Douglass, which stress the family-centered, private "capabilities of Black Men" (1865: 83), Hopkins's biographies revitalize the heritage by insisting upon public biographies as the intimate ground of history. Passages celebrating the family possibilities of the emancipated sphere – Douglass discovering in New Bedford "the colored people owning their comfortable little homes and farms, schooling their children and transacting their business" (Hopkins 1900–1: 123) – yield to the larger framing emphasis placed on the didactic aims of biography and history.

The inherited rhetorical demands of the representative life served Hopkins well when she dealt with figures she deemed heroic. The received structure, however, broke down rather early, necessitating reconstruction along different lines, as she began to cope with the eccentric nature of her "representative men." The Booker T. Washington sketch (*CAM*, October 1901, 436–41), which concludes the series, offers insight into the problematic nature of the genre for Hopkins as she turns nineteenth-century heroic conventions on her contemporary and rival. By its very nature, biography demands belief in the subject-embracing rhetoric, and this portrait must bear the polemical weight of the entire series. Whereas Toussaint's and Douglass's lives seemed divinely inspired, Washington's (in his autobiography as well as Hopkins's sketch) seems decidedly secular, deliberate, and forced.

Hopkins's strict accounting of this representative man is perfunctory from the start. Public presence and authority do little to animate this "subject of [a] sketch" whose influence in "words and acts on the future history of the Negro race will be carefully scrutinized by future generations" (1900–1: 436). Her intricate and personalized rhetoric slips into the indifferent air of an all-too-familiar biography. The exceptional qualities of Washington's *The Story of My Life and Work* are nullified by her strained indifference: "No one will question the assertion that Dr. Washington and Tuskegee are one. . . . Tuskegee Institute is the soul of the man outlined in wood, in brick and stone" (436). Hopkins refuses to animate this "outlined" man, withholding both dramatic narration and fictional dialogue. Rather, she allows him to seem limited by his own tide of accomplishments and honors, divorced from a larger sense of community. Halfheartedly she notes, "Dr. Washington's public career as a speaker is full of interest" (439). The absence of the expected generic elements contribute to the sense of diminished form and compromised rhetoric.

Hopkins concludes with a lifeless, cautionary epilogue in which "motives" turn suspect in the harsher light of history: "When the happenings of the Twentieth Century have become matters of history, Dr. Washington's motives will be open to as many constructions and discussions as are those of Napoleon today, or of other men of extraordinary ability, whether good and evil, who have had like phenomenal careers" (441). Readers recalling the series' initial depiction of Toussaint's subversion of Napoleon were certain to perceive the ironic weight of the equivocating "whether good or evil" judgment on Washington. Embedded in this invocation is Hopkins's unwritten warning, which seems like a revision of Emerson: If Washington is the race, it is because the people he sways are little Washingtons.

The suspension of authorial moral judgment is but one way that Hopkins signals her ambivalence toward Washington and his prescription for black America. The collapse of rhetoric in the Washington sketch suggests the power of biography, when aesthetically charged, to sustain the representation. It also serves to intensify the sense of peril for contemporary readers. The accomplishment of the series is not simply that it emphasizes the triumph of race heroes over slavery, but that it encourages those survival traits as a means of securing full citizenship. The withdrawal of authorial passion in the Washington sketch italicizes the persistent subtext of the series: that these life stories are "interwoven inseparably with the political history of the United States in the most critical period of its existence" (*CAM*, February 1901, 301). Portraits of more regional "famous men" demonstrate Hopkins's skillful adaptation of the genre, favoring those with the moral complexity, fervor, and capacity that she considers worthy of visionary race models.

Of the remaining nine portraits, all but one share Boston roots or obligations, and most of the careers originate in the Oberlin-Boston nexus of liberal reform and abolitionist fervor. "The history of abolition was," as Hazel Carby has noted, "a constant reference point for Hopkins; the possibility of the revival of such a force for political change was the source of her political optimism" (1987: 121). Not only was this invocation of regional history essential to capturing her audience but it informed the dominant rhetoric of each sketch. Hopkins relied upon the intertextual resonance of these portraits to demystify for her readers the received history of place and origins so that they might find the life of history itself in their own genealogy.[12] Through the rhetorical reiteration of slave ancestry, readers might recover the inventive passion of the abolitionist movement as these regional figures are invested with historical weight, circumstance, and obligation. Their public lives, when subjected to the art of biography, turn exemplary as well as historical. They become a lens through which history appears as both perceivable and participatory.

Experimenting with authenticating history through these exemplary lives, Hopkins – biographer and mediating voice – moves beyond history as a static past to that great force of history's literal presence. Readers inspired by the opening portraits of Toussaint and Douglass could turn to these successive sketches of citizens seemingly in their midst to chart a course for their own improvement, their own contributions to the race. Hopkins exploited her fictional talents to lend dramatic narration and enlivening dialogue to her biographies. She wrested African-American history from the "maelstrom of slavery" and situated it in a larger cultural continuum (*CAM*, January

1901, 236). Unlike the portraits of the cultural icons, those of Hopkins's less "Famous Men" rely upon rhetorical and narrative strategies that introduce the notion that race history precedes and empowers individuals. They also emphasize the precarious nature of African-American citizenship in their insistence upon participation in history through public roles.

"Lewis Hayden" (*CAM*, April 1901, 473–7) is a stylistic case in point. Reinvoking and then upsetting the conventions of hagiography, Hopkins begins with an insistence of Hayden's spirituality in the face of his seemingly unexceptional nature. Though not "great as a scholar, nor one gifted with eloquent speech," he nonetheless "consecrated all that he had" to the Lord's work (473). Readers insert themselves into the biographical space made apparent in the ordinariness of the unfolding life. After an Emersonian meditation on the nature of "genius," Hopkins concludes: Hayden "coveted no man's genius, but did the best with his own special gifts, and at his death held the respect of all persons – white and black – from the governor down to the lowliest citizen of the grand old commonwealth of Massachusetts" (473). Hopkins targets the public life as a means of integrating the representative man with his history. For those of less than heroic stature, recognizable patterns of service authenticate their lives.

Conventions of the slave narrative enable Hopkins to establish a framework within which to contend with her anxiety of influence. She must recover the vitality of the received form of the antebellum slave narrative and put it into the service of her contemporary representative lives: "Mr. *Hayden* was born in *Kentucky*, but the date is lost in the dark annals of slavery. He escaped with his wife, *Harriet*, when quite a young man. It was the usual thrilling story of hiding in barns, swamps, and forests by day, and travelling by night ever toward the North Star, then the beacon-light in the travail that preceded the birth of liberty" (473; emphasis added). Biography rescues from "the dark annals of slavery" the specific and the general trials of race history: from chattel slavery to flight to Oberlin to Boston.

Hopkins multiplies these familiar dramatic effects through dramatic narration and fictional dialogue, italicizing authorial exhortations to readers. In her sketch Hayden's life was one of fictional imperatives – "adventures," "sacrifices," and "events" – inscribed on the tablets of public (because verifiable) history. Cascading layers of specific reference inform the more recent Boston history – "having a store on Cambridge street, just above North Anderson street (then known as Bridge street)" (474) – privileging the local in its creation of an intimate dialogue with the readers. She expands the context beyond the immediate neighborhood to the State House where Hayden was a member of the Massachusetts Legislature and, "at the close of his public career," secretary of state. This trajectory of public success is confirmed by the fact that state offices closed for the "funeral exercises" of this public servant (474).

The epilogue militantly announces the relevance of race history and welfare to African Americans: "The deeds of men of a past generation are the beacon lights along the shore for the youth of today. We do not rehearse deeds of riot or bloodshed from a desire to fire anew the public mind, but because our traditions and history must be kept alive if we hope ever to become a people worthy to be named with others. We must pause sometimes in the busy whirl of daily life and think of the past, and from an intelligent comprehension of these facts read the present signs of the times" (476).

Advancing the private mind into the public arena, Hopkins seeks coherence and immediacy in her biographical histories. The twin axes of slave history and citizenship recur in each profile but are made explicit in Hayden's sketch: "The question then was: Has the Negro a right to resist his master? We settled that in the Civil War. The question now is: Has the Negro a right to citizenship? This last question cannot be settled by strife" (477). The impersonalized generalizations concluding Hayden's biography characterize the way in which Hopkins moves quickly from history to the urgent, present-tense citizenship implications with the collective authorial voice "We." The recurrent emphasis throughout these narratives remains that history for black America is what *is*, not what *was*.

While the "Famous Men" series forms a relatively uniform rhetorical chorus, it is more than simply a race miscellany. Hopkins sought figures whose newly emerging public roles would underscore their moment in race citizenship and history. This necessitated a departure from prior models like Emerson's *Representative Men*, where every figure is canonical. Although the *Colored American* exploited the serial nature of these biographies (to enhance readership), contemporary critics committed to the expansiveness and depth of Hopkins's historical grasp need to appreciate the intertextual subtlety of her collection. For example, the literacy and authority of William Wells Brown would "stimulate the soul thirsting for the springs of knowledge" (*CAM*, January 1901, 236); the Emersonian self-reliance of state representative Edwin Garrison Walker would illumine the "thrilling occurrences . . . [and] sacrifices made of money and of personal safety by the colored men of New York and New England for the amelioration of their race" (*CAM*, March 1901, 361); the valor of Sergeant William H. Carney, volunteer in the Massachusetts 54th Infantry Regiment, would incarnate New England's noble African-American history when, as color-bearer, he "held the emblem of liberty in the air" at Fort Wagner (*CAM*, June 1901, 87).

Senators, jurists, soldiers, and authors form a human bridge of historical recovery and continuity, embodying the "benefits of sacrifices, hopes and prayers . . . for future Afro-American[s]" (*CAM*, June 1901, 89). Authentic history originates in the biographies of just such standard-bearers. In an echo of her fictional project, Hopkins muses on the genealogical import of race history: These lives "are about all we can claim as absolutely our own; we are of one blood, and of one kind with them" (*CAM*, September 1901, 337). Yet, uneasy with a celebration of merely individual paths, Hopkins decided to expand her representative kinship into a community notion of race biography and history in her "Famous Women of the Negro Race."

Although "Famous Women of the Negro Race" (November 1901–January 1903), like its predecessor, historically and culturally anchors readers through familiar iconographic portraits – in this instance, "Sojourner Truth" and "Harriet Tubman" – it departs significantly from the earlier series (with its reliance upon the representative individual) in favor of group portraits of community endeavor, privileging the public and spirited contributions of African-American women to culture and society. The series begins with one such collective portrait, "Phenomenal Vocalists," as if to signal a radical departure from Hopkins's earlier representative individual strategy. The restricted, public historical focus of the "Famous Men" series proved inadequate to the needs of previously marginalized contributions of African-American women.

By inaugurating her new series with a collective portrait, Hopkins inserts a contextualizing group identity that informs even the heroic figures of Sojourner Truth and Harriet Tubman, transforming them from indecorous race heroines (women deemed excessively public and opinionated for the day) to exemplars of a race history and ongoing community. As Claudia Tate notes in her incisive discussion of the turn-of-the-century revision of patriarchal texts and models in African-American fiction: "Even though the black Victorian model permitted professional activity outside the home for the wife and other females of the household, modesty and reserve were essential. Those middle-class women (like Mary Church Terrell and Ida B. Wells-Barnett) who asserted positions of leadership, thus resisting that decorum, were often regarded as aggressive and immodest" (1992: 151–2).

"Sojourner Truth: A Northern Slave" (*CAM*, December 1901, 124–32) occasions an immediate revision of life in the abolitionist North and an attendant challenge to Hopkins's own generation of readers. Moving swiftly from a globalized capsule history of slavery to a regional account, Hopkins advances the theory that this life is "remarkable because she experienced that Northern slavery of which we know so little at present" (125). This "Ethiopian Sybil" is the very incarnation of what her biographer finds most difficult to capture without yielding to contemporary clichés of women's spirituality. Lacking the fictional spurs of characterization and plot, the sketch grounds its discussion of the revelatory spectacles of one "who knew religion only by revelation!" (131) in a sequence of domestic framings of personal and racial family history.

Ever conscious of the bourgeois probity of her audience, Hopkins as mediating biographer enables this life to emerge as both family narrative and assertive self-construct, seeming to sanction as it subverts the "append[ed] certificate of character given Sojourner Truth by men . . . as a guarantee of the authenticity of this woman's statements" by privileging the subject herself: "The subject of this biography, Sojourner Truth, as she called herself – but whose name was originally Isabella – was born between the years of 1797 and 1800" (125). While the culturally significant subject of "this biography" is the woman who "called herself" Sojourner Truth, not the one who "was named" Isabella, the sketch must still account for the chattel history.

Sojourner Truth joins Hopkins's established pantheon of male race heroes (Douglass, Toussaint, Langston, Washington, and Elliott) who seem equal when seen through the leveling experience of slavery. Through this reiteration of secular saints, Hopkins (now bound by race *and* gender) rejects received history and reconstructs the essential narratives of representation and history in the black community. Here the biographical project depicts an ongoing race history as the complementary revelation of domestic dramas: Sojourner as sexual victim under slavery, as mother of five children, as rescuer of her son. These fictionally embellished escapades (familiar to readers of *Uncle Tom's Cabin*) sound the reassuring notes of turn-of-the-century domestic fiction.[13] But within the blurred genres of history, fiction, and biography, one might detect a subtext of a black heroine, which announces what Tate identifies as "domestic allegories of political desire." Under the genteel surface beats an aggressive and assertive life.

Unlike the slavery thresholds in the "Famous Men" sequence, this historical antecedent risks presenting Isabella's experience of sexual, emotional, and physical traumata as general to the condition of slave women. Marriage, motherhood, and morals "suffered" because slaves were not allowed to have those social roles and characteristics. In third-person narration, Hopkins makes communal Sojourner's/Isabella's plight and then turns to yet another contemporary instruction regarding Southern race policies and fear of amalgamation. Neither womanly attributes nor maternal instincts assume dramatic form until the narrative turns to the authentic subject, Sojourner Truth. As in Harriet Jacobs's *Incidents in the Life of a Slave Girl*, agency resides in women as complex and complete individuals, as Hopkins privileges the intimate components of this public life.

Only Truth's slave and family roots require male authentication. Hopkins liberates her from domesticity into a series of spiritual and global travels, noting that "she sent her children word of her whereabouts" (132). This nod toward maternal responsibility both acknowledges and severs Truth's connection with her family circle in order that she may perform on a grander, public stage. Traveling throughout New England, Sojourner Truth translates knowing into telling, "lecturing, preaching, and working by the day" (132). She surmounted her illiteracy with "her commanding figure and dignified manner" as she gave voice to her racial history and her gender. With her "remarkable gift in prayer and great talent in singing" (132), Truth embodies the spirituality and artistry Hopkins explores in the remaining sketches.

The subject of Harriet Tubman presented greater challenges than the lesser-known Sojourner. Because Tubman (like Toussaint and

Douglass) had an archetypal presence in race history, Hopkins sought to make "the Moses of her people" anew, to render this already familiar cultural figure in an immediate and pertinent way.[14] In "Harriet Tubman ('Moses')" (*CAM* January/February 1902, 210–23), the present political struggles – "the strange Providences which have befallen us as a race" (210) – become the historical extension of Tubman's own struggle seen as parable. Evoking a "paradise lost" familiar to readers of "Toussaint L'Overture," the sketch announces its Christian correspondence to the "life of Jesus." Simultaneously a martyr – "side by side with . . . Joan of Arc, and Florence Nightingale" – and a survivor, Tubman exceeds even these Christian prototypes: "for no one of them has shown more courage and power of endurance in facing danger and death to relieve human suffering than has this woman in her heroic and successful endeavors to reach and save all whom she might of her oppressed and suffering race, and pilot them to the promised land of Liberty" (212). Hopkins relies upon this image of the feminized Christ throughout the sketch, as she draws Tubman through her "stations of life."

Echoing the slave narrative, Hopkins introduces a range of possibilities regarding Tubman's being named and self-naming and is herself intrigued by the fictional potential of the authorial act of naming. The catalogue of identities mimics the itinerary of this extraordinary life as it merges the domestic with the public life. As "Moses," she becomes the very idealization of motives; as "conductor," she, like Christ, epitomizes "the Way"; as "Moll Pitcher," she incarnates a national and racial folk hero; as Araminta, she announces the circumstance of her birth; as one who "married," she confirms self-agency and self-authority. Like Toussaint and Truth, Tubman presents no written record for biographer Hopkins to shape, thereby liberating fictional instincts to dramatize and characterize the emerging historical record. Literal kinship is subordinate to the grander panorama of Tubman's larger racial family. So inherently dramatic is this historical record that Hopkins, as if to deny its seeming fictional excesses, stresses Tubman's humanity: "One of the most ordinary looking of her race; unlettered; no idea of geography! asleep half the time" (215).

When read against the subsequent iconographic sketches, the initiating "Phenomenal Vocalists" is grander in concept and scheme than first appears (*CAM*, November 1901, 45–53). Now its affirmation of "the pathos and trueness to nature" (46) of African-American music and its testimonial to the nobility and sacrifice of the African-American woman must be read through the lives of Truth and Tubman, investing the sketch with larger race ambitions. Whether to appease the sensibilities of her Victorian readership or to enlarge the historical ground to include an expanded notion of family, Hopkins depicted "the achievements of Negro women who were beacon lights" (46) within a suitably decorous frame. Only the bold eccentricities of the series' icons violate decorum for Victorian women.

In the remaining generalized portraits of educators, literary workers, college elite, and club women, Hopkins explores the women's communal or "lift while climbing" cultural work. During these turn-of-the-century years, as Angela Davis has noted, "a serious ideological marriage had linked racism and sexism in a new way" (1981: 121), compelling African-American women to transform seemingly innocent social activities, like the Boston Women's Era Club, into politically intense circles for social change (Giddings 1984: esp. chap. 6). The national club movement, far from being a race-blind sisterhood, broke along politically practical and racially circumstantial lines.[15] While the casual reader of the *Colored American* might view these sketches as simple testimonials to culture and taste (offering the imitative socialization of the bourgeoisie), Hopkins invested these life studies with the broader cultural ambitions of the national club movement. An insistence upon generational continuity as well as collective identity pervades each installment. Family or name recognition would be preserved while a historical race identity would be proposed. Hopkins sought to displace cultural ignorance with a schooled intelligence sharpened by fragile and incomplete citizenship.

Unlike earlier portraits celebrating historical moments and individual courage, these communal portraits memorialize individuals (complete with genealogical specifics) because they categorize public work and opportunities for the race. Hopkins assumes that individual achievement is but one way to "mark an era in the progress of the race" (as she notes in "Phenomenal Vocalists," 1901: 51). In modifying received biographical strategies, she imposes on the individual life story the imperative of cultivating race consciousness through collective identity. The rising generation must draw individual and race inspiration not simply from the heroic, historically distant few but from their cultural identity as African Americans. Cognizant of her authorial duty to fulfill readers' expectations, Hopkins balances her political agenda of extolling learned and independent womanhood with a socially realized series which, at least superficially, accommodated the ethos.

If Hopkins's men embodied an instructive historical authenticity through sharply focused public lives, these "Famous Women" bridge family and culture to bring progress to the race. Salvation resides in a union of the private and public lives of women *and* men. As Hopkins asserts at the close of "Literary Workers": "Why is the present bright? Because, for the first time, we stand face to face, as a race, with life as it is. Because we are at the parting of the ways and must choose true morality, true spirituality, and the firm basis of all prosperity in races or nations – honest toil in field and shop, doing away with all superficial assumption in education and business" (*CAM*, April 1902, 371). Such physical confrontation requires more than a historical regard for the exemplary: it necessitates a generational continuity with the future. Hopkins, in a manner familiar to readers of her fiction, deliberates on the race's inability to compensate for the "stress and pain of that hated past" (371). Advancement, she suggests, depends upon the construction of an authentic history that can point to as well as lead beyond slavery.

Awareness of such tense issues as accommodation and generation dominate the biographer's historical review at the midpoint of her series on "Educators." Here she simultaneously seems to acknowledge the inferiority of African-American cultural contributions even as she suggests the originary force of African culture. Her historical review undercuts the privilege accorded Anglo-Saxon "race" accomplishments in its commanding restoration of historical antecedents. Wresting "race" from its current Anglo-Saxon moorings (A. Davis 1981: 110–26; Horsman 1981), Hopkins seeks primary cultural moments like the one narrated in *Of One Blood*. Rhetorically, this reversal serves the double-voiced pattern of the text so that the novelist can both please an accommodationist – black or white – and inform the militant race-and-culture reader. When Hopkins's many contributions to the *Colored American Magazine* are considered intertextually, she appears more militant and savvy than either Carby or Gwendolyn Brooks allows. What Carby labels her "unashamed sycophancy" (1987: 130) and Brooks declares to be reverence for "the modes and idolatries of the master" (1978: 404) seem upon further reflection to be the linguistic manipulation of one conversant with the signifying power of the double-voiced narrative. This dialogic interplay allows the novelist to inform the historian-biographer of the interplay between master and slave, polemicist and accommodationist.

Through these collective portraits, the biographer privileges the public roles of black women in American society over the customary celebration of "nobler women, more self-sacrificing tender mothers" (*CAM*, November 1901, 46), so that she may include them in the larger race tapestry. Nowhere does the domestic sphere receive the attention she would pay it in her fiction. Not only did the audience for these biographies require the sustaining citizenship instruction that public lives could give, but the genre demanded it. The series encouraged a move from the preoccupation with moral suasion and genteel education to the "organized intelligence" called for in "Club Life among Colored Women" (*CAM*, August 1902, 273–7). Repeatedly asserting the "intellectual capacity" of African-American women, she advanced the cause of "a new race of colored women" (*CAM*, October 1902, 446–7).

In those turn-of-the-century years at the *Colored American Magazine*, Hopkins as editor, biographer, historian, and fiction writer understood the intertextual potential of the periodical press. It is difficult from this historical distance to appreciate the synergic relationship between her individual contributions and her century-distant audience. Although the single-volume republication of her magazine novels has made her serial fiction readily available to a new generation, it obscures the larger, instructive context of Hopkins's cultural mission at the *Colored American*: to restore "the fire and romance which lie dormant in our history" (*Contending Forces*, 1900: 14). While her biographical sketches may lack the literary "fire and romance" of her fiction, when read individually in the pages of the *Colored American* they nonetheless significantly enhance our understanding of the ways in which Hopkins, as Elizabeth Ammons has claimed, "changed history" through her revisionary reconstruction of the novel (1991a: 85). Most immediately, these sketches represent an African-American woman novelist's attempt (paraphrasing Hopkins) to throttle evil by invoking the power of "an upright manhood and an enlightened womanhood" (*CAM*, July 1902, 213). Though they lack the "distinctiveness as a discourse" that Elizabeth Fox-Genovese finds critically so compelling in some autobiographies of black women, these biographies adroitly manipulate a host of generic strategies, generating a sense of the dramatic and historical depth of the African presence in America.

Pauline Hopkins's "talented" fate committed her "to teach life" (Du Bois 1903b: 861). Long before she joined the Colored American Publishing Co-operative, and for the remainder of her life, she wrote as a conscientious African American with a duty to her race, her gender, and her intellectual and artistic gifts. In reconstructing the inherited rhetorical conventions of the exemplary life, she sought to authenticate not simply race history but also black America as an equal partner in the larger national experience. If Mather and Emerson seem to constitute an unlikely rhetorical inheritance for an African-American woman writer, readers need only recall that Mather's *Magnalia* and Emerson's *Representative Men* were also attempts to construct *American* history ex nihilo. For Hopkins, the appropriation of generic strategies from the dominant white culture was not a concession to oppressive cultural values; it was a dignified and accessible way of rendering homage to the African-American past.

READING RIOT

"A STUDY IN RACE RELATIONS
AND A RACE RIOT IN 1919"

The streets were like avenues of the dead. They only caught a ten-year-old Negro boy. They took his clothes off, and burned them. They burned his tail with lighted matches, made him step on lighted matches, urinated on him, and sent him running off naked with a couple of slaps in the face.

> – James T. Farrell
> *The Young Manhood of Studs Lonigan* (1935)

In the twentieth century . . . the idea of community scarcely means anything anymore . . . except among the submerged, the "lowly" . . . called communities because they are informed by their knowledge that only they of the community can sustain and re-create each other. The great, vast, shining Republic knows nothing about them – recognizes their existence only in time of stress, as during a military adventure, say, or an election year, or when their dangerous situation erupts into what the Republic generally calls a "riot." And it goes without saying that these communities, incipient, wounded, or functioning, are between the carrot and the stick of the American dream.

> – James Baldwin, *The Evidence of Things Not Seen*
> (1985a: 123–4)

The determining of a relationship between news and its subsequent privileging as history takes on a renewed urgency in the aftermath of the 1992 spring riot in Los Angeles. Daily newspapers assume what Sterling Brown calls, in "An Old Woman Remembers" (1989: 188), the power to "name," as familiar headlines declare "VANDALS ROAM CITY" and a news story, generic in its observations, unfolds: "Social order broke down today across a broad area of the nation's second-largest city as vandals and looters roamed the streets, carloads of young men attacked pedestrians and uncounted fires burned out of control" (*New York Times*, May 1, 1992: 1). Once again a president expresses shock, fear, and bewilderment, and forms a commission to investigate the causes of what the Kerner Commission had decades before termed "socially-directed violence." The lack of an ongoing public dialogue concerning riots stems from what Cornel West sees in the case of the Los Angeles riot: "The narrow framework of the dominant liberal and conservative views of race in America, with its worn-out vocabulary, leaves us intellectually debilitated, morally disempowered and personally depressed" (1992b: 24). The tension between privilege and disempowerment pervades the polarized discourse evoked by public violence. Kenneth Clark, before the Kerner Commission in late 1968, recalled the history of all such riot commissions:

> I read that report . . . of the 1919 riot in Chicago, and it is as if I were reading the report of the investigating committee of the Harlem riot of '35, the report of the McCone Commission on the Watts riot. I must again in candor say to you members of this Commission – it is a kind of Alice in Wonderland – with the same moving picture shown over and over again, with the same analysis, the same recommendations, and the same inaction. (1965: 483)

Read individually, these reports bear traces of exhaustive scholarship, active citizenship, and remorse. Unfortunately, as Clark suggests, when read in succession, they inadvertently expose how decisively African Americans have been left to sink in twentieth-century urban America. Competing stories of Chicago's 1919 riot mark the beginnings of Clark's "same moving picture syndrome" and offer a complex literary and social weave of anecdote, report, and journalism that illustrates the genre-defying nature of such narratives.

By 1919, racial and class tensions, coupled with the burden of post–Great War anxiety, proved too heavy for many American cities to bear. The end of the war for African Americans signaled a time of an intense diasporic consciousness that revived interest in territorial and cultural nationalism. Black journalists, reflecting cynicism and disillusionment as they reconsidered Mr. Wilson's war for democracy, sought an enlarged racialism and an assured citizenship. If Georgian complacency died in the trenches of the war, black acceptance of compromised citizenship perished in national service. As columnist William Colson, formerly a lieutenant in the 367th U.S. Infantry, trenchantly summarized the mood in "The New Negro Patriotism" (published in *The Messenger,* August 1919):

> The Negro soon found that the treachery of the white American was infinitely more damaging to him than that of the Hun. He was refused a square deal in the army and navy, and discriminations became more gruelling in the South. . . . Intelligent Negroes have all reached the point where their loyalty to the country is conditional. The patriotism of the mass of Negroes may now be called doubtful (Vincent 1973: 67, 69).

In Chicago, a carefully engineered though rigid vision of city planning that involved calculated racial and ethnic segregation became an ad hoc reaction against change. What Bertolt Brecht called the "great city jungle" of Chicago (1966: 12) convulsed with demands made by new constituencies, as recent Southern migrants were pitted against more established immigrants and the old neighborhood boundaries failed to contain or restrain the burgeoning new populations. Chicago in the summer of 1919 erupted into racial conflict.[1]

Like most outbreaks of social violence, the 1919 riot was occasioned by a random, cruel event. By the spring of 1919 the postwar labor, class, and racial tensions in Chicago were at an all-time high. Black laborers were in demand, but tensions at the neighborhood level exacerbated a long-held animosity between Irish and black workers. Expectations of social and economic opportunities carried home from the Continent by African-American veterans brought pressures to bear in the workplace and in the neighborhood. Soldiers who had fought for freedom in Europe were certain to fight for their liberties at home. It was a "critical year," as Arthur Waskow explains, when Americans were forced to rethink their "attitudes toward the public and private use of violence in dealing with intense social conflicts" (1966: 1).

Nationally, the spring had brought racial violence. Riots from Arkansas to Washington, D.C., erupted from years of discontent. Journalists had warned Chicago that the unaddressed issues of unemployment and poor housing would surely lead to violence. In fact, Carl Sandburg's "riot report," actually a series of articles commissioned by the *Chicago Daily News* (a paper often cited by the *Chicago Defender*'s Robert Abbott as the only evenhanded daily in Chicago), was written just before the riot and warned of imminent social unrest. On Sunday July 27 riot came to Chicago. All morning, groups of blacks and whites had been vying for the territory between the 26th and 29th Street beaches. Unofficially segregated, the turf broke along racial lines. A group of black teenagers who had "trespassed" into imagined white swimming territory were stoned by a lone white man; one boy, Eugene Williams, drowned. Officer Daniel Callahan ignored the pleas of bystanders to arrest the man they thought had caused the drowning, instead arresting a black for harassing a white man. Someone fired shots; a riot was on. In a week, twenty-three blacks and fifteen whites were dead.[2]

Almost from the moment of its eruption, this riot became the subject of intensive historical, sociological, economic, and multidisciplinary investigations into Chicago's failure to accommodate and assimilate its new populations. The nation turned its national attention to Chicago to answer "the question of questions for America – the race question" (Kerlin 1920: v). Although the various forms of discourse generated by the riot have provided generations of scholars with information about class, nationality, religion, and party affiliation, scant attention has been paid to the rhetorical strategies of these competing communities.[3] The disinterest of scholars in the discourse of riot as a subject of literary and social inquiry has fostered impatience with the various narrative accounts surrounding the event.

Of these narratives, four offer exemplary aesthetic constructions of the riot: Robert S. Abbott's *Chicago Defender* editorials, Carl Sandburg's stories for the Chicago *Daily News*, the Chicago Federation of Labor's rallying cries for *The New Majority*, and Charles S. Johnson's scholarly race advocacy in *The Negro in Chicago: A Study in Race Relations and a Race Riot in 1919.* Each of these responses to the city's race crisis had an alternative agenda as well in its dialogues with sociologically definable constituencies too complex to speak with a single voice.[4] Diverse in their contexts and rhetorics, these writers made the riot into readable social dramas that countered certain hegemonic traditions that formed the way the history of the riot has been written and understood. The militantly political *Defender* and the *New Majority* would assume the authority to speak for, as well as to, the neglected masses. The officially concerned *Daily News* and *The Negro in Chicago* would speak for the leadership of the city. The attempts of the *Defender* to embody and define race aspirations nationally; of the

New Majority to promote the class interests of mostly white recent immigrant laborers and blue-collar workers; of Carl Sandburg, for the *Daily News*, to reflect assumptions of earlier, more fully assimilated immigrants; and of Charles Johnson to sculpt race awareness into the very body of *The Negro in Chicago* all provide insights into a range of rhetorical strategies and assumptions about Chicago's diverse and competing communities. Rhetorical analysis demonstrates that news is less a strict accounting and more a signifying upon ideas or assumptions of community circumstances. And though this knowledge may seem commonplace, it is often neglected. These documents have a prismatic effect on the event, refracting history into many bands. If, as Martin Luther King, Jr., concluded, "a riot is at bottom the language of the unheard" (1967: 112), then attempts by others to translate that language into more socially benign forms say a great deal about what those others think of the unheard.

Since cultural bias and commitment shape the coercive race rhetoric of these competing stories and the assumptions (not the historical accuracies or inaccuracies) their authors make about audience and community values, I am interested in uncovering what Clifford Geertz would call the "principles of mapping" implicit in their rhetoric (1983b: 20). A further level of theory would consider the extent to which these competing rhetorics expose the tension between a desire for authority and a regard for historic or objective accuracy. The rhetoric of journalism, like most forms of public discourse, tends toward hegemony and authority. Bakhtin's distinction between the centripetal and centrifugal forces in language may help to explain the tendency of public discourse to marginalize competing authorities and reject the objectivity that would recognize alternative readings of history and the news.[5]

For Robert Abbott, marginal discourse is the voice of the large white community newspapers, a voice that finds its way into his writing as the voice of resistance; for Sandburg, the marginal is both his own latent or suppressed racism, which creeps into his riot articles in various ways, and a self-effacing liberal discourse that, like a siren song, would lure him from his privileged cultural position to become a genuine voice of the oppressed. For the *New Majority* writers, a language of class solidarity attempts to marginalize the voice of racial distinction; for Johnson, the distant and objective voice of historicized authority drifts away amid the various political voices he tries to relegate to the margins. All of these publications, because they address communities with definite expectations, privilege the centripetal force of their language through the rhetorical means available to them, though the centrifugal force cannot be entirely suppressed. But, as Bakhtin has argued, discourse is always particularized.

Although these documents share a national effect or resonance, I am interested in their local setting and their projections of collective identity in a time of crisis. I will not compare daily news accounts but will reflect instead upon the rhetorical strategies of a range of documents – headlines, editorials, proclamations, feature stories – anticipating, reporting, and reflecting the riot, writings that have formed the historical chorus of the event. Close consideration of the rhetorical stances taken in these four narratives will demonstrate that this partisanship inheres in the writers' use of language and often exposes itself despite their stated intentions, sometimes in a counterproductive way, as the centrifugal force of marginal discourse intrudes.

In 1905, Robert Abbott recognized that if black Chicagoans were to have a voice, they must have a paper that would, on a weekly basis, assert through conscious definition the place of the "Race" in the United States. And by 1925, his dream of a national race paper realized, Abbott secured international recognition through Charles S. Johnson's contribution to Alain Locke's anthology *The New Negro*. In "The New Frontage on American Life," Johnson reflected:

> There was Chicago in the West, known far and wide for its colossal abattoirs, whose placarded warehouses, set close by the railroad, dotted every sizable town of the South, calling for men; Chicago, remembered for the fairyland wonders of the World's Fair; home of the fearless, taunting "race paper," and above all things, of mills clamoring for men (1925: 278).

Abbott refused a reactionary stance – to appropriate "Negro" or "colored," labels inherited from and used derogatorily by whites – working to forge a positive identity in the pages of his "race paper." By 1919 the *Defender* was by no means the only race paper in the city. In fact, as James Grossman's *Land of Hope* demonstrates, the Chicago *Whip*, founded in 1919 in reaction to Abbott's own "rhetorical ambivalence" to trade-union issues, became the paper of choice for race members interested in labor issues (1989: 234–6). But the national as well as local circulation of Abbott's paper made the *Defender* a social force.[6] As Frederick Detweiler noted in *The Negro Press in the United States*: "The paper seeks to live up to its title of *Defender*. Colored people from all over the country turn to it when in trouble" (1922: 65). Chicago's leading race paper was read and revered by family and friends still in the South. Relatives could compare notes with those already in the North, intensifying the subtexts of the news and its rhetorical strategies. Readers of the *Defender* were a "family" with "understandings" about Abbott's worldview.

What Robert Park and James Weldon Johnson independently surmised about newspapers Abbott already believed: that they were "circulated and read" (Park 1925: 80), not just printed; that newspapers nourished and reflected community interests as well as disseminated news. What Park asserted for working-class immigrants was as true for many South Side families: Their "only literature was the family newspaper" (1925: 94–5). Perhaps even more central to the needs of the community, Johnson declared, was the certainty that newspapers "converted masses of Negro Americans into Readers" (1938: 31).[7] Because of the fear that innocent rural migrants would be manipulated by industrialists, the *Defender*, like the newly formed Chicago Urban League (UL), committed time and money to "Americanization" efforts, trying to enable new arrivals to fit into Chicago.[8] Abbott redirected the energized rhetoric of war, making the *Defender*'s headlines concerning the great migration into proclamations of hope and near military zeal: "Millions to Leave South" . . . "Northern Invasion Will Start in the Spring – Bound for Promised Land" (January 6, 1917). "Invasion" here represents aggressive enthusiasm, a flow of energy, and an uplifting of hope rather than a threat, but the threatening connotations linger. Many white northern papers also resorted to the term "invasion," but with trepidation and barely concealed hostility.

An example of such hostile northern response may be found in a Beloit, Wisconsin, *News* editorial (August 25, 1916):

> The Negro *problem* has moved north. Rather, the negro problem has spread from south to north; and beside it in the South is appearing a stranger to that clime – the labor problem.
>   It's a double development brought about by the war in Europe, and the nation has not yet realized its significance. Within a few

years, experts predict the negro population of the North will be tripled. It's your problem, or it will be when the negro moves next door.

Italians and Greeks are *giving way* to the negroes in the section gangs along northern railroads, as *you can see from the train windows*, and as labor agents admit. Northern cities that had only small colored populations are finding their "white" sections *invaded* by negro families, strangers to the town.

Many cities are in for the experience that has *befallen* all communities on the edge of the North and South – gradual *encroachment* of colored folks on territory *occupied* by whites; depreciation of realty values and lowering of rents, and finally, moving of the white families to other sections, leaving the districts in *possession* of colored families with a small sprinkling of whites.

This means racial resentment – for the white family that moves to *escape negro proximity* always carries, justly or not, a prejudice against the black race. It hits your pocket too. . . .

With the black *tide* setting north, the southern negro, formerly a *docile tool* is demanding better pay, better food and better treatment. And no longer can the South refuse to give it to him. It's a *national problem* now, instead of a sectional problem. And it has got to be solved. (Grant 1972: 40–1; emphasis added)

Within a hundred miles of Chicago, Beloit was already registering the confusion and fear of the white voyeur looking out at race through a train window. Unlike the battle-royal rhetoric used by Abbott, this editorial inverts the vocabulary of war into one of a siege mentality. The standoff here is between territory held by whites and that threatened by the oncoming "tide" of migrants. The message is not merely one of economics but of classical, class-driven race tensions. The assumption of this editorial is that "negro proximity" alone is enough to incite war between the races.

Crucial to my rhetorical analysis of the riot is an awareness of the larger, regional concern prompted by the first wave of migration that reverted to a social policy of containment. Long before African-American veterans returned home with "continental" expectations, communities ringing the northern cities impacted by the migration were already bristling with indignation and fear. A Chicago *Whip* editorial (August 9, 1919) generalizes the concern of many black editors in the region:

"Has the Negro Been Fighting for Social Equality?"

We have made an accurate survey of the claims of the New Negro. We have censored his activities since his return from France. And we even aided the investigators of Chicago dailies as they followed the color line. We have gathered first hand information from Washington, D.C., as to the feeling of its colored people. WE HAVE YET TO OBSERVE WHERE THE NEGRO HAS MADE ANY FIGHT FOR SOCIAL EQUALITY. . . . Yet they claim the Negro is fighting for social equality when he buys property in sections where he was a stranger. THEY CALL THIS AN INVASION. We admit that the Negro is tired of being a 'half-man.' We admit that he is tired of the heel of white oppression. We admit that he has been pushed to the wall and even now he stands and shows his teeth. We even admit that the Negro desires social EQUALITY ON THE BASIS OF MERIT. BUT WE CANNOT BE INTELLIGENTLY HONEST AND TRUTHFULLY ADMIT THAT HE HAS MADE A FIGHT FOR SOCIAL EQUALITY. HIS FIGHT HAS BEEN A DEFENSIVE ONE. THIS SEEMS SURPRISING AND ALARMING TO OUR WHITE FRIENDS, WHO SEEM TO THINK THAT HE SHOULD BE PASSIVELY SUBMISSIVE. . . . (Kerlin 1920: 66).

Borrowing from the rhetorical strategies of the race and labor presses (and anticipating the pronominal tide of Gwendolyn Brooks's "We Real Cool"), the *Whip*, like the *Defender*, militantly subverts the equally bellicose rhetoric of the mainstream white press. Such rhetorical appropriation was particularly advantageous for minority readers who read both the mainstream dailies *and* the race or labor weeklies.

Rather than being intimidated by such hostility, however, Abbott seized upon its blunt racism in language that recalled the fervor of the abolitionist. After years of recording the plight of black Americans in the South, Abbott used the agency of the *Defender* to once again "free the slaves." In answer to those who attempted to dissuade blacks from coming to the "freezing" North, Abbott editorialized: "IF YOU CAN FREEZE TO DEATH in the north and be free, why FREEZE to death in the south and be a slave, where your mother, sister and daughter are raped . . . where your father, brother and son are . . . hung to a pole [and] riddled with bullets?" (February 27, 1917). Clearly Abbott saw himself as the leader of this hegira in spite of opposition by forces clearly beyond the circulation of the *Defender*. Only a few years later, however, black sociologist Charles Johnson would declare the migration to be a "leaderless mass-movement."[9]

By spring of 1919 the postwar labor, class, and racial tensions in the city appeared to Abbott to be at an all-time high. Black laborers were in high demand. But in spite of rhetorical support from the Chicago Federation of Labor (CFL), the American Federation of Labor (AFL) offered no commitment to racial equality in the workplace.[10] Tensions at the neighborhood level exacerbated the long held animosity between Irish- and African-American workers. The quarrels here went beyond issues of race or the workplace. They grew out of a history at least as old as the 1863 anti-Emancipation Proclamation draft riots and the ensuing constituency interests: the urban, immigrant, Democratic, Catholic Irish in perpetual conflict with the rural, native, Republican, Protestant blacks. In spite of shared economic and social concerns, such cultural differences precluded a common language. Irish Americans and African Americans seemed doomed to perpetual conflict as they struggled for the freedom of self-definition. Unlike recent central and southern European immigrants, the Irish, in James Baldwin's words, "began rising." They had worked their way into positions of ward rule and neighborhood distinction and therefore became not merely competitors in the workplace but agents of political order – and, therefore, oppression.

In response to the Irish rule of the precincts and the ballot boxes, Abbott editorialized on the issue of neighborhood gangs, in particular the Irish "athletic clubs" surrounding black neighborhoods.[11] By the summer of 1919, in the pages of the *Defender*, "police" became synonymous with "Irish." Articles as well as columns denounced the Irish as "cheap ruffians" (see, for example, February 23, 1919). "Cheap" became Abbott's code word not only for those who were recent immigrants without means but for those who simply acted that way. Unlike in the black community, where the more established business class often held itself aloof from the migrants, the Irish communities, at least in Abbott's eyes, fused into a common political, ward identity.

The *Defender* began to pair accounts of white assaults on race members in Chicago alongside reports of lynchings in the Deep South. Readers learned to decode headlines like "White Policemen Cause So. Side Riot" (April 26, 1919) to mean "Irish assault race member." The familial association between the many Irish "athletic clubs" and the police enraged Abbott. As he noted, members were "sons and relatives of a number of policemen of the Stock Yards station and, as a result, their depredations seldom occasioned an arrest" (July 12,

1919). Such street gangs had come to seem untouchable to him because they were part of the armed leadership of the city itself. And this immunity intensified the sense of colonization and disfranchisement. Abbott seized every opportunity to invert the expected syntax of white press headlines (e.g., "Ragan's [*sic*] Colts Start Riot") to counter the impression of African Americans as the agents of socially directed violence.

Alienated from the official power structure and segregated from a larger urban identity, it was as if black Chicago were being held captive and silent by a foreign power. This expands the context within which Abbott's extravagant editorial practices might be judged. Those offended by his flamboyant disregard for facts must weigh that violation of journalistic ethical practice against his intent to give voice and political clout to a race that otherwise was without agency.

Barely represented on the city's police force, black police did seem to fall into the "last to be hired, first to go" category. A lead story in the Chicago *Tribune* (July 11, 1919), two weeks before the riot, offers a glimpse into life on duty for the African-American police officer: "COP'S RACE FEUD BRINGS CHARGES AGAINST THREE / COLORED MEN TAKE WHITE ONES' BEDS AND THREATEN THEM." The front-page follow-up (July 29, 1919): "MERIT BOARD PUTS 3 COLORED COPS ON TRIAL." By the end of the month, the officers, whose sole offense was to sleep in beds designated for white officers, had been fired (see Tuttle 1970: 264–5).

In weariness and dismay the *Defender* expressed the sense of futility felt by the race; on April 12, 1919, Abbott editorialized: "We have arrayed ourselves on the side of capital to a great extent yet capital has not played square with us; it has used us as strikebreakers, then when the calm came turned us adrift." Almost poignant in its resignation, this editorial makes manifest the nativist race commitment to Americanism, patriotism, and capitalism. Curiously, the race found itself on the side of management, which it used against fellow workers. With palpable dismay Abbott confesses, "capital has not played square with us." The race had entered freely into a compact with the northern, industrial world of labor and capital even as it had given of itself in the Great War. And it had suffered a cruel betrayal. The reasoned, impassioned tone of this editorial suggests the range of Abbott's rhetorical ability as it pronounces race policy within the context of white racism.

No matter how lurid and sensational the front page became, Abbott reserved a measured temperament for his editorials. A meditation on the larger implications of the race problem preoccupied his columns throughout the spring, culminating in "Reducing Friction" (May 3, 1919). The occasion for the piece was the continued bombing of South Side residences, but the larger concern was the seemingly undying hatred between the races. Swept away by metaphor, Abbott literalizes, as he attempts to make the crisis seem immediate and palpable to citizens and journalists alike:

> Friction generates or evolves heat, no less in human bodies than in cold, lifeless metal. The clashing of two racial groups, it matters not what the cause may be, brings the heat of passion to each, and if carried far enough fans the burning brain of a sane, normal man into a white fever heat and makes of him, for the time being at least, a star graduate of his satanic majesty's school. It is not an uncommon thing to pick up a daily newspaper and read a highly colored account of a race riot. And what is a race riot?

Because the column touches on the hyperbolic treatment of racial incidents by the white dailies – "Perhaps a few school children, white and Black, have some petty differences" – it serves as a critical marker regarding Abbott's insight into the deliberative tensions between the white and black press. By its very nature, the black press was a weekly supplement and spiritual corrective to the omissions and distortions handed to the race on a daily basis.

Front-page dissections of neighborhood gangs culminated in a terse, pre-riot editorial. In "Ruffianism in the Parks" (July 12, 1919), Abbott forged a crucial link between the socializing effect of journalism and actual behavior. He associates the outbreak of residential bombing with "an exhibition of ruffianism in our public parks" (the pronominally integrationist emphasis on public spaces is characteristic of Abbott's style). In order to expose the utter lack of civility and citizenship in the white community, the editorial feigns sympathy with

> these young hoodlums, many of them yet in their teens, [who] get their inspiration from what they read in the yellow press. It is there that they receive suggestions for their lawless acts. Added to this is the influence of bad home surroundings, and the ill-advised counsel of their elders. They listen to the comments of their parents and

then start out to put into execution the evil judgments of the family circle.

Inverting the usual white rhetoric, Abbott concludes that "it is inconceivable that young men of any education and respectable home training could be guilty of such acts as are laid at the door of these young savages." His target is more than the tough on the street: It is the unchristian, "savage" family circle that perpetuates such hateful behavior in and out of city hall.

Confronted with the news of a genuine uprising, the *Defender* shuttled between pulp sensationalism (not unlike the white dailies) and editorial austerity as it struggled to cover the riot. On August 2, 1919, the front page read:

RIOT SWEEPS CHICAGO
GHASTLY DEEDS OF RACE RIOTERS TOLD

Defender Reporter Faces Death to Get Facts of Mob
Violence; Hospitals Are Filled with Maimed Men and Women

GUN BATTLES AND FIGHTING IN THE STREETS
KEEP CITY IN AN UPROAR

4,000 Troops in Armory Ready to Patrol City;
Scores Are Killed

FRENCH GIVE OPINION OF RIOT

The *Defender* staff, conscious of its four-day lag behind the white dailies, sought the cinematic immediacy of charged imagery – "sweeps," "ghastly," "maimed" – as well as the legitimizing objectivity of international censorship – "French Give Opinion of Riot." Box scores of "slain" and "injured" gave a vaguely athletic cast to the grisly event.

"Reaping the Whirlwind" – an editorial with a biblical charge that anticipates James Weldon Johnson's editorial for the *New York Age*, "Reaping the Whirlwind" (August 2, 1919) and Gwendolyn Brooks's "The Second Sermon on the Warpland" – asserts Abbott's race pride in the midst of upheaval. Proclaiming the riots in Washington, D.C., and Chicago to be "a disgrace to American civilization," he returns to an indictment that had been the refrain of the *Defender*: "It is not chargeable . . . to the general unrest now sweeping the world. Nor are we witnessing anything new in these disgraceful exhibitions of lawlessness. America is known the world over as the land of the lyncher and of the mobocrat. For years she has been sowing the wind and now she is reaping the whirlwind." For Abbott the riot signaled a larger, spiritual crisis in the ongoing assumption governing race relations and the attendant obligations of the race press. Historians who claim, as William Tuttle has, that the *Defender* "erroneously informed its inflamed readers" mistake both the local intent and the governing mission of the paper (1970: 49). Blending the sensational and some-times fabricated "news" story with the censoring pulpit rhetoric of his editorials, Abbott hoped to create an alternative chorus for his read-ers. If we move beyond the "hideous and totally fabricated" nature of the account to a reading grounded in an appreciation of its rhetorical and "performative" use of language, we glimpse what Dominick LaCapra has called a "dialogical understanding of discourse and of 'truth' itself in contrast to a monological idea of a unified authorial voice providing an ideally exhaustive and definitive (total) account of a fully mastered object of knowledge" (1985: 36). The voices of histo-ry compel Abbott to see the riot in an altogether different cultural matrix. The riot-as-lynching, in his usage, becomes a trope, a literary empowering of historical material. This trope in turn becomes a com-mon motif in the *Defender*'s campaign against race-based crimes. Race murder and lynching were so repugnant, such an indictment of white America, that the facts of the instance no longer mattered as much as the emotional power generated by lynching as a dramatic motif.

However, despite the sensationalism of the *Defender* in response to that of the white mainstream dailies, Abbott never forgot his respon-sibility to his ideas of community, as evinced by this handbill distrib-uted by the *Defender* during the riots:

> The present lawless conditions prevailing throughout the city are only aggravated by loose talk and foolish actions by irresponsible of both races.
>
> We urge you to do your part to restore quiet and order.
>
> Keep yourself and your children off the streets. Remember the innocent bystander generally gets the worst of it.
>
> Remain at home and urge your friends to do likewise. Avoid crowd-ed street cars, and corners.

The police can handle rowdies better if you are not in their way.

Every day of rioting and disorder means loss of life, destruction of property, loss of money for you and your families, and for some of us these losses will be large and irredeemable.

Measures are being taken now to give adequate police service and protection.

This is no time to solve the race question.

Never mind who started it. Let proper authorities finish it.

We must have order at once for our own good and the good of Chicago.

We need cool heads and steady nerves. The police are playing no favorites.

Follow their example.

If you do your part as real citizens regardless of your color, responsibility can be easily and more justly placed.

MAKE YOURSELF a Committee of one to make things peaceful.

OBEY ALL POLICE ORDERS

Yours for Peace,
ROBERT S. ABBOTT [12]

With its emphasis on individual accountability ("Committee of one"), its socially constructive advice, and especially its insistence that the suppression of violence preempts racial issues, this handbill asserts, at the moment of crisis, the role of the urban citizen as a member of a community larger than those defined by race or ethnicity. The rhetoric in this moment of upheaval is one of integration and reflects Abbott's long-term goals as much as his fears for the moment. However, the anxiety and passion of his captioned assertion that "This is no time to solve the Race Question" compromise his long-standing attempt to shape the rhetoric of racial concern into a language of political hegemony.

Subsequent editorials throughout the fall would situate the riot in the larger historical and national context. Abbott, convinced that news is just the beginning of how we remember, sought to keep the historical record favorable, or at least neutral, to African Americans. As he intones in "Mr. Hoyne's Mistaken View" (September 6, 1919):

State's Attorney Hoyne it seems is of the impression that Colored gamblers started the race riots in Chicago. Mr. Hoyne is mistaken. He fails absolutely to grasp the underlying causes of the race clashes in this community. When he charges our people with having brought on the disgraceful happenings centering about the first week of August, he flies in the face of the real facts.

"Real facts" authenticate history and validate community. Abbott knew that this riot was a formative event in race history but that through historical purification it would lose its essence. Subsequent summer editorials would ask Chicagoans to commemorate what happened to Eugene Williams. As "The Joys of Summer" (July 9, 1921) challenged: "Less than a dozen of our group were to be seen on the beaches Friday, when the whites were out by the thousands. And why? Surely the 29th Street episode some two years ago has not frightened them away. If so they are out of place in a Northern city. Chicago especially has no room for quitters or spineless individuals." Abbott, a journalist of outrage as well as social construction, believed that control over the news was but the beginning of the invention of African-American history. The "Race Question" would never be solved by "quitters or spineless individuals," but only by those capable of authenticating their existence in the news of the day.

By the summer of 1919 the Chicago dailies were reflecting the explosive tensions in the city's race relations. Veterans' issues, prohibition, and labor strife shared front-page space with race issues in the nation's urban press. The *Chicago Tribune*, the self-proclaimed "World's Greatest Newspaper," carried daily editorials on the "Race Question." Returning repeatedly to the twin demands of housing and employment, editors feared that what had happened in the nation's capital would soon come to Chicago. Headlines, captions, news stories, editorials, and cartoons conspired to present all African Americans as disturbing, if not utterly hostile, residents. On July 22, 1919, for example, the *Tribune* ran on its front page:

Martial Law for Riot in Capital?

5 Dead, Scores Hurt, 200 Jailed; Savage Battle Near White House Negress Kills Detective; Negro Shot Seven Times

On the front page of its second section, the editors featured a nine-panel political cartoon, entitled "The Responsibility for the Industrial

Unrest," in which a man, gesturing to unskilled labor signs, pro-claims: "The restriction of immigration is responsible. We used to get hundreds of thousands of unskilled labor from Europe – men who would do the kind of work the native born doesn't want to do. Now we have no immigrants, haven't had for four years, and may not have for a considerable time more." Without showing a single black strike-breaker, the cartoon delivers its message: Restrictions upon European workers mean jobs for blacks. Editorially, the *Tribune* surmised a lack of understanding between the better elements of both races:

> and there is only violent expression of resentment on the part of the heedless and ill tempered . . . [who] have, or at least employ, only one means of expression, and that is violence.
>
> Continuance of this sort of expression can only result in recruit-ing to the aid of each violent factor all those either similarly dis-posed or by *racial instinct* inclined to take part. (July 23, 1919)

Though the *Tribune* repeatedly ran stories on the class tensions be-tween Irish immigrants and black migrants, it stereotyped only the African Americans.[13] Readers of the *Tribune* expected dialect and race-biased political cartoons whenever blacks were involved.

Outraged by the editorial actions at the *Tribune*, the *Daily News* (as Carl Sandburg would recall) assigned its own reporter to "investigate the situation three weeks before the riot began" (Sandburg 1919: 4). Published by Harcourt, Brace and Howe later in the year under the somewhat misleading title *The Chicago Race Riots, July, 1919*, Carl Sandburg's articles were heralded at the time as a central investiga-tion into what went wrong in the Black Belt and may be considered now as a subtle literary news-fiction that literally anticipates the riot.[14] Introduced by a passionately indignant Walter Lippmann, who saw the "race problem . . . as a by-product of our planless, disordered, bedraggled, drifting democracy," the articles link the "Negro prob-lem" to economic status, especially housing and employment (1919: iii). Informed by the pretense of street savvy familiar to readers of Sandburg's poetry, the articles are illuminating journalistic exercises in established liberalism grounded rhetorically in social bombast and based structurally upon imagistic tableaux vivants.[15]

Relying upon the journalist's strategy of letting folks talk for them-selves (not unlike the more recent personal journalism of Studs Terkel or Nelson Algren), Sandburg offered the stories of those who had experienced the history and the news of the riot. Though recognized at the time, by a seeming majority of black and white journalists, as "true and friendly," the series today exposes more than Sandburg's generation's veneer of liberal sentiment; it also reveals the ways in which his rhetoric corrupts the very history in his investigative report (Detweiler 1922: 152). Within months, Sandburg's serial account formed national public opinion as it was preconceived into a concerned, liberal document bearing the imprimatur of Walter Lippmann. Ranging freely from an overview of the migration's impact on Chicago to the particular concerns of housing, employment, and larger issues of opportunity, the series effects a double-voiced dialogue with its national white liberal audience as well as Chicago's black weeklies, especially the *Defender*. Direct interview techniques were used by Sandburg to unseat the irrational or unlearned pleas from his subjects. The controlling intelligence throughout the articles is Sandburg's.

For the pamphlet reprint from the *Chicago Daily News*, Sandburg appended an introduction, "The Chicago Race Riots," in an offhanded, disinterested voice that provides a startling contrast to the Lippmann introduction. Obviously influenced by the residual effects of social Darwinism, the poet-journalist projects these chaotic news events into a world apart from the one he inhabits. He finds in this world primitive social forces at work, ruled by "the most ancient ordeals of the jungle," though he calls into question the underlying social factors by describing the origin of the riots in the anecdotal language of historical randomness: "The so-called race riots in Chicago during the last week of July, 1919, started on a Sunday at a bathing beach. A colored boy swam across an imaginary segregation line. White boys threw rocks at him and knocked him off a raft. He was drowned" (1). Like Abbott's earlier "Reducing Friction" editorial, the introduction, with its offhanded phrase "so-called," subverts the severity and significance of the event. And yet, by recasting the stoning of Eugene Williams into simply an act of "white boys," he writes, not to avert riot, but rather to deny its community significance and its attendant historical significance. In spite of its national packaging, the pamphlet is stripped of its larger human import by making the catalytic incident into just another childish prank.

But because the conflict involved black migrants from the South and Irish immigrants scrambling for turf and authority – groups removed from the journalist's immediate circle – Sandburg, as he closes his introduction, presents a binary opposition of socially distant factions: "So on the one hand we have blind lawless government failing to function through policemen ignorant of Lincoln, the Civil War, the Emancipation Proclamation, and a theory sanctioned and baptized in a storm of red blood. And on the other hand we have a gaunt involuntary poverty from which issues the hoodlum" (1919: 2). Not unlike Abbott in his condemnation of "ruffians," Sandburg and most of his readers saw the crisis at hand as a primitive competition between poorly socialized and educated groups. He does not fully examine either the singular event that triggered the riots or his competing assumptions about the root cause, one of which is that the ignorance of a particular social group caused the unrest, the other, that poverty generated a lawless atmosphere.

Readers of the *Chicago Daily News* as well as their national counterparts may have felt secure, like Walter Lippmann, in their conscience-stricken liberal sympathy with the "race problem." Sandburg directs his surging, dialogue-laden prose at those who have a vested interest in the status quo, those directly threatened by the instability and aggression of the new factions. Although he discusses the emerging brotherhood of the unions as the best hope of imposing order on migrants and immigrants alike, his social Darwinism precludes the subordination of competing interests, and the crisis situation, dominated by a "blind Lawless government," indicates that the projected brotherhood would be a fragile and temporary one at best. In "Unions and the Color Line," he uses a black union man, secretary of Local 651 of the Amalgamated Meat Cutters and Butcher Workmen of America, subtextually to unseat the validity of his own testimony:

> "If you ask me what I think about race prejudice, and whether it's getting better," he said, "I'll tell you one place in this town where I feel safest is over at the yards, with my union button on. . . .
>
> "We had a union ball a while ago in the Coliseum annex, and 2,000 people were there. The whites danced with their partners and the colored folks with theirs. . . . Whenever you hear any of that race riot stuff, you can be sure it is not going to start around here. Here they are learning that it pays for white and colored men to call each other brother." (1919: 45–6)

Central to Sandburg's presentation of union brotherhood is the strong current of "knowing one's place" in the evolutionary cycle. This social Darwinist view largely negates the socialist faith in integration expressed by this union man. Even the black middle class, in Sandburg's eyes, is useful primarily as a socializing force to contain unruly ambitions. In a curious way, then, neither class nor race is as important in Sandburg's scheme as a comfortably hierarchical status quo.

However well-intentioned the individual articles, most are prejudiced by their very organization. Perhaps believing that the marginal is what is newsworthy about the series, Sandburg begins most discussions with an anecdote of backward, ignorant folks crowding into an ever accommodating Chicago.[16] With prose as vivid and garish as turn-of-the-century "darky" art, "The Background" strives to provide an honest encapsulated review of the migration, but collapses under the weight of its own deafness: "There is apparent an active home buying, home owning movement, with many circumstances indicating that the colored people coming in with the new influx are making preparations to stay, their viewpoint being that of the boll weevil in that famous negro song, 'This'll Be My Home'" (8).[17] The use of the insect metaphor admits at least two ways of reading Sandburg's liberalism. When he equates the migrants with the boll weevil, he either intends his readers to chuckle over the sly suggestion of "infestation" ("Boll-weevil's coming," as Jean Toomer explains in "November Cotton Flower," "and the winter's cold, / Made cotton stalks look rusty" [1988: 24], encouraging the migration in the first place) or he hopes that they will admire his homespun depiction of the "folk." The sinister undercurrent of his phraseology becomes evident when we consider the effect the weevil migrants had upon their new (cotton) homes. Sandburg exploited another popular stereotype as well: that of the country hick (the cotton picker) come to the Big City. Reliance upon such comfortable and familiar portraits ensured his readers' distance and superiority, while allowing them conceptual space for pity and understanding.

Sandburg, aware of the *Defender*'s encouragement of the migration as well as Abbott's relentless antilynching campaign, repeatedly subsumes lynching under the category of economic deprivation. In spite of contradicting testimony by Willis N. Huggins, an Alabama migrant who taught manual training at Wendell Phillips High School (CCRR 1922: 10–11), he insists that

> it is economic equality that gets the emphasis in the speeches and the writings of the colored people themselves. They hate Jim Crow cars and lynchings and all acts of race discrimination, in part, because back of these is the big fact that, even in the north, in many skilled occupations, as well as in many unskilled, it is useless for any colored man or woman to ask [for] a job. (22)

By equating lynching with other forms of racial discrimination, Sandburg deprives the word and the historical event of their horror and violence. Unwilling to accept the basic tenet of the *Defender* that, as metaphor or fact, lynching was the central race news in America, he disparages, as too gullible, both the readers and the writers of black newspapers. He pities "the illiterate colored people" who "believed" the following lynching story:

> In Vicksburg, in the third week of June, the story goes, a colored man accused of an assault on a white woman was placed in a hole that came to his shoulders. Earth was tamped around his neck, only his head being left above ground. A steel cage five feet square then was put over the head of the victim and a bulldog was put inside the cage. Around the dog's head was tied a paper bag filled with red pepper to inflame his nostrils and eyes. The dog immediately lunged at the victim's head. Further details are too gruesome to print. (53)

Particularly striking about this instructive fable is Sandburg's class-conscious reticence to print the indecorous or perhaps inappropriately ridiculous final details. In this subtle censure of the kind of journalism practiced at the *Defender*, he disengages himself from the very community he professes to know and assess. Dismissive and patronizing, he reflects on the dubious standards of journalism practiced by the black press: "Whatever may be the truth about this amazing story, it is published in the newspapers of the colored people . . . " (53). The characterization of black journalism as "amazing" is developed in succeeding articles on "Negro Crime Tales" and "Colored Gamblers," which consciously utilize the rhetorical strategies of popular fiction to impress upon the reader the outlandish self-dramatization and comic-opera

events that characterize a world too utterly apart for Sandburg to feel
any but the most remote imaginative participation.[18]

Even so well-documented a crime as home bombings (widely discussed in the dailies and weeklies) is subjected to Sandburg's domesticating pen. The article on "Real Estate" begins:

> Eight bombs or dynamite containers have been exploded within the
> last five months on the doorsteps of buildings in the south division
> of the city, all of these buildings being situated in streets adjacent
> to the residence district popularly called the "black belt," where the
> population is about 80 per cent colored. . . . The police began their
> work with two theories in mind: one that explosions were the result
> of race feeling, the other that there was a clash between two real
> estate interests. As a result of their work, the police now believe that
> the second theory is more likely to be correct. (13)

Swiftly Sandburg dismisses the fear and anger expressed in the black
weeklies as simply "the propaganda of the colored people." Pairing
responses to the bombing crisis, he pits L. M. Smith of the Kenwood
Improvement Association, who fears that African Americans "injure
our investments . . . hurt our values . . . and taint our neighborhoods," against Charles S. Duke, a Harvard-educated city engineer
who sees real-estate dealers as being in the "business of commercial-
izing racial antagonisms" (CCRR 1922: 14). Ceding authority and
authenticity to the police, Sandburg cavalierly rejects Abbott's thesis,
as he concludes:

> In the series of bombings there is little or nothing to indicate a
> motive to destroy life. In one case a child was killed. The police
> have evidence that in the flat next door an Italian girl was to be
> married and jealous suitors had sent threats of violence. The theory
> is that the dynamiters put the bomb on the wrong doorstep. (16)

It is curious to note how Sandburg's anecdotal insertion in the passive voice – "a child was killed" – is offset by the paragraph's competing, subversive concerns: that there was no motive to destroy life and
that swarthy Mediterranean types might destroy life.

While Sandburg purports to allow the citizens of Black Metropolis
to speak for themselves, he nonetheless projects a voice more characteristic of DuBose Heyward or Eugene O'Neill than of a serious
journalist. The denizens located through his explorations seem to

have migrated from Catfish Row, where even the sharpest black characters are sly, not intelligent. Into this chorus Sandburg mixes the centripetal, unitary voices of reason, including the perspective of an anonymous packing official, an interview with Julius Rosenwald (president of Sears, Roebuck), and an appeal by Joel Spingarn to "the intelligent whites of America" to see the "race question as national and federal" (69).

The pamphlet represents a retrospective anticipation of violence and a historical, anecdotal acknowledgment of the riot as fact, with no effort to reconcile these distinct perspectives.[19] As Sandburg recalled, "Publication of the articles had proceeded two weeks and were [*sic*] approaching the point where a program of constructive recommendations would have been proper when the riots broke and as usual nearly everybody was more interested in the war than how it got loose" (4). His obvious frustration in not quite reaching the point where "a program of constructive recommendations would have been proper" suggests his perspective on race and social policy (4). Because he shared the tone of liberal good fellowship of his newspaper, he inevitably endorsed many of its generalizations and distortions. Although not so blatantly racist as its competitors, the *Daily News* still resorted to racial exaggerations and outright stereotypes.[20] One of its most popular features was the cartoon "Meditations of a Hambone," which exploited hateful stereotypes and Remus mock-wisdom.

However impure or complex its motives, the *Daily News* nonetheless sponsored one of the more exhaustive examinations of the "Race Problem." The paper's willingness to underwrite Sandburg's series, as well as its relatively evenhanded coverage of the riot itself, won praise from the Charles Johnson-led Chicago Commission on Race Relations. Yet even editor Victor F. Lawson would have to be told by a black former American Expeditionary Force officer, Stanley Norvell, that "Negroes [in Chicago] have become highly suspicious of white men, even such white men as they deem their friends ordinarily" (quoted in Tuttle 1970: 226). The articles reveal a blend of liberal concern and cultural misunderstanding characteristic of those comfortable with the status quo.

When seen in the light of Sandburg's private correspondence, his cultural bias and intolerance become manifest. Writing on July 8, 1919, to his father-in-law, Edward Steichen, the journalist exposes his bigotry: "I have spent ten days in the Black Belt and am starting a series in the *Chicago Daily News* on why Abyssinians, Bushmen, and Zulus are here" (Sandburg 1968: 167). A sympathetic reader might rationalize Sandburg's lapse as merely intergenerational "good ol' boy" banter; but when read in conjunction with the articles themselves, this comment seems to reinforce the contempt suggested, for example, by the boll weevil metaphor and the belief in the infinite gullibility of black newspaper readers.

Even Lippmann compromised his introductory plea to provide "complete access to all the machinery of our common civilization" in his assertion that, "since permanent degradation is unthinkable, and amalgamation undesirable, both for blacks and whites, the ideal would seem to lie in what might be called race parallelism" (1919; iv). Lippmann clearly did not detect the racism embedded in the very concept of "race parallelism," itself a curious permutation of conflicting notions of Du Bois and Washington, for he confidently expanded on this utopian vision: "Parallel lines may be equally long and equally straight; they do not join except in infinity, which is further away than anyone need worry about just now" (1919: iv). Such a vision of "separate-but-equal" provides a means of liberalizing the present without risk. This amendment to Lippmann's original plea for "complete access" puts into perspective the social doctrine of well-educated liberals of the era.

But however impure or condescending Sandburg and Lippmann may seem to us, they were positively enlightened in comparison to any of the competing accounts in Chicago's mainstream white dailies. A mid-riot report in the *Chicago Tribune* (July 30, 1919) is typical of the reporting in the majority of urban white dailies:

RIOT REFUGEES
FLEE TO POLICE
FEARFUL OF MOB COLORED CITIZENS
JAM STATIONS;
GO HOME IN CLOSED VANS

"Uncle Tom's Cabin" in a modern setting – that was the central police station yesterday. Like *fugitive slaves* of the antebellum south, colored citizens *huddled* in the squad room and awaited their turn *to be taken home under escort*. All day long they streamed into the station. Some came of their own accord. . . . Not far away stood a middleaged colored man whose *costume* was topped by an old black derby.

"No, suh, Ah'm not takin' no chances," he said. "If Ah was bul-let-proof, like one of them there dug-outs, it's be different. Some-thin' tells me Ah better stick right here with the parlice."

A policeman entered the room with a couple of colored men marching before him. "Sit down and we'll take you home just as soon as we get a wagon," they were told. At long intervals a *closed delivery auto* from one of the downtown department stores would halt at the curb and the *human merchandise* would climb aboard. Some of the *refugees* wore bandages. (n.p.; emphasis added)

Beyond the obvious transformation of citizen or migrant into "refugee" or "human merchandise," the article breeds contempt in other, more subtle, ways. The policeman, officer of the status quo and embodiment of The Law, is in no way caricatured or even visu-alized. Whereas the blacks are drawn as cringing provincials, unlet-tered and cowardly, the neutral voice of authority sounds merely the letter of the law. Dehumanized and dependent, these citizens have reverted, in the eyes of this journalist, to the condition of chat-tel slavery.[21]

Proclaimed the "Lincoln of Our Literature" by several biogra-phers, Carl Sandburg possessed many of the Great Emancipator's blind spots. He would consider himself a liberal visionary throughout his life and believed these articles to be some of his most insightful journalism. Writing in 1956 to a friend in Flat Rock, North Carolina, Sandburg cagily inserted a greeting: "Tell Charles S. Johnson I'd like a good long talk with him and that sometime I would like to meet his student body with one of my programs and that if anybody asks me what Brother Johnson and I are Alumni of it is The Chicago Race Riots and 'the score' thereof" (1968: 508). While never a participant in or veteran of the riot, Sandburg remembers his role in the narra-tive. Available as a pamphlet, Sandburg's series had a national impact on the way a settled white readership began to view its relationship to the dynamic of race in America's cities. The collaboration of Sand-burg and Lippmann, the very axis of liberal equanimity and sensibili-ty in postwar America, made this an essential document. Although Sandburg's conscious attempt to move beyond personal prejudice and empower a language of accommodation and harmony has been eclipsed by the Chicago Commission's report, it nonetheless provides a crucial voice in the dialogue between the black and white press, between news and history.

*   *   *

The New Majority, a sporadic publication of the Chicago Federation of Labor, added to the rhetorical ferment of post-riot Chicago a language of its own (Spear 1967: 39–42). Though not essential to a discussion of the race rhetoric, I include its mid-riot, two-page broadside "PROCLAMATION: Concerning the Race Riots by the Chicago Federation of Labor" to suggest how the heteroglossia of racial discourse crosses a more authoritarian discourse of class solidarity. The indictment of Chicago's class situation is evident from the opening sentence: "The profiteering meat packers of Chicago are responsible for the race riots that have disgraced the city" (August 9, 1919).[22] Coincident with but rhetorically unlike Abbott's mid-riot appeal for law, order, and regard for the well-being of Chicago itself, the CFL broadside intends to polarize and politicize as it capitalizes on the riot's residual anger and energy. Like the *Defender*, the *New Majority* sought to give voice to a silenced constituency, in this case, blue-collar workers. For this constituency the privileged discourse concerned labor, not race. Race was merely a public circumstance, a divisive issue. Despite the paper's attentiveness to class issues, it shared a generational deafness to race issues, relying upon racist language and stereotypes (Grossman 1989: 241–3). Yet, as if to sound a note of race solidarity, the Chicago Federation rhetorically projected the industrial "plutocrats" as the new slaveholders: "These colored men and women *are not brought here* for their own improvement, but are enslaved at low wages and have been used by the packers to undermine union conditions." As in so many other white visions of the migration, this version denies agency. The passive voice casts doubt on the ability of the migrants to decide and act independently. Sandburg's anonymous "official of the packers," in a vehement denial, absolves the packers of any antiunion activity:

> In the yards it is not a race question at all. It is a labor union question. We have no objections to the negroes joining the union. We are running an open shop. The unions want us to run a closed shop. . . . The unions have done everything to get the negro into their membership, but they *haven't got him*. . . .
>
> At one time, we heard, they had about 90 per cent of all the negroes in the unions. But they don't stay. The trouble is that the negro is not naturally a good union man. He doesn't like to pay union dues. (63)

Typical of so much of the white rhetoric surrounding the event, this official's statement denies the importance of race as a political and polarizing force while acknowledging it as a dominant personal characteristic. The packer's argument is centered in a property dispute: Who has the right "to get the negro."

Like Lippmann and Sandburg, the Chicago Federation of Labor, through the *New Majority*, mouthed concern for the best interests of the migrants as well as the new immigrant populations. Anxious to recast this occasion to stress race-blind solidarity, the union moved beyond the distraction of race to promote its own capsule history:

> Some weeks ago the *unions* redoubled their efforts to get the negroes in. *Squads* of union organizers held street corner meetings as the workers left the yards. The *packers* called on Captain Caughlin of the stockyards station for mounted police to break up these meetings, and Captain Caughlin, *tool* of the packers, sent his bluecoats there to *ride down* the men who gathered to listen to the speakers. This caused a strike of stockyards workers until the federation officials and the officials of the Stockyards Labor Council stepped in and secured the transfer of Captain Caughlin away from the yards and the cessation of this *Cossack* practice. (emphasis added)

Written in the aftermath of the Russian Revolution, the broadside employs aggressively visual prose that anticipates the sweep of citizens on the Odessa steps in Sergei Eisenstein's *Potemkin* (1925). The narrative proceeds cinematically, scene by scene, as if scripted for the camera, each group of actors placed in an appropriate setting, direct and minimal prose indicating principal actions. The ideological process behind this aggressive fictional historicizing reveals itself when we recognize that the actors in the scene are union men. Irish-American Caughlin, like the African-American migrant, loses the power of agency and becomes one more "tool" of the industrial powers. The reliance on the passive voice subordinates the opposition while enhancing the power of the union. In this interpretation of the world at hand, the war is waged between the union and the packers, a historical revision that marginalizes the fact that the actual conflict was fought between African-American migrants and Irish-American immigrant police. The union's larger political reading of the text necessarily subsumes the question of race. Like Abbott at the *Defender*, the federation had to downplay any competing issue if it hoped to refocus attention on the strike and other long-range labor issues.

By refusing to privilege race as the central issue, the *New Majority* retained its own political interests in this time of crisis, failing to seize the opportunity honestly to promote race and class solidarity. For the federation, race prejudice is *of use* only when it serves the union's purpose: to indict the packers. Labor-angled rhetoric demands that the packers be agents of violence and deceit, the union men partners in fraternity and equality:

> At every opportunity the packers and their hirelings fanned the fires of race prejudice between strikebreakers and organized workers, hoping for the day to arrive when union white men would refuse to work beside unorganized colored men, so that union men, white and black, could be discharged and nonunion workers, white and black, put in their places, until the spark came that ignited the tinder piled by the packers and the race riot ensued.

This reading reorganizes the world into competing classes, race being relegated to an incendiary, causal distraction. For the Chicago Federation of Labor, clarity of political vision dictated such dogged polarity. One might believe from this construction that workers, black and white, if left to their own devices, would forge a new political and social reality. However different the rhetoric, this vision echoes Sandburg's own in its unrealistic marginalization of race.

As if to move beyond the crisis of the riot itself, this proclamation elects to celebrate the union. Familiar rhetorical assaults on "the packers and their hirelings" would not destabilize the fragile brotherhood the way an open discussion of race in class issues would. Pronouncement after pronouncement reinforces and extols the fraternal nobility of the cause and its organizers:

> The only thing that saved the city from becoming a shambles was organized labor. . . . It stands to the credit of the union workers of Chicago that neither black nor white union men participated in the rioting, despite the *lying accounts published daily by the kept press, bought body and soul* by the advertisements of the packers and other crooks of big business.

As in so many of its political cartoons, labor organizes itself into the persona of The Worker, who towers above deceit and dishonor to save the very soul of the city. Not only does labor celebrate itself, but the *New Majority* seizes the opportunity to distinguish itself from the "kept" press, the "prostitute" newspapers. The *New Majority* sculpts its political identity and constituency as finely as Abbott's *Defender* does. While Sandburg and the *Daily News* had a casual, assumed investment in the status quo, the *Defender* and the *New Majority* had an immediate and reactionary political stake in their riot coverage. Both the race and the labor papers needed to reach beyond the crisis to the struggle beyond. Rhetorically as eager and unpredictable as the riot itself, the *Defender* and the *New Majority* told their disfranchised constituencies how the world was arranged, how the struggle would be resolved.

The discourse of riot fades quickly into the discourse of history. With the publication of *The Negro in Chicago* in 1922, the charged rhetoric of the *Defender*, the *Daily News*, and the *New Majority* slips into the ephemera from which history is constructed. The significance of an active relationship to history is seen by Ralph Ellison to be a product of memory; as he reiterates in "The World and the Jug": "Negro American consciousness is not a product (as so often seems true of so many American groups) of a will to historical forgetfulness. It is a product of our memory, sustained and constantly reinforced by events, by our watchful waiting, and by our hopeful suspension of final judgment as to the meaning of our grievances" (1963/4: 171). Johnson's report, in spite of its official nature and committee design, subtextually initiates the conversion of grievance into historical meaning. Though *The Negro in Chicago* demands its own rigorous reading, I include a brief assessment of it as an immediate and local rhetorical response to the riot. It offers, in the guise of a contemplative and "official" report, another contemporary partisan reading of the news. A black student of Robert Park at the University of Chicago, Johnson had distinguished himself as research director for the Chicago Urban League and was at the beginning of a career devoted to encouraging fellowship between the races. "*The Negro in Chicago: A Study of Race Relations and a Race Riot,*" as David Levering Lewis has recently asserted, "was doggedly optimistic" (1981: 47).[23] Johnson believed that mutuality and community between the races could displace immigrant and migrant racism. Though it was published as a statement of a twelve-member biracial committee (including Robert Abbott and

Julius Rosenwald), the investigation is primarily Johnson's.[24] Funded privately by some of Chicago's wealthiest citizens, the commission struggled against its patronage as well as through a series of financial crises to produce an acceptable report. As Arthur Waskow has noted, Johnson's report was corrupted by final revisions suggested by former Governor Lowden, who

> gave the proofs a final look in order to write a foreword . . . and had one suggestion to make. Whereas in the proofs the commission called the notion that "Negroes have inferior mentality" a "prevailing misconception," Lowden explained that he was "not persuaded that the commission had acted upon sufficient evidence." [Citing Army intelligence tests] Lowden expressed the belief that although recent Negro progress had been great, Negroes were still inferior to "the race which furnished . . . [the world] with Aristotle more than 2000 years ago." (Waskow 1966: 88)

Although Lowden did not insist upon revision, the "offending" passage was first amended and then deleted altogether. In spite of dubious sponsorship and vigorous political tampering, *The Negro in Chicago* in its expansive structure and rhetorical subtext remains a monument to Johnson's scholarship and race advocacy.

The nearly seven-hundred-page assessment – replete with overviews, interviews, charts, maps, and graphs – as it classifies and organizes the news and the history of the riot, undermines its official neutrality. Its partisan nature is most evident in the visuals accompanying the text. Johnson lends dignity to the migrants' plight by placing photographs of immigrant violence against migrants beside views of workers, families, mothers with children. A survey of the captions – "Negroes under protection," "The militia and negroes on friendly terms," "Milk was distributed for the babies" – suggests how the report sought to move beyond the ugliness of the riot itself to a larger social, human context for the race in Chicago. Even the initial summary of the riot leaves the impression that the riot was bad primarily because it brutalized the black family.

The report criticizes newspapers for resorting to anger-stoking rumors. Though forgiving the press for relying upon "misinformation" or "exaggeration" because of the "crowding of events" during the riot (26), Johnson provides more than ample evidence – statistical analysis as well as citation – of racially motivated distortion and outright falsehood.

In the commanding final chapter, "Public Opinion in Race Relations," an extensive review of competing newspaper accounts gave grounds for hope. At the suggestion of Victor Lawson, commission member and Sandburg's publisher at the *Daily News*, representatives of the city's papers testified, acknowledging the centrality of the press in forming the news and the history of the riot (Waskow 1966: 82). In comparing the news accounts Johnson found that migrants and immigrants shared the same fears – loss of jobs, violence to women and children. Because of this common ground, he concluded, there was hope for a truly integrated community. An editorial reprinted from the *New Majority*, strategically placed at the end of the riot overview, underscores Johnson's belief in common humanity through an assertive rhetoric of empathy:

FOR WHITE UNION MEN TO READ

Let any white union worker who has ever been on strike where gun-men or machine gun have been brought in and turned on him and his fellows search his memory and recall how he felt. . . .

Well, that is how the Negroes feel. They are panic-stricken over the prospect of being killed. (4)

Able to read through the inflammatory rhetoric to the essential sub-texts, however damning the racism or distortions, Johnson had the sense that migrants and immigrants could not merely coexist but together could build a new Chicago.

By comparing headlines, sources, and fact bases, Johnson's final chapter draws attention to a range of distortion and error without explaining why the news media, in his opinion, so utterly failed the communities they presumed to serve. If Johnson wavered in his inter-pretation, it is because he believed that somehow the white establish-ment press was inherently less political than the black. In claiming that blacks did not "rely upon the Negro press for *authentic general news* [but only for] news concerning Negroes," he inadvertently con-ferred a dubious respectability upon Chicago's dailies (563). In spite of what seems a double standard of journalism, there can be little doubt that Johnson intended his authored report to be a genuine and hopeful reconciliation in the guise of official reportage.

Chicago's 1919 riot offers more than the opportunity to quarrel with the hyperbole and inaccuracy of contemporary accounts. For it is a linguistic moment as well as a historical one and, as such, shares languages to assess in terms of social and political efficacy. For too long we have worried over the unreliability of the news without taking interest in what its community inspiriting, if not actually forging, rhetoric might say to readers today. Newly arrived as well as newly assimilated migrants and immigrants, when they became journalists and scholars, continued to fight for the right to express a selfhood situated in their ideas of community. Such partisanship breeds rhetoric. As late as 1950, reflecting upon the twentieth-century history of the black press and race relations, P. L. Prattis of the *Pittsburgh Courier* suggested the nature of the partisan press in general:

> The behavior of the Negro press is mirrored in the behavior and writing style of the Negro reporter. The Negro reporter is a fighting partisan. He has an enemy. That enemy is the enemy of his people. The people who read his newspaper, or read after him, expect him to put up a good fight for them. They don't like him tame. They want him to have an arsenal well-stocked with atomic adjectives and nouns. They expect him to invent similes and metaphors that lay open the foe's weaknesses and to employ cutting irony, sarcasm and ridicule to confound and embarrass our opponents. (1950: 273)

Prattis's rhetoric of simple assertion attempts to counter the partisanship of Negro reporters with their "atomic adjectives and nouns."

This counter-rhetoric of simple words and brief sentences intends to reassure and calm the readers of the *Daily News*. The riot, after all, involved only those excitable ("atomic") migrants and immigrants. Sandburg, for all his liberal inclination, was in rhetorical effect a partisan fighting for the status quo that had served him, and others like him, well. To use language that challenged the social hierarchy would be to open himself up to the possibility of slipping into a less lofty, less secure position in relationship to the fractious ruffians. The trade unionists of the *New Majority* saw both race and riot as an opportunity to reassert, with the "atomic adjectives and nouns" of the class struggle, the hope for worker solidarity against the tyranny of industrial might. In its unsuccessful struggle for objectivity and neutrality, Johnson's official report ignored and fell victim to the enduring power of such charged rhetoric. In his vision of fellowship, Johnson neglected the linguistic significance of the varied and often competing utterances on the issues that most concerned him.

*   *   *

In hindsight, the Chicago riot has become the "ideal type riot . . . [one of] clarity" (Waskow 1966: 10), one of "parity" (Grossman 1989: 259), for in an almost athletic fashion, the migrants and immigrants struggled for self-identity and neighborhood control. What has been lost in the numerous historical accounts is an awareness of the ways in which these communities generated competing languages of selfhood and assurance even as they increased the tension between the competing discourses. Repeatedly, the centripetal force of authority – which would have claimed objective, historical status – yielded under pressure to marginal voices in ways that underscored the incompatibility of differing social and cultural dynamics. This powerful and varied response offers a rare opportunity to understand the way in which news outlets attempt to create, to respond to, or to reflect community needs and belief systems. As Arna Bontemps pondered his community's relationship to the race press in a 1942 letter to Langston Hughes:

> Du Bois takes some of the steam out of my plan to do a Negro press article by making the main point in his first *Defender* article: namely, that the black press is a symptom, not a disease; a result of the Negro's lack of participation in American life, not a cause of anything. The thing to treat is the condition which makes the daily press insufficient for the needs of the Negroes. The justification of the Negro press, according to my argument, is that it fights for goals which if attained would liquidate itself. Thus it proves its essential integrity. Its essential patriotism and Americanism. In sum, we shouldn't ask why this or that is printed by Negro papers, but what is it that causes Negroes to want to read such and such. (Bontemps and Hughes 1980: 122)

The implications of such rhetorical awareness of community journalism become clearer when one returns to a work as challenging as Richard Wright's *Native Son,* a novel thoroughly informed by the role of popular journalism in the African-American imagination of the 1930s. Writers and readers immersed in the conventions of the race press should enter into an enriched relationship with many of the important African-American literary works of the twentieth century. But if literary works read differently in light of the rhetoric of the popular press, so the journalism seems to respond to a literary-critical approach. The Chicago riot, exhaustively analyzed by so many disciplines, must now be read as a powerful exercise in discourse. Until the race and immigrant presses are valued as sources of community identity and purpose, and as crucial instances of the authority of language in community building, the working-class and minority literature growing up and out of the news will be incompletely read or misunderstood.

RENDEZVOUS WITH MODERNISM, FASCISM – AND DEMOCRACY

THE CASE OF MELVIN B. TOLSON

> France is a country and Great Britain is several countries but Italy is a man, Mussolini, and Germany is a man, Hitler. A man has ambitions, a man rules until he gets into economic trouble; he tries to get out of this trouble by war.
>
> – Ernest Hemingway, "Notes on the Next War"
> (*Esquire*, September 1935)

> As I see it, the doctrines of democracy deal with the aspirations of men's souls, but the application deals with things. One hand in somebody else's pocket and one on your gun, and you are highly civilized. . . . Desire enough for your own use only, and you are a heathen. Civilized people have things to show their neighbors.
>
> – Zora Neale Hurston, *Dust Tracks on a Road* (1942: 792–3)

Melvin Tolson began his weekly "Caviar and Cabbage" column for the *Washington Tribune* on October 9, 1937.[1] Author of an unpublished collection of poems (*A Gallery of Harlem Portraits*),[2] assorted unpublished fiction, and two plays (*Moses of Beale Street* and *Southern Front*), and professor of English at Wiley College in Marshall, Texas, Tolson was the very embodiment of what he called "the New Negro in action," anxious to forge an honest democracy out of the "verbal democracies" (1982: 118) hewn by "two-bit radicals and 2x4 liberals" (117). He was an avid reader of *Chicago Defender* columns by Langston Hughes and *Pittsburgh Courier* columns by George Schuyler and believed in the local immediacy and global reach of the African-American weeklies. As coach of the Wiley College debating team, Tolson had achieved a national reputation for his team and for himself – a reputation that might have stimulated the *Tribune*'s offer of a column. Tolson's picture, as biographer Robert Farnsworth notes, appeared in the *Tribune* on September 25, 1937, with a brief caption celebrating "the recent publication in the Omega Psi Monthly, Tolson's fraternity publication, of his article 'denouncing colored leaders . . . which caused much discussion'" (Farnsworth 1984: 9).

The *Washington Tribune*, unlike many other weeklies, served a local constituency that was national – a fact underscored by the banner's caption "ONLY NEGRO NEWSPAPER PRINTED and PUBLISHED in the NATION'S CAPITAL."[3] For though its readership did not extend beyond the District of Columbia, the fact that it served the federal center of the union encouraged a national perspective in its consideration of the promises and failures of democracy. Deeply entrenched in the depression well into the Second New Deal, the district was more likely to see national compromises in policy as a sequence of intense, local failures that required representation in its weeklies. The published manifesto of the *Tribune*, elaborating upon its banner motto of "LIBERAL. PROGRESSIVE. INDEPENDENT," scaled human rights down to the immediate indignities of daily life for its citizens:

Our Policy

Newspapers, like people, should have an excuse of living. Our excuse, which is also our purpose for living, forms our policy, expressed as follows:

To ever uphold, contend for and defend Human Rights, which should dominate over property rights. Therefore, our policy is formulated into a nine-point program

1. Unemployment and Relief.
2 A Positive Purpose on Economic Security.
3. Law Enforcement and Law Observance.
4. Recreation and Citizenship.
5. Good Housing.
6. Good Health.
7. Suffrage for the District.
8. Comfort Station at Triangle at Tenth and U Streets, Northwest.
9. A Representative on the District Commission Board.

(Farnsworth 1982: 12)

The *Tribune*'s unlikely and expansive redrafting of the promises of the Declaration of Independence distilled and localized the Jeffersonian parameters of "life, liberty, and the pursuit of happiness" into the community necessities of "law, citizenship, and comfort."

Tolson's depiction of W. E. B. Du Bois projects essential qualities of Tolson as well: "an artist turned into a scholar by the awful alchemy of racial prejudice" (1982: 64). Prominently displayed above a syndicated column by Dale Carnegie ("a quack," who, in Tolson's words, wrote "bunk" [1982: 41]), "Caviar and Cabbage By M. Beaunorus Tolson" (with cameo photograph of the author) shared its folksy topicality, scholarly acuity, and aesthetic inventiveness in the service of democracy.[4] In the midst of his tenure at the *Tribune*, Tolson described his commitment to and definition of the First Amendment by way of explaining his stature. "In the *Washington Tribune* I Write as I Please" (January 6, 1940) describes a journalist who simultaneously exemplifies the "talented tenth" and the folk, one in touch with the powerful and the great:

> My contacts with editors and publishers, white and black, are very extensive. I know what they preach . . . and what they practice. I know what gets to the readers and what does not for political, social, and economic reasons. . . .
> When dumbbells talk about "the freedom of the press," I know they are dumbbells. When I hear idealists denouncing the dictatorship of the press in foreign countries, I smile cynically.
> . . . My pals are aristocrats and scrubwomen, scholars and dumbbells, millionaires and tramps. I am at home in a penthouse on Fifth Avenue or a boxcar on the C. & A. (1982: 172)

Wielding a superficial class-leveling rhetoric, Tolson speaks with an egalitarian ease and charm that recalls the American grain of Walt Whitman, Vachel Lindsay, William Carlos Williams, and Carl Sandburg, and the Marxist inflections of Langston Hughes.[5] Tolson situated himself in a direct line of descent from Whitman who, he claimed, "was compelled to emphasize and glorify the Americanism of his art [even as he attempted] to decolonize American [literature]" (quoted in Nielsen 1994: 53).[6] Lingering at the margins of the publishing world, this son of a Methodist minister shows enormous presence as he drives home his sermon to a Christian-rich, capital-poor democracy. He projects himself as a truth seeker brutalized by energetic redaction. As he notes in the subsection "Where the *Tribune* Comes In," "Now in the *Washington Tribune*, I write as I please. When my articles come out, I can recognize them. In some other papers and magazines I've been compelled to ask the editors if I wrote articles bearing my name. . . . I had the manuscript of a book turned down because I wouldn't rewrite it the way the editor wanted it rewritten" (Tolson 1982: 173). Whether to buoy the spirits of the reader or himself, Tolson casts himself as a David in mortal and moral combat with the Goliaths of a fallen, or at least scandalously compromised, civilization.

Unlike Pauline Hopkins, who elevated racial discourse through exemplary biographies, or Robert Abbott, who exhorted southern rural readers northward to citizenship, Tolson favored a preacherly, down-home manner that sought to chide his readers into action. His rural diction and rhetoric recall the expressive, ancestral cadences of many of his readers, themselves recent arrivals to the District of Columbia from the South. As a journalist Tolson marginalized the literary discourse he had sought to perfect in order that he might better address the victims of what he often called the "mouth Christians" of "the land of the spree and the home of the Burma Shave." A conversational yet literary vernacular invests his ministerial persona. Shifting from the avuncular to the bullying, he relentlessly upbraids the imaginary "Sambos" and "Hagars" (taunting his readers with received racial designations) from "Chittling Switch" for "white" pretenses he associated with the African-American bourgeoisie and insists they face their *African* blackness, which they can then transcend.[7] In a parodic inversion of Robert Abbott's exhortations of his readers (in which the city speaks to the country), Tolson disarms his urban dwellers with the cadenced bluntness of a country preacher. Congregational refrains of "No lie" or "Ain't it the truth?" voice a rhetoric familiar to readers who themselves may have migrated to the ambiguously southern District from Dixie.

The voice that surfaces with most assurance is one that speaks of uncompromised democracy but retains the authority of the elite.[8] The "I" who "hate[s] the guts of Hitler and Governor Talmadge of Georgia, because they hate Democracy" and who "believe[s] the little people of all nations want the Four Freedoms," reserves for himself an insightful perspective: "Two-bit minds scorn the little people. I am not one of these. If we had real Freedom of Speech, Governor Talmadge would be hooted out of Georgia by the little white people of

Georgia. The trouble is the press and schools and radios of Georgia are controlled by the Big White Boys." Proclaiming the "importance of the Little Negro (LN)," Tolson, superficially in the manner of Sandburg or Frank Capra, locates the authority of his column in the voice of the fighting partisan himself: "So I like to write for little Negroes. They are important. Of course, they don't know it. The little Negro is thinking today. Like the ants and the bees, the little Negroes are getting together. The salvation of America is in the hands of the little Negroes. If the Race problem can't be solved, America cannot lead the world" (1982: 97). The progressive effacement of direct address, shifting from the aggressive "you" and intimate "we" into the collectivity of class, modulates the closure into speculation, as Tolson turns the "Little Negro" into an Emersonian "Man Thinking." In keeping with earlier columns in which he celebrated the Soviet triumph over race prejudice,[9] "the ants and the bees" serve as collective and poetic similes of political possibilities.

Langston Hughes offered the immediate source of inspiration for Tolson's enthusiastic reception of the Russian Revolution. Seeing Christianity as the prototype of the model communist state, Tolson perceived capitalism as not simply the agent of colonialism but of all assorted tyrannies as well. As Hughes suggested "Let America Be America Again" (first published in *Esquire*, July 1936), so Tolson projected a politicized aesthetic of Pan-African liberation that materialized in "Rendezvous with America" as "To keep a rendezvous with Justice now" (1944: 8). For Tolson, democracy, resisting or affirmative, had to evolve as a denationalized construct. While white invocations of democracy and freedom might be seen as a wartime exigency, black claims in democracy addressed an abiding, idealistic concern. Liah Greenfeld defines the phenomenon in *Nationalism*: "The idealistic loyalty to national values, which could be and usually was as ardent a patriotism as the more earthly love of country, was by its very nature a stimulus for disaffection and revolt, for the more intense the commitment to the ideals, the more sensitive, the more intolerant, one became to the imperfections in their realization" (1992: 412). Read through the black experience of Woodrow Wilson's "War for Democracy," Franklin Delano Roosevelt's "Four Freedoms" could serve as that "stimulus for disaffection and revolt."[10] The cultural and civil coordinates of the principles underlying the liberation goal of the war – "to make the world safe for democracy" – enforced a compromised black citizenship even as they, as Patricia Sullivan has noted, "intensif[ied] the flagrant disparities between the promise and the practice of democracy" (1996: 135).[11] For the majority, the war encouraged a museumification of democracy that curator-citizen Tolson challenged in his projection of reciprocal discourse in the ideal democratic state. Unlike his imagined poetry coterie, thought to share the more private sphere of aesthetic concerns, his "Caviar and Cabbage" readers constituted a public sphere eager for racially inflected readings of citizenship and democracy. Anxious that the *Washington Tribune* receive his full attention, Tolson left the events of the war to the reporters, reserving his genius for investigations into the problematic nature of American democracy – a consideration occasioned by the plight of Ethiopia.

As Roi Ottley (1943b: esp. chap. 8) and others have noted, the interwar years had a particular significance for the increasingly racialized nations, what Benedict Anderson calls "imagined communities," which were global in scope and historical in orientation.[12] Within these cultural and political circumstances, Arthur Schomburg's assertion in Alain Locke's *The New Negro* (1925) that "The American Negro must remake his past in order to make his future" becomes less a rhetorical aside and more a culturally grounded political imperative for the new decade.[13] Race papers and journals continued the foundational work of turn-of-the-century editors like Pauline Hopkins and Robert Abbott as they emphasized, through history features and exemplary biographies, the centrality of black history.[14] Race increasingly became the bridge between the public and private spheres of history and genealogy, as it realigned marginalized and collectively atomized social identities into conceptual political actualities with a trajectory of past, present, and future. Nominal nationalism, territorially associated with citizenship and patriotism and rights, gave way to the supranationalism of Pan-Africanism. Previously held notions of national order, solidarity, and union (emphasized throughout the Great War) yielded to the grander racial union only hinted at in Du Bois's "Make Way for Democracy!" armistice editorial in *The Crisis* (April 1, 1919).

Despite its global aspirations and cultural impact, the black nationalism of these years foundered in the subnational quandary of eruptive politics and incomplete assimilation. But by the autumn of 1935, all this would change: Italy's invasion of Ethiopia, by signaling a convergence of regional fascism and nationalism into an international force, mobilized an intensely racialized public opinion in the black press, nationally and internationally. The sincerity of journalistic preoccupation was celebrated the following year in Langston Hughes's "Broadcast on Ethiopia," published in the *American Spectator*: "Addis Ababa / Across the headlines all year long. / Ethiopia – / Tragi-song for the news reels" (1992: 35). The invasion was more than an isolated case of belligerence on the part of what *Fortune*'s editors had described as "a moth-eaten colonial empire" (July 1934, 45); it was a crucial display of the means by which the systematic deployment of fascism would secure its future role in Italy's national culture. As Benito Mussolini boasted, in his introduction to *The War in Abyssinia*, an extravagant commemorative volume written by his field commander Marshal Pietro Badoglio and published in London by Methuen: "the war which lasted from October 3rd to May 5th may with full justice be termed a 'Fascist' war, because it was waged and won in the very spirit of Fascism: speed, decision, self-sacrifice, courage, and resistance beyond human limits" (Badoglio 1937: vii).

A threatened Ethiopia, independent black nation as well as conceptual lodestar for Hopkins, Du Bois, George Schuyler (see in particular his columns for the *Pittsburgh Courier*), and countless other black writers, served, in Roi Ottley's words, to "put the nationalist organizations on sound agitational footing" (1943b: 105). For not only did the plight of the beleaguered African nation appeal to racial sensibilities, it struck to the very heart of white liberal and radical sympathies regarding victims of Fascist aggression. It was, as Joseph E. Harris concludes, a war that motivated "the reaffirmation of a common historical identity for Africa and its diaspora" (1994: xi). The Italo-Ethiopian war also inspired a wave of aggressive global citizenship on the part of many black Americans. By midsummer of 1935, many black weeklies were reporting or advertising news regarding recruitment activities in support of Ethiopia. The *Washington Tribune* carried several front-page articles concerning recruitment and boycott activities in the nation's capital. On July 13, 1935, one such story, detailing events at Howard University, bore the headline "Colored Group Recruits Here for Ethiopia" and discussed a "boycott and war move against Italy."

The international race war in Africa, with its attendant partisan activity in the United States, was not without its ethnic political implications at home, as ethnicity and race fractured along new lines of religion, nativity, and language. Publications like the *Voice of Italy* and *Il Progresso Italo-Americano* drew discussion away from fascism, racism, or international law, preferring to rally support for the embattled fatherland in the form of recruitment efforts as well as fund-raising; while New York's *Voice of Ethiopia*, national organ of the international United Aid to Ethiopia, sought to establish the relations among colonialism, racism, and fascism. The war exacerbated tensions between the "foreign," necessarily of mixed cultural and national allegiances, and the "native," perpetually compromised in their citizenship. In "War Comes to Little Italy," an early wartime essay written for *Common Ground* (edited by Tolson's fellow Gurdjieffian Margaret Anderson), Michael De Capite sought to explain the Italian-American response by the time of the American declaration of war against their homeland:

> I had read what the papers hurriedly reported of the war's effect on Little Italy, of the sense of *vergogna* – shame – that Italian Americans felt, the patriotic fervor for America and its ideals. . . . It was not fascism which moved the older people to doubt and question. They had understood only that Mussolini was a great man, headlined in the news, respected by people in high places. They who first clustered in Little Italy, who never belonged in human terms to the city and the country, took a natural pride in Duce's stature. For many he was a compensation for their inferiority. (1942: 51–2)

For many huddling in the real and conceptual ruins wrought by the Great War, fascism promised just such a compensatory pride. Roosevelt and his 1936 reelection advisors, believing the Italian voting bloc essential, courted Italian-American ethnic and religious concerns regarding Ethiopia and the "fatherland," while slighting those of African Americans.[15]

Political pressures from recent European, "new-stock" immigrants, celebrated in the popular press by writers like Louis Adamic, whose *From Many Lands* (1939) had been a best-seller,[16] escalated black America's claims for its "old-stock" native sons, stressing an already fragile Roosevelt coalition at odds on race. And this "G.I." war, like its "doughboy" predecessor, did little to resolve the crisis of compromised citizenship. By war's end, racialized globalism would drift into an international nativism that at once privileged black America's native sons and castigated Europe's foreigners. As the reiterative end-of-the-war patriotism of Langston Hughes's "My America" suggests, the weariness of perpetually suspended citizenship diminished hope for the promised interracial democracy:

> This is my land, America. Naturally, I love it – it is home – and I am vitally concerned about its *mores*, its democracy, and its well-being. I try now to look at it with clear, unprejudiced eyes. My ancestry goes back at least four generations on American soil and, through Indian blood, many centuries more. My background and training is purely American – the schools of Kansas, Ohio, and the East. I am old stock as opposed to recent immigrant blood. (1944: 299)[17]

Even such compelling ancestral lines, in Hughes's case African and Native American, were likely to complicate even as they authenticated complete and unfettered citizenship as a birthright. Hughes's personal genealogical and linguistic markers of citizenship inscribe and authenticate the race's claims to a long suspended democratic birthright.

The Ethiopian beginnings of the "next war" encouraged a renewed interest in the community weeklies that provided antiphonal and antagonistic complements to the dailies. As Ottley would reflect in *A New World A Comin'*:

> I know of no event in recent times that stirred the rank-and-file of Negroes more than the Italo-Ethiopian War.
> Doctor Huggins once said it marked Ethiopia's return to the black race. Finding insufficient material in the white dailies, Negroes were eager for information about Ethiopia, its people, and the progress of the war. (1943b: 111)

Ethiopia, an international theater of more than war, grew quickly into a racialized backdrop for many global liberation movements. Weeklies like the *Chicago Defender*, the *Pittsburgh Courier*, and the *Washington Tribune* eagerly provided both news of the war and the history of the conflict: for in the retelling came an affirmation of a historically grounded identity itself.[18]

While the Second World War was for Parisians and Poles and Czechs the War of '39, it was, for Melvin Tolson, the War of '35 – one in which Ethiopia resisted corporate and imperial domination of the world's colored populations. With a fervor equal to that of George

Schuyler at the *Courier*, Tolson devoted his columns to the defense of ordinary Americans, his African-American readers, questioning what "democracy" meant under certain, given circumstances. For Tolson, there may have been an aesthetic difference but little difference in social purpose between writing journalism and writing poetry; each summoned a mediational instinct in the Marxist-inclined writer as he stood between the Big Guys and the Little Guys, hoping to level a field that was at once political and aesthetic. A chronological survey of his columns, written in the rhetorical wake of the New Deal from 1937 to 1944, reveals strong resistance to the "mouth Christians and democracy whoopers" who demanded the fulfillment of the American promise. Washington, Jefferson, Lincoln, and Roosevelt were authentic sources of inspiration, but they remained unfulfilled preachers of a still promised text in which the Declaration of Independence and the Constitution both encouraged and mocked the current, ongoing struggle for equality. His journalism, often motivated by an isolationism spawned by a reluctance to engage in foreign affairs while domestic circumstances were so bleak, results in more than a home-front chronicle of black America's struggle for democracy; it anticipates the passionate Americanism of Tolson's first published collection of poetry, *Rendezvous with America* (1944).

"Caviar and Cabbage" reaches well beyond the *Tribune* audience as Tolson reacts to the currents of cultural nationalism, born of colonial ruptures and global economic instabilities, that drove political and aesthetic centers to the margins of fascism or communism. These columns, when read against essential period texts such as Roosevelt's New Deal rhetoric and Ezra Pound's *Jefferson and/or Mussolini*, betray a literary sensibility comfortable with a Bakhtinian centrifugal authority that denies the fascistic unitary force inherent in modernist aesthetics and politics, a reign of what Charles Bernstein deplores as "totalitarianism masking as authority, racism posing as knowledge, and elitism claiming the prerogatives of culture" (1992: 121).

*　　*　　*

As I write this 18th September, anno XI, there is NO American daily paper contemporary with the F. D. Roosevelt administration, there are several papers *favourable* to the administration, but that is not the same thing. . . . I have never quarrelled with people when their deductions have been based on fact, I have quarrelled when they were based on ignorance, and my only arguments for 25 years have been the dragging up of facts, either of literature or of history. Journalism as I see it is history of to-day, and literature is journalism that *stays* news. (Ezra Pound, *Jefferson and/or Mussolini* [1935b: x])

By the time of Ethiopia's invasion, Mussolini for many Americans represented a political constant of order and efficiency imposed on a previously ungovernable nation. So seductive was the Duce's declaration of the triumph of the will that Walter Lippmann would remark, in his "Today and Tomorrow" column just weeks before Roosevelt's first inauguration: "Any group of 500 men, whether they are called congressmen or anything else, is an unruly mob unless it comes under the strict control of a single will" (January 17, 1933; quoted in K. S. Davis 1986: 36). In February, Lippmann took his appeal directly to the president-elect, counseling Roosevelt "to assume dictatorial powers" to deal with the leaderless drift of national and international chaos;[19] in March, Roosevelt challenged the nation to accept his leadership:

> For the trust reposed in me I will return the courage and devotion that befit the time. I can do no less. We face the arduous days that lie before us in the warm courage of national unity; with the clear satisfaction that comes from the stern performance of duty. . . . We do not distrust the future of essential democracy. The people of the United States have not failed. In their need they have registered a mandate that they want direct, vigorous action. They have asked for discipline and direction under leadership. They have made me the instrument of their wishes. In the spirit of the gift I take it. (quoted in K. S. Davis 1986: 32)

The liberal New Dealer's rhetorical consistency with Italy's Fascists was noted in Mussolini's party journal, *Il Giornale d'Italia*: "The whole world feels the need for executive authority capable of acting with full powers of cutting short the purposeless chatter of legislative assemblies. . . . This method of government may well be defined as Fascist" (quoted in K. S. Davis 1986: 37). While the extreme right called for a dictatorship of the executive branch and the extreme left a dictatorship of the masses, Roosevelt projected a charismatic redemptive personality that promised a disciplined democracy of capitalistically inspired executive zeal. (As Amiri Baraka would later reflect in "What Does Nonviolence Mean?": "most of the socio-economic policies of Roosevelt's New Deal were not meant to change society, but to strengthen the one that existed" [1966: 136].) The actual and perceived turbulence of structures (economic, social, aesthetic) as well as the confusions of political hierarchies produced a convergence of politics and culture. Fascism and its attendant fields of cultural production become the essential intermediary text by which Tolson's journalism, "the history of to-day," and poetry, "journalism that stays news," may be read.[20]

The ideological contest between fascism and communism inspired events to cohere around the leaders of the day, characterizing the plot of the unfolding historical narrative. Individuals informed news with an immediacy that was both theatrical – as world leaders shaded into personae – and personal. Columns by Langston Hughes and George Schuyler often shared Tolson's tendency to see history as a contest between exemplary individuals. And yet comparison with these cosmopolitan race journalists fails to illuminate the contestatory modernist realm Tolson shared with Ezra Pound and his cantankerously willful world of *Jefferson and/or Mussolini*. Unlike these other writers, Tolson in his poetry embraced many of Pound's modernist aesthetic aspirations, while in his journalism he echoed Pound's concern with economic subjugation.

Unlike his persona Hugh Selwyn Mauberley, the Pound of the 1930s had been dramatically affected by "'the march of events'" that would keep him as "out of key with his time" (Pound 1926: 185). Written in 1933 and published in the year of Italy's invasion of Ethiopia, *Jefferson and/or Mussolini* debates the status of government and the individual, rejecting Germany with its "Hitlerian yawping" (1935b: 127) in favor of "Italy organic, composed of the last ploughman and the last girl in the olive-yards" (1935b: 34). He sees the figure of Mussolini as a logical, twentieth-century extension of Jefferson's agrarian democracy, one that superficially resembles Tolson's "democratic dictator." Rejecting, as Tolson would, the "infinite evil of the profiteers and the sellers of men's blood for money" (Tolson 1982: 61), Pound rooted the spiritual crisis of his day in materialism:

> But Jefferson saw machinery in the offing, he didn't like it, he didn't like the idea of a factory.
>
> If you are hunting up bonds of sympathy between T. J. and the Duce, put it first that they both hate machinery or at any rate the idea of cooping up men and making 'em all into UNITS, unit production, denting in the individual man, reducing him to a mere amalgam. (1935b: 63)[21]

70

It was a case, as Pound would note in an essay written the same year, of "Murder by Capital," a world in which "England grovelled in an utter terror, flat on her belly before banks and bankers' touts. The Press lied, economic discussion was taboo, though a huge camoflage of mystification was kept up by licensed economists" (1935b: 61). The colonial powers were "going mouldly" – London, "a terror of thought," Paris, "tired, very tired" – only Italy was "full of bounce" (1935b: 49). By the time Pound located a publisher for his essay, Italy's pastoral "bounce" surrendered to the machinery of war.[22]

Tolson, like Pound, believed the historical moment an auspicious one to seek a redefinition of democracy, leader, citizen, and free-dom – concepts essential to America's sense of national identity. Drawn to the historical rhetoric of Jefferson and Lincoln, both Pound and Tolson situate the origin of this chaos in the long, corrupting his-tory of industrialism and capitalism. As Tolson reflected on May 31, 1941 (in a column ominously linking Thomas Hardy's poem of the Great War to the chaos about him):

> Nazism has been coming for One Hundred Years. Its seeds were planted during the Industrial Revolution. For fifty years, men had been losing faith in men. Cut-throat competition had reduced men to predatory animals. . . . The scientist had reduced God to $qp - pq = ih/2$". Everybody looked out for himself. $$s spelled success. We start-ed worshipping titles and degrees instead of brains and character.
>
> The wise guys told us that Big Business could save humanity. Of course, I wasn't fool enough to believe that. (Tolson 1982: 143)

Modernist preoccupations with the cultural implications of industrial, urban societies inform the essays of both Tolson and Pound. Where Pound saw the atavistic return of an idealized peasantry and fascist agrarianism, Tolson envisioned a fascist state crushed by imperialist and capitalist evil.

Although Pound's provocative equation of Jefferson and Mussolini came well before the Duce's invasion of Ethiopia, Mussolini's imperi-alist gesture prompted Pound's renewed endorsement. Praising Mus-solini's "acquisition" of Ethiopia, Pound went on to write several articles for *The British-Italian Bulletin*, an English-language supplement to *L'Italia Nostra* (a newspaper for Italian-speaking Londoners), in which he defended Mussolini. As he proclaimed in the issue of December 27, 1935: "No man living has preserved the Peace of

Europe as often as Benito Mussolini" (1: 8).[23] While the intellectual complexities and aesthetic proprieties of modernism continued to fascinate Tolson, its fascistic political orientation, represented in part by the Italo-Ethiopian War, repelled him.

Mussolini's assault on Ethiopia dichotomized Tolson's thinking about national identity, democracy, and citizenship: on the one hand, it fostered the need for imperiled people (and by extension an endangered race) to bond in mutual support; on the other, it encouraged isolationism and a fight for democracy at home. His earliest response to the invasion was *The Lion and the Jackal*, a prose meditation that begins:

> It was Tuesday on the morning of October 1, in the year 1935. The deep red explosion of the tropic sunrise had purpled the peaks of the hinterland beyond the blue-green tiers of the eucalyptus forest and burst in savage splendor upon the port of Dijibouti, the front door of Ethiopia.
>
> Along the sprawl of the quay, built of native wood and rock, helmeted Europeans and bushy-hairy Somalis had already begun the grind of the day. Against a background of monoliths of salt evaporated from the Gulf of Aden, the toilers of empire fell into the rhythm of loading and unloading inboard cargo. (quoted in Farnsworth 1984: 68)

The exotic palette of Tolson's lush scene ironizes as it dramatizes the cultural and material disjunctions between the invading force and the domesticated ("front-door") Ethiopians. The "toilers of empire" transform Ethiopia from an Eden of natural rhythms and savage splendor into a mere link in the mechanistic chain of imperialism. The foreign rhythms of colonial production and appropriation, with its elliptical allusion to Gandhi's 1930 Salt March, supplant the metres of nature – and, for a time, of poetry. In July 1936, shortly after Mussolini's poison gas victory over Ethiopia, deposed Emperor Haile Selassie would report to the League of Nations:

> I decided to come myself to testify against the crime perpetrated against my people . . . and to give Europe warning of the doom that awaits it if it bows down before the *fait accompli*. . . . If a strong government finds that it can with impunity destroy a weak people, then the hour has struck for that weak people to appeal to the League

of Nations to give its judgment in all freedom. God and history will remember your decision. (quoted in K. S. Davis 1986: 596)

The League stalled, and within weeks the Spanish Civil War began.

Mussolini's "annexation" for America's president was a moral embarrassment, an inconvenience without international complications, but Spain signified the chaos he most feared. At his nomination ceremony on June 27, 1936, Roosevelt would forsake the popularly sanctioned dictatorship invoked by his first inaugural address and proclaim a return to the originary force of democracy. Sounding the concerns of intellectuals right and left, regretting that "man's inventive genius . . . released new forces in our land . . . the age of machinery, of railroads; of steam and electricity; the telegraph and the radio; mass production, mass distribution," he envisioned an attendant peril in this new civilization:

> For out of this modern civilization economic royalists carved new dynasties. New kingdoms were built upon concentration of control over material things. Through new uses of corporations, banks and securities, new machinery of industry and agriculture, of labor and capital – all undreamed of by our fathers – the whole structure of modern life was impressed into this royal service. . . . Faith – in the soundness of democracy in the midst of dictatorships. Hope – renewed because we know so well the progress we have made. Charity – in the true meaning of that grand old word. . . . In place of the palace of privilege we seek to build a temple out of faith and hope and charity. . . . There is a mysterious cycle in human events. To some generations much is given. Of other generations much is expected. This generation of Americans has a rendezvous with destiny. (quoted in K. S. Davis 1986: 637)

Roosevelt's rhetoric, suffused with a radiant democracy that seems a model of Christian charity, provides a crucial intertext for the reading of Tolson and Pound. Corrupt economic structures, fraudulent governance, and tyrannical visionaries serve as agent, practice, and institution in this projection. Acknowledging the nation's formative distrust of monarchic institutions, Roosevelt asks the masses to draw upon the Judeo-Christian ("temple out of faith and hope and charity") roots of American democracy. This immediate claim to "destiny" will be reformulated and reclaimed in Tolson's *Rendezvous with America*.

73

Tolson's "Drama: 'The Tragedy of Ethiopia'" (May 28, 1938), detailing Haile Selassie's "dramatic 11th hour appeal to the conscience of nations," moves from consideration of the event itself to contemplation of the more abstract demons of imperialism and capitalism:

> When Mussolini's savage hordes invaded Ethiopia to spread civilization with machine guns and high-powered rifles and syphilis, I was sitting in a Negro drug store near the courthouse square of a Southern town. . . . A prominent physician got to his feet and exclaimed: "Mussolini will never take Ethiopia!" The gentleman became eloquent. He said the country was too rugged, too mountainous. I told him quietly that bombing planes eliminate mountains. That poisonous gas seeks out the hiding places of guerilla warriors. That spears and old-fashioned guns are no match for mechanized modern warfare. (1982: 104–5)

Anecdotal and dramatic, Tolson turns the news into a morality play about the victims of Big Boys and Big Business. The report of Selassie's plea occasions another treatise on "the octopus of capitalism," in which specific global and local concerns telescope into an indictment of the corrupting principles of the world order. As if in answer to Poundian economics, Tolson concludes:

> A Negro who believes in capitalism is a Negro who believes in the rape of Ethiopia, the peonage system of Georgia, and the infamous exploitation of all weaker peoples. . . . Ethiopia was the victim of capitalism in the form of imperialism; Mussolini was put in power by the financiers of Italy. He sold out the Italian people. Today they groan under financial and psychical burdens. (105)

While Pound was willing to charge England and France with moral turpitude, Tolson enlarged the circle of accusation to include Italy, constituting the "Unholy Three . . . [that] sold out the League of Nations for thirty pieces of filthy silver" (106).

Such unholy alliances with their long histories make essential the "fearless Negro newspaper" in which readers can "interpret the race problem in America" and discover "the history of the world, yesterday and today" (107).[24] Conflation of the anecdote with event-centered reportage and philosophical rumination characterizes Tolson's response columns, inspired by the pressure of the war news. Simultaneously internationalizing the news (seeing, for example, Chittling

Switch, Mississippi, from the perspective of Tirana, Albania) and localizing it (recognizing, for example, Hitler and Mussolini in the characters of Al Capone and John Dillinger) invested Tolson's war reflections with a startling intensity. A proposed disquisition on Hitler and Mussolini, "Two Madmen and Two Damn Fools!" (April 22, 1939), becomes an "indictment of American education and European civilization" (109), as Tolson, with a ministerial sleight of hand, defers discussion of the treacheries of the "Big Men" to depict the consequences for a particular victim:

> We are informed that a fear of war and a haunting dream that he was forced to kill his fellowman drove this 17-year-old to suicide.
>
> The mother of little Buddy Merrill found his body swaying from the end of his book-strap in the family garage.
>
> I am wondering about the books he carried in that book-strap. Did those books give the boy the facts of life? Did they shoot him a lot of bunk about idealistic platitudes? Did they let him know who made wars? Did they tell little Buddy about the profits big men derive from patriotism? Did they tell him about our dollar-democracy? (1982: 109)

Among so many columns of war news and philosophical posturing, Tolson pauses to locate and nourish a portrait gallery of the war's victims, the little guys he will soon commemorate in his poems.

Fundamental to Tolson's construction of the democratic ideal was economic equality, since he believed that the financial solace of middle-class status, black or white, dimmed the prospects for social action. He defines the social imperative in "A Discussion of Hogs, Dogs, Fish, and the Declaration of Independence" (July 22, 1939):

> And hunger is going to make whites and blacks in America declare a new Declaration of Independence. An empty stomach is the greatest defender of liberty. "Taxation without representation" is the cry of the exploited men. "All men are created equal" is the cry of jim-crowed men. "Give me liberty or give me death" is the cry of underprivileged men. "A government of the people, by the people, and for the people" came from the lips of a poor white man who was the son and the grandson of poor white men. . . .
>
> These words mean nothing on Independence Day, to the 400, whether the 400 are black or white, yellow or brown. (1982: 77)

Liberating patriotic clichés from their historical remove, Tolson reinscribes a national rhetoric from one of failed promise into one of perpetual revolution.

Tolson's war columns lack the urgency of his prewar indictments of the imperialistic nations, especially Great Britain, seeking profit and territory from war. Railing against the "gangster methods" of England and France, he targets "our international banking system and our economic loyalties [to] England." This echoes Pound's response to "*all* them buggarin massacres . . . caused by money,"²⁵ yet Tolson's conclusions could not have been more different. The imperial path of treachery – from Chamberlain to Mussolini to Hitler, from England to Ethiopia to Poland – led to deeper colonial enslavement. As Tolson concludes "The Second World War: International Crooks" (September 9, 1939):

> We Americans must stay out of this war. We must not listen to the siren of the war lords. We Negroes certainly have nothing to gain in a war. Too many Negro soldiers have already served as cannon fodder for the big white boys. Keep up with the European developments. This war is going to change the world. I'm looking for uprising in India and in other colonies. I predict that Chamberlain will be the last imperialistic premier of England. (1982: 113)

Few columns articulate Tolson's historical, philosophical, economic, and theological reading of the democratic ideal as clearly as "There Can Be No Democracy without Dictatorship" (February 10, 1940). Structurally and rhetorically it recalls Lippmann's 1933 projection of leadership as it epitomizes Tolson's advocacy of the "little Negro" in the midst of "white intellectuals." Appropriating current events, political philosophy, New Testament economics, global and local transgressions, Tolson redefines the promise of American life as he shuffles the historical deck and ponders the question of leadership. First Judas, then Al Capone; Caesar, then Douglass; Du Bois, then Roosevelt. Caught in the midst of "New York . . . white intellectuals . . . whooping it up for democracy," he turns their global consciousness into a local crisis with his "self-evident" assertion: "There can be no democracy . . . without dictatorship" (1982: 176).

For his immediate auditors as well as his readers, the exchange occasions a contested history of Western philosophy (exploring such inheritances as Athenian "democracy") and a Christian indictment of capitalism ("Judas knew that the Big Boss who holds the money bag dictates what the boys shall do and what the boys shall not do") that liberates the column's fundamental lesson: It takes a dictator to control dictators. As he explains in the vital subsection "Why Mr. Roosevelt Was Called a Dictator":

> When Mr. Roosevelt went into office, he discovered a dictatorship of Big Business, and for Big Business. Mr. Roosevelt should have known that before he went into office.
>
> Thomas Jefferson discovered it 150 years ago. . . . Now when Mr. Roosevelt started putting the screws to the economic royalist dictators – they began calling the President a dictator! That let the cat out of the bag. Only poor Negroes and poor whites and Uncle Toms believe we have democracy! When democracy comes per se, there will be no government. So don't be fooled. Think it over.[26] (1982: 177)

Roosevelt's pretense of discovering the dominance of big business absolves him of capitalist allegiance and makes way for a more activist and beneficent use of the federal government. Of course Roosevelt then must function as a counterdictator. In Tolson's rendering, only victims of wage slavery (the unlikely biracial union of the poor and the Uncle Toms) "believe" the government can serve them instead of business. But if democracy is to transform an inspirational ideal into an agency of change, it will happen only when the federal government ceases to serve either the dictatorship of capital or the dictatorship of beneficence. Then government itself will dissolve in the heady broth of democracy.

The failure of the democratic ideal surfaces whenever a dictatorship requires a counterforce to check it. Tolson alerts his readers to the fundamental lesson of American history: "All governments are brutal if you violate their laws . . . and get caught. Look at the Jews in Germany and the Negroes in the Capital of our verbal democracy" (1982: 177). Jeffersonian democracy remains unfulfilled because, "at the present time in the history of the world, there can be no democracy without a dictatorship" (1982: 178). Roosevelt, "a man with a social conscience," and Congress become the dictatorial agents of the Declaration of Independence and the Constitution:

> Now in the United States a few people are living off the fat of the land, while millions stand around crying for bread. . . . So Uncle

Sam will have to do what Jesus did when He went into the temple among the money-lenders. . . . I want Congress to dictate that every citizen shall enjoy the rights of life and the pursuit of happiness. I want Congress to dictate the abolition of poverty in a land of plenty. I want Congress to dictate the enforcement of the Constitution.

Otherwise our boast of democracy is a joke before civilized peoples. (1982: 178)

These democratic equalizers – the President and Congress – must serve as temporizing agents until America learns to tolerate its own professed ideals.[27]

But the war profiteers triumphed; war broke out, and Tolson sought solace, reaching beyond the war, in a vision of a global democracy. Speculating upon dictatorial force as an agent of right and wrong leads him to an enlarged sense of history. As he surmises in his comically poignant rendering of Oswald Spengler (and indeed of Pound), "The Merry-Go-Round and the Ferris Wheel of History" (October 19, 1940): "The history of man heretofore has been the history of the rise and fall of nations" (1982: 90). Citing Edgar Allan Poe's "To Helen," Tolson muses upon the aesthetic and historical difference between Greece's "*glory*" and Rome's "*grandeur.*" Rome, Mussolini's ancestral state, "was materialistic and pragmatic like ours, huge geographically and financially . . . 'All roads lead to Rome.' That means the Big Boys said to the little Sambos: 'Bring us the dough'" (1982: 91). Through this carnivalesque depiction of the inevitability of national collapse (what Spengler had called *The Decline of the West*), Tolson leads his readers on a whirlwind tour of Western civilization. His cyclical view of history enables him to "discover" the foregone conclusion: "Now, here is something that's an eye-opener. Every nation at the top got there by force – and force caused its downfall. Every nation at the top invented a theory that proved to itself its own superiority. Each top-nation scorned all other nations" (1982: 91). Tolson's global narrative of success and failure assumes particularity and force as a Christian parable of pride and fall, one of seemingly inescapable eternal verity and ultimate justice.

Tolson's Ferris Wheel metaphor hardly allows his stark oppositions to shade into their opposites, projecting instead a cinematic rush of black and white, big and little, rich and poor, winners and losers, until history itself blurs into the ambiguity of a never-decided or always-already-decided narrative. Force as the agent of imperial power and worldly success fails in the tyranny of Tolson's reading, which renders illogical, because doomed, any script of racial or ethnic superiority. History's wheel, with leisurely ascent, momentary stay, and rush of descent, carries all in its unvaried circuit. Such a reading of history requires death, slavery, and misery to oppose life, liberty, and happiness.[28] It also finds that, whether capitalist or feudal lord, fascist or communist, rulers are invariably blinded by power. Seizing upon the economic roots of this hierarchy, Tolson concludes: "A fascist is either a capitalist with capital or a capitalist without capital. A Communist is a man with an empty belly knocking at the door of a capitalist. Until the Big Boys see through these two definitions, they'll continue to put nails in their own coffins" (1982: 92). As long as leaders require dictatorial power and nations rely upon force, the "Ferris Wheel" will produce only an endless, shape-shifting stream of success and failure. Halting this continual vertical movement requires an economic realignment of history from the vertical to the horizontal: "The Merry-Go-Round of History" (1982: 92).

"The Merry-Go-Round and Ferris Wheel of History," a philosophy undoubtedly born out of Tolson's experience in organizing rural sharecroppers, and perhaps animated by images of the exhaustively advertised New York World's Fair, imagines a Jeffersonian democracy, requiring an "economic and racial brotherhood" (1982: 92),[29] that anticipates A. Philip Randolph's March on Washington Movement even as it recalls his earlier appeals in *The Messenger* for "justice," not "patriotism." Randolph's Brotherhood of Pullman Porters would have found solace in Tolson's "merry-go-round" state, in which "nobody goes up therefore nobody has to come down. That is democracy . . . all members are equal" (1982: 92).

Although Tolson ponders the democratic ideal, he sees it as an unfulfilled rhetorical exercise in a colonial and capitalistic world and correspondingly shows little sympathy for Europe in his columns leading up to the American entry into the war. Whether England, which "walked the earth as conqueror for centuries, exploiting weaker peoples" and ignored "the pleas and prayers of black men in Africa and brown men in India," or Belgium, which "cut off the hands of Africans in the Belgian Congo, when the Africans didn't bring in enough rubber," or white America, which "paid no attention to the appeals of black men," the industrial imperial state had reaped what it had sown (1982: 132).³⁰ African Americans "must fight on the American Front," Tolson declares in "While Britain Is Getting Bundles, Let Sambo Get BVDs" (March 15, 1941), "Not the European Front [because] We'll never live under Adolf Hitler. We shall live under the Bilbos" (137). Tolson's war-within-a-war repudiates colonial perceptions at home and abroad,³¹ his democracy demanding a global realignment of the heart and mind:

> The earth is big enough for all of us. Democracy was made for the earth not for the stratosphere of politicians. I don't believe in postponing the Constitution. The Stars and Stripes should be in the heart as well as the buttonhole. Take democracy out of the stratosphere. When a man says democracy to me, I ask: "What are you doing to wipe out economic, political, and racial injustices?" (July 20, 1940, 184-5)

Seldom are "mouth christians and democracy whoopers" able to enact the sentiments lodged in a patriotic rhetoric that has ultimately defiled their religious and national heritage. For them, ideological display stands in place of action.

No Washington insider mobilized the rhetoric of the president's "Four Freedoms" better than Eleanor Roosevelt. She was throughout her husband's presidency the agent of his rhetoric, as she brought the issues home, literally domesticating them as she seemed at times to be the White House agent of the *Courier*'s "Double V" campaign. She shared with Tolson a political engagement that was at once intensely intellectual and practical. Uncomfortable with her husband's cozy relationships with his racist Warm Springs, Georgia, neighbors, Eleanor worked publicly, in private, to aid the integrative efforts of the Southern Tenant Farmers Union.³² So powerfully did the First Lady articulate her convictions that Tolson, like John Johnson at *Negro Digest*, joined her in domesticating the war aims of the campaign into a home-front issue.

In "The Four Freedoms of Mrs. Roosevelt" (September 11, 1943), Tolson reassigns the famous proclamation by envisioning it through a foundational, Enlightenment lens that refracts into the spectral truth of Christianity: "Who wants to abolish Jim Crow? I'll tell you. Only those who have been washed in the blood of the Constitution. . . . Only those who would have followed Tom Jefferson, Abe Lincoln, Garibaldi, and Sojourner Truth!" (1982: 156). The exuberance with which

Tolson notes his appreciation is unrestrained: "My God, the First Lady has a punch like Joe Louis. Pardon me, for the comparison, but it's all I can think of, at the moment . . . I am glad Mrs. Roosevelt has bearded the lion of race hate in his den" (1982: 157).

As the war progressed, Tolson grew increasingly impatient with a white liberal patronage that "admired Negro genius . . . but [didn't] accept . . . the Negro masses . . . as citizens" (1982: 98).[33] Bored with the promises of an ever illusive democracy and eager to see black America respond to its "native land,"[34] he proclaims in "Our Good White Friends Get Cold Feet" (January 23, 1943): "The battle is on for the Four Freedoms, at Home and Abroad. The interracial chicken dinners are things of the past" (1982: 98).[35] The integrity of what Pound had called those "few clean and decent pages in the nashunul history" was dependent upon the accommodation of all citizens. As Tolson explained to his readers, only blacks can reclaim a citizenship held in suspension by "the biggest lie ever told in America. . . . 'This is a White Man's country'" (1982: 99). Unlike columns by white liberal "friends of the race" (such as the "If I Were a Negro" guest columnists for John H. Johnson's *Negro Digest*), Tolson's essays insist upon full citizenship now, admitting no extenuating limitations due to the war. To do so would "mean the death of the Declaration of Independence, the Bill of Rights, the Emancipation Proclamation" (1982: 99).

The *Washington Tribune* offered Tolson the presence and authority of a genuinely independent journalist capable of an unedited advocacy, because (as Tolson noted) the black press was "the only Free Press in America" and was "responsible to the Negro readers alone" (1982: 233). By the end of his tenure there, he concluded: "the Negro newspaper is a Declaration of Independence. And it costs only 10¢" (1982: 234). The journalistic freedom Tolson located in what Pound had called the "history of to-day" animated his subsequent literary productions, in particular his second collection of poetry, *Rendezvous with America*. Eager to draw his weekly readers to the pages of *Common Ground* (publisher of the title sequence, "Rendezvous with America") and the *Atlantic Monthly* (publisher of "Babylon" and "Dark Symphony"), Tolson explained on April 24, 1943, the differences in poetic language:

Some people say the language of my poetry is very different from the language of "Caviar and Cabbage." Well, when you go to a formal ball of the Big Boys, you have to put on evening clothes. No lie! When I'm at home, among friends, I go about the house in my patched pajamas. A woman doesn't cook cabbage in her Sunday best. In "Caviar and Cabbage" I try to be so simple that only a Howard professor can tell I am a professor. (1982: 269)

A formality of expression, drawn here as "the formal ball of the Big Boys," attends the literary world and reflects an aesthetic hierarchy of a discourse that aspires to stay news.

By the 1940s Tolson's search for a poetic of "democracy" would further necessitate the narrowing of the gap between his journalism and his poetry as it sought to mediate between the war and its history. Nearly a decade after his failure to see *A Gallery of Harlem Portraits* through to publication, Tolson prepared a new manuscript as distinct from his previous "portraiture" as his columns. A series of eight independent, yet complicit, sequences reveal Tolson's *Tribune*-honed and lyrically inspired adeptness at resituating the reader within the floating significations of those linked and unanchored signifiers, "America" and "democracy." Though stimulus for his refined discussion of nationality and democracy might have been Herbert Croly's *The Promise of American Life* (1909), a treatise that enjoyed a renewed popularity during the Great Depression and the war, it more likely originated in his abiding interest in Hamilton and Jefferson's debate over nationality and democracy.[36] Years at the *Tribune* had bred an awareness of the public sphere that challenged the purity of his lyric sensibilities, encouraging a hybrid discourse that was at once journalistic and epic in scope. Lyric compression relaxes into editorializing; abandoning intimacy of detail and privacy of emotion, Tolson's poetry now turns to the epic address of a nation's citizenry. Yet unlike the *Cantos*, *Rendezvous with America* employed none of Pound's fractious techniques. The collection did, however, share Pound's interest in the lyric's ability to transform epic into historical collage.

Ethiopia, most importantly, resurfaces throughout *Rendezvous with America* as a somewhat paradoxical, unanchored signifier. Poems as diverse as "A Song for Myself" (with its visually paradoxical take on Whitman),[37] "Vesuvius," "The Bard of Addis Ababa" (with its revision of Sandburg; see Sandburg's own "yellow dog" poem, *The People, Yes*, 1936: sec. 51; 510), "The Idols of the Tribe" (with its cautionary reflection on Pound), and "Tapestries of Time" (with its culminating

indictment of "the calendared March of the Global Man" [121])
return to the lessons of Ethiopia – for nations and for poets. From
the epigrammatic insights of "A Song for Myself" – "Caesars / Without, / The People / Shall rout; / Caesars / Within, / Crush flat / As
tin" (46) – to the oracular vision of "Tapestries of Time" – "Time /
Saints the unity of blood and clime, / Martyred by Caesars of the
Undersoul / Who rape the freedoms and their crimes extol"
(107) – democratic or Christian retribution befalls those who betray
the trust of the people. For Tolson, steeped in the classical philoso-
phers, the decline of Rome manifest in Mussolini's Italy signifies a
near fatal flaw in the Western conceptualization of the individual and
the state, while Ethiopia, what Tolson idealizes as a monarchical
Christian democracy, offers a living alternative.

Throughout the collection, Tolson, as he had in "Caviar and Cabbage," invests the body politic with the flesh and blood of its constituents, rendering it living – and therefore mortal, perishable. The
fluidity of his construct *democracy* comes not from an abstraction but
from its eccentric, palpable presence (or absence) in a citizen's life.
And though it is a commonplace to suggest that a *nation* is its *people*,
Tolson collectivizes (racially, ethnically, generationally) even as he
individualizes the notion of *citizenship* in the land of *e pluribus unum*;
for *Rendezvous with America* as well as "Caviar and Cabbage" fix the
reciprocal nature of Tolson's survey of nation-people-citizen, socially
recalibrating Huey Long's utopian projection of *Every Man a King*.[38]

Rendezvous with America, when read as a progression of Tolson's
work, represents a series of bridges between epic and lyric, history
and news, nation and citizen, community and race. The invasion of
Ethiopia, the Spanish Civil War, and the Second World War inspired
poets and journalists alike to meditate upon the promise and reality
of democracy in America. Langston Hughes, after topical responses
in *Opportunity* ("Call of Ethiopia" [1936] with its Pan-African, centrifugal response to the invasion – "Ethiopias free! / Be like me, / All
of Africa, / Arise and be free! / All you black peoples, / Be free! Be
free!" [184]) – and *New Theatre* ("Air Raid over Harlem" [1936] with
its national, centripetal scenario for Harlem – "Kill ME! / Sure, I
know / The Ethiopian war broke out last night: / BOMBS OVER
HARLEM / Cops on every corner / Most of 'em white / COPS IN
HARLEM" [186]) – broadened his wartime disquisition on the nation
in "Let America Be America Again."[39]

Carl Sandburg, oblivious to the significance of Mussolini's march on Ethiopia, turned his ever anxious liberal attentions to the splintering "family of man" in *The People, Yes* (1936). His seemingly all-inclusive America, with its tides of "migratory harvest hands and berry pickers, the loan shark victims, the installment house wolves, / The jugglers in sand and wood who smooth their hands along the mold that casts the frame of your motorcar engine, / The metal polishers, solderers and paint-spray hands who put the final finish on the car" (sec. 21: 462) in a land of infinite freedoms and geographic diversity, shrinks in proportion to Sandburg's liberal remove, a distance that turns his presumed sympathy into a shrill ventriloquism of partial if not complete misunderstanding. Throughout this celebratory epic, the "people," in their economic and political impotence, more often than not fall subject to an earnest vision of social engineering.[40]

Librarian of Congress Archibald MacLeish committed to the democratic epic in *America Was Promises* (1939). Once as interested in matters of leadership as Pound or Tolson (see, in particular, his Pulitzer Prize–winning *Conquistador* [1932]), MacLeish increasingly reveals a mistrust bordering upon disgust as he contemplates totalitarianism in radio plays such as *The Fall of the City* (1937) and *Air Raid* (1938). *America Was Promises*, with its rhetorical questioning and historical insistence on America's role in the world, answers Pound and Sandburg. The exile lost in a sea of Social Credit bunk, he dismisses: "The Aristocracy of Wealth and Talents / Moved out: settled on the Continent: / Sat beside the water at Rapallo: / Died in a rented house: unwept : unhonored" (14); the populist of the Family of Man, he reiterates: "Tom Paine knew. / Tom Paine knew the People. / The promises were spoken to the People. / History was voyages toward the People. / Americas were landfalls of the People. / Stars and expectations were the signals of the People" (15). MacLeish turns abruptly from the historical that had so intrigued Pound and Sandburg – "Truth now from John Adams . . . Tongues from Thomas Jefferson . . . Justice from Tom Paine" – to the news of the day. And yet in his inventory of crimes, "Spain Austria Poland China Bohemia / . . . dead men in the pits in all those countries" (18), Ethiopia is missing, thereby limiting his call of "Brothers! Generation! / . . . / Listen ! Believe the speaking dead!" (19). If, however, "America is promises to / Take!" Tolson would be there to seize the day.

While all of these war-inspired epics were written by poets who were seasoned journalists representing a range of political beliefs, only Hughes and Tolson addressed the subnational constituencies bordered by race and class, the "little guys" Sandburg only imagined. Though the pages of periodicals such as Margaret Anderson's *Common Ground* and Henry Luce's *Fortune* bear testimony to the national anxiety regarding the meaning of America, few reveal the urgent idealism and speculative reserve of *Rendezvous with America*. Tolson, fresh from his segregated conversations on national identity and citizenship in the *Washington Tribune*, could assume the poetic *and* political mantle of modernism, retrieving "America" and "democracy" from the dustbin of a racialized history. The journey toward deterritorialization begins with his war-inspired nationalization.

Seemingly a product of (in Pound's sense) a racially inscribed "national culture" as well as a challenging extension of Roosevelt's "warm courage of national unity" (proposed in his First Inaugural Address), *Rendezvous with America* has the audacity to splinter *and* cohere even as it forces the patriotic abstraction of *democracy* to conform to the national borders of *America*. As contestatory as his journalism, Tolson's poems move effortlessly within the aesthetic and political matrices of America's many, often competing narratives. Exemplary figures, quotation, polyvocality, and personae enter a stream of narrative ventriloquism that, while derived from any number of his contemporaries (in particular, Eliot, Pound, and Sandburg), is his own. Workers, rebels, tyrants, bawds, and presidents populate this riposte to earlier and contemporary poems and promises of America by Whitman, MacLeish, Hughes, and Sandburg. *Rendezvous with America* prefigures his subsequent attempts to move Americanism from an institutionally enforced and ultimately empty signification to a spiritually, spatially, and aesthetically rendered one according to the precepts of G. I. Gurdjieff. What Arnold Rampersad reads as the volume's "militant pro-Marxism" and Werner Sollors as its "melting-pot catalogues"[41] originate in poets as diverse as Archibald MacLeish and Carl Sandburg, William Carlos Williams and Ezra Pound. Sympathies with the "masses" or "people" or "folk," though frequently prompted by contemporary and often contrary political currents, more often than not originated in literary considerations and affiliations.

If, as Aldon Nielsen suggests, Tolson's ultimate poetic ambition was to "deterritorialize" modernism (see Nielsen 1994: 48–70), his short-term, wartime goal, achieved in *Rendezvous with America*, was more modest in its inscription of the immediate and national, the temporal and territorial. Democracy's failure as experienced by black America was due to its presence as a guiding abstraction rather than an abiding reality in a citizen's life. In revising national identity into a form of knowing democracy, Tolson triangulates democracy, America, and citizenship into a complex of rights that are universal, natal, and inalienable. As he notes in the locationally and chronologically imperative title sequence:

> *Here,*
> *Now,*
> The Pilgrim Fathers draw
> The New World's testament of faith and law:
> A government of and by and for the People,
> A pact of peers who share and bear and plan,
> A government which leaves men free and equal
> And yet knits men together as one man.
> ("Rendezvous with America," sec. 8: 10)

Unlike the self-construction of the infinitely mythologized American individualist, Tolson's citizen is a nationally created participant in an equally constituted society. Sandburg's Lincoln as depicted in *The People, Yes* suggests a model for Tolson's national conversation, in which the truly democratically inspired leadership blocks the "insidious debauching of the public mind" (Sandburg 1936: 523–4). Emboldened by his journalistic respite from the trials of modernism, Tolson assumed a poetic and political role that ultimately would enable him to contest the polemic of Pound and the sentiment of Sandburg as well as the vision of FDR.

When read as an extension of *A Gallery of Harlem Portraits* and "Caviar and Cabbage," *Rendezvous with America* forms a spatial and temporal axis to the discontinuous history, the dialectic between nationality and democracy, initiated in his columns. The fraying of the national fabric evidenced in the hyphenate sprawl of *Gallery*'s closing "The Underdog" –

> Sambo, nigger, son of a bitch,
> I came from the loins
> Of the great white masters.

86

Kikes and bohunks and wops,
Dagos and niggers and crackers . . .
Starved and lousy,
Blind and stinking –
We fought each other,
Killed each other,
Because the great white masters
Played us against each other.

Then a kike said: *Workers of the world, unite!*
And a dago said: *Let us live!*
And a cracker said: *Ours for us!*
And a nigger said: *Walk together, children!*

WE ARE THE UNDERDOGS
ON A HOT TRAIL!
(Tolson 1979: 229–30)

– prefigures the ethnically and racially inflected common ground of class that will inform his journalism and wartime poetry. The literal force with which Tolson appropriates and deploys Roosevelt's "rendezvous," an individualized presentation at a specified time and place, intensifies the figurative passion of its immediate and historical occasion as it emphatically resituates its "destiny." Laced with Marxian topics and tropes while suffused with a messianic theology tempered by the constative vision of a retrospective prophet, the sequences attempt to redeem the past through a poetry predicated upon both the immediacy of news and a long and complex racial history. More Christian than Marxist, Tolson seems to invert Brecht's famous "First comes grub, then morality" as he proffers a socially comprehensive, religious sustenance.

Ultimately, the centrifugal daring of *Rendezvous with America* stems from its willingness to sustain poetically and politically the voices of America and to entertain the promises of democracy.[42] Tolson, obviously liberated by his racialized sojourn at the *Tribune*, brings to the harsh white intricacy of modernism and the "Big Guy" world of New York publishing a range of intertextual challenges. For those who follow his poetic and journalistic modes, *Rendezvous* offers a complex lyrical indictment of American race history and political promise; for all those familiar with the liberal fellowship of Tolson's well-meaning literary associates, the volume reveals interstices within which his

response to their democratic and epic appeals may be heard; and finally, for those who have followed Pound's descent into that special
national craziness peculiar to what William Carlos Williams labeled "the
pure products of America," the poems claim that democracy is embedded in a land and a people destined to be accountable for its promises.
Seasoned readers of his journalism will certainly detect the historical
rap and contemporary pulse of the newspaper columns throughout
Rendezvous, as its poems course through the history and poetry of
democracy in America. The relevant past of these poems may be found
in the columns: It is America's unfinished business of democracy. Black
America's claim to the promise of American life, secured by its
birthright, seems in Tolson's mind as quintessentially American as Herbert Croly's biblically cadenced, turn-of-the-century assertion:

> From the beginning Americans have been anticipating and pro-
> jecting a better future. From the beginning the Land of Democracy
> has been figured as the Land of Promise. Thus the American's loy-
> alty to the national tradition rather affirms than denies the imagi-
> native projection of a better future . . . In cherishing the Promise of
> a better national future the American is fulfilling rather than
> imperiling the substance of the national tradition. (1909: 3)

And it is in that spirit of "fulfilling rather than imperiling" that Tolson
offers us his narratives of America.

4

"IF I WERE A NEGRO"

LIBERALISM AND CITIZENSHIP AT NEGRO DIGEST

Liberals like people with their heads, radicals like people with both their heads and their *hearts*. Liberals talk passionately of the rights of minority groups; protest against the denial of political and voting rights, against segregation, against anti-Semitism, and against all other inhuman practices of humanity. However, when these same liberals emerge from their meetings, rallies, and passage of resolutions and find themselves seated next to a Negro in a public conveyance they tend to shrink back slightly. . . . Intellectually they subscribe to all of the principles of the American Revolution and the Constitution of the United States, but in their hearts they do not. They are a strange breed of hybrids who have radical minds and conservative hearts. They really like people *only* with their heads.

– Saul Alinsky, *Reveille for Radicals* (1946b: 19–20)

In January 1968, for *Fortune* magazine's special issue on "the urban crisis,"[1] John H. Johnson recalled his quintessentially American, rags-to-riches saga. A visit to the 1933 Chicago World's Fair convinced the young Johnson and his mother to move from rural Arkansas to Chicago's South Side. In 1936 Johnson, an honors student at Du Sable High School, spoke at the annual convocation on "America's Challenge to Youth," was heard by Harry Pace, the president of a local insurance company, and was awarded a scholarship to the University of Chicago as well as part-time employment at the Supreme Life Insurance Company. Impressed by Johnson's energy and wit, Pace gave him "an assignment that changed [his] life" (1989: 113): "to read magazines and newspapers and prepare a digest of what was happening in the Black world" (1989: 133). Johnson's surfeit of race news made him the social epicenter of events in the black community. From the lunchroom to the conference table, he shared the nation's perspectives on race. His work as editor of the company's newsletter (and his skill in operating "the Speedaumat, an addressing machine which kept the names and addresses of the twenty thousand people who paid their insurance premiums quarterly, semiannually, or annually" [1989: 114]) prompted his decision go into publishing for himself.[2] As he recalled in his autobiography: "The next step was so obvious that I'm ashamed to say that I didn't immediately recognize it. I'd been riding the social circuit for several weeks, reciting my stories of Black achievement and aspiration, before it occurred to me that I was looking at a black gold mine" (1989: 114). Johnson used his mother's furniture to raise collateral for a five-hundred-dollar loan to pay for his direct-mail campaign for *Negro Digest* (*ND*). Using a corner of the law library at Supreme Insurance as his headquarters and official address, he sought his first readers. His appeal to twenty thousand black Americans, sent in the spring of 1942, offered subscriptions at two dollars each and brought in three thousand subscribers.[3]

As Ben Burns,[4] a white editor for the *Chicago Daily Defender* and managing (though unattributed) editor of *Negro Digest,* notes in his memoir *Nitty Gritty: A White Editor in Black Journalism,* Johnson was convinced of the commercial timeliness of his first publishing venture:

> I asked Johnson, "How are you going to sell a quarter magazine when the Negro papers are just getting through by the skin of their teeth on a dime?"
> "You know there's a war on," countered Johnson. "Big things are in the air and we can get in on them if we make the right moves. The magazine can't miss." (1996: 30)

Embedded in Johnson's nod to the war is the tacit admission that for black Americans "the war" was always already "on." And though expressing little interest in politics per se, urging the *Fortune* interviewer to "Remember, I am a businessman, not a social worker," Johnson nonetheless worked tirelessly to create a culturally insistent, linguistically sophisticated context within which African Americans might discover a success rooted in a racialized, bourgeois identity that would equal if not challenge the economic self-destiny of white America. "Lift while climbing" signified at Johnson Publishing a racialized economic liberation cycle epitomized by a personal corporate philosophy. Countering those who would consign the "Negro . . . to the little man who wasn't there," Johnson lived the philosophy reiterated in his autobiography: "going first class is the best revenge" (1989: 197).

Recognizing a "demand for a magazine to summarize and condense the leading articles and comment on the Negro now current in the press of the nation," Johnson financed and Burns assembled a monthly "dedicated to the development of interracial understanding and the promotion of national unity . . . for the winning of the war and the integration of all citizens into the democratic process" (*ND*, November 1942, 1–2). Wishing to assess "the impact of the war and [further] attendant discussion of what [blacks were] fighting for," Johnson and Burns culled the best commentary from a wide range of American periodicals – I. F. Stone from *The Nation*, Norman Cousins from *The New Republic*, Dalton Trumbo from *Crisis*, S. I. Hayakawa from the *Chicago Defender* – to accompany feature articles by writers ranging from W. E. B. Du Bois and Langston Hughes to Gwendolyn Brooks and Richard Wright.

Although the wartime *Negro Digest* reflects the absurdity of the conflicted and contested rights of America's black citizens – fighting for liberty abroad while fighting for freedom at home – it quickly won praise from governmental agencies as the premier interracial publication (thereby securing a generous wartime paper allowance). Johnson transformed these bureaucratic encomia into the promotional "Comment" page, prefacing his January 1943 issue:

> Because of the quality of the articles contained in the first two issues, I am sure Negro Digest will serve to promote inter-racial understanding and will serve as an outstanding contribution to the war effort.
>
> *G. R. Ragland, Jr.,*
> *Superintendent*
> *Oklahoma State Training School*
> *Taft, Oklahoma*

Considering the need for national unity and participation of every

American in the war effort, the publication of a magazine such as yours is particularly valuable at this time. I am sure that it can contribute to understanding and cooperation between the races.

Donald M. Nelson, Chairman
War Production Board
Washington, D.C.

(n.p.)

The inaugural issues of the *Digest* appropriated this officious rhetoric to promote the complacencies of interracialism, but subsequent numbers reflected real tensions in America's communities of color. From California's Japanese- and Mexican-American citizens to Harlem's African, race-based abridgments of civil rights were egregious.[5] Though Burns's compilations emphasized the deplorable state of black America's rights, resentment and discrimination played only a small part in the overall substance, context, and tone of Johnson's publishing vision.

Unlike the direct missions of the *Colored American Magazine* and the *Chicago Defender*, which sought to nurture bourgeois material and cultural aspirations even as they helped create a black middle-class, or the adversarial charge of "Caviar and Cabbage," which privileged the "Little Negroes" and scorned "interracial chicken dinners," the editorial and market strategy of *Negro Digest* whetted the material and intellectual appetites of an increasingly metropolitan black bourgeoisie alert to name recognition. Even as Hopkins wrote for those unlettered in history, Johnson published for those appreciative of his manipulation of the cultural and philanthropic elite contributors. He was, in Kenneth Clark's description, "one of the few Negroes who has succeeded in breaking out of the constricted standards of the ghetto" (1965: 172).[6]

The ability of *Negro Digest* to realign the liberal critique of race even as it subverted the dialectic of black and white places Johnson at the very center of Bakhtin's dialogism, Foucault's counterdiscourse, and Habermas's fields of discourse. Reversing the centripetal tide in the language of the contributors' original sites of publication, the *Digest* employed a counterdiscourse in its editorial and publishing apparatus, supplanting, incorporating, and enslaving the public discourse on race even as it challenged the very notion of linguistic unity. *Negro Digest* initiated a publishing vision that anticipated the "deformation of mastery" that Houston Baker locates in African-American literature. Johnson and Burns, through cunning appropriation and manipulation of the "master texts," became interracial agents of the medium and message of the "dynamic democracy" of the participating citizens envisioned by Saul Alinsky in his *Reveille for Radicals* (1946b: 47).

From its inaugural issue, *Negro Digest* circulated in a contestatory public sphere in which the discourses of race and liberalism, whatever their local or internal organizing principles, were unable to maintain their boundaries in relation to a larger and national public as they were edited and reset by a black publisher and white editor for a primarily black audience, becoming the very embodiment of Bakhtinian heteroglossia. While Johnson campaigned for the financial security of his magazine, Burns harvested a compendium of notable guest columnists, all to some extent embodying the racial and ethnic complexities they sought to address. These various and contradictory visions generated *Negro Digest*'s fields of discursive connections.7 And while all marginalized journalism represents defensive structures (recall the *Colored American Magazine*, the *Chicago Defender*, or the *Washington Tribune*), *Negro Digest*, interracial editorially as well as philosophically, is a startling example of the sabotaging of ideological hegemony through the readerly and visual imperatives of the print medium itself.

Of enduring interest is *Negro Digest*'s solicited feature column "If I Were a Negro." Appearing monthly from December 1942 to October 1946, "If I Were a Negro" quickly became a financial asset for the fledgling journal and secured the journal's national status. Unlike the selected articles that formed the bulk of each issue (works of black and white authors from journals with primarily white audiences), these "written expressly for *Negro Digest*" columns continued the social drama of advocacy on the part of "officially concerned" white agents for black America. Within the racialized speech negotiations of these columns, the signature cultural bias and vocabulary of American race liberalism constitute enforced imaginings of the racial "other" with little or no hope for the reader's reciprocal reimagining or understanding. Recalling the New England abolitionists of Hopkins's biographical sketches (who assumed the right to rescue) and the Sandburg–Lippmann axis of a "race liberalism" predicated upon "race parallelism" (who embraced even as they marginalized African

Americans), these earnest, agitated, and plaintively sympathetic "guest Negroes" clasped black America in the rhetorical embrace of liberal philanthropy.

Though a popular feature, the columns signified yet another dimension of the perennial grip of a cultural and political elite. Even such self-aware columnists as self-avowed radical Saul Alinsky, whose "Beware the Liberals" ended the series in 1946, presumed they had the authority to instruct as they guarded the racially subordinate class. Ralph Ellison, in 1945 reviewing Bucklin Moon's *Primer for White Folks* (the column's spiritual twin: an anthology of "aroused efforts by liberal whites"), could but conclude:

> Since hardly any aspect of our culture escapes the blight of hypocrisy implicit in our social institutions, it is not surprising that many of the pieces mix appeal for fair play with double-talk; or that most are much too fearful of that absolute concept "democracy," circling above it like planes being forced to earth in a fog. They seemed concerned most often with patching up the merry-go-round-that-broke-down than with the projection of that oh-so-urgently-needed new American humanism. (1945b: 147)

At the end of the column's first year, *Time* magazine's reviewer dismissed the transracial empathy of "If I Were a Negro" as excessive, indeed so extreme that its voluntary "Negroes" were more "hot and bothered about the race question" than Johnson himself (Burns 1996: 35).[8]

Unlike previous depictions of transracialism by W. E. B. Du Bois and Langston Hughes,[9] the "If I Were" columnists resisted the severity and penetration of literary depiction, favoring instead a race-defined empowerment that drifted rhetorically and politically between prescriptive counsel and proscriptive admonition. Excluded from the reality and circumstance of being black, the white guest columnists, despite their intellectual sympathies, generally advocated a status quo of liberal authority and agency. Burns shared their fate. Though well aware of his editorial manipulation of liberals and radicals, he could not transcend his own racially inscribed identity. This dilemma curiously anticipates the dreamily estranged and intellectually hip projection of the young Norman Mailer in his polemic "The White Negro," published a decade later.[10]

Left to his own devices, Burns might have allowed such subversive hipster currents to surface in the content and layout of the magazine, allowing the language of marginalization to testify to the rents in the national fabric. Certainly the predominantly northern solicited contributors shared his intensity and, to some degree, even his guilt regarding America's systematically abridged citizenship for African Americans. Such feelings seemed endemic to a white liberal community that was simultaneously proud of and embarrassed by Gunnar Myrdal's internally funded, externally inspired reading of America's "Negro problem."[11] Ralph Ellison's assessment of the psychopathology of the liberal conscience, that "philanthropy on the psychological level is often guilt-motivated, even when most unconscious," may be extended to the editorial and authorial aspects of this column (1944: 331).[12] And had there not been a war, these social philanthropists might have expressed their rancor and discontent with constitutional abridgments of citizen rights even more stridently. But the complexities of the war sanctioned, for the duration, restrictions upon citizens of color intolerable to the nation's professed sense of justice and democracy, enabling the most high-minded to rest content in what Ellison called their "corny notion . . . [of] . . . obligation" to the Negro.

Because its record of distinguished service during the First World War did nothing to forestall the citizenship crisis of the Second, black America turned to a home-front campaign for full, participatory citizenship. The ongoing segregation of the armed forces and defense industries, the emergency "relocation" of Japanese-American citizens and their "alien" relatives from the West Coast in the spring of 1942, the "zoot suit" riots in Los Angeles in the summer of 1943,[13] and Myrdal's Carnegie-funded study of "The Negro Problem and Modern Democracy" confirmed Ellison's suspicions that "the solution of the problem of the American Negro and democracy lies only partially in the white man's free will. Its full solution will lie in the creation of a democracy in which the Negro will be free to define himself for what he is and, within the large framework of that democracy, for what he desires to be" (1944: 328–9). The propulsive desire of Ellison's review reflects Johnson's actively bourgeois vision of America as a nation in which economic agency signifies liberty. Of the magazine's many highlights, no feature better foregrounded the disabling effects of interracialism than "If I Were a Negro."[14] Individually, these guest columns form a dialectic of celebrity and agency; collectively, they constitute a curiously monological epic of philanthropically inclined and ultimately condescending liberalism.

*   *   *

> The claims of the Negro minority to democratic recognition
> were vastly heightened by the war. Resentment against exclu-
> sion from many branches of the armed forces and from
> defense industries, coupled with segregation, flared in the
> Negro press and was vigorously voiced by Negro agencies. . . .
> Cast upon the larger world stage of exploitation of the darker
> races in the colonies of the democracies, their cause in the
> United States is taking on a new significance in the conduct
> and aims of the war.
>
>   – *The Bill of Rights in War* (ACLU 1942: 8)

Unlike the predictable structure of Hopkins's single-authored biographical profiles, the "If I Were a Negro" columns situated formulaic
and political rhetoric in a visual field dictated by the print medium
itself. Substantive and accidental texts form and re-form as readers
respond, often subconsciously, to semiotextual directions that ask
them to look as well as read. The very material form of the magazine
becomes part of the overall signifying system of the journal, corrupting the tensions and intentions of individual selections. The gravitas
of "If I Were a Negro," for example, is modified if not completely nullified by the blithe spiritedness of the black-authored "If I Were Young
Again" (featuring a complement of black celebrities such as W. E. B.
Du Bois detailing what they would do "if they had their lives to live
over again"). Typographical devices, vignetted cartoons, and editorial
juxtapositions (often at odds with the text at hand) further personalize
the appropriated layout of *Negro Digest*, altering the temperament of
the individual contribution as they optimize the whole. Few "guest
Negroes" could emancipate their homilies from the editorial
pressures imposed by a print medium that wanted to have "everything – laughs, controversy, tragedy, excitement, entertainment,
knowledge – a complete, well-rounded magazine that does the job of a
dozen others" (*ND*, December 1943, frontispiece). And yet, when liberated from the journal's contextual boosterism, the series prompts
more than an indictment of liberal authoritarian inconsistencies: It
exposes the referential instability of the race-shifting representations
themselves. America's "officially concerned," whose utterances honor
the centripetal forces of hegemony and authority, consigned black
America to a subnational, colonial status (Polenberg 1995: 11–24).

     Of the forty-four columns, few escape the expected vocabulary of a
sympathy predicated upon retention of agency and the earnest dispen-

sation of justice. All but the first in the series, Royal F. Munger's " . . . I Should Be So Proud" (originally published in the *Chicago Daily News*, November 9, 1942), were written for *Negro Digest*. In the tradition of Carl Sandburg's status quo liberalism at the *Daily News*, this borrowed, inaugural column in the second issue of the *Digest* established a model for future lapses of insight and expression; Munger begins: "If I were a Negro, I should be so *proud* of being an American *citizen*, and so *grateful* to my country that I could hardly find words to express that emotion. It is a far bigger thing to be an American Negro, and a far greater achievement, than to be a Negro in any other country in the world" (*ND*, December 1942, 48-9; emphasis added). With astonishing rapidity, the assumed racial identity lapses, and by the second paragraph Munger cedes the racialized speaking "I." In his forgetfulness, his "song of himself" turns into a hymn *to* "the Negro . . . and his own conduct." Munger relaxes into the familiar rhetoric and experience of white hegemony as he depicts a "darky" familiar to his readers from minstrel shows and the cinema and projects a collective identity for this racial other: one that has moved from "downtrodden . . . to hardworking, merry, kindly, and usually trustworthy" (48).

Innocent of his journalistic pretense and wholeheartedly rejecting his self-assigned role, Munger turns voyeur in this supplemental disquisition on race. His black world, unrelieved by irony, is peopled by those who "have genuine worth as . . . human being[s]" and "gave full value according to . . . their abilit[ies]." Pretense of individual worth quickly succumbs to a collective identity resistant to the perils of full humanity; as Munger determines the evolution of (what Ralph Ellison would characterize as) "pre-individuals":[15]

> Gradually he [the Negro] began to enter the more skilled trades and even the professions. All this took time, but the progress in terms of decades has been plainly visible. In the meantime, the individual Negro need not feel discouraged because he does not always obtain instant recognition; he is one of a group, and all members of groups are judged somewhat in the mass. The group is advancing steadily. (49)

As a tactician or historian, Munger is challenged; but as a Negro, he is a failure.

In spite of their dusky guises, these voluntary Negroes were unable to descend from their racialized prominence and assume the dialectic of the politically compromised other. Employing such central value words as *proud* ("If I were a Negro, I would be proud . . . "), *bitter* ("I would not be bitter"), *democracy* ("I would see in democracy the one hope"), *thankful* ("I would be thankful for my heritage"), and *citizen* ("being an American citizen"), the columnists, regardless of their peacetime preferences and agendas, succumbed to the liberal contradictions common to the earlier wartime writings of Sandburg and Lippmann. Readers expecting a radically redeployed vocabulary of insight and consequent understanding found instead a model exercise in which rhetoric shades into epistemology. Black Americans familiar with the absolute space between "liberalism" and "democracy" would hear an intertext foregrounded, though perhaps unsuspected, by the columnists themselves.

Embedded in the style, presentation, and argument of these transracial offerings was a conspiracy of the ideational and interpersonal in which linguistic assumptions betrayed epistemological presumptions. The series renewed the Jeffersonian commitment to "government by its citizens in mass, acting directly and personally," while acknowledging the gradualism encoded in all such promises. Tribute to race pride becomes reason for contentment with the status quo; appeal to analogous circumstances (authors writing as women, Catholics, Jews), excuse for inaction; counsel to acceptance, relinquishment to racialized hierarchy. Their distinction and celebrity rendered most contributors incapable of deprivileging individual rhetorical and political stances. To insist that professional role players (actors, writers, politicians, ministers and priests, musicians, attorneys) modify their inherited premises of racial circumstance and authority would have compromised Johnson's and Burns's separate, though curiously equal, visions of the symbolic function of this self-indicting feature. *Negro Digest* could savor the circulation-building power of its famous crossracial writers while it showcased their moral myopia.

Structurally, visionary disturbance impaired many columns, encouraging authors to stray from a forced racial empathy to a condescending interpersonal sympathy. In this way, Eleanor Roosevelt saw through race to women, Pearl Buck to Chinese, Ted Le Berthon and Bishop Sheil to Catholics, Bucklin Moon to southerners, and Milton Mayer to Jews. Unwilling (or perhaps ultimately unable) to suspend their racial disbelief, few moved beyond the dominant modality of the lecture, an encumbered discourse unlikely to seduce "the other." Though each began boldly through assertion or apology as either "I am" or "I could never be," the columns encompassed the extremes of consolation and instruction. The representational uncertainties become most evident when the authors straddle the boundary between personal roles and social relationships inscribed in the columns. Seeming to display a catalogue of modal logic, the race-determined attitudes drift from apparent *truth* to sense of *obligation*, from extending permission to arguing *desirability*. The intimate orality of the columns, at once conversational and lectural with their periodic disrupted syntax, bespeaks an impositional hierarchy that is linguistic, social, and characteristic of liberal sensibilities.

Nowhere is this racialized class stratification more apparent than in columns plagued by pronominal instability. Often, regardless of introductory sympathies or apologies denoting awareness of their roles, these voluntary Negroes drift from their assigned black "I"s into signature gradations of white privilege and class in which the speakerly "I" recedes and the racialized subject turns into the racialized object signified by "they." The momentary natal exuberance for race circumstance and history disintegrates into the reappropriated lexicon and society of the status quo. Whether these lapses are representational or epistemological is less interesting than the effect they have on these race homilies. For, as empathy pales into sympathy, sermons lapse into lectures exposing a core of ideational and interpersonal ignorance. And yet, despite its superficial and formulaic predictability, "If I Were a Negro" sometimes surpasses its immediate purpose, fracturing national metanarratives into economically and racially defined local narrative communities.

Few submissions had the aplomb or the market impact of Eleanor Roosevelt's in the final issue of the magazine's first year. Appearing in October 1943 (8–9), "Freedom: Promise or Fact" both extended and personalized the First Lady's earlier contribution to the *Digest*, her objective supplement to FDR's "Four Freedoms," the "Four Equalities."[16] Her rhetorically balanced, comfortably binary imagination, accommodating bitterness and patience, produced ideal copy for the ambitious and inexperienced editor and publisher; what Johnson recalls as the "georacial" impact of the issue was strategic:

an October 1943 cover story by the wife of the president of the United States – marked a major turning point in the fortunes of

Negro Digest. . . . Southern White newspapers picked up the part about the great patience. Black newspapers and northern White newspapers picked up the part about great bitterness. And our circulation jumped, almost overnight, from 50,000 to 100,000. After that, we never looked back. (1989: 132)

The perfect balance or "fit" of Roosevelt's central rhetorical constituencies (deftly modulated among the local, the national, and aspirant global components of her model, united nations, world) make this a particularly rewarding example of the series' strengths and weaknesses.

Roosevelt's nuanced presentation of self-as-other relies as much upon the reader's reception as the author's representation. Within her linguistic and structural expression rests an intricately encoded message of liberal sympathy and presumed agency. These ideas are fluid, not static, constantly being authorized or dismissed by a racialized sphere of readers: hence, the congenial nature of the column for northerners and southerners alike. Readers seeking affirmative consolation would latch onto that linkage, while those yearning for the status quo would secure themselves to its complementary opposite. Though, from Johnson's editorial and publishing perspective, the ideal reader of the column was the black bourgeoisie, the accidental white audience discovered in the shifting planes of text and context a geopolitical and transracial complexity that belied the clarity and innocence of Roosevelt's "black" subjectivity. In this way, the symbolic morality inherent in her national (though unelected) office, when wedded to the sincere superficiality of her racial guise, yielded a language of caprice and authority.

Even the title suggests a First Lady engagée, playing a rhetorical zero-sum game in which "promise" cancels "fact," "faith" voids "bitterness." In the opening two paragraphs, Roosevelt sustains her projected identity only briefly, as she moves from empathy to condescension. Even her opening rhetorical gesture shrinks into tentative concession – "If I were a Negro today, I would have moments of great bitterness" – as the subjunctive yields to a passivity that accommodates a momentary biracialism that shades into a qualified conditional: "It would be hard for me to sustain my faith in democracy and to build up a sense of goodwill toward men of other races."

Roosevelt's dispassionate writing shifts imperceptibly from the rhetoric of experience to that of the lecture, disclosing a neocolonial remove in the language of this race impostor: "I think, however, that I would realize that if my *ancestors* had never left Africa, we would be worse off as '*natives*' today under the rule of any other country than I am in this country where my *people* were brought as *slaves*" (1943b: 8; emphasis added). When coupled with the qualifying caution of her introduction – "I think, however, I would realize" – the genealogical and historical imperatives of these unanchored signifiers produce a countertide of white-inflected reference that privileges "ancestor" over "'natives,'" "people" over "slaves" and ultimately neglects the dialectical verbal tensions between "had never left" and "were brought." The surface sincerity of her assumed racial sympathies lapses into the instructional discourse of white on black.

Diminishing the history of chattel slavery to a "comparatively short period of time," Roosevelt proclaims "slaves . . . free men . . . that is, as far as a proclamation can make them so" and returns to the paradoxical nature of her column's title: "There now remains much work to be done to see that freedom becomes a fact and not just a promise for my people." Roosevelt, resolute in her austere sympathies, never wavers from the pronominal certainty and rhetorical gesture of her pose. And yet this three-paragraph passage from bitterness to faith, slavery to democracy, Africa to America seems to have unduly strained Roosevelt's representational reserves, prompting her defection from race to gender.

The civility with which Roosevelt slips from race-based into gendered prejudice – "I know, however, that I am not the only group that has to make a similar fight" – masks the ease with which she has mastered the unitary force of language and resituated her "authentic" self. Although she appears to enlarge the imaginative potential of her representation, she generalizes a host of discriminations into but a momentary stay in the progress of democracy. For as she notes: "Even women of the white race still suffer inequalities and injustices, and many groups of white people in my country are the slaves of economic conditions. All the world is suffering under a great war brought about because of the lag in our social development as against the progress in our economic development" (1943b: 8). The rhetorical decomposition is subtle, as the phrasal alliance of "women of the white race" dissolves into the generalizing taxonomic vagaries of "many groups of white people in my country." This expressive breach transforms the discourse of race into a diminished category of compromise: "the slaves of economic conditions." The mutual nullification inherent in these conjoined sympathies liberates Roosevelt from the confines of either race or gender, supplanting her racialized epistemology with the rhetoric of spunk: "Even though I was held back by generations of economic inequality, I would be proud of those of my race who are gradually fighting to the top in whatever occupation they are engaged in" (1943b: 8). Such spirited gradualism, familiar to readers of Lippmann and Sandburg, typifies what Gerda Lerner has called the "all-powerful benevolence" of the Roosevelt administration's liberalism, which perpetually suspended black America in a netherworld of marginalized citizenship.[17]

Roosevelt's magnanimous comprehension of racially marginalized citizenship shifts in mid-sermon to home-front boosterism that compromises liberty in the name of a wartime higher good. No longer an issue of the national commonweal, the status of citizen becomes a global function of the promised land of the United Nations: "I would still feel that I ought to participate to the full in this war. When the United Nations win, certain things will be accepted as a result of principles which have been enunciated by the leaders of the United Nations, which never before have been part of the beliefs and practices of the greater part of the world" (1943b: 8–9). The transmutation of "allies" into the geopolitically higher form of "United Nations" should not be read as an accidental or rhetorical effect. Committed to the postwar ideal of a global community, Roosevelt consigns freedom's "promise" to the nation, its "fact" to the world. And yet, imbedded in her altruistic projection of a brave new world rests an inverted liberal text in which the agents of this new order remain the allied Euro-American force.

Roosevelt's gesture to the postwar world of revisionary association signals a retreat from her contrived posture of race empathy because the speakerly text counsels wary striving. Citizenship and economic equality for black America regrettably remain something to "go on working for"; "real rights as a citizen" have priority over "social relationships." White opposition to full citizenship should be respected "until certain people were given time to think them through and decide as individuals what they wished to do." Marginalized citizens must "not do too much demanding" and must take "every chance . . . to prove [their] equality and ability . . . and if recognition was slow . . . continue to prove [themselves], knowing that in the end good performance has to be acknowledged." Roosevelt's sense of citizenship as a performative circumstance makes explicit her acceptance of the existing state in which race-circumscribed national subjects, like the "minor" nations of the world, must await national recognition of their political existence.

As Roosevelt enlarges her sermon from racial to gender discrimination, she notes that solidarity with more diverse, special-interest groups is in order. The segregated army and navy offer the possibility of "advance," though, as she quickly cautions, "I would not try to bring those advances about any more quickly than they were offered." The labor movement, frequently noted by the other "guest Negroes" as a means of political empowerment, offers the potential of a brotherly affiliation in which "men . . . work side by side and find out that it is possible to have similar interests and to stand by each other, regardless of race or color."

Anxious to find honor in this degraded state, the First Lady closes with an ascetic rendering of the spirituality of "her people":

> I would try to remember that unfair and unkind treatment will not harm me if I do not let it touch my spirit. Evil emotions injure the man or woman who harbors them so I would try to fight down resentment, the desire for revenge and bitterness. I would try to sustain my own faith in myself by counting over my friends and among them there would undoubtedly be some white people. (1943b: 9)

This extranational conception of humanity neglects the unconstitutional nature of black America's plight. The language center of this culminating projection announces the linguistic and social elitism of this sublime forecast. At its acute extreme, "Freedom: Promise or Fact" conveys the intimacy of a race voyeur; at its blank opposite, the column reveals the ideological self-deception of an earnest spectator. The sincerity of this attempt to bridge the bifurcated rights of "we" and "they" buckles under the weight of the First Lady's experience and privilege. Wishing to draft a grid of liberal suasion in which injustice no longer figured, Roosevelt assumed the power of authentication at odds with her fictive kinship. Ultimately, no matter how well-meaning her representation, the speech relations of her contrived world confirm the social and linguistic roles in place. Readers convinced by Eleanor's minstrelsy were perhaps dismayed to read "If You Ask Me" (*ND*, February 1945, 9–10), in which she spoke as First Lady, counseling: "Sometimes it is wise not to move too fast."

Curiously, Roosevelt's column exemplifies the very whiteness that anthropologist Ruth Benedict had warned against in "I Wouldn't Forget" (*ND*, July 1943, 20–1). Acknowledging the limitations of her racial purview, she confesses: "I am on the top looking down and that is inevitably different from being on the bottom looking up. I can forget. If I were a Negro I couldn't" (20). She alerted her audience to the dangers of the "thousands of whites who would have conspired to teach me a passionate demand for human decency" even as they are "pushing some people into the outer darkness – of hopeless poverty, or racial caste, of bitter subjection to the whims of other men?" (20–1). Yet her anthropological skepticism does little to ward off the temptation to promote the fight against bitterness and for a protest "clear and bright" that would result in a "common cause with millions of people on this earth, black and white and yellow" (21).

Roosevelt's global circumstance becomes in Carey McWilliams's "The Economic Roots of Race Hate" (*ND*, August 1944, 53–5) an archetypal national crisis, one resolved through the enactment of the democratic principles of America's "great basic documents." McWilliams's experience as head of the California Division of Immigration and Housing from 1939 to 1943 inspired a belief in the sociopolitical and economic foundations of equality. In the spirit of Johnson's own publishing credo, he advanced the notion that because the Constitution and the Declaration of Independence are "wholly free of race bias" the very existence of discriminatory practices "must be accounted for quite apart from these basic documents" (53). As the author of *Brothers under the Skin* (1943), a history of the "vicious mistreatment of Negro, Indian, Mexican, Japanese, Chinese, Hawaiian, Puerto Rican, and Filipino" and a declaration that discrimination "was no longer a local problem," McWilliams challenged America's citizens to fulfill the promise of their history.

McWilliams's career is a study of regional crises begging for federal intervention. As California commissioner of immigration and housing, McWilliams moved from general historical and literary studies (*Louis Adamic and Shadow-America, Ambrose Bierce: A Biography, The New Regionalism in American Literature*) to an investigative journalism (*Factory in the Fields*, a study of migratory labor practices in California;

Brothers under the Skin, a wartime consideration of discriminatory practices against persons of color; *Prejudice: Japanese-Americans: Symbol of Racial Intolerance,* a case study of the War Relocation Agency) that used state issues as the evidentiary base for federal intervention. Unlike Roosevelt, who foresees an egalitarian world of the future, McWilliams "insist[s] that the race problem is essentially a national problem, and that the federal government must recognize its responsibilities toward racial minorities" (1944a: 55). The apparent directness of an activist shades into a more complex displacement in which the hierarchical superior achieves the dreams of the subordinate. Now, when read against Roosevelt, McWilliams seems a kindred spirit. For him, the federal government supersedes the state; for Roosevelt, the "united nations" relieves the nation: each looks to the larger authority to "repair democracy" (55).

McWilliams, too, fails to see beyond the blinders of liberal philanthropy. In "What We Did about Racial Minorities," his contribution to *While You Were Gone: A Report on Wartime Life in the United States* (1946), he isolates minorities from the prospect of change, noting:

> Great changes have taken place in race relations in America since the beginning of the war. By accelerating processes long at work in our democracy, the war has quickened the pace of cultural change. It has telescoped pre-existing tendencies, brought to light long-dormant issues, and sharpened numerous contradictions. By focusing public attention upon "the race problem," in all its ramifications, it has aroused *a new national interest in racial minorities* and stirred to life *a new national conscience toward these groups.* (1946: 89; emphasis added)

Nowhere is this spirit of national community more in evidence than in *Negro Digest*'s subscription campaign. Periodically, throughout the war, the endpaper would carry a sales appeal that aligned the health of the magazine's circulation with the world of "the Fuller brushman, the itinerant peddlar, the any-bonds-today man . . . welcomed at the front door." Imbued with the transracialism of the "If I Were a Negro" columns, the solicitations posited a "nation" of "neighbors," some of whom earn "themselves some spare-time income for the enjoyable pleasure of chatting with their neighbors about 'The Tenth American,' who is the theme of *Negro Digest.*"

Region, ethnicity, and national ideal warred endlessly in these columns, as Johnson's race guests sought to locate their experiences and their ideals squarely on the side of justice. Bucklin Moon, author of the novel *The Darker Brother* as well as the anthology *Primer for White Folks,* used the authority of his southern roots to declare the social and theatrical bankruptcy of white supremacy in his guest column, "Dixie Bottleneck" (*ND*, July 1945, 59–60). Whether viewed locally or internationally, white supremacy lost ground in Moon's eyes because "more and more whites are seeing what a comic show they are staging, not only for their fellow Americans but for the whole world" (59). And with the authority of a homeboy, he notes: "The white South is certainly the bottleneck holding up the integration of the Negro into the American lifestream, but even the South is showing signs of cracking at the edges" (59).

Few contributors had the point-blank rhetorical empathy of Milton Mayer. A columnist for *The Progressive, The Nation,* and *The New Republic* and a well-known conscientious objector, he conflated the bonds of race and ethnicity in a particularly poignant essay: "If I Were a Negro? Say, brother, I *am* a Negro. I don't take as bad a beating as the rest of the Negroes because I'm a *white* Negro; in other words, a Jew" (*ND*, March 1944, 21–23). His personal inventory of injustice does little to restrain the resignation or the resolve apparent in his summary: "I'm lucky to be an American, even a second-class American, because being an American gives me the best chance on earth to fight for human freedom. I'm not *proud* to be an American, because I didn't do anything to be one except to be born here" (22). Yet the intensity of circumstance, Hitler's race war, does little to attenuate the superficiality of conclusion or closure as Mayer resorts to the commonplace:

> And so I try to forget I'm a Negro, white or black, and I try not to be bitter about my lot, and I try not to repay hate with hate or prejudice with prejudice because I've got a job to do, a radical job to do, and hate and prejudice get in the way of doing my job. And when anybody asks me who I am or what I am, and tries to make a Republican, a Democrat, a Communist, or a Fascist of me, I say, "I'm a man, not a white man, a black man, or an American, but a man, fighting in all of humanity's war for emancipation." (23)

Such problematic closures intensify the question of national space, national responsibility. For if, as Homi Bhabha suggests, "the margins of the nation displace the centre" (1990: 6), where does the authority of "the people" reside?

For Louis Adamic, the request from *Negro Digest* touched upon conflicting circumstance and belief. Born in Carniola, a Yugoslavian region of the Austro-Hungarian Empire, and reared in the mill towns of Pennsylvania, he served in the American Expeditionary Force, fought at the Battle of the Somme, and upon discharge migrated to yet another new world, Los Angeles. Known for such popular Americanization texts as *A Nation of Nations* and *Two-Way Passage*, Adamic also authored works invested in the class-war world of the immigrants. *Laughing in the Jungle* (1932), an "autobiography of an immigrant in America," contributes what Mike Davis calls "an extraordinary documentary of Los Angeles in the 1920s from the standpoint of its radical outcasts and defeated idealists" (1990: 31). Unlike his earlier affirmations of assimilation, "There Are Whites and Whites" (*ND*, March 1946, 47–50) complicates, perhaps terminally, the very notion of nationality and citizenship. Adamic, a marginal citizen of fading nations, identifies borders as essential marginal constituents of mid-century identity. Rejecting Myrdal's defining terminology, he lays bare the complex interweave of circumstance and alliance that is the American nation:

> If I Were a Negro, I think my attitude to the general situation of Negroes in the United States would be the same as it is now. There is no isolable "Negro problem." It is not a "Negro problem" – it is an American problem. It is an element in the American situation, which consists of the interplay between and among, say, the Negro, Italian, German, Jewish, Protestant, Catholic, Mexican, Polish and old-line Anglo-Saxon "problems." (Adamic 1946: 47)

Grounded clearly in Marxist readings of class stratification and rights, Adamic had, as Carey McWilliams notes in *Louis Adamic and Shadow-America* (1935), "an instinctive hostility to typically middle-class concepts" (32). Such philosophical aversion should have made him an unlikely contributor to Johnson's bourgeois digest. And yet the column's tendentious and formulaic inheritance liberated an unexpected synthesis of Adamic's experiential and intellectual social philosophies. Clearly, at war's end he located culture and identity at the boundary of an increasingly tangled national sensibility. History and prospects were simultaneously to blame for the "prevailing view, indirectly insisted upon by the dominant channels of information. . . . that the United States is a White-Protestant-Anglo-Saxon country whose White-Protestant-Anglo-

Saxon civilization must either reject or engulf and overwhelm the 'alien' civilizations of Negroes and 'foreigners'" (Adamic 1946: 48). Having slipped from a conversational into a lectural mode, Adamic iterates his newly synthesized vision of "America":

> It is a heterogeneous, multi-national, multi-racial, multi-religious country. . . . Our industrial, social, and political developments hinge on that point. . . . The pattern of the United States is all of a piece – it is something new – it is American. . . . It is a blend of cultures from many lands. It has been – and is still being – woven of threads from all corners of the earth. (48)

Anticipating poet Jay Wright's bicentennial "imaginative dissolution and reconstruction" of American materials, Adamic declares in a curiously modern way that "Diversity is the American pattern, is the stuff and color of the fabric" (48). As he would elaborate in his postwar reading of American history, *A Nation of Nations*:

> There are two ways of looking at our history.
> One is this: that the United States is an Anglo-Saxon country with a White-Protestant-Anglo-Saxon civilization struggling to preserve itself against infiltration and adulteration by other civilizations brought here by Negroes and hordes of "foreigners."
> The second is this: that the pattern of the United States is not essentially Anglo-Saxon although her language is English. Nor is the pattern Anglo-Saxon with a motley addition of darns and patches. The pattern of America is all of a piece; it is a blend of cultures from many lands, woven of threads from many corners of the world. Diversity itself is the pattern, is the stuff and color of the fabric. Or to put it another way: The United States is a new civilization, owing a great deal to the Anglo-Saxon strain, owing much to the other elements in its heritage and growth, owing much to the unique qualities and strong impetuses which stem from this continent, from the sweep of its land between two oceans, the mixture and interplay of its peoples, the plentitude of its resources, and the skills which we all of us have brought here or developed here in the past three centuries. (1945: 6)

Unusually candid in its assessment of the failure of earlier Americanization cycles, "There Are Whites and Whites" explains without excusing the effective double bind in which recent immigrants find themselves:

As a result of the wrong kind of "Americanization," some members (including, if not especially, leaders) of the new immigrant elements have taken on, like a kind of protective coloring, some of the old-line White American attitudes; among them, some of the worst.

Thanks to our education, thanks to our whole cultural atmosphere, Negro-hating is near the core of the "Americanism" of many immigrants and their American-born sons and daughters. Although they are White, they are in inferior social and economic circumstances, and they turn to anti-Negroism for compensation. (1946: 48)

Unlike the patrician austerity of Eleanor Roosevelt's disquisition or the suavity of Carey McWilliams's reading, the experiential intensity and political sophistication of Adamic's text expose the interstices of *e pluribus unum,* the subnarratives of American democracy. The particularities of his own outlandish American journey illuminate this point: "some Yugoslav Americans are anti-Negro in part because they are naturally reactionary, and pro-Mikhailovich and Royalist in reference to Yugoslavia, while most of the liberal, progressive or radical Yugoslav Americans who favor Tito – a majority – are not anti-Negro, not anti-Semitic" (1946:49). In many ways Adamic's contribution to this dialogue reveals what Homi Bhabha calls "the trials of cultural translation" (1990: 314), in which the course of empire dissolves the accepted status of subject and empire, citizen and nation. Cognizant of the cultural flux inherent in America's national experiment as well as of the ontological suspension necessary for its realization, Adamic acknowledges that "Life in this country works in two directions at once – splitting us up into racial, national, religious minorities, and on the other hand weaving unity from out of many diverse threads." He warns that "the disintegrative impulse seems to have the upper hand. Anti-Negroism, anti-Semitism, anti-alienism are sharply rising along with strikes and crimes" (1946: 50).

Few columnists apprehended the wealth of liberal tradition as a form of federal interventionism better than Helen Gahagan Douglas. Unlike the weary wisdom of socialist Norman Thomas's "Too Proud for Bitterness" (*ND*, November 1944, 85–6), Douglas's "Racial Progress with a Plan" (*ND*, August 1945, 49–50) possessed a programmatic acuity uncommon in the series. As a former actress, she was comfortable with assigned roles and scripted lines. But as a newly elected congresswoman pledged to a national office, she endorsed the "constituted authority" of the federal government: "I would realize that not once since the beginnings of this nation has a liberal step forward been about-faced, not once has a law designed for the betterment of any segment of our people, dark or white, been rescinded or repealed" (50). Her commitments were justified; for not until the summer of 1996 were such liberal reforms reversed. And yet in the month of Hiroshima and Nagasaki, her pledge to "liberals of all faiths, all shades" and plea for our "common humanity" drowned in the deafening silence of the bombs and revelry of VJ Day.

Descendants of abolitionists would have their say as well. Oswald Garrison Villard (former editor of *The Nation*) and John Beecher (descendant of Harriet Beecher Stowe and purser on the Negro-skippered *S.S. Booker T. Washington*) bore names and advocacy with authority. Early in the series, Villard's "No Time for Pessimism" (*ND*, March 1943, 9–11) preached fulfillment and caution. Never conversational, always lectural, Villard is the sole columnist to enlarge the grievance of compromised civil rights within the framework of a paean to American civil liberties. The centripetal force of his opening recognition scene presumes that "if Negroes can be disfranchised and segregated and refused participation in any branch of the war effort, the next to be put outside the pale could be Jews or some of the foreign-born, or the American-born Japanese who have now on the Pacific coast been placed in concentration camps behind barbed wire merely because their parents were born in Japan" (9). Perceiving a threat to "our whole democratic structure," Villard, never comfortable with his racialized persona, reverts to the reserve and authority of his abolitionist forebears: "Now as to methods: I would have the Negro adopt as his motto the words of my grandfather, William Lloyd Garrison, which adorned the first issue of his *Liberator* devoted to the freeing of the slaves. He said: 'I will be as harsh as the truth, and as uncompromising as justice. . . . '" Secure in his family's traditional role of liberal mediator and dispenser of justice, Villard, all but abandoning his guise, prescribes the martyrdom of principles and patience: "The point is that the individual Negro is under a double obligation for good conduct, for he represents not only himself but his race, and upon his behavior depends, as I have said, how the battle for complete legal equality will come out" (11). By relegating the Negro to passivity Villard abandons the many and the one in a representation of American blackness that disallows contumacy as emotional or tactical response. Endowed with the unskep-

tical spirit of his grandfather, Villard accepted white America's role
as "liberator."

John Beecher, merchant mariner and regional director of the New
York Fair Employment Practices Commission, was moved to a poetic
response. "Their Blood Cries Out!" (a three-part individualized narrative of circumstance and resolve) initially resists the assigned blackness, favoring the empathetic depiction of two black martyrs: one a
lynching victim, one a war hero. The former, a black sharecropper,
"got his own piece of this earth / bought from the county for back
taxes," died at the hand of "the white men who had owned the land /
but hadn't paid the taxes"; the latter, a black merchant seaman, who
"was needed" in the "next war," perished "when the planes struck /
and he was at the wheel" (*ND*, January 1945, 13–14). Though the
final section presumes a racial guise, Beecher continues to narrate:

> If I were a Negro
> I would swear the same oath I am swearing now
> to avenge these men
> and all the men like them and the women and children
> white black yellow and brown
> whose blood cries out for vengeance
> all over the world
>
> Being a Negro would change nothing
> the same men would be my brothers
> for brothers are not known by the color of their skins
> but by what is in their hearts
> backed up by their deeds
> and by their lives
> when it comes to that   (1945: 15)

Though contradictions abound in this vendetta bound to a presump-
tive charity, Beecher's (what editor Burns captioned as) "creed," for
black and white, advances the Christian distinction between false and
true teachers: "by their fruits ye shall know them" (Matthew 7:20). In
spite of the ordinariness of its message, "Their Blood Cries Out!"
packs an unexpected aesthetic and emotional wallop. None of the
novelists contributing to the series had Beecher's stylistic daring or
passion. Readers familiar with the works of Howard Fast, Wallace
Stegner, Pearl Buck, and Fanny Hurst, trained in the art of characterization, were undoubtedly surprised by their authors' fixed adher-

ence to formula. Perhaps the most disappointing in this regard is Howard Fast's "Proud To Be Black" (*ND*, March 1945, 5–6). Readers of his best-sellers – *The Unvanquished* (1942), *Citizen Tom Paine* (1943), *Freedom Road* (1944) – would certainly have been disappointed and somewhat surprised by the triteness of his wartime homily: "I would be proud – so damned proud – because today, laying aside their wrongs, their hurts, their miseries, my people have joined fully and whole-heartedly in this war to liberate all people, putting the cause of humanity before petty causes, dying on foreign soil, so that men may be free" (6). Only Beecher, himself not a creative writer, risked an aesthetic and emotional rawness in his message.

Tensions in these scenarios of challenged American citizenship are nowhere higher than in the opening and closing columns of the series's final year. By December 1945, its monthly harvest of race articles betrayed resurfacing tensions regarding Americanism as a postwar cover for ongoing racism. Bold narrations of national commitment effecting closure to the trauma of the war, including Marian Anderson's "This Is My America" and Frank E. Bolden's "My Favorite War Hero," were countered by acerbic challenges in Zora Neale Hurston's "Crazy for This Democracy" and Walter White's "My Most Humiliating Jim Crow Experience." Perhaps the most editorially destabilizing feature appeared on the issue's back cover. A public service appeal from Sachs Furniture Stores, originally appearing in the *New York Post*, entitled "The Shape of Things to Come" seems to sound the editorial sentiments of the race press: "A new era has been born. What kind of era will it be? . . . This much is crystal clear; another war may mean the suicide of civilization. Now if ever, the people of the world must learn to live together." In spite of its closing exhortation to domesticate "get our own house in order," the commercial appeal succumbs to an apparent impossibility: "to avoid prejudice, to fight for justice, to BE AMERICAN." The liberal rhetoric takes an unexpected turn as the editorial elisions emphasizing the announcement's attempt to domesticate ("get our own house in order") nationalism ("BE AMERICAN") deny closure to the war narrative. The militarism and racism of fascism had not been destroyed, only displaced. For the foreseeable future, the First Amendment would be modified by "national security."

Whether Burns scheduled the contributions by Leonard Feather (*ND*, November 1945, 45–7) and Saul Alinsky (*ND*, October 1946,

33–4) to bracket the expected and routine rhetoric of the series with an aggressive dissonance is unknown. The energy and textual play they possess, however, introduces into the dying year of the series a pair of sensibilities both challenging and alien. Fueled by the hypocrisy and superficiality of the white liberal thinking in earlier contributions, Leonard Feather, jazz critic for *Esquire*, erupts in righteous indignation in "Wanted: A White Mammy":

> If I were a Negro I'd resent the vague idealism and lack of specific detail that has characterized most of the articles . . . nobody has stopped to interpret the question precisely. Does it ask what I would do if I were the same person I am today in every respect except my color? Or does it mean what would I do if I were just *any* Negro? Does it ask how I would have lived my life if I had been born a Negro, or does it demand what I'd do if I woke up tomorrow and found myself colored? (1945: 45)

These rhetorical questions clear the slate and enable Feather to embark upon a pointed "general and impersonal" agenda for postwar black America. Benefiting from the struggles of earlier columnists to detail a compelling vision, he abandons the inherited dispassion of the task and offers a cagey program in a streetwise vernacular. The twin imperatives of his program require a move from the South, though "not necessarily to a big city, where there's too much economic competition and social congestion" and "as soon as I had brains enough to realize the need for education, I'd spend every moment of my childhood and adolescence cramming myself with educational equipment to fight Jim Crow" (45). Speaking as if he were Johnson's protégé himself, Feather sees money and "string-pulling, 'connections' and political pressure" as the sources of "finagling" in the white business world. And yet, despite this initial stridency, Feather's passion leaches into a familiar field of temperance and caution. Even his personal appeal to all national exiles is cushioned within parentheses: "(I'd also make a special effort to cultivate Jewish people and point out the many similarities between their problems and mine)" (46).

The racial and ethnic uncertainties embedded in American assimilation become all the more evident in Feather's equivocation: one moment, he'd "sue the hell out of every restaurant, every public place, every official and every other person involved in such incidents"; the next, he'd "think very long and seriously before contemplating [interracial] matrimony, realizing the enormity of the social obstacles" (1945: 47). He attempts to recover his initial bravado by "going out of [his] way to break down Jim Crow by buying real estate in what are snobbish-ly known as 'high-class' districts" (47) – evoking the world of Gwendolyn Brooks's "In the Mecca" – and hiring an "ofay maid" so that he might tell his friends: "Why, I have nothing against white people. Why, we've even had a dear old white mammy in our house for years and I just don't know *what* we'd do without her!" (47). Nevertheless, unable to sustain the verve and determination of his projected policies, Feather disintegrates into the ambiguous resignation of earlier columnists:

> I'd be scared of having children, of bringing more possible objects of bias into the world. But I'd leave the decision up to my wife.
> If we did have children, I would bring them up to live the same kind of life I had, and fight the same kind of fight. Because, if I were a Negro, I'd figure that would be the only way to build the brave new world that's supposed to be coming, but is taking so trag-ically long. (47)

Feather's lamentation over the state of race relations has more in com-mon with the blues than this jazz critic might have intended. For even in this cool presentation of race crossing, postwar readers of *Negro Digest* and the *Los Angeles Tribune*, "the most articulate and literate of all Negro newspapers" (46), are left to mourn as "dangling men" endlessly sus-pended from a constitutionally guaranteed but unrealized citizenship. The bluesy, tapering temporality of Feather's "long time comin'" antici-pates the frustration that James Baldwin would subsequently express in "Negroes are Anti-Semitic Because They're Anti-White," an essay pub-lished in The *New York Times Magazine* on April 9, 1967.

Readers familiar with organizer Saul Alinsky's best-selling *Reveille for Radicals* could hardly have been surprised by the harsh tone of his "Beware the Liberals" (*ND*, October 1946, 33–4). His career as a rad-ical organizer, most recently as leader of Chicago's Back-of-the-Yards Neighborhood Council, fostered an impatience with the rhetorical surface and inertia of America's liberals. Dismissive of authority that sanctioned either the status quo ("one of prejudice, segregation, hatred, second-class citizenship, and a denial of the basic premise of the Declaration of Independence of Life, Liberty, and the Pursuit of Happiness" [33]) or endorsed gradualism, Alinsky risked imagining a communal structure of progressive groups "in a united crusade to make this a human world" (33). Labor organizing in Chicago's ethnically and racially divided neighborhoods had schooled him in the liabilities of such familiar clusters, be they national, social, fraternal, religious or "what have you" (33).

Alinsky dispensed with liberals, especially those columnists of earnest goodwill who counseled patience and patriotism, declaring them "phonies" (34), and thus undermining the very editorial basis for the column. Seeming to declare the entire run of "If I Were a Negro" suspect, Alinsky castigates liberalism for an essential tolerance that is incompatible with American citizenship:

> If I were a Negro, I would not fear the Rankins, Bilbos, or the Talmadges (for they cannot survive their own venom), as much as I would the tolerant middle-of-the-roader who boasts of his liberal attitude, who fraternizes only with the top Negro intellectuals in conditions of luxury and whose friendly well-intentioned *practical* counsel is much more retarding in the long run. . . . There can be no compromise on the concept of equality. People cannot be given equality in certain spheres of life and denied equality in others. (34)

Perilously close to describing the "top Negro" that John Johnson himself would become, "Beware the Liberals" agitates still in its insistence that equality resides in action beyond mere conceptualization. Alinsky would reiterate his concern over imperiled citizenship in his afterword to the 1969 edition of *Reveille for Radicals*:

> I suggest that those who live in the past don't want a confrontation with the present. I believe that white Americans welcome the present race violence and that under the surface reactions of horror and shock is very deep relief. Now white Americans are back in the familiar jungle. Now the confrontation is in terms they can understand and in accord with their prejudices. Now they can have a confrontation because they think they know the answer to violence, and the answer is force, and furthermore they welcome the use of force. Now they no longer have to talk or think about injustice, guilt or the immorality of racism. Now it is simple: "Law and order must be upheld before we get around to anything else." (1946b: 210–1)

* * *

She read *Sepia, Tan, True Confessions, Real Romances,* and *Jet*. According to these magazines, Woman was a mindless body, a sex creature, something to hang false hair and nails on. Still, they helped her know for sure her marriage was breaking up.
– Alice Walker, *Meridian* (1976a: 65)

Alice Walker's bicentennial reflections upon the lack of enlightenment in John Johnson's race magazines, casting them as analogues
to mainstream lurid pulps, challenge contemporary readers attempting to understand the subversive editorial control of Johnson's sustained integrationist, aggressively bourgeois platform during the first
decade of his first publication, *Negro Digest*. Partisans of Hoyt Fuller's
later, black nationalist reincarnation of the magazine, *Black World*, are
understandably restrained in their discussions of this early, wartime
prototype. The unfashionable surface of the later, subscription-scram-
bling postwar years of *Negro Digest* (with such cover articles as "I Am
the World's Oldest Father" and "What's Wrong with Negro
Women?") repels contemporary readers, discouraging interest in the
beginnings of this vital community journal.

Increasingly drawn into the *Life*-vying world of his photojournal
Ebony, Johnson would suspend publication of *Negro Digest* in 1951.
Lacking commercial sponsorship (the second series, which began in
1961 under Fuller's editorial management, carried endpaper advertisements for black publications like *Black Power, U.S.A.* and cosmetics manufactured by black firms such as Supreme Beauty Products of
Chicago), *Negro Digest*, in spite of a literary and historical stature that
derived solely from its cavalcade of race articles, was ultimately
unable to meet either its editorial or its circulation expectations.

Of particular interest to contemporary readers are the ways in
which *Negro Digest*'s editorial compression and presentation of national race news foregrounded the racialized differentiation of self from
not-self, minority from majority community structures, and liberal
agency from community activism, so essential to its feature column,
"If I Were a Negro." Belief systems of radical otherness are instructive because they encode what Edward Said calls the "dialectic of self-
fortification and self-confirmation by which culture achieves its
hegemony over society and the State . . . now based on a constantly
practiced differentiation of itself from what it believes to be not itself"
(1983: 12). By reimagining *Reader's Digest*, rendering DeWitt Clinton's
master text a *Negro Digest* manqué, John Johnson exploited just such a
dialectic as he simultaneously decontextualized and recontextualized
race and citizenship in America.

PART TWO

DECOMPOSING UNITIES, DECONSTRUCTING NATIONAL NARRATIVES

I am no prophet – and here's no great matter;
I have seen the moment of my greatness flicker,
And I have seen the eternal Footman hold my coat, and snicker,
And in short, I was afraid.

> – T. S. Eliot
> "The Love Song of J. Alfred Prufrock" (1917)

America is Good   An Apple Pie
and maybe   Emmett Till
in the small Negro pages of *Jet*
magazine in my soul where Words are fine
clothes   for the Negro to die in

– Sam Cornish, "Langston Variations 1955"

5

REPORTAGE AS REDEMPTION

GWENDOLYN BROOKS'S IN THE MECCA

========

The tradition of the oppressed teaches us that the "state of emergency" in which we live is not the exception but the rule. We must attain to a conception of history that is in keeping with this insight. Then we shall clearly realize that it is our task to bring about a real state of emergency.

> – Walter Benjamin, "Theses on the Philosophy of History, VIII" (1940: 257)

Let us pass through the arched doorway of the Mecca; let us see what the Mecca looks like inside, see who the people in it are and how they live, when they came and why they stay.

> – John Bartlow Martin
> "The Mecca: The Strangest Place in Chicago"

On August 22, 1962, Gwendolyn Brooks wrote to Elizabeth Lawrence, her editor at Harper and Row, about her fixation upon the Mecca Building, the turn-of-the-century apartment complex John Bartlow Martin (an essayist who would in 1968 serve as Robert Kennedy's urban policy counselor in the wake of Martin Luther King's assassination)[1] had declared "the strangest place in Chicago." The building, described with curatorial gusto by Martin in *Harper's Magazine*, had "become one of the most remarkable Negro slum exhibits in the world" (1950: 87).

For Brooks, however, the Mecca (site of her first employment and subject of a series of unpublished prose narratives)[2] registered more than urban blight: it signaled the "material collapse" of a community dependent upon white agency as it indexed the possibility of recovering the subjectivities trapped within. Assembling what Homi Bhabha has called "signs of national culture . . . the scraps, patches, and rags of daily life" (1990: 297), she recognized the potential for "Construction" at the site of ruin – a place where *e pluribus unum* (dis)integrates, freeing the "many" from the totalizing force of the "one." Brooks recalled in her autobiography the "high hopes" for what would be her final collection for a white publisher: *In the Mecca* would "touch every note in the life of this block-long block-wide building . . . [and would] capsulize the gist of black humanity in general" (1972a: 190).

The publication of *In the Mecca* in 1968 marks a caesura in Brooks's career that is retrospective and prophetic, historical and contemporary, cultural and ideological. This assertive poetic transgression of the bounds of genre, when read as a progressive abandonment of her white liberal support and an ideologically charged aesthetic reconfiguration, transforms a poetic sequence into a document essential to understanding her conception of a poetry that is historically informed, journalistically inflected, and indigenously directed. The consequent afterhistory of Brooks's last submission to Harper and Row – her move to independent black publishers (Dudley Randall's Broadside Press, Haki Madhubuti's Third World Press, and her own David Company) and adoption of a "blackened" aesthetic – has been reasonably documented.[3] The rhetorical complexities of that journey – her intertextual subordination of the "master's" voice (the language of official reports, planning documents, and mainstream journalism) and cooptation of literary antecedents – and the metajournalistic ambitions of her evolving aesthetic are my concern here. For *In the Mecca* – title sequence and its subsequent "After Mecca" poems – when read as a systematic deformation of the "master's" discourse (the rhetorical strategy Houston Baker calls "deformation of mastery") yields a counterdiscourse that locates the redemptive force of journalism within the subjective reach of poetry. The intense and enduring commitment Brooks brought to the journalistic imperatives of presses like the aptly named Broadside (publisher of *Riot*, her first original publication after leaving Harper and Row)[4] begins with this "Super-reporter's" investigative report into life *in* the Mecca.

*   *   *

The Mecca, like the "rotten from the inside out" Gardener Building of Frank London Brown's *Trumbull Park* (1959: 1), fulfilled Walter Benjamin's prophetic surmise that "in the process of decay, and in it alone, the events of history shrivel up and become absorbed in the setting" (1928: 179).[5] Built in 1891, the Mecca at the zenith of its social prominence had become one of the city's featured stops for tourists. Demolished in 1952,[6] at the nadir of its fortunes, the Mecca embodied a fragmented aesthetic. Once its representational value had transcended its architecture, signifying the very order of commodity culture, defining the physicality of prestige; once its facade had announced the associational worth of Chicago's middle class, while its address revealed the status of first its white, then its black residents. The building was, in the words of a reporter writing on the eve of its razing, "a mecca for Chicago's rising rich until the South Side became less stylish" ("The Mecca." *Life*, November 19, 1951: 133).[7] But its reduction to "a great grey hulk of brick" that contained poverty within squalor reflected the latent instability of America's commodity culture. The architectural ruins starkly disclosed "the transitoriness and fragility of capitalist culture [as well as] its destructiveness,"[8] transforming Benjamin's theoretical argument into a real (e)state of emergency. The Mecca essentialized Chicago's debilitating and persistent racism, a liberal bigotry that distinguished itself, in the words of Nelson Algren, as "a soft and protean awareness of white superiority everywhere, in everything" (1951: 82).[9]

From her childhood recollections of her father's stories of the 1919 riots[10] to her adult recognition of the forces contributing to Emmett Till's death, Brooks had witnessed America's race narrative unfolding on Chicago's South Side. In the wake of the 1965 Voting Rights Act and the Selma campaign, Martin Luther King's 1966 crusade to promote economic justice in Chicago encountered a hardening resistance that confirmed Brooks's deepening suspicion that the nation was irredeemably racist.[11]

King, dismissing Bayard Rustin's prediction that he would be "wiped out" in Chicago, advanced with a characteristic faith in his ability to employ the tactics of the rural south in the urban north.[12] Civil society predicated upon civil rights and redistribution of the country's wealth had been the key to King's evolving sense of social justice. On August 1, 1965, just days before the Watts riot and a few months before he journeyed to Chicago, King, speaking in Philadelphia, revealed the ideological shift central to his forthcoming northern campaign: "We need massive programs that will change the structure of American society so there will be a better distribution of wealth" (quoted in Hampton and Fayer 1995: 298). Throughout the Chicago crusade, seemingly aware of the geopolitical complexities of Mayor Richard Daley's wards, he reclaimed the language of urban renewal:

> There are two possible ways to concentrate on the problems of the slum: one would be to focus on a single issue, but another is to concentrate all of our forces and move in concert with a nonviolent army on each and every issue.
>
> In the South concentration on one issue proved feasible because of a general pattern of state and local resistance. However, in Chicago we are faced with the probability of a ready accommodation to many of the issues in some token manner, merely to curtail the massing of forces and public opinion around those issues. Therefore, we must be prepared to concentrate all of our forces around any and all issues. (quoted in Garrow 1986: 456–7)

Throughout the summer, while Brooks was revising her Mecca manuscript, Dr. King's protest against Chicago's segregated housing met with such hostility that it ultimately degenerated into what King called a "riot" and Mayor Daley termed a "juvenile incident" (quoted in Hampton and Fayer 1995: 309).[13] And as King's "war on slums" collapsed, so did Brooks's hope for an integrationist path to social and economic justice.

Each knew that the secret to the "massing of forces and public opinion" resided in the appropriation of the "master's" rhetoric, the language of oppression that had institutionalized racism as it had sanctioned the concomitant erasure of lives. A stunning example of the rhetoric they sought to subvert – the logical positivism of city planning that results in a historicism wedded to mechanistic progress – may be found in Harold M. Mayer and Richard C. Wade's 1969 architectural history, *Chicago: Growth of a Metropolis* (see, in particular, chap. 6). I quote at length from this secondary source because in its effortless ventriloquization of generic renewal rhetoric – a language of war and disease and a teleology of Progress – it retrospectively sanctions and explains the demolition of the Mecca.[14] The quantifiable human cost, the erasure of identities, that so preoccupied Brooks and King may be read as the intertextual silences in this unskeptical text:

> The *physical problems* of postwar Chicago were only too obvious. Just south of the Loop was the Near South Side, once the city's *most fashionable* neighborhood, now its *worst slum.* . . . The most recent arrivals to Chicago settled there first; for some, especially Negroes, there was *no escape.* The *cancer* stretched for miles. . . . As early as 1943 the Plan Commission's *Master Plan of Residential Land Use* called for *total demolition* in twenty-three square miles of *blighted and near-blighted* residential areas. The solution could, no doubt, have been better, but any city which left these slums standing could be *rightfully indicted for callous injustice* as well as for shortsightedness.
>
> Part of the attack on this *enormous wretchedness* came from private sources, for the *spread of deterioration* not only scarred the lives of those who lived there, but it also jeopardized important institutions. On the Near South Side, the Michael Reese Hospital, at the time the largest private hospital in Chicago, and the Illinois Institute of Technology were almost *engulfed in blight.* Both occupied old buildings; both had ambitious expansion programs on the drawing boards. For each, a critical decision was at hand: whether to *remain in the area and help transform it,* or to move to some other place where land was cheaper and the neighborhood more desirable. Both *courageously* decided to stay and to throw their weight into the effort *to create a new environment.*
>
> Once committed to remaining, both institutions *girded for battle.* Michael Reese became the first hospital in the nation to hire its own professional planning staff with Reginald R. Isaacs as director. I.I.T. responded similarly, and appointed the celebrated architect Mies Van der Rohe as chairman of its Department of Architecture with the responsibility of designing its new campus. . . .
>
> Michael Reese's expansion *eliminated many substandard structures* while producing an attractive "campus" of new hospital buildings. I.I.T. *transformed its neighborhood* into a showplace for the architectural talents of Mies Van der Rohe. (Mayer and Wade 1969: 378–80, 386; emphasis added)

Institutional rhetoric bonded to corporate and civic gusto reduces citizens to invisible denizens of "slums" and "substandard structures." Neither political nor social status adheres to these anonymous poor.

The renewal rhetoric of planning documents (such as the cited *Master Plan of Residential Land Use* [1943], in which the city explained its plan for the "total demolition of twenty-three square miles of blighted and near-blighted residential areas") and of the white dailies resulted in a deformative poetic that would serve journalistic and poetic needs by coopting the "master's" documents, relegating them to an intertextual role in Brooks's dominant report. The textual bravado of her demolition dialectic of the indigenous and the intruder envisions Houston Baker's subsequent understanding of the dynamics of black rhetoric: "first, the indigenous comprehend the territory within their own vale/veil more fully than any intruder. . . . Second, the indigenous *sound* appears monstrous and deformed *only* to the intruder" (1987: 51–2). *In the Mecca* meets Baker's primary and secondary qualifications, demonstrating Brooks's indigenous comprehension of the territory even as it vexes intruding readers with its monstrous and deformed sound.

Stylistic deformities announce the collection's cultural and ideological shift. The Mecca's shifting significations of law and cultural order – previously mediated for Brooks by such mainstream publications as *Harper's*, *Life*, and local white dailies and official commissions – registered more than the inherent deformities of national progressive ideologies: They disclosed the tensions between Brooks's public (as delineated by the "intruder") and private (defined by the "indigenous") selves. Read as a metanarrative, *In the Mecca* encapsulates a critical rereading of her public success within its assessment of national failure. She began to read the celebrity manifest in her Harper publications, two Guggenheim Fellowships, and the Pulitzer Prize as products of a dying and deadly culture. Turning from what Frank London Brown in "Chicago's Great Lady of Poetry" had called "the 'hollow land of fame,'"[15] Brooks sought to channel the epistemic significations flowing from the Mecca into her "now-*urgent* business" of a new history, a new poetry of her community.[16] Liberation from the race-betraying supreme fiction of a national community of cultural hegemony and consent was imperative; distance from her liberal white audience, essential.

Such cultural realignment and personal imperatives, when brought into the public sphere, are bound to confuse. Reviewers and readers, once braced by what Louis Simpson called her "lively pictures of 'Negro life,'"[17] responded uneasily to the alienating discomfort of *In the Mecca*. For unlike earlier Bronzeville poems that stunned bourgeois readers with their quiet spectacle and dignity,[18] the Mecca sequence, through its intricacies of racial and local reference, encouraged an indigenous readership that would follow Brooks into the interior world represented by the Mecca. Weary of considering an indifferent and intrusive liberal audience (afflicted with what Ralph Ellison had called the "Aren't-Negroes-wonderful school of thinking" [1945a: 137]), she abandoned *épater les bourgeois* as a strategy and device, dismissing white readers and the superficialities of their world.

Although it sold briskly, 2,986 copies in its first week, *In the Mecca* was cautiously received by a corps of loyal reviewers who, preferring the consolations of Brooks's earlier work, challenged the racialized stance of the collection.[19] Black reviewers, many of whom had been her students and had been made uneasy by the "whiteness" of her success, were thrilled by the obvious and immediate impact the younger generation of Black Arts writers had exerted on Brooks.[20] As Haki Madhubuti, a veteran of Brooks's writing workshop who represented the sentiments of many in the Movement, wryly explained the perverse redirection and tensions of the moment: "*In the Mecca* 'blacked' its way out of the National Book Award in 1968" (1972a: 21).

By the 1960s, Brooks was experimenting with a fusion style inspired by the documentary verve of contemporaries like Lorraine Hansberry and Frank London Brown. This stylistic pastiche, what she would soon call "verse journalism" (1972a: 186), matured into a focused aesthetic of political engagement and witness that would retain the reportorial function of journalism while possessing the lyric charge of poetry. Though long fond of the dispatch (consider, for example, the news trace in the bulletin prefacing "Appendix to 'The Anniad' – leaves from a loose-leaf war diary": "('thousands – killed in action')" [1949: 110]), Brooks became increasingly estranged from the conventions of journalism, finding even local venues like the *Chicago Defender* and *Negro Digest* inadequate to meet the pressures of the news. Yet she kept the investigatory temperament of a reporter. The reportorial themes that Brooks's editor Elizabeth Lawrence had found unimaginative and tedious in Brown's *Trumbull Park* beckoned to Brooks, inspiring her transformation into "a Watchful Eye; a Tuned Ear; a Super-Reporter" (*In the Mecca* dust-jacket copy).[21] Such kaleidoscopic refractions of authorial roles declare Brooks's immediate intentions even as they recall her earlier flirtations with a poetry of witness and report.

Attentive readers of *The Bean Eaters* (published in 1960 and reprinted in its entirety in *Blacks* [1987]) had noted an evolving political consciousness in Brooks's adaptation of the urban modernism of Baudelaire, Eliot, Sandburg, and Hughes. Stylistically unsettled, especially when compared to the sonnet formality of her Pulitzer Prize-winning *Annie Allen*, these poems of the first decade of the modern civil rights movement reflect a growing impatience with the aesthetic and political constraints of poetry and journalism. At least a decade before such cultural anthems as Amiri Baraka's "SOS" and Madhubuti's "Don't Cry, Scream," Brooks agitated in "The Explorer" (a poem dramatically self-conscious of its searching imperial subtext) for the subjective collectivity of a poetry derived from "spiraling, high human voices, / The scream of nervous affairs, / Wee griefs, / Grand griefs. And choices" (1960: 327).

The political urgency of *The Bean Eaters* anticipated the socially active and journalistically alert poetic that critics would come to associate with *In the Mecca*. Poems like "A Bronzeville Mother Loiters in Mississippi. Meanwhile, a Mississippi Mother Burns Bacon" (1960: 333) and "The *Chicago Defender* Sends a Man to Little Rock" (1960: 346-8), with the banner-headline display of their titles, share a critical anxiety over the inadequacy of poetry or journalism to deliver the news. The national vision that had underwritten Brooks's poetry of the Second World War (such as "Negro Hero") had by the 1960s withered into politically tentative, morally emphatic inquiries. By the time of Emmett Till's murder, a decade before she would concede that the Mecca was where "fair fables fall," news had overrun her aesthetic. Even the ballad, with its long prejournalistic history of carrying the news of murderous deeds, failed to accommodate the horror of Till's death.[22] "A Bronzeville Mother Loiters in Mississippi . . . " (1960: 333–9), admitting disjunctions that will compel her conjunctive genre of verse journalism, affirms the inability of the Anglo-American ballad to comprehend as it delivers the "last bleak news of the ballad. / The rest of the rugged music. / The last quatrain" (1960: 339).

Forecasting the deformative mastery of the Mecca poems, "The Lovers of the Poor" initiates Brooks's disengagement with liberal philanthropic agents. Black weeklies so conditioned readers to be suspicious of the socio-solicitudes of do-gooders that they would never mistake Brooks's portrayals, as Henry Taylor has, as the "reduction of characters to cartoons" (1991: 126);[23] the acute composites of liberal tourists from various social agencies were familiar personalities in their daily lives. The broad strokes of characterization belie the complexities of historicized indictment. Economic privilege drives the betterment philanthropy while shielding the ladies from the history underpinning "the puzzled wreckage / Of the middle passage" where the largely irrelevant white dailies carpet the floors of "this sick four-story hulk." The indecorousness of the poor disgusts these *real* ladies, who have never seen such "make-do-ness as / Newspaper rugs . . . the oozed, the rich / Rugs of the morning (tattered! the bespattered . . .), / Readies to spread clean rugs for afternoon" (Brooks 1960: 351).[24]

If, as Hugh Kenner has suggested, "poems remember their beginnings" (1971: 278), then *In the Mecca* recalls through reconfiguration the squalidness incompletely perceived by the intrusive "Lovers of the Poor." Historical construction from the narrative material of the Mecca entails the salvage of "a large variety of personalities [placed] against a mosaic of daily affairs, recognizing that the *grimmest* of these is likely to have a streak or two streaks of sun" (Brooks 1972a: 189) – the recovery of the "many" from the "one." The narrative of these sick rooms, resistant to the aesthetic of poetry, yields to the report; the vitality of these lives, evasive of facts, succumbs to the poem. Once stripped of its objectifying commodity shell[25] – leveled into "slum" by *all* intruders, black and white – the Mecca could disclose to the public the multiple subjectivities trapped within its intimate sphere. Retrieving the "many" from the lethal "singlicity" of "slum" is but a beginning: social individuation through naming and cultural distinction through cultural and historical awareness are essential to Brooks's black nationalism. Her benevolent comprehension of these interior lives led William Stafford, in his review of *In the Mecca*, to declare the poet "a writer avowedly a spokesman . . . a writer who 'looks in' . . . [with] languages that attempt to hold that existence in human perspective that is local, indigenous" (S. C. Wright 1996: 26).[26]

*   *   *

The appetite for architecture, however, is inconsistent with the older nothing-to-do-with-me with which the republic's various social classes used to negotiate their downtowns. It means the city, certainly, and it means the free-standing building, preferably blocks of stone, whose shape in space does you some good to see, if that is the right verb. What is in question here is the

> monumental; it does not need contemporary rhetorics of the
> body and its trajectories, nor is it basely visual in any of the
> color-coded postmodern senses. You don't have to walk up the
> grand staircase personally, but it is not some mannerist parabo-
> la, either, that you can miniaturize with a quick look and carry
> home in your pocket. . . . Postmodernism . . . went on to abol-
> ish . . . the distinction between the inside and outside. . . .
>   The consequence is, however, that as spatially exciting as
> the new thing may be, it becomes ever more difficult in this
> urban landscape to order a high-class architectural meal of
> the older kind.
> – Frederic Jameson, *Postmodernism: Or, the Cultural Logic of
> Late Capitalism* (1991: 98)

Discussing architecture's "words of built space" and proposing a new "text-grammar of the urban," Jameson questions the referential identities of exterior and interior space that enable class-savvy Americans to negotiate their downtowns (1991: 105). Long before postmodern theory facilitated such playful discussions, Brooks created a "text-grammar of the urban" to meet the sociocultural challenge of her title narrative, "In the Mecca." Perceptual and structural realignments stage an investigation that will reveal an evidentiary chain of reference to move beyond the exterior image and the myth of the building, beyond the significance of its name and address, to the sequestered narratives of its tenants. A reconstructive report of the Mecca's interior life, a redemption of its "peoplehood," necessitates a systematic consideration of the intrusive media(ting) forces that have created the Mecca's image.[27]

Serial epigraphs to "In the Mecca" delineate the documentary lineage of Brooks's reconstruction. The twin epigraphs from Martin's *Harper* essay (as well as the *Life* photographs that Brooks had hoped to use) – a vividly stark description centered upon a "dirt courtyard . . . littered with newspapers and tin cans, milk cartons, and broken glass" and testimony from an anonymous "Meccan" – suggest her fascination with mainstream media depictions of black America that betray the homogenizing force of poverty to the eyes of even the most sympathetic white Americans. Successive epigraphs from the named and indigenous Blackstone Ranger Richard "Peanut" Washington ("' . . . there's danger in my neighborhood'")[28] and Chicago activist Russ Meek ("'There comes a time when what has been can never be again'") intiate a social recovery strategy dependent upon oral and ephemeral confirmations of identity. Between the epigraphs and the poem proper, tacitly signaling an aesthetic revolution (or at least split), Brooks insinuates a "tribute" to the new black artists of Chicago (including Walter Bradford and Don Lee [Haki Madhubuti]). The distance traveled in these epigraphs traces out the boundaries of the poem. Neither the received aesthetic nor the history of the Mecca accounts for the preoccupation of the poem with its status as a self-consuming artifact of a waning culture. If Brooks interrogates the building as a representative space, she does so through deconstruction of the documentary legacy of the space and a sympathetic reading of the lives within.

Exploiting the archetypal ordering force of religion – one at once aesthetic and legal, cultural and social – Brooks complicates the literary and moral structures of "In the Mecca" by conflating the strands of Christianity and Islam into a secondary, solemn epigraph – "Now the way of the Mecca was on this wise" – that draws upon the branching (and local) consequences of the building. Reinscribing the religious signification of "Mecca" by alluding to Matthew 1:18 ("Now the birth of Jesus Christ was on this wise . . . ") initiates the poem's cycle of liberation from binding orthodoxies, whether religious or aesthetic, enacting the injunction of "Riders to the Blood-Red Wrath": "Democracy and Christianity / Recommence with me" (1963: 392).[29] The archaic formality of the Christian text fades as "Mecca" substitutes for "Christ," recalling through this stratagem Elijah Muhammad's Black Muslim suspicion of the Bible.[30]

Brooks disrupts the literary formality established by her tidal epigraphs, aligned on the facing page, with an opening stanza of three end-stopped lines that substitute for the apostrophe associated with an epic: "Sit where the light corrupts your face. / Miës Van der Rohe retires from grace. / And the fair fables fall" (5). Verbal patterns – "sit," "corrupts," "retires," "fall" – in which a noun, "fables," feigns verbal form, initiate the associational dislocation of Brooks's linguistic world and signal her departure from the aesthetic discourse of modernism (literary, architectural) to the "official" discourse of urban planning. Readers accustomed to the subjunctive, invitational civility of T. S. Eliot's "Let us go then, you and I . . . " are meant to be stunned by the abruptness of the opening command, its vaguely postlapsarian gesture dismissive of aesthetic and religious antecedents, and alert to the shift in reference. Embedded within its superficially respectful rejection of the European modernism of Mies is an abandonment of modernism and censure of the neocolonial ambition of the Illinois Institute of Technology that, in the words of architectural historians Mayer and Wade, "transform[ed] its neighborhood into a showplace for the architectural talents of Mies Van der Rohe" (386).

As director and architect of the new campus of the Illinois Institute of Technology, Mies incarnated what Brooks had come to view as the intrusive and destructive Eurocentrism of modernism. John Bartlow Martin, in his isolation of competing modernisms, had visualized a forbidding landscape of predetermined contests, a vision that for Brooks distilled the essential moral and aesthetic blankness of Western art:

> Across an expanse of new-turned earth stretches a new public housing project, with a playyard for the children, and at 32nd Street begins the new campus of the Illinois Institute of Technology, sleek brick-and-glass buildings surrounded by new trees and new grass. And just beyond the Institute rises a great gray hulk of brick, four stories high, topped by an ungainly smokestack, ancient and enormous, filling half the block north of 34th Street between State and Dearborn. It is the Mecca Building. (1950: 86)

With deliberative force, "In the Mecca" subordinates Martin's vivid mediation, in which Mies personifies modernism and the Mecca embodies its social and aesthetic collapse, transforming it into a documentary intertext to her dominant narrative.

Within the Mecca, all ideas of order are suspect. And so, before Brooks can turn to journalism, she must demonstrate the inadequacies of her primary genre, poetry. The poem adopts a strategy of abandonment in which literary allusion fails to support or clarify the news. In theme and trope, the poem relies upon, even as it competes with, the ornate diction and cadences of the King James Bible, rendering the appropriated scripture vernacular through the voices of the Meccans. Such artful confiscation empowers the display of her increasingly cumbersome aesthetic heritage as she debates the aptness of the literary and the vernacular. "Low-brown butterball" triumphs over "prudent partridge"; "armed coma" dislodges "fragmentary attar"; "district hymn" succeeds "fugitive attar" – the local and immediate superseding the inherited and removed. The baroque artifice of *Annie Allen* would disintegrate under the pressure of this new aesthetic.

Codes as complex as the Twenty-third Psalm, which announce the art and law of God, retreat into cultural traces,[31] complementary but not essential to the text at hand. In the immediacy of enactment, ritual turns into patterned ecstasy for St. Julia Jones:

> . . . who has had prayer,
> and who is rising from amenable knees
> inside the wide-flung door of 215.
> "Isn't He wonderfulwonderful!" cries St. Julia.
> "Isn't our Lord the greatest to the brim?
> The light of my life. And I lie late
> past the still pastures. And meadows. He's the comfort
> and wine and piccalilli for my soul.
> He hunts me up the coffee for my cup.
> Oh how I love that Lord."
>
> (1968: 5–6)

Mingling the language of spirituals and popular culture, St. Julia improvises a communion adequate to her circumstance and her soul. Far from the green pastures of biblical promise, Meccans seek their pastoral pleasures and communion in the indigenous: wine, piccalilli, and coffee. Brooks fragments the potential force of the psalm's consolation, the immediacy of which may have been inspired by the 1961 televised hearings of Adolf Eichmann, when she recasts it as a rebuke in the voice of Meccan Loam Norton, who "considers Belsen and Dachau" and concludes that "The Lord was their shepherd. / Yet did they want" (15–16). Here the Middle Passage and the Holocaust stream into the commonality of diasporic circumstance, intimately implicated in Brooks's indictment of Christianity, and entwine in Boontsie De Broe's memory of "the extract / of massive literatures, of lores, / transactions of old ocean; suffrages" (16).

Allusions crowd the stale corridors of the Mecca but fail to create sustainable social or cultural systems. Mrs. Sallie recalls her Lord as "an incense and a vintage" (6), her literature as "the whiskey of our discontent!" (8); Prophet Williams, "rich with Bible," succumbs to lust and wife beating (6); Emmett and Cap and Casey, "skin wiped over bones," wonder "What shall their redeemer be?" (12); Alfred troubles over "The faithless world! / betraying yet again / trinities!" (12);

Pops Pinkham is "doubtful of a specific right / to inherit the earth or to partake of it now" (30); "Jamaican / Edward denies and thrice denies a dealing / of any dimension with Mrs. Sallie's daughter" (31). Even the mimicry of political rhetoric – such as the intertextual silencing of the Gettysburg Address and the Pledge of Allegiance in "Don Lee wants / not a various America. / Don Lee wants / a new nation / under nothing" (21) – underscores the impoverishment and irrelevance of Western quotation to the reality of black life. Don Lee's "new nation / under nothing" italicizes the eruptive originality of a venture that abandons the secular or spiritual potential of American art, religion, or law.

The breaking story of the disappearance and murder of Mrs. Sallie's daughter, Pepita, defeats the anomie of the collapsing cultural context by converting social alienation into community activism, allowing "In the Mecca" to construct its narrative sequence in a "barbarous rhetoric / built of buzz, coma and petite pell-mells" (20) from the material ruins. Though epic in intention, the narrative relaxes into an aesthetic that readers would soon associate with her composite genre, verse journalism. Typography and orthography, variable stress of event and rumor, alternating emphasis and descriptive paralanguage, naming, syntactical and morphological structures, and speech – all strategies familiar to those conversant with the visual and linguistic conventions of the press – underwrite the news in Brooks's poem. As a dispatch, "In the Mecca" slips from the expected discontinuities of modernist collage into a coherent and familiar journalistic layout, one that moves comfortably between the public and intimate spheres. The design conventions of the black weeklies empower these otherwise random narratives, linked only by neighborly proximity, to recontextualize the otherwise linear unfolding of the news event.

The dramatic vignetting essential to "In the Mecca" relies upon the self-contained partiality of journalistic practices that Brooks explored in *The Bean Eaters*. Timely occurrences lure the intimate into the public sphere for a duration explicitly determined by their intertextual viability with the dominant narrative, the breaking news story. Through a seemingly random juxtaposition, Brooks achieves a transient compositional unity of daily events at the Mecca as she contextualizes the lead narrative. A whole-page perspective on the poem intensifies its potential as journalism, visualizing the narrative stratification of the dependent subnarratives. Readers familiar with the conventions of the weeklies would automatically compartmentalize Mrs. Sallie's suppers and St. Julia's recipes as community news; Prophet Williams's wife who "died in self defense" [6] and Pepita's murder as front-page; Alfred's liaisons with "Telly Bell / in 309, or with that golden girl" (7) and Yvonne's lovers as gossip; displays for "spiritual adviser" Prophet Williams's "love charms" – "Drawing and Holding Powder, Attraction Powder, Black / Cat Power" (25) – as advertisements – and so on.

Visual correspondences between "In the Mecca" and the black weeklies (obvious to Brooks's intended audience) reveal a stylistic intertextuality in which narratorial commentary may be read as editorial suasion. The ministerial reply to the Christian docility of Mrs. Sallie's "What can I do?" – "But World (a sheep) / wants to be Told. / If you ask a question, you / can't stop there. You must keep going" (8–9) – transforms the sermonic rhythms of Robert Abbott's hortatory editorials for the *Defender* into the "music, mode, and mixed philosophy" of the Mecca (8).

Although central to the conception of Brooks's revolutionary aesthetic, journalism remains suspect in its local indifference and deception, its global pretensions of concern. Through Melodie Mary, who "likes roaches, / and pities the gray rat" (10), the poet's suspicions surface:

> To delicate Melodie Mary
> headlines are secondary.
> It is interesting that in China
> the children blanch and scream,
> and that blood runs like a ragged wound
> through the ancient flesh of the land.
> It matters, mildly,
> that the Chinese girls are grim,
> and that hurried are the seizures
> of yellow hand on hand
> . . . .
> Where are the frantic bulletins
> when other importances die?
>
> (10)

Though disparities between the "Caucasian dailies" and the "Negro weeklies" had long preoccupied Brooks (finding perhaps their boldest expression in "Negro Hero" [1945: 48]), the essential value of journalism had never been questioned. But the Mecca, in its harsh reciprocity between a commodified domain and community, renders news inimical to the social and psychological welfare of its tenants. The "importances" of these "frantic bulletins" resist the conventional powers of journalism to inform or console, forcing a temporizing conclusion: "One reason cats are happier than people / is that they have no newspapers" (11). The "terrified standstill of the heart" (6) that earlier had menaced Alfred and his creations also threatens the progression of the news, resembling the transformative temporal arrest that Walter Benjamin termed *Stillstand.*

Mid-narrative, exhausted by the conceptual limitations of the report, Brooks questions the authority of the written text by privileging an orality that is indigenous and true. The single line stanza – "What else is there to say but everything?" (13) – yields to a two-line, orthographically distinct and linguistically and syntactically blackened insertion – "SUDDENLY, COUNTING NOSES, MRS. SALLIE / SEES NO PEPITA. 'WHERE PEPITA BE?'" – that resembles even as it rewrites the conventions of journalism. The master narrative of Pepita's disappearance abandons the chronicle, proceeding in lyric counterpoint between the never-ending community chant in which polyvocality is distinguished by italics – "*Ain seen er I ain seen er I ain seen er // Ain seen er I ain seen er I ain seen er*" (14) – and the individual, aestheticized despair is articulated through a doubling of complete sentences that deepens the display of grief through partial reiteration – "'One of my children is missing. One of my children is gone'" (15). An ever-widening historical context centers Pepita in the long history of many thousands gone.

Historical recontextualization occurs as well in the person of Great-great Gram, who draws Pepita's plight into the ceaseless narrative of the black diaspora. Ventriloquially, she sounds the narrative's established community voice and "mumbles, 'I ain seen no Pepita. But I remember our cabin,'" collapsing the Mecca's architecture into a slave's dwelling. Like the "one disremembered time" of Robert Hayden's "'Mystery Boy' Looks for Kin in Nashville" (1985: 68), this summoning of the racial past is what Melvin Dixon calls "re-membering, as in repopulating broad continuities with the African diaspora. This movement is nonlinear, and it disrupts our notions of chronology" (1994: 21).[32] The temporal and spatial dislocations of Gram's recollection of slavery bear the traces and share the immediacy of Frederick Douglass's depiction of the slave's world, in which all are "registered with four footed beasts and creeping things" (1950–75, 1: 282); her world is one with things that "creebled in that dirt / for we wee ones to pop" (15).

Contextualizing Pepita's individual victimization with the collective racial plights of Africans and Jews loosens the bonds of history as it relaxes the poem into memory's (and journalism's) present tense.[33] With the recovery of racialized memory comes a community authority capable of countering the received systems of art, religion, and law. Imbued by a literariness distinguished by Nelson Algren as "a conscience in touch with humanity,"[34] Brooks directs her poem toward the parallel investigatory pursuits of Mrs. Sallie and the Meccans – and The Law.

Poverty relegates the Meccans to a subsocial caste outside the equality of consideration essential to the rule of law. Contingencies of social circumstance objectify them into an ascriptive identity signified by "slum," denying the significance of individuation or the legitimate collective expectation of justice as fairness. "For the historically disempowered," as Patricia Williams reflects in *The Alchemy of Race and Rights*, "the conferring of rights is symbolic of all the denied aspects of their humanity: rights imply a respect that places one in the referential range of self and others, that elevates one's status from human body to social being" (1991: 153). This denial that is at once cause and effect retains historical volatility in its literal presence: as Williams cautions:

> It must be remembered that *from the experiential perspective of blacks*, there was no such thing as "slave law." The legal system did not provide blacks, even freed blacks, with structured expectations, promises, or reasonable reliances of any sort. If one views rights as emanating from either slave "legal" history or from that of modern bourgeois legal structures, then of course rights would mean nothing because blacks have had virtually nothing under either. And if one envisions rights as economic advantages over others, one might well conclude that "because this sense of illegitimacy [of incomplete social relations] is always threatening to disrupt into awareness, there is a need for 'the law.'" (1991: 154)

"Reasonable reliances," insofar as they exist at the Mecca, derive from the extralegal civility some neighbors share with Mrs. Sallie in its overcrowded precinct.

The swarming subjectivities of the Mecca (the "many") yield momentarily to the threatening objectivity of The Law (the "one"). Moving beyond familiar ethnocentric vilifications of the Irish cop, Brooks constructs The Law reliant upon official collectivity as it intensifies the anonymity and invisibility conferred upon her community. Individual and community vulnerability converge as the progressive diminution of the victim – "child," "tot," "little girl," "little lost girl," "lone," "languid" – sharpens the taut parallelism of the circumstance and the crime in which the true tragedy of the Mecca becomes manifest. Assurance turns into suspicion, a stanza break underscoring the alienation embedded in the fracture of "everyone" into "every one": "Kind neighbor. // 'Kind neighbor.' They consider. / Suddenly / every one in the world is Mean" (18). A widening and estranging tide prefaces the declarative (not interrogative) quandary – "How shall the Law allow for littleness!" – that establishes the social tensions of Brooks's evolving aesthetic – "How shall the Law enchief the chapters of / wee brown-black chime, wee brown-black chastity?" (18). An inexorable linkage – signaled by the invariable *ch*s – of law and order on the one hand, art and sexual vulnerability on the other, plots procedural objectivity and maternal subjectivity onto a grid of social and aesthetic reconstruction.

Abstraction meets abstraction as external agency (its dubious intentions insinuated by "fetch," confirmed by "lariat") confronts a representative exemplarity (characteristic of Pauline Hopkins's biographical sketches and anticipatory of Brooks's subsequent aestheticization of Senghor's "art-lines / of Black Woman" [20]) that is in itself a parodic rendering of earlier heroic portraiture: "The Law arrives – and does not quickly go / to fetch a Female of the Negro Race" (19). The "lariat of questions," recalling the troubled Christianity of "The Chicago *Defender* Sends a Man to Little Rock" with its deplorable "lariat lynch-wish" (1960: 348), betrays little in the way of benevolence, shares less in the sense of justice. The Law retains its hierarchical disengagement while the mother, at once described and overheard, drifts from punctuated reiteration, and then chant: "The mother screams and wants her baby. Wants her baby, / and wants her baby wants her baby" (19). In this alternative maternal script that recalls "The Mother" (1945: 21), the "crime" is authentically that of "the other."

The textual and social authority of The Law erodes as Brooks suspends its definite article. Sheriffs, as agents from their distant racist precinct of "South State Street" (the geopolitical designation nation-alizing as it literalizes the north into the south), regard the Mecca as a "Postulate," its inhabitants socially dead. Brooks inserts a counter-cau-tionary discourse in the intimacy of the second person – "Until you look. You look – and discover" – that attempts to realign The Law and victims. But its crime-scene objectivity sees only "paper dolls . . . terri-ble and cold" (19): Pepita as statistic.

Dialogue and narrative conspire to particularize Richard "Peanut" Washington's intimate assertion that "there's danger in my neighbor-hood." Parallel counterdiscourses compete for the news of the Mecca: Aunt Dill assists with the grotesqueries of the near history of this most recent crime – "Little gal got / raped and choked to death last week . . . / . . . and her tongue / was hanging out (a little to the side); / her eye was all a-pop, one was; was one / all gone" – while The Officer, in Aunt Dill's reiteration, says "that something not quite right had been done that girl" (19). Recalling Carl Sandburg's objec-tion to "the too gruesome to print" embellishments common in the black press, Aunt Dill's micronarrative underwrites as it stages the subjective horror of the crime and the circumstance, forcing, through her graphic vernacular, The Officer "to look" – and to see.

Physical markers turn linguistic as Brooks, abandoning the reduc-tive personalization of The Officer, concedes the objectification of the circumstance. Mounted police, recalling the depictions in the *New Majority* of such forces of law and order, invade the interior of the Mecca with an equestrian impatience that intensifies the abstract and brute letter of this genderless and singular force: "The Law returns. It trots about the Mecca. / It pounds a dozen doors" (19).

Invisible citizens who "can speak of Mecca" (20) and its contin-gencies of social circumstance testify to a material and spiritual dis-integration representative of the community's internal collapse. Three denials – Alfred, who "has not seen Pepita Smith," surrenders to the removed and received aesthetic of Leopold Senghor; Hyena, who "has not seen / Pepita – 'a puny and a putrid little child'"; "Mazola / [who] has never known Pepita S." (21) – presage the unsparing narratorial concession that death itself is never the news: "Mazola / has never known Pepita S. but knows / the strangest thing is when the stretcher goes! – / the elegant hucksters bearing the body when the body / leaves its late lair the last time leaves. / With no plans to return" (21).

The summary confusion of literary corpus and corpus delicti confirms the apocalyptic nature of Brooks's revelation. The subsequent chronicle of the Meccans' indifference to the plight of Pepita and her "chirpings oddly rising" (31) suggests the progressive alienation Brooks senses in the "intruder's" constructions of community. The stanza dedicated to Don Lee's "new art and anthem . . . / a new music screaming in the sun" (21-2) insinuates a potentially redemptive breaking story of an indigenous aesthetic ultimately more revolutionary than the "illustrious ruin" of Amos's projected "long blood bath" (22–3). Neither Alfred's Negritude nor Edie Barrow's ballad can resuscitate received artistic forms dead to the realities of the Mecca.

Little exemplifies the internal alienation of the Mecca's ruins better than the predatory and extralegal world of Prophet Williams, in which the commercial and the journalistic conspire to promote the false prophet. His complicity with mercantile and legal structures of the oppressor is signaled by his appetites and his advocate: "He is not poor (clothes do *not* make the man). / He has a lawyer named Enrico Jason, / who talks. The Prophet advertises / in every Colored journal in the world" (24). Through his solicitor, The Prophet represents an internal agent of the objectifyingly indifferent Law: "Enrico Jason, a glossy circular blackness, who / sees Lawmen and enhances Lawmen, soon / will lie beside his Prophet in bright blood, / a rhythm of stillness / above the nuances" (25). Like The Prophet who "advertises," Jason, himself a "circular," becomes part of the commodity flux of journalism and capitalism that consumes the idle and corrupt of the Mecca.

Brooks's agitation to get the report right draws its oppositional strength from the crookedness of an alienating external medium, one that she has drawn upon extensively in rewriting the story of the Mecca, that distracts the community from itself. The "mischievous impromptu and a sheen" of *Vogue* – in which the Black Atlantic of Boontsie De Broe's "massive literatures . . . lores . . . transactions" is subsumed by Laddie Sanford of Palm Beach, Florida ("I call it My Ocean. Of course, it's the Atlantic" [27]) – seduces Darkara away from the cares of the Mecca and care for "what befalls a / nullified saint or forfeiture (or child)" (27). The enlarging significance of Pepita's story depends upon the self-destructiveness of a community reliant upon external agencies of law and report. With such indifferent witnesses, Brooks asks, who will tell the tale? A reverse inventory of Meccans (a folk cast mirroring Sandburg's Chicago poems) – "The painter, butcher, stockyards man, the Typist, / Aunt Tippie, Zombie Bell, / Mr. Kelly with long gray hair who begs, / . . . Gas Cady . . . the janitor . . . Queenie King . . . Wallace Williams" (27) – testifies to the crippling indifference of the powerless tenants.

The aimlessly repetitive, participially insistent motion and utterance – "gruntings," "outwittings," "shufflings," "starings," "spittings," and "wanderings" – warn of the linguistic riot potential in such places of social death and silence – places where boys break glass: "If / you scream, you're marked 'insane.' / But silence is a *place* in which to scream!" (26). The perverse census of indifferent and distracted identity categories betrays an unofficial nation contrary to the governance, regulation, and orders of The Law – its emergent postcolonial silence the site of a prelinguistic howl searching for indigenous ideology, grammar, and classification.

Counterdiscourses resolve into a narrative that telescopes The Law and the Mecca into a single condemned structure irrelevant to Brooks's community. In a demoniac projection of Walter Lippmann's idealistic race parallelism, Brooks exposes this quandary in a mortuary and floured minstrelsy that recalls the elderly of "Beverly Hills, Chicago" – "It is just that so often they live till their hair is white. / They make excellent corpses, among the expensive flowers . . . " (1949: 129) – and anticipates the considered and apocalyptic ruin imagined by Way-Out Morgan:

> Officers!
> do you nearly wish you had not come into this room?
> The sixtyish sisters, the twins with floured faces,
> who dress in long stiff blackness,
> who exit stiffly together and enter together stiffly . . .
> stare at the lips of The Law . . .
> and stiffly leave Law and the Mecca.
>
> (28)

Unlike Aunt Dill who, presaging the Mahalia Jackson-bolstered Reverend Doctor Purify and wife in Spike Lee's *Jungle Fever*, sustains a "happy" normalcy in denial, the sisters confront imminent collapse with a postmortem absolutism born of longevity and recognition.

Alfred the aesthete, his ruinous frailty imitative of the building itself, contemplates the forgiveness potential in this knowledge of coming collapse and, like the entropic subject of Eliot's "Gerontion," he "stiffen[s] in a rented house" (Eliot 1920: 23):

> I hate it.
> Yet, murmurs Alfred –
> who is lean at the balcony, leaning –
> something, something in Mecca
> continues to call! Substanceless; yet like mountains,
> like rivers and oceans too; and like trees
> with wind whistling through them.
>
> (31)

Nature – rendered *un*natural by the crushing interiority of this urban setting where inhabitants customarily take their "peek at the sun," like Hattie Smith, "from the insides of the door" (1945: 51) – settles with conjunctive force into Alfred's figurative other. Similes, weakening the epiphanic potential of the romantic sublime, contribute to the force of revolutionary reason – "an essential sanity, black and electric" – and suggest the deallegorization of poetry.

Even as Pepita's disappearance impelled this social text of reality and authority, so her subsequent murder generates its own imperatives, as it surveys an emerging aesthetic that, in Houston Baker's terminology, "can be fittingly characterized as the establishment of a mode of *sounding* reality that is identifiably and self-consciously black and empowering" (1987: 71). Having broken the news of the tragic consequences of ruinous capitalism, Brooks turns impatient with the sociopathological details of "the murderer of Pepita" and the crime itself. Jamaican Edward "looks at the Law unlovably" and underscores his crime against innocence by reenacting Peter's betrayal of Christ – "denies and thrice denies a dealing / of any dimension with Mrs. Sallie's daughter" (31). By nativity and deed the most marginalized of Meccans, he is denied access to the redemptive closure of the poem.

Recalling the inadequacy of headlines and "frantic bulletins" to Melodie Mary's world of little "importances," the news of Pepita's demise dictates a literary closure that will accommodate the significance of her squalid death. Elegiac in its catalogue of absence – "never went to kindergarten . . . never learned that black is not beloved" – Brooks's inventory of Pepita's aborted life joins "The Mother" as a reflection upon "the children you got that you did not get" (1945: 21). Yet unlike those earlier children who "were born . . . had body . . . and died," Pepita *had* "giggled," "planned," and "cried." The wrenchings – linguistic and emotional – of yet another "last quatrain" effect transition, not closure, as the poem struggles with a resurrectional force that is spiritual as well as aesthetic. Betraying a mastery of modernist form that warps Pound's Provençal bird with its "sweet chirps and cries" into Eliot's "notion of some infinitely gentle / Infinitely suffering thing," Brooks retrieves a field of linguistic possibility from Pepita's final, preliterate soundings:

> She whose stomach fought the world had
> wriggled, like a robin!
> Odd were the little wrigglings
> and the chopped chirpings oddly rising.
> (31)

Ultimately, the eccentricity of Pepita's (e)motions and utterances anticipates an indigenous aesthetic, born from the "chopped chirpings" (echoing the earlier unanswered challenge "How shall the Law enchief the chapters of / wee brown-black chime, wee brown-black chastity?") that will "allow for littleness!" Brooks, resisting the temptation to apotheosize Pepita, translates her fate into an aesthetic construction that opens onto the communal field of the "After Mecca" poems, a social matrix of what Melvin Tolson had called "Niagras of the little people" (1944: 5).

* * *

> It was as if the historical temperature in America went up
> every month.
> – Norman Mailer, *Miami and the Siege of Chicago* (1968: 188)

The "After Mecca" sequence, with its startling recapitulation of topics and tropes and its confident deformation of "master" Eliot's aesthetic, itemizes the aesthetic transformation (re)sounding throughout "In the Mecca." Within Walter Benjamin's desired "state of emergency," Brooks had transformed Walt Whitman's "many item'd union" into the racially reconfigured mass democracy of "All / worship the Wall" (43). Her editor's request that she supplement "In the Mecca" with additional poems, transforming her prophetic narrative into a collection, provided an unexpected opportunity to display the consequence of her redemptive reportage: the re-presentation of deformative strategies as ultimate mastery of "intruding" and "indigenous" traditions, thereby completing the socially charged aesthetic contract of *In the Mecca.* When read against "In the Mecca," these seemingly unrelated poems exhibit an aesthetic recalibrated to the historical temperature of her community.

The opening four poems betray topical continuities within an increasingly relaxed aesthetic. "To a Winter Squirrel," its end-stopped tercet forcefully recalling the opening of "In the Mecca," resituates Alfred's "substanceless" literary epiphanies (and Eliot's forbidding "sill")[35] within the spectatorial indigenous purview of "Merdice / the bolted nomad" (35), whose life force forbids self-pity.[36] "Boy Breaking Glass," a resituation from "In the Mecca," here conjoins citizenship, class, and race in its reformulation of art as social identity or presence that creates: "'If not a note, a hole. / If not an overture, a desecration'" (36). In "Medgar Evers" and "Malcolm X," hagiographic as befitting Famous Men of the Negro Race, Brooks transforms the obituary into a verse necrology that acknowledges poetry's superior power to register loss.

"Two Dedications" – a paired sequence of "The Chicago Picasso" ("commissioned" art) and "The Wall" (interactive and improvisational art) – reflect upon art in the public sphere. Demonstrating mastery of form and deformation of mastery, Brooks gives the "trick to white expectations, securing publication for creative work that carries a deep-rooted African sound."[37] Mimicry of modernist collage and journalistic convention – datelines, news epigraphs, stage directions – signifies ongoing commitment to the aestheticization of the news. "The Chicago Picasso," with its epigraph from the *Chicago Sun-Times,* weds the geopolitical and commercial to the commissioned in its assessment of the public-subordinating nature of Art in the public sphere: "We / may touch or tolerate / an astounding fountain, or a horse-and-rider. / At most, another Lion" (40-1). The aesthetic machinery that contrives a Mies van der Rohe produces a "Flower / which is as innocent and as guilty, / as meaningful and as meaningless as any / other flower in the western field" (41). Such intruding art demands compliance, makes Man "squirm." "The Wall," with its epigraphic notice from *Ebony,* trumps "The Chicago Picasso" in its display of indigenous mastery through a bold revision of "Portrait of a Lady," silencing Eliot's "'false note'" of "a dull tom-tom" with its deferential chant: "A drumdrumdrum. / Humbly we come" (42).[38] Previously disputed ideas of order – art and religion – coalesce into a natural realignment that denies the oppositional force of "We" by the totalizing "All / worship the Wall" (43). At once an advertisement, yet another city surface for visual display (a "broadside"), and a monument consistent with the categorical sweep of A. B. Spellman's "I Looked & Saw History Caught" ("I looked & saw history caught / on a hinge" [Major 1969: 126]), this Art registers: "Heroes. / No child has defiled / the Heroes of this Wall this serious Appointment / this still Wing / this Scald this Flute this heavy Light this Hinge" (43).

The territorial imperative of "In the Mecca" – "There is danger in my neighborhood" – matures in "The Blackstone Rangers," a sequence of three poems delineating resultant local structures of The Law. Withdrawing from such totalizing classifications as "Leader" and "nation," Brooks reviews the "Black, raw, ready" energies of this "organization, not a gang."[39] Media constructions like Harry Belafonte, Martin Luther King, Jr., Stokely Carmichael, and Malcolm X, what Brooks calls "Bungled trophies," owe their celebrity to the totalizing powers that read the nation genealogically. Such leaders are unavoidably "dupes of the downtown thing," and as such irrelevant to the "footloose" bureaucracy of the Rangers: "Their country is a Nation on no map" (45).

The deformation of mastery that Houston Baker asserts "secures territorial advantage and heightens a group's survival possibilities" (1987: 51) is on full display in the concluding "The Sermon on the Warpland" and "The Second Sermon on the Warpland." Brooks's audacious subordination of Eliot's *The Waste Land* and the Sermon on the Mount to her racialized "commonwealth" of the "whirlwind" loudly sounds the "assertion of possession," the "report" that Baker associates with the drama of deformation. Such mastery exacts a price, as Brooks concludes: "It is lonesome, yes. For we are the last of the loud. / Nevertheless, live. // Conduct your blooming in the noise and whip of the whirlwind" (54).

"In the Mecca" (re)solved essential tensions in the professional and community aspects of Brooks's career.[40] Its historicized aesthetic transgressions moved her poetic from the necessary aesthetic and political rebellion inherent in counterdiscourse to the formation of a cultural and ideological community poetic evident in the "After Mecca" poems. By recognizing the sincerity of Brooks's reportorial role, we may begin to read the powerful journalistic intertext in sub-

sequent poems like *Riot*, a three-part poem that recognizes its immediate antecedent:

GUARD HERE, GUNS LOADED.

The young men run.
The children in ritual chatter
scatter upon
their Own and old geography.
The Law comes sirening across the town.
("The Third Sermon on the Warpland," 1969: 475)

More than a vestige from the *Mecca*, the news formulation of *Riot*
announces a subordination (not supplanting) of the "old geography"
of the dailies that is essential to the racialized report of communities
chattering to "their Own." Within this newly reconfigured (and necessarily transient) world, the reciprocal structures of community news
and the mainstream press realign into the intertextual coherence of
the prophetic (and apocalyptic) present:

Nine die, Sun-Times will tell
and will tell too
in small black-bordered oblongs **"Rumor? check it
at 744-4111."**

(1969: 477)

6

KINSHIP AS HISTORY

SAM CORNISH'S GENERATIONS

––––––––

... solemnly pledging myself anew to the sacred cause, I subscribe myself.
   – *Narrative of the Life of Frederick Douglass: An American Slave*

I hope to embrace a generation of people living through
history.
                                   – Sam Cornish, personal interview

The family signature is always a renewing renaissancism that
ensures generation, generations, the mastery of form and the
deformation of mastery.
                  – Houston Baker, *Modernism and the Harlem Renaissance*
       (1987: 106)

In 1971, at the height of the Black Arts Movement in poetry, Beacon
Press published Sam Cornish's *Generations*, a powerfully ordered
sequence of brief but highly focused poems on black historicized kinship. The book received favorable reviews in the white press but little
attention from Cornish's peers in the black community. Although his
family and social background gave Cornish a thorough firsthand
understanding of the stresses of contemporary black urban America, it
was apparently insufficient, in the opinion of some in the movement,
to authenticate his poetic vision of "people living through history."

   Born into the austerity of urban poverty in Baltimore (a place Tolson had called "the city of contradictions, at the mouth of the Patapsco River" [1982: 271]),[1] Cornish early developed a poetic flexible
enough to accommodate the vernacular of his neighborhood and

learned enough to depict fully the culture he both inherited and invented. In 1964, while part of Baltimore's developing political and literary underground, Cornish self-published (under his Beanbag Press imprint), a sixteen-page pamphlet entitled *Generations and Other Poems*. A subsequent edition of the collection, *Generations*, appeared in 1966, when Cornish was editing *Chicory*, a journal of children's writing, living at Fell's Point, and working at the Enoch Pratt Free Library. Though these antecedent *Generations* lack the organizing structure of the Beacon Press collection and fail to cohere in the larger sense of a poetic sequence, they nonetheless testify to Cornish's sense of himself as a walker in history and reflect the growing social and cultural tension both in his community and in himself.

While few of the original poems have survived the revisions and restructurings that led to the final version published in 1971, the same insistence upon historical contingencies pervades each version of this generative vision. By 1971 Cornish, represented in the LeRoi Jones (Amiri Baraka) and Larry Neal anthology, *Black Fire* (1968), as well as in the Clarence Major collection, *The New Black Poetry* (1969), seemed destined to become a central figure in the decade's black aesthetic movement. His poems answered Baraka's call for "Black Art": "We want a black poem. And a / Black World" (1969: 220) while transcending what Gwendolyn Brooks recalls, in *A Capsule Course in Black Poetry Writing*, as "condition literature" (Brooks et al. 1975: 5).

But in the wake of Brooks's migration from Harper and Row to Dudley Randall's Broadside Press (*Riot* [1969]), Cornish's publishing *Generations* with Boston's Beacon Press may have seemed a compromise with what Brooks would soon call "those professional Negro-understanders, some of them so *very* kind, with special portfolio, special savvy"(1972a: 85–6). Beacon Press was – and is – a self-consciously liberal, nonprofit press concerned with social issues.[2] Renowned for publishing such definitional works as James Baldwin's *Notes of a Native Son* (1955), C. Eric Lincoln's *The Black Muslims in America* (1961), Martin Luther King's *Where Do We Go from Here: Chaos or Community?* (1967), Daniel Berrigan's *The Trial of the Catonsville Nine* (1970), and Raymond Mungo's *Famous Long Ago: My Life and Hard Times with the Liberation News Service* (1970), Beacon Press had secured a comfortable reputation as the press of choice for liberal concerns.[3] It was quite different (and perhaps more offensive because of its liberal sincerity) from the profit-making New York presses like

William Morrow, E. P. Dutton, Random House, and Grove Press that were publishing Nikki Giovanni, Lucille Clifton, and Amiri Baraka.

Further, the presentation and reception of the book may have grated on sensibilities alerted to the dangers of white cultural colonization. In the highly politicized as well as polarized culture of the Black Arts Movement, the source of approbation mattered. In "The Explosion of Black Poetry," Clarence Major claims centrality for black poetry by arguing that "[t]he most common themes in black poetry . . . have been universal ones" (1972: 36). But such claims seemed authentic only when expressed from within the black community. In her preface to *Generations*, Ruth Whitman, having established her own Jewish-historical sense of victimhood, describes Cornish as "a poet who speaks authentically and deeply from his own human history. His vision goes far beyond the passing trend; it is, in fact, universal" (1971: x). Such conviction might persuade a less polarized audience, but as a well-intentioned white liberal Whitman could hardly persuade black critics that Cornish's publication by a press owned by the Unitarian Universalist Association was not a betrayal of his racial identity. Whereas the book received numerous favorable reviews in the white press, black journals such as *Black World* and *The Journal of Black Poetry* ignored it. Instead of attaining centrality in the Black Arts Movement, Cornish, after 1971, drifted toward the margins.

It was a time, as Henry Louis Gates, Jr., reminds us, "in which we [felt] the unrelenting vise of the poet's grip upon our shoulders" (1987: 32). Those preoccupied with the community-level struggle of the Black Arts Movement would reject with particular contempt the liberal pretense of race-blind intentions as culturally blank and socially corrupt. The formative years of the new black aesthetic, Haki Madhubuti recalls, were preoccupied with "the area of definition":

> How does a black poet (or any black person working creatively) define himself and his work: is he a poet who happens to be black or is he a black man or woman who happens to write? The black and white "art for art's sake" enthusiasts embraced the former and the black nationalists expanded in the latter adding that he is an African in America who expresses himself, his blackness with the written word and that the creativity he possesses is a gift that should be shared with his people and developed to the highest level humanly possible. (1972a: 26)

And so, however pleased Cornish and Beacon Press may have been with Joel Conarroe's *Shenandoah* review or with Michael Heffernan's *Midwest Quarterly* review, the terms and the sources of such academic approval were irrelevant to the community-based Black Arts Movement.[4] Eugene Redmond, in *Drumvoices: The Mission of Afro-American Poetry: A Critical History* (1976), noted Cornish's marginality and deplored it; but already in major aesthetic and political publications, such as Dudley Randall's *The Black Poets: A New Anthology* (1971), Abraham Chapman's *New Black Voices: An Anthology of Contemporary Afro-American Literature* (1972), and Stephen Henderson's *Understanding the New Black Poetry: Black Speech and Black Music as Poetic References* (1972), Cornish had become an idea under erasure.[5]

From this distance in time, however, it seems clear that *Generations*, as centrally as much of the work embraced by Black Arts editors and critics, deals with the important aesthetic and thematic issues of the movement. The poems not only anticipate but embody the current critical concern of kinship and history as the twin axes of African-American literature. As Michael Cooke explains in *Afro-American Literature: The Achievement of Intimacy*: "It is not kinship in the sense of consanguinity or descent, with all its formal systems and restrictions. Rather *kinship* means a social bonding, a recognition of likeness in context, concern, need, liability, value" (1984a: 110). Cooke carefully distinguishes between "kinship by exhortation" (Baraka, Ron Karenga, Madhubuti) and kinship through "intellection, retrospection, and experience" (1984a: 131). And though he identifies Michael Harper as the leading practitioner of the latter, he might as well have turned his contemplative definition back on the poetic sequences of Cornish's *Generations*. For, like Harper, Cornish knows that the poetry of statement is condemned to a short, unhappy life. Best to move (in Gates's words) "from blackness as a physical concept to blackness as a metaphysical concept" (1987: 28).

Cornish's project in *Generations* is both lexical and commemorative, as he seeks to continue a master narrative of black culture within a lyrical metanarrative. He accomplishes this, not in the nativist profiles of Melvin Tolson (which superficially owe much to Edgar Lee Masters and Edwin Arlington Robinson), nor in the experimental modernism of Jean Toomer, but rather by topically dwelling in the historical present and discovering the aesthetic energy of a minimal yet rhetorically enhanced lyric line that depends upon imagery as compressed as that of William Carlos Williams. Cornish situates his poetic in a nexus of imagistic modernism and a black aesthetic. Whether his "fatless" lines derive from Williams or Baraka or both, it is the narrative sequencing and rhetorical sophistication of these minimalist lyrics that intensifies the lyric moment, even as it invokes the culture's master narratives.[6]

The recent efforts of African-American theoreticians (like Henry Louis Gates, Jr., and Houston Baker) and new historicists (like Stephen Greenblatt) encourage this rereading of the structure, language, and aesthetic of *Generations*. For here is a collection that prompts reconsideration of the aesthetic and historical relationship between African-American ancestral narratives and black lyric poetry through its representation of the "family signature" that Baker has declared to be a topical as well as stylistic definition of black modernism.

Houston Baker's individual-and-society reassessment of narrative structures in Richard Wright – "A Meditation on the Black (W)hole" in *Blues, Ideology, and Afro-American Literature: A Vernacular Theory* – guides this demonstration of the ways in which *Generations* redefines a poetic of African-American history. Adapting anthropological rites of passage to literary tropes, Baker (responding to René Girard, Roland Barthes, and Mikhail Bakhtin) formulates the progression of what he calls "Black (W)hole Rites (Rites of the Underground)." His trajectory of selfhood, embedded in the narrative texture, offers a way into the governing, ordering principle of Cornish's work, enabling us to sense the transformation of topic and narrative line into poetic. Baker sees the movement from "zero image" (borrowing from Carolyn Fowler) to "rites of separation (conflagrational departure)" to a "liminal" state in which the "initiand [is] outside of History" (where the Rites of Liminality consist of "ancestral wisdom; historicization of self; negation of the negation") to a "black expressive wholeness." This theoretical line of development suggests ways of comprehending the narrative strategy underlying Cornish's lyric, offering a means of assessing both the stations of the identity journey and the whole. The justification of a narratological theory applied to poetry resides in the way that Cornish's harshly reduced lyrics, when drawn into poetic sequences, redefine the nature of master narrative and history for the black poet.

Generations consists of six (what the poet considers to be) "symphonic" movements: "Generations," "Slaves," "Family," "Malcolm,"

"Others," and "Afterward." Baker's four-stage progression serves to define as well as foreground the sections, making the symphonic movements visible as well as audible. The sequence moves from the death of social identity represented by slavery, where self is object, to the deployment of a marginalized or "liminal" self, outside of the oppressor's defining society yet without a self-defining context. Each movement tests the potential of self as well as community definition, expanding a naming project into poetry that eventually makes blackness manifest and irreversible. Though the voices never speak from underground, they echo a marginal remove in their witnessing.

Cornish initiates his project with the trope of naming. In "Generations i" (the sole poem of the first section, "Generations"), an anonymous, unnamed though "named" figure begins his progressive deconstruction (and reconstruction) of the role of witness in history, which for him begins in prehistory:

> he had a name
> and no father
> packed his books
> in milk crates
> never reading them just watching
> the colors in the afternoon dust
> (1971: 3)

An authentic name is a link to social identity. But because the subject's name lacks the historical resonance of acknowledged paternity, the world of record keeping doesn't recognize him, and his place in family and community remains undefined. Packing his books without reading them, he seems to be what Orlando Patterson defines in *Slavery and Social Death* as a "genealogical isolate" (1982: 5), alienated from language itself yet, in this instance, freed of inhibiting historical characterization. This originating, ahistorical poem of poverty and beginnings defines what Patterson sees as the core of a slave's "natal alienation": "the loss of ties of birth in both ascending and descending generations" (1982: 7). It also underscores a freedom from paternal inhibition and family responsibility that, if unwelcome and chilling (especially in the era and context of slavery), still offers an unusual opportunity for self-historicizing.

Such self-historicizing, however, comes at great emotional and social cost. The poem's abrupt shift to enactments of adolescent sexual initiation and loss depicts the emptiness of an individual and a race stranded from parents and community, generation having been reduced to a sexual act rather than a genealogical fact:

> when he was thirteen
> . . . .
> he would come into her cold apartment
> wondering if he had the special knowledge
> that women wanted from men
> endured the pain she moaned
>
> (3)

The paradox of "a name / and no father" hovers over the poem's closure, invoking as it does the larger social sense of the world and its commerce:

> and wanted god to remember
> he was young
>
> and in much trouble
>
> with himself
>
> (3)

Whether God the Father will invest this life with a larger community, history, or purpose remains unanswered in this mute apostrophe. The adolescent upon whom Cornish hinges the introduction lacks an inspiriting context; he has only the fatherless, unnamed moment. And yet the invocation of the Lord securely places the poem in the larger context of the "sorrow song," recalling a tradition of a people in trouble.

With the section entitled "Slaves," *Generations* moves into representations of the historical present as it posits a community. In order for artifacts or historical extensions to thrive, as Stephen Greenblatt suggests, there must be "the imagined ethnographic thickness" (1990: 176).[7] Rooted in a sense of place (see "Home": "home / where my / ground / is" [9]), a procession of secular saints – from Harriet Tubman to Rosa Parks, Nat Turner to Frederick Douglass – speaks history in a double-voiced dialogue with the present. In paired history-and-news poems, Cornish violates the temporality of the narrative to allow Tubman to speak and be spoken to. The historical Tubman ("Harriet

Tubman #1") shares a contemporaneous existence, as she "sing[s] to hide / . . . dance[s] to conceal / the pistol under [her] apron." Tubman as historical referent ("Harriet Tubman #2) epitomizes blackness – racial consciousness and memory itself. Cornish celebrates Tubman and her mother in this reading of generation as propagation and survival:

> Lord, while I sow earth or song
> the sun goes down. My only mother
> on a dirt floor is dying, her
> mouth open on straw and black
> soil, the smell of stew or chicken
> in a pot her only memories. I think
> of the children
> > made in her and sold.
> > > (10)

The harsh though natural rhythms of life ("sow earth," "sun goes down," "mother . . . dying") are violated by the commodification of propagation itself ("the children / made in her and sold"), yet are commemorated for representing the persistence of the will to live.

"Frederick Douglass" extends this celebratory disclosure of maternal determination:

> my mother carried me in the fields and slept
> on black ground as i turned within our skin
> and as a child white fingers walked into her
> mouth to count the teeth and raise the price
> > (12)

The continuous, stark sentiment of such compressed imagery of earth and mother intensifies the daily heroism of women in chattel slavery. Cornish's simple past-tense, preposition-driven constructions encourage the sensation of historical recurrence, achieving what Baker would term "an 'ahistorical,' 'metaphorical' sense of the black self's *historicity* or placement within a diachronic series of Afro-American events" (1984: 154). The strands of historical circumstance and inevitability force a logical redefinition of slavery and history: slavery is what *is*, not what *was*.

In "Montgomery," Rosa Parks partakes of the energy and nobility of her ancestors when she declares, "i walk for my children / my feet two hundred years old" (19). These historical extensions work not merely because of the complexity of the ongoing struggle, but also because of the lean elegance of the poetic line. Cornish exploits an image-driven poetry that infuses history with a present-tense urgency, making it literally present, thus enacting Brooks's declaration that "ESSENTIAL black literature is the distillation of black life," a declaration that encompasses the historical as well as social sense of "black life" (Brooks et al. 1975: 3).

Because voice and personality alone lack the strength to bear such history, Cornish historicizes the peculiar institution of slavery as he depicts what Winthrop Jordan has called "the mental margin absolutely requisite for placing the European on the deck of the slave ship and the Negro in the hold" (1969: 97). The patriarchal white culture is dehumanized, stripped of emotion, reduced to meager sensation: "white men [who] feel teeth   arms / ass" are deaf to "the noises / tangled / in the breaking / of families" ("Slave Market," 14). In "A Dog Looking," the fierce equation of "meat" and "nat turner" demands an absolute acknowledgment of slavery as a dishonorable, commodity-based institution. Borrowing a taste for social homily from Douglass, Cornish telescopes all matters of selfhood and identity in "Age":

> age
> is for those
> with fathers
> (17)

The collapse of social rituals of identity – age, name, genealogy – as well as the sheer physicality of the "breaking / of families" demonstrate the means by which patriarchal white culture attempted to strip slaves of history *and* time. In Baker's formulation, this "abnormal condition" of utter estrangement places the "initiate without status, outside society, outside time" (1984: 153). While the introductory poem claims generational center stage, these biographical and historical glimpses encourage the linkage of dog, meat, and slave, insisting upon the brute fact of slavery. The poet's fondness for participials and present-tense constructions encourages a sense of the historical present. In Cornish's world one cannot get to the point of history, if by "history" one means that which is lived through. For a black poet, there is no getting to the other side of slavery.

The sequence "Family" begins the self-definitional "passage rites" central to Baker's view of self-definition and authority. Cornish peoples a historical landscape with immediate kin. In "Generations 2" the poet dons a covertly autobiographical mask: "sometimes he walked to occupy / his feet." Seeking a relational context, he mimes his ancestral linkage to the Middle Passage and the Black Atlantic as he "sail[s] ship for the new world / in the kitchen sink." His reenactment of his place in history requires articulation: "when asked about his ambition / he always held // his words" (25). The ambiguous marginality enforced by "held" (to keep, to store, to maintain, to bind, to assert) reflects the progression into liminality, while the physicality of his grasp underscores the reality of his text. Unlike the "never reading" adolescent of the first poem, this figure appears to have secreted away a lexicon for future use. As Baker suggests, "an enduring *Black Difference* is the only world available to the initiand" (1984: 154). Denied the actuality of his race's history in the New World, the writer confronts reality in an estranging world that simultaneously contracts and expands around him.

Yet the procession of unnamed family members contributes to the progressive historicization of the emergent self. Memory, history, blood, and ancestry fuse to form a historical community:

> brother to brother
> skin to skin this
> is the way the young sleep
>
> now we have entered
> the street   i think
> of him he remembers me
> ("Brother" 27)

If in fact the speaker (and his kin) are decentered, something must be made of the memories, the history of the marginalizing self-identity of "black difference" manifest "skin to skin." Only the brother seems tough enough to withstand the forces of history *and* news:

> my brother is homemade
> like he was the first real
> black boy i ever knew
> ("My Brother is Homemade" 29)

This poem has a talismanic presence in Cornish's oeuvre, appearing as it does in several collections and finally becoming the core of his memoir, *1935*.[8] The brother who "came into this / color thing lighter / than [the poet]" signifies race and its attendant cultural heritage: "Richard Wright / or James Baldwin." "First," "real," and "black" – equally weighted modifiers – coalesce to define what Cornish means by black power and a black historicized aesthetic: an affirmation of kinship as well as a projection of literary ancestors and descendants.

A bridging sequence concerning the poet's present-tense, married existence comes to an uneasy rest with "April 68":

> somewhere cities burn
> my wife is sleeping
> i touch her face
> and find the cheeks
> are wet
> there is something
> being said
>
> (34)

The world where "cities burn" and "something [is] being said" is removed from the poet's circumstance. Curiously, the "barn" and "bird" world of the wife – Lenox, Massachusetts – requires punctuation and capitalization, signaling (what in this context is) an estranging formality, which in turn liberates the intense autobiographical prose poem, "Winters."

An emerging "we-ness" (Baker's phraseology) or near-historical identity displaces the white bourgeois world of wealth in the pastoral Berkshires. In the prose poem "Winters," Cornish, sifting through previous impressions and representations of his family, escapes this suspended, almost deathlike world and centers the genealogy on himself. While this may be read as a repudiation of the privileged circumstances of his wife's family and the rest of the white middle-class world, it may also be seen as a return to the authenticating historical implications of the collection. "Winters" provides Cornish with the opportunity to authorize his genealogy, reflecting upon and anticipating the text as a whole. Like Douglass, he "subscribe[s]" or underwrites himself, and in so doing must incorporate the identity that he is relinquishing. In spite of the prosaic elaboration, the sequence is as spare and intense in expressive imagery as the lyric poems, in their evocation of what Houston Baker calls "the everyday world occupied by our grand, great-grand, and immediate parents – our traceable ancestry that judged certain select sounds appealing and considered them efficacious in the office of a liberating advancement of THE RACE" (1987: 100):

> I suppose there is a sadness to this: images of women alone in their rooms unable to drink or dance life into their long and vacant lives without husbands or relations, winters so cold the toilet freezes under you, and most of all the rats that squeak in the night, the mice that walk through the kitchen looking for food, as you must have looked for food, and candies. But you lived and while you are alive there is the joy of living, this is what keeps. (39)

Here are the musical possibilities Baraka defined in "LEADBELLY GIVES AN AUTOGRAPH": "To pick it up and cut / away what does not singularly express" (1969: 213). The processional prepositions recall the prior histories of "the joy of living." The struggle, tense and elemental, unifies the historical and the genealogical as it proffers a broader text of circumstance and reality.

Beyond the issues of genealogy and history, "Winters" explores the wintry, writerly calling itself. In both summary and investigation, Cornish circumscribes the potential of writing:

> I think this is what I want to write about: the life behind the broken faces or finished hands. Something goes on, even death picks the life out of your legs. I have seen it. The streets where men dig in the dust of their pockets to fool themselves. A man unable to kill because we are brothers and his knife is at your throat, and must be at his also. Hunger so deep your eyes cannot attend to the things before them. Winters so cold that the fingers break off and the hand hangs there. (40)

Writing reverses the agency of death and supplants it with the articulated life and riffs of language. The facts of death and hunger are so real, so physical, that writing seems done with fingerless hands. Only love and community can stave off the unutterable consequences of such abandonment and poverty:

> The only recollection we have of poverty was the day we came home and there was nothing to eat for lunch, and my grandmother made gravy from flour and water. We went back to school ready

to read our books with a warm and friendly belly. This was the way I remembered it. I'm certain this was the way it was. (41)

With the power of an alchemist or of Jesus with his loaves and fishes, the grandmother (recalling Mrs. Sallie in her Mecca kitchen with her "hock of ham" and "ruddy yams") turns paste into gravy, "nothing" into "lunch," hunger into "a warm and friendly belly." The community kinship encourages but cannot supplant the individual's urge to create, but it forestalls descent into the urban hell of discontinuity and ruin where "the fingers break off and the hand hangs there." Such inversions are recollected transformations, the poet insists, rather than imaginative translations. However inspiriting personally, they fail in a literary sense because they are "the common work of memory." The poet, realizing how self-limiting this kind of recollection is, admits, "Now when I want to know myself, there is nothing for me to work with." Given the extremity of the moment, Cornish requires more than a recollected past or a historical narrative. As he had lamented in "Turk," published in the Baraka and Neal anthology *Black Fire*: "there is no space / to move do not come / too close i am a private / me" (1968: 399).

Recognizing the possibility of what Baker calls "reintegration," Cornish extends the search initiated with "my brother is homemade" as he seeks a public figure who is both "real" and "black." No leader epitomizes the quest for independent self-identity and stature better than Malcolm X. He was, in Gwendolyn Brooks's eyes, "Original. / Ragged-round. / Rich-robust" (1987a: 441). As Michael Cooke suggests: "Malcolm X did not only brandish defiance before a white society. He flourished, unpredictably and irresistibly, *within* himself. He was the power of the ordinary black individual made manifest, in many modes" (1984a: 135). The "Malcolm" sequence quickens with the moment, sounding remarkably like the prose of Malcolm X in moments of grave rhetorical urgency, like this passage from his autobiography: "Anyway, now, each day I live as if I am already dead, and I tell you what I would like for you to do. When I *am* dead . . . I want you to just watch and see if I'm not right in what I say: that the white man, in his press, is going to identify me with 'hate'" (1965: 381). The scrim of matriarchal endurance is lifted; no longer is memory's gentle blur able to muffle the surge of expression: Malcolm is dead, the poet discovers, and history is obscene.

157

In the title poem of the sequence Cornish addresses the martyr, recalling the assumptions of his own earlier attempts at history and identity. "Malcolm" contrasts the emotionally manipulative, charged rhetoric of the news – disseminated by "boys on winter street / corners selling the newspapers late / into the night, the next day, the day after / and the following weekend" – with Malcolm's appeal to race pride in a world of urban decay:

> Malcolm, I think of you when I wash
> my hair and look at a can of grease,
> or young punks seeking old men
> with ice picks and broken bottles,
> wanting nickels for wine.
>
> (47)

The poem calls into question the very mythology of leadership. As evidence, the poem shows how the fact of John Kennedy's minor role in the black community is overshadowed by his apparent martyrdom:

> Malcolm, I think of you when I remember
> the death of JFK and black children
> who for no reason wet their eyes.
>
> (47)

Cornish challenges the silent conspiracy of news and, eventually, history to revise reason and emotion so that new, more acceptable, identifications (to use Malcolm's formulation) can be made between leaders and their followers. Such recognition of false historical extensions marks the progression of the poet's consciousness into the irretrievable world outside of white consciousness. America has become a plague-ridden world of brutal inversions, violent hypocrisies:

> Malcolm, I think of you when I walk home
> after leaving a street of poor white and
> hear you are dead and see all the white
> faces behind their own prisons and windows.
>
> (47)

Culture and antecedent skew historical resonance. Black children are programmed to grieve the death of Kennedy while whites seek mute refuge "behind their own prisons and windows." The poem's imponderable topics, delicate and obdurate as the class issues raised in "Winters," are the weight of circumstance and fact of racism as well as Malcolm's death. Anaphora – "Malcolm, I think of you" – binds the split quandaries of community and writerly identity. Malcolm, who died while shedding his "own prisons and windows," must squarely face the impoverishment of the oppressors.

Both the death and the life of Malcolm X enter into a vernacular, oral culture, as the poet records "I hear Malcolm X is dead" and grasps the larger cultural truth that "indians are falling in the streets" ("Empty Doorways"). Like James Baldwin before him, Cornish – schooled in white American cultural mythologies from the films of John Ford and Sam Peckinpah – comes to the despairing conclusion that all minorities are at risk in white America.[9] In "Remembered," the crucifixion of a black Christ separates time into before and after: "he measured his world / and made it black" (51). What survives him is a world in which a racist, capitalist economy bears severe consequences for both black and white citizens:

> now the summer crumbles into fall
> and the CIA recruits on black campuses
> white housewives take target practice
>
> the white man buys his ground
> and moves his children, his taxes,
> while black women crowd their families
> into their bodies and small apartments
> growing smaller each year
>
> (51)

Cornish detects no agency of "central intelligence" at work here. Invoking the legacy of slavery's perverse commerce, he depicts an inverted economic growth cycle, pairing the expansion and contraction of parturition with the racially determined fate of the economy.

"You Can Burn a City with a Rent Book" (combining the images of book destruction – "burn," "rent" – and economic coercion) and "Low Income Housing" preface the angry, exacting "White Town," a two-part poem of urban decay and emotional collapse. When read in context, this world of real estate mirrors the slave world in which families are safe only in utero. The obligation to define a self and a language ruptures the sequence, exposing a rhetorical and social fault line:

> repeat
> in me
> repeat again the places
> the history
>
>> of people kept
>> to themselves ugly
>> and unwilling to work
>> who push their lives
>> against us
>> ("White Town #1," 55)

The places vie with the history as appropriate signifiers of race and class estrangement. If not continuity, history should offer a refrain, but the poet finds no available hook, no way to enter a larger sense. The sequence that began with the elegiac "Malcolm, I think of you" turns harsh and brutally ironic in the final inversion of the earlier "george washington / was for the rights / of man" ("Other Nat Turners," 18), "Crossing Over into Delaware during the Newark Riots":

> on the streets
> headlines rolled
> into fist
>
> between the river
> city and bridge
> a darkness
> in the air
> the wind is spreading
> (57)

News, memory, and history conflate in the violence of the moment. Recalling the newspaper rugs of Brooks's urban poor and anticipating the newspaper logs of Walker's rural poor, these "headline fists" of Cornish's unheard convert yesterday's news into today's weapon of what the Kerner Commission would decorously refer to as "socially-directed violence." What Malcolm had identified as the "human combustion" of "black social dynamite" (1965: 312) threatens to annihilate all possibilities of continuity: generation, family, history.[10] The "darkness / in the air" is a formless cloud of oblivion.

The final sequence succumbs to the liminal, *entre les deux* world of "Others." No longer bound by historical or genealogical rubric, this progression of poems acknowledges the severance of news from history. Here is the price of the ticket: Members of the black expressive community, in Baker's terminology, can "never 'return' to the affective and perceptual structures of an old, white dispensation" (1984: 154). The final investigatory work commemorates the community relevance in a tally of lives cut short. From Dorie Miller ("black man who earned a purple heart at Pearl Harbor") and Bobby Hutton ("Panther . . . murdered by the Oakland Police") to Martin Luther King, Jr., and Robert Kennedy, the sequence incarnates the "darkness / in the air" of the "Malcolm" section, literally to assume bodily form(s) in an effort to thwart the violent oblivion of the moment. Identity itself is at stake in every lyric. Deaths from riots, drugs, and despair claim the famous and unknown alike. Leaderless and estranged, the country sows the seeds of its own destruction.

In an extreme reduction of Malcolm, Cornish lays bare the crisis for the family and community identity in "Black Child":

> if jesus
> eyes
> are blue
> I
> stay
> with my
> doll
> (72)

Unlike the "black children / who for no reason wet their eyes" over "the death of JFK," this child has noted the signaled duplicity of the conditional *if*, and has opted for *her* doll. Spare and absolute, in the wake of utter devastation and despair, the poem recalls Malcolm at his sermonic best: "Brothers and sisters, the white man has brainwashed us black people to fasten our gaze upon a blond-haired, blued-eyed Jesus! We're worshiping a Jesus that doesn't even look like us!" (1965: 220). Because the narrative strands of religion, like history, must (in William Andrews's formulation) "explain and justify the self" (1986: 1), Cornish and Malcolm signify upon the very notion of *regard* in their challenges to blue-eyed Christianity. "Others" grimly vindicates Malcolm's stance and vision, as it fades into a world where Good Friday is followed not by Easter but simply by Sunday morning (see "Good Friday and Sunday Morning," 73).

In the sequence's final moments, history assumes the role of literary "ancestor" as Cornish turns to what Baker terms the "signal black (w)holeness of Richard Wright" (1984: 140).[11] In "Bigger Thomas Says Some Bad Niggers Is Over Thirty," the poet seizes the time and sets Wright's avenging angel loose "with a pillow as a weapon":

> Bigger Thomas in Cleveland
> breaking the heart of Carl Stokes
> looking for Malcolm
> for Stokely
> for Rap
> . . . . . .
> Bigger Thomas cutting up the pool table
> pissing in the collection plate
> what is that boy worth?
> . . . .
> Bigger Thomas on the roof cleaning
> a rifle
> "What kind of progress is this?"
> asks Edward Brooke
>
> (76–7)

Unlike the mission-directed Harriet Tubman "with a pistol under [her] apron," Bigger Thomas (in whatever incarnation) is both violent and self-destructive, embodying rage and death twinned. The genuine vernacular – "what is that boy worth?" (itself *un*quoted) – contrasts sharply with the *quotable* platform speech of Edward Brooke – "'What kind of progress is this?'" Cornish prefers an openly parodic interplay between utterances over a Bakhtinian "hidden polemic"; the boundaries here are the boundaries of the poem.[12] Building upon what Barbara Johnson sees as "the distorted strength of the black folk hero" (1990: 146) in Bigger Thomas, Cornish attempts historical generation only to stumble at the gate of genocide:

> the first
> and last
> the one who the convoy
> comes for
> the new man in the ovens
> ("A Black Man," 78)

Biblical resonances merge with holocausts from the pages of history and *Time*, consuming past and present as history deigns to repeat itself. Unable to straddle the "black (w)hole" to gain a "black expressive wholeness," Cornish effects closure with a singular poem that both embodies and satirizes the universality Ruth Whitman praises in her preface to *Generations*. The "Afterword," consisting of a single poem entitled "Forecast," renders fate as a general proposition:

> All will die
> watch out for
> the man with the soap
> and the towels
>
> (81)

A volume that began with anonymous procreation ends with a general but sanitary annihilation in which Armageddon fails to be followed by the millennium.

The poet of *Generations* assumes that the act of writing by its very nature isolates and estranges the writer from all but the commodity of language itself. But in Cornish's vision of the marketplace, words transcend commercial and temporal exigencies to thrive in the realm of a community-bred aesthetic and narrative. These poems have survived the ravages of two decades in part because of their dedication to a culture's literary and ancestral narratives, honestly aestheticizing and thereby ensuring historical resonance and life. They epitomize what Houston Baker describes in the historical instance of the Harlem Renaissance as "a sounding field called *renaissancism*, their contribution and value as national resources and as audible signs of the human will's resistance to tyranny" (1987: 107). *Generations* has the audacity to be both a social and a literary project, demanding an accounting as its ledger of poems confronts the failures, not successes, of fin-de-siècle America. Unseating the aesthetic he associates with a perhaps exaggeratedly universalized but nonetheless seemingly hegemonic white middle-class culture, Cornish substitutes an African-American poetic of uncertainty and pride.

The journey of *Generations* is incomplete and leaves the poet temporarily stranded in the liminal world Baker describes, a place unbounded by conventional history yet defined by its resonance. But although the intervening children's books, other poems, and the generous and evocative memoir *1935* have edged Cornish closer to expressive wholeness, they do not diminish the risk and achievement of his early refusal to go underground and relinquish his claim on American culture. *Generations,* even after twenty years, retains its prophetic sense of history as selfhood and still seems a book suspended, not in the contingencies of its era, but in the process of the poet's self-invention. Unlike the more stridently eruptive lyrics from the apocalyptic late 1960s, the poems of *Generations* command recognition for their aesthetic of empathy, historical immediacy, and rapport. Cornish, like James Baldwin, believing in history's literal presence, maps as he "embrace[s] a generation of people living through history." And in so doing he suggests ways of redefining a black poetic that draws the full range of its cultural ancestry into the present.

7

NATION-NESS AS CONSCIOUSNESS

ALICE WALKER'S MERIDIAN

'Revolution' said Mr Adams 'took place in the
   minds of the people
     in the fifteen years before Lexington'
                    – Ezra Pound, Canto 50 (1937)

I have given you a motive
         to run down a flag.
          – Jay Wright, *Dimensions of History* (1976a: 23)

"Nobody can change the past," says my mother.
"Which is why revolutions exist," I reply.
  – Alice Walker, "Beyond the Peacock: The Reconstruction of
    Flannery O'Connor" (1975a: 58)

In 1974 Alice Walker journeyed with her mother to rural Georgia to visit her deserted childhood home just down the "Eatonville-to-Milledgeville road," the axis of her aesthetic ancestors, Zora Neale Hurston and Flannery O'Connor (1975a: 42). This return occasioned more than a consideration of her fellow southern writers: It prompted daughter and mother to contemplate the character and quality of the old and new South, its ways of abidance or revolt. With some impatience, Walker's mother seeks a rationale for this return:

> "When you make these trips back south," says my mother . . . "just what is it exactly that you're looking for?"
> "A wholeness," I reply.
> "You look whole enough to me," she says.

"No," I answer, "because everything around me is split up, deliberately split up. History split up, literature split up, and people are
split up too. It makes people do ignorant things." (1975a: 48)[1]

The wholeness that Walker aspires to, one of a binding community
and an indigenous voice, would be realized in the beatific closing of
her epistolary novel, *The Color Purple* (1982);[2] the "split" worlds of history, literature, and people would structure her bicentennial novel,
Meridian.

Walker completed the manuscript of "Atonement and Release"
(her working title for *Meridian*) during the televised spectacle of the
nation's birthday celebration. Unintentionally parodic performances
of idly constructed history, sentimental reenactments of "the Revolution," and formulaic dramas of exemplary forefathers,[3] obliterated
the still raw news of the 1960s. The regularized reenactments of the
nation's own incendiary birth rhetoric rendered frozen the originary
metaphors of "life" and "liberty" and "happiness" so embedded in the
national historical consciousness. Unlike the Centennial, which had
marked the end of Reconstruction and had projected a reunified
nation, the Bicentennial proved notable only in that the country was
being governed by a nonelected president and vice president. The
"mild indifference in the United States towards the bicentennial of
Independence in 1976" (Kammen 1991: 695) may be read as the
national exhaustion with things national in the wake of Watergate
and the fall of Saigon. Within this contextual frame, the civil rights
movement surrendered and became the property of nationalized
memory, a closed, historical narrative at odds with experience. What
June Jordan recalls as a time of "unabashed moral certitude, and the
purity – the incredibly outgoing energy – of righteous rage" (1994b:
178) was engulfed by the willed amnesia and contrived historical
recall of the Bicentennial.

Citing chronological ideas of order as particular stumbling blocks
to her historical and narrative conceptions for *Meridian*, Walker abandoned the "rigorous realism" of her first novel, *The Third Life of
Grange Copeland*, and adopted a new aesthetic, "like a crazy quilt, or
like *Cane*" (Tate 1983: 176).[4] Such a constitution accommodated both
the active memory and the willed amnesia of the recent revolutionary currents of the civil rights, women's, and antiwar movements.[5]
News and history, chronicles and novels succumb to the asynchrony

of discourse time – whether story time or history time – and lead to a realignment of historical and narrative possibilities. The "split," if it were to be linguistically realized, necessitated a systematic reevaluation of received history, textual and televisual, and fictional narrative. Examination of the novel's historical field and narrative frame opens both to reassemblage, to representation, and to reenactment in the hope of maintaining a historical vitality that addresses the future as well as the past.[6] Walker commits her novel to a cycle of historicized and interchangeable enactments of public and private histories, stories without insistent narrative logic or coherence.

Walker's interrogation of national narratives, social identities, and historical forms results in a latent narrative construction of stories available for reassembly into a later narrative whole – in a more favorable time. A preoccupation with the failure of narrative design, in fiction and history, dictates a fate (suggestive of Derrida) for Meridian: to be a character outside of but central to a narrative. External to the logic of either contemporary history or fictional plot rests Meridian's social, performative function. Unable to inhabit or accept the available social roles, she reconceptualizes herself within intertextual silences unavailable to the other characters, individualizing a persona alien to all received roles. Successive liberation is necessary before she can locate a neutral space where self-definition and narrative (fictional or historical) truth are possible.

As the protagonist slips her narrative constraints, so does the novel abandon other received, totalizing narratives. Television must be countered because it insinuates an obstructive focus that frames, edits, and normalizes with its fraudulent narrative certainty. True to repeated corporate assertions that television was primarily an "entertainment medium," networks tended to subordinate news imagery into the fabric of prime time. National viewers read the sporadic texts of civil rights and war through the persistent barrage of sitcoms celebrating a white, rural South independent of current complications.[7] This country projection of America was so abhorrent to jazz-poet Gil Scott-Heron that he celebrated in "The Revolution Will Not Be Televised" (slogan and anthem for a generation) a near future when "Green Acres / Beverly Hillbillies / Louisville Junction / Will not be so damn relevant" (1970). Black nationalism had to be rescripted, because, in its present form, it offered an inherited, violent patriarchal rhetoric which perpetuated the worst of the master's script. If meaning is to be found or restored, it must come through negation of corrupt legacy. For, as Michael Riffaterre insists, "Significance cannot be produced without first voiding, displacing, or repressing an established meaning, whether this meaning originates in the sociolect or in the context" (1990: 83). Every personal, historical, and literary fault line must be italicized if *Meridian* is to initiate Walker's search for wholeness and complete the quest of Jean Toomer's "Blue Meridian": "to enact a mystery among facts – " (Toomer 1988: 71).

*   *   *

> Whatever part one's parents as teachers played, and whatever part one's enchantment in the charm of the story-telling played, the stories, the music, the pictures that belonged to one's own life story seemed at once to be recognized and to recognize. "Thus every sort of confusion is revealed within us," Plato warns. And to speak at all of the operation of design, I would bring back the fullness of that warning. The city that is within us haunts all of Poetry.
> – Robert Duncan, "The Truth and Life of Myth" (1985: 8)

The facts of Walker's fiction-made-from-history are combative and restless, resistant to coherent patterns, textual or visual. Even her substitution of the "crazy quilt" for what Robert Duncan calls "the operation of design" introduces a spatial frame to the narrative alien to the ordering of the novel's tensions. The invocation of history, with its insistence upon locality and temporality, prompts a search for retrospective significance and encourages the reader to discover narrative logic within textual and contextual fields.[8] If Walker displays unusual confidence, it is in her willingness to allow the text to recover not only her "own life story" – her years as a civil rights worker in Mississippi – but that of her nation as well. *Meridian* rescripts the national narrative to include the silences and potential of a social movement and a personal revolution beyond the camera's lens.[9]

A plot summary may serve as rehearsal for the essay. *Meridian* explores the personal and public maturation of Meridian Hill,[10] a black woman from the rural South whose experiences – domestic and political – resonate with the political crises of the sixties and early seventies. Her schooling at the historically black Saxon College provides the initial social matrix of politics and personality even as it represents the ways in which Meridian emblematizes the benefits of liberal endowment. Anne-Marion, classmate and aspiring revolutionary, offers the initial challenge to Meridian's sense of political justice and vision when she challenges, "Will you kill for the Revolution?" Truman Held, black activist and college student, draws Meridian into love and activism while they cooperate in early voter registration drives. Their relationship deteriorates as Truman falls in love with a succession of northern white activists, including Meridian's friend, Lynne Rabinowitz. Truman's marriage to Lynne, the birth and death of their child, and the progressive failure of their relationship represent the broadest social dynamic in Meridian's world. The stages of Meridian's involvement with and rejection of her rural heritage, her liberal aspirations (family, education, endorsed political activity), and her marked friendships animate this story of spiritual and social growth through disengagement and commitment.[11]

Witnessing the civil rights movement growing as mummified as "The True Story of Marilene O'Shay" (incarnated in the barely preserved, sideshow corpse that serves as Meridian's foil in the opening scene), Walker skirts the easily iconographic tribute to the "revolution" in favor of a spare, reflective meditation on the shifting planes of representative lives, revolutionary struggles, and historical antecedent and accident. In so doing she hopes to avoid what Benedict Anderson calls the "museumizing imagination" (1983: 178).

Critics and reviewers have noted this figurative displacement or reconstitution of the *historical* from many angles[12] without considering its relevance to Walker's reconstruction of the narrative whole. Often *Meridian* as a historical construction is discussed with little sense of its critical and transformative challenges. Writing in the historical abyss between Watergate and the fall of Saigon, Walker seeks to restore the aura of a movement captured by television.[13] She strikes repeatedly at the media-intercepted history, resolving to capture the ambiguity and vitality of passionate human endeavor as well as its indecisiveness and spirituality. As she explained in her interview with Claudia Tate (1983: 179):

> I mean [civil rights workers] were often stricken because of their flaws which at the same time kept them going. I was fascinated by the way you hardly ever saw their flaws. And yet, they were there, hidden. The image you got on television showed their remarkable control, their sense of wholeness and beauty. In short, they were heroic. It's just that the other side of that control was the cost of their heroism, which I think as black people, as Americans, we don't tend to want to look at because the cost is so painful.

Inhabiting the conceptual space of Albert Camus's *The Rebel*, *Meridian* dwells in a historical space in which past, present, and future seem simultaneous, rendering history problematic and atemporal – a void of perpetual deliberation.[14]

Displacement of established constructions begins immediately as Walker introduces Meridian – "'that woman in the cap . . . staring down the tank!'" (3) – in the shadow of a memorial that echoes the "Courthouse Square / On the Fourth of July" of Tolson's "The Town Fathers" (1944: 22):[15]

> The town of Chicokema did indeed own a tank. It had been bought during the sixties when the townspeople who were white felt under attack from "outside agitators" – those members of the black community who thought equal rights for all should extend to blacks. They had painted it white, decked it with ribbons (red, white, and of course blue) and parked it in the public square. Beside it was a statue of a Confederate soldier facing north whose right leg, while the tank was being parked, was permanently crushed. (4)

The shifting axes of history and region, generation and allegiance, lock in a chronology-confounding present tense. Meridian enters at the seeming confluence of the Civil War, the Centennial, the civil rights movement, and the Bicentennial. Alliances, once clear to contemporaries, cloud with indeterminancies as the Confederate memorial faces north in an apparent appeal to the reconstructed Union – emblematized by a tank bedecked in national colors – for help. Lest historical foes seem carelessly realigned in Walker's vision, the Yankee tank turns predictably ugly in this alien setting and crushes the Confederate statue's right leg. Meridian's action enters a realm of historical performative language, a confrontational one independent of time.[16]

The liberty to "move back and forth in time" enables Walker to restage the Movement, resituating herself relative to memory and amnesia. She acknowledges that historical fixity distorts even as it preserves, and risks unsettling the historiographical structure to liberate the life of the dead-because-historical movement. To counter the fossilizing stability of historical record, Walker opens her text to patterned, cyclical reenactment, independent of narrative or episodic sequence. Historicity intrudes subtextually and allusively, as when, for example, *Meridian* opens onto a scene of "po' kids . . . too young to 'member when black folks marched a lot" (7). The Movement, referred to in the past tense, lives only in Meridian's performative displays. In a series of returns to the sites of personal memory and historical resonance, Meridian subverts history into retrospect and project. More than a reverse migration to "go back to the people, live among them, like Civil Rights workers used to do" (18), she commits herself to a life of momentary intrusions and perpetual migration within a deterritorialized space.

The design of *Meridian* reflects the relinquishment of narrative logic embedded in chronology, favoring a synchronic progression of self-awareness over a determined advancement of historical, not historicized, plot. The alternation of private and public spheres, what Melissa Walker has termed a world of "personal needs and public commitments" (1991: 169), insists upon a necessary and observed dialectic. But, as Benedict Anderson suggests, "nation-ness is virtually inseparable from political consciousness" (1983: 135). Meridian's "split" narrative comes to resemble that of her nation.

Meridian, "a woman in the process of changing her mind" (12), effectively bridges her self and her society and becomes a floating signifier of liberation from relational conventions. Successive relinquishment of defined or strictured roles – daughter, student, wife, mother, lover, activist – allows Meridian to mediate between two socially determined collectives: the educated and politically empowered world of the Movement and that of the inarticulate and disfranchised, her "people." The totalizing mythic substrata of the text – race, ethnicity, and ideology – successively yield to Meridian's urgent displays of virtue and courage.[17] Unencumbered by ideology, she embodies the abstractions essential to communal self-understanding. Such attributes, which failed to surface in or sustain her personal life, contribute to sporadic and unnerving performances of authority and valor.

Activism as defined by Meridian legitimates the momentary fusion of the public and private spheres, obliterating the distinction between contemplating "the good" and exercising it. Accountability to (in Duncan's words) "one's own life story" requires simultaneous public and private recognitions that may not contribute to a narrative or historical whole. Central to the novel's "operation of design" is the commitment to protagonist as interlocutor, one able to speak the silences between the interlocking stories while unable to articulate the coherence or chronology necessary to either narrative or history. Her ponderous inarticulateness can peacefully void established meanings with little immediate requirement for restorative significance.

*   *   *

> With the major Civil Rights battles televised, the most militant of black leaders photographed for the covers of *Newsweek* and *Time*, and my own sense of having come of age at the most visible of all times for black people in America, it had often seemed to me incredible that my parents and their parents and their parents before them had acted out the drama of their lives with none to observe what they did but themselves. . . . How naïve I was not to suspect that those hidden lives, generations old, were the constant reality of the race and that they would continue – without benefit of TV or newsprint exposure – to be its great strength. I should have known the truth of a popular saying among people in the black movement who chose not to become its stars and instead remained paranoid about interviews and persistently camera shy: "The revolution, when it comes, will not be televised.". . . .
>   And yet, there is a reality deeper than what we see, and the consciousness of a people cannot be photographed. But to some extent, it can be written.
>   – Alice Walker, "Recording the Seasons" (1976b: 227–8)

If, as Benedict Anderson suggests, "the novel and the newspaper . . . provided the technical means for 're-presenting' the *kind* of imagined community that is the nation" (1983: 24–5), then television consolidates the national spectacle of image and narration, dictating a collective and marketable imagination and foreclosing upon memory. The imaginary public of television suffers an immediacy that mimics face-to-face communication and threatens to obliterate the significance of textual forms. The collectivized, particularized imaginary "I" of the television intensifies the sense of immediacy while rendering the "I" nonexistent. Though a mixed media, television subverts its text (whether script, anecdotal reportage, or captions) by the very power of its imagery, projecting a surface that is at once inviting and impenetrable.[18]

The interposition of television as a controlling factor in the construction of national and cultural memory dominates Walker's consideration of the personal and public histories intertwined in

Meridian. Of particular interest is the televisual actualization of the public careers of Martin Luther King, Jr., and John F. Kennedy – in life and death – as they serve as paradigms for the ways in which Americans understood their national narratives and the notion of exemplarity.[19] Metajournalistic in its inquiry, the novel asks serious questions about how participants in history are transfigured through media documentation into spectators of the news that will become the national history. Historical record is the outcome of such a process and therefore remains suspect in Walker's mind, because the images retrieved evoke simplistic and sentimental responses to ever-shifting, ponderous questions for individuals, communities, and nations.

Well before television further corrupted the relationship between event and visual perception, Walter Benjamin reflected upon the revolutionary functions of film in "The Work of Art in the Age of Mechanical Reproduction": "Evidently a different nature opens itself to the camera than opens to the naked eye – if only because an unconsciously penetrated space is substituted for a space consciously explored by man. . . . The camera introduces us to unconscious optics as does psychoanalysis to unconscious impulses" (1936b: 236–7). The camera radically alters the thinking and perception of the "world of the unarmed eye" (1936b: 223). Voyeuristic and teasingly unconscious, televisual representation of the world blurs the distinction between presence and absence, and in doing so intensifies the "split" between viewer and participant.

Meridian is grounded in a series of meditations on the relationship among the mass media as generational arbiters of celebrity ("black leaders photographed for the covers of *Newsweek* and *Time*") and false historical accounts. Walker, willing at the end of *The Color Purple* to call herself "author and medium," is attentive to the limitations of corporate mediation. Print journalism's whole-page design[20] seems a textual analogue to her quilt aesthetic, accounting in part for the ways in which she preserves the disjunction among the episodes or "pieces" of her history. Not only has she resolutely abandoned chronological order, but she has advanced a network of stories that dictate alternative coherences or reject the notion of unity altogether. Only by displacing the media spectacle of news and history could Walker locate the authentic, experiential core of the lived and living historical text.[21] The epigraph from Black Elk bespeaks the consequences of such disjunctions between experience and historical record.

In a two-page untitled "chapter" abutting Anne-Marion's nationalist challenge – "Will you kill for the Revolution?" – Walker reflects
upon the linguistic and graphic, quiltlike intertexts of the news and
its embedded narratives. The stark typography that opens this chapter subverts journalistic conventions of headlines, as the names swim
in a broken field of unconsummated, nonlinear historical narratives
where plots suggestively align and recombine but fail to lead into
their expected stories:

MEDGAR EVERS/JOHN F. KENNEDY/MALCOLM X/MARTIN LUTHER
KING/ROBERT KENNEDY/CHE GUEVARA/PATRICE LAMUMBA/
GEORGE JACKSON/CYNTHIA WESLEY/ADDIE MAE COLLINS/DENISE
MCNAIR/CAROLE ROBERTSON/VIOLA LIUZZO (21)

This telegraphic necrology rejects chronology or context, shuffling
the martyrs into an unfamiliar and therefore uncomfortable arrangement. Though stripped of historical narrative, the names, singly and
collectively, carry individual as well as interlocking stories.

An emphatic double space further isolates the italicized block
quote following the martyr display. An extranarratorial voice deliberates, enlarging the context and setting of the Movement. The names
of the martyrs spawn a grander historical reading in which a random
continuity supplants the expected historical order:

*It was a decade marked by death. Violent and inevitable. Funerals became
engraved on the brain, intensifying the ephemeral nature of life.* (21)

The conjunction of "violent" and "inevitable" recalls Black Elk's cryptic pronouncement that "something else died there in the bloody
mud" (x), reinscribing American history as a cycle of catastrophic
inevitabilities. The cascading names become an invention of headline declarations, typographic reliquaries storing the sacred and
sealed truths of recent history. The narratives sepulchered in these
names recall *"earlier times, when oak trees sighed over their burdens in the
wind; Spanish moss draggled bloody to the ground; amen corners creaked with
grief"* (21).

The tide of nominal recall relaxes momentarily into a new isolating order imposed when *"television became the repository of memory, and
each onlooker grieved alone"* (21).[22] "[T]he first televised Kennedy
funeral" (21) initiates the nationalization and collectivization of grief,

televisually sealing the narrative of John Kennedy's death (even as it announces the theme of the fallen patriarch) and displacing the memories of the earlier victims. Television's spectacular intervention into this personal and public display produces the sensation of experience and memory, of being-there and having-been-there even as it enforces the sense of isolation upon the viewer. Television converts the national audience into witnesses and analysts because of filmed behavior's precision and isolation.[23] "Meridian's face, grayish-blue from the television light" (22), projects not simply the adequate though somewhat unexplainable grief of the moment but also recalls that other 1963 marker, "when Medgar Evers was assassinated" (22).

Although televisual subversion of historical, text-based narratives introduces the "split" between record and occasion, it is by no means the only corrupting agent. Accounts, linguistic and imagistic, consume much of the text. Meridian (who often seems both destination and incarnation) – "He had gone to Meridian three years after he married Lynne" [137]) – becomes a transient locus of the Movement as she instigates clarification of every abstraction and account. The teasingly unattainable trappings of the white world circulate throughout Truman's reconsideration of their relationship. Not only was Lynne white, but "she had read everything" (138). Reading itself becomes suspect cultural baggage, a freighted signifier. Lynne's commitment to evident abstractions – "freedom" and "justice" – seems indigenous to her possession of the enslaving print record. Meridian becomes a lyrical counterpoint in her "relative inarticulateness" as her presence suggests an alternative, unwritten script, a future history: "no matter what she was saying to you, and no matter what you were saying to her, [Meridian] seemed to be thinking of something else, another conversation perhaps, an earlier one, that continued on a parallel track" (139). Meridian's revolution subverts the print and televisual media, refusing to succumb to any form of framed narrative.

Truman's counterhistory is one invested in the symbology of racial and class distinctions and committed to a patriarch. The Movement blurs many of the interior dialogues framing his notions of intellectual and social elites. Only Meridian can rhetorically draw forth Truman's insecurities and the longing that attaches itself to Lynne as wife, wife as white. Curiously personal history and attachment become central to Truman's definition of intellect, and perception centers on his ongoing relationship with white women. To Meridian's biting and hurtful challenge – "But what do you *see* in them?" – he could but reply "in a way designed to make her despise the confines of her own provincial mind: 'They read *The New York Times*'"(141).[24] Truman, who "loved all the foreign cultures of the world . . . [and] believed that anything said in French sounded better" (95), succumbed early to his self-loathing adoption of his cultural "other." And it is that attitude, captured by the *New York Times*, that Meridian hopes to counter. Imitative in the extreme, Truman cannot reach the level of artistic autonomy essential to true creation; he is left to respond to the Bicentennial with his ordinary sculpture of Crispus Attucks. Their intended dispute over sexual and racial politics recedes in the face of a larger, unelaborated gesture of received history and borrowed aesthetics, the very notion of artistic commission.

It is the self-mythologizing, historiographic display of the front page of the *Times* ("All the news that's fit to print") and its "imagined community" that Meridian voids. Truman's obeisance toward the *Times* suggests the level of his uncritical and, indeed, learned regard for the official record of power and of note. Prisoner of the establishment in both his affections and disaffections, Truman becomes the ideal target for Meridian's reconsideration of events, historical record, and commemorative art. Corporate aesthetics, news, history, and education have manipulated his coming of age. Every break with the status quo came preapproved by the orchestrating recorders of events and collective memories. Meridian, though removed from their circle, remains troubled by Truman and Lynne, who represent immediate victims of the manipulation of politics, youth, and art.

The closing "Ending" dispenses with a range of potential recorders and records of the Movement. Personal recollections, vituperative correspondence, displacing newsreels, and newspapers in turn suffer from an individual as well as collective inability to sustain the oral narrative thread of living history, oral testimony. Each in its own way offers to conceal, distort, and preserve life in the historical frame of a static past. If *Meridian* seeks closure to matters personal and historical, it does so in a patterned alleviation of strictures imposed by various forms of media – including fiction.

"Free at Last: A Day in April, 1968," the closing two-page compression of martyrdom and narrative dissolve of the Movement itself, carries an especial burden as it summarizes and equalizes Meridian's witnessing and survivorhood.[25] No longer transfixed by the grayish-blue of the television screen, Meridian participates in Atlanta's alternative display of grief and resignation, beyond the frame. She moves within and without the spectacle of Dr. King's funeral, as tangential and parallel enactments perform within a silenced and silent sphere extraneous to the scripted media display of presidential aspirations and orchestrated sorrow.

The funeral occasions a recuperative display of unbroken, local histories and genealogies, as "nearby families" tell "their children stories about the old days before black people marched, before black people voted, before they could allow their anger or even exhaustion to show" (189). Cultures intertwine as sustaining oral histories point the paths to memories: "myths of strong women and men, Indian and black, who knew the secret places of the land and refused to be pried from them" (189). Such events cannot be recorded on film or in the pages of newspapers or history books; they are sounded simply among survivors, witnesses of history anchored in life not death. Even as the folk press forward, "with their tired necks extended, to see, just for a moment, just for a glimpse, the filled coffin" (189), they recede into their own state of perpetual remembrance for those who have passed on.

Unlike the innocence of the first Kennedy funeral, this telecast bristles with the collective competence of broadcasters and citizens too aware of the media-dictated conventions and their appointed roles: the congestion as "the senators running for President . . . and the horde of clergy in their outdone rage . . . and the movie stars glided . . . as the pitiable crowd of nobodies . . . hungered to be nearer" (190). State funerals have become part of the apparatus of national campaigns in this election year. The competing public and private lives, with the need to be seen countering the need to see, form the ebb and flow of the ritual. Jostling bodies search for their appointed roles in the historical performance, the genuine mourners are eclipsed by the telegenic and famous. And yet, as the funeral procession moves from the televised recesses of the church into the unframable clutter of the streets, it walks to a local and ancient cadence quite alien to the visiting tongues:

> Later, following the casket on its mule-drawn cart, they began to sing a song the dead man had loved. "I come to the gar-den *a-lone.* . . . While the dew is still on the *ro*-ses. . . . " Such an old

> favorite! And neutral. The dignitaries who had not already slipped
> away – and now cursed the four-mile walk behind the great dead
> man – opened their mouths eagerly in genial mime. (190)

Such slippage serves Walker well throughout *Meridian* as she exceeds
the parameters of the camera's framing eye and its duplicitously suspect historical narrative.[26]

This enactment of simultaneous and parallel historical constructions offers Meridian the opportunity denied her when she was frozen
in the flickering glare of television's broadcast of the first Kennedy
funeral. Present in Atlanta, she substitutes an alternative trajectory for
the equally, and in some ways increasingly perfected, mediatized event
of King's funeral, and in doing so, she offers a stubborn critique of
more than television as a repository of history. Walker, however, complicates this community gesture by freighting "the filled coffin" with
more than the martyred King: She stores the Movement itself.

The street scene, which promised Meridian the intimacy and community that had been denied her by the isolating commercialization
of *national* civil rights events, collapses inevitably into a carnivalesque
display (one that anticipates the novel's opening scene, chronologically, while recalling it episodically): "Ahead of Meridian a man
paraded a small white poodle on a leash. The man was black, and a
smiler. As he looked about him a tooth encased in patterned gold
sparkled in his mouth. On the dog's back a purple placard with white
lettering proclaimed 'I have a dream'" (190).[27] What may have started as genuine commemoration turns sour, exploitative, and cruelly
comic in the expanded context of the event. Like the "genial mime"
of the famous visitors, this notation seems but another signifier without signification, a trace of an already dead movement. The disjunction between the closed televisual narrative and its actual
complement hastens the decontextualization of the Movement itself.

Historical past and committed future succumb to an ahistorical
abidance in which sociolect and context are perpetually at odds. The
dog with the purple placard reorients Meridian so that she witnesses
the relinquishment of the people's grasp of a history of public utterance and a relieved acceptance of the inconsequence of their lives:

> Then she noticed it: As they walked, people began to engage
> each other in loud, even ringing, conversation. They inquired about
> each other's jobs. They asked after members of each other's fami-

lies. They conversed about the weather. And everywhere the call for
Coca-Colas, for food, rang out. Popcorn appeared, and along their
route hot-dog stands sprouted their broad, multi-colored umbrel-
las. The sun came from behind the clouds, and the mourners
removed their coats and loosened girdles and ties. Those who had
never known it anyway dropped the favorite song, and there was a
feeling of relief in the air, of liberation, that was repulsive. (190)

Leaderlessness prompts the unconscious loosening of physical constraints that symbolize the abandonment of moral imperatives.
Relapse into an irony of contentment seems imminent; aspiration has
vanished.

Caught between her leaderless people and the shade of the fallen
leader himself, Meridian seeks a projection of leadership, community,
and history that will sustain her story in the absence of a contextualizing narrative. Significance may be found only in the repression or
voiding of the corrupt enactments. She awaits a time when King will
imperceptibly slip from martyr to man and his death and life be
accorded narrative, historical, and fictional truth. Until then, the historical formulation of narrative and significance haunts Meridian:

> "Meridian," Truman said. "Do you realize no one is thinking
> about these things any more? Revolution was the theme of the six-
> ties: Medgar, Malcolm, Martin, George, Angela Davis, the Panthers,
> people blowing up buildings and each other. But that is all gone
> now. I am, myself, making a statue of Crispus Attucks for the Bicen-
> tennial. We're here to stay: the black and the poor, the Indian, and
> now all those illegal immigrants from the West Indies who adore
> America just the way it is."
> "Then you think revolution, like everything else in America, was
> reduced to a fad?" (192–3)

Truman's Bicentennial project, like King's funeral, becomes little
more than a confused enactment of honest and corrupt history, both
spawned by martyrdom and claiming a sincere hold on the national
historical imagination. Thematized and aestheticized to the point of
being simply a "fad," revolution (whether in 1776 or 1976) becomes
little more than a developmental stage, lost in acuity and sense in the
recall of mature entropy. Truman's recounting devitalizes the names
(this time race-specific) and events as it shuttles familiar mythological
and historical threads into a meaningless weave.

In "Travels," Walker reduces the journalistic tedium to startling utility, thereby providing the final symbolic revision of the news. The episode, both timeless and chronologically determined by the voter registration movement, attempts little or no linkage surrounding installments; it works steadfastly and simply to crystallize Meridian's fundamental withdrawal into momentary local gestures for her people. Singled out by a child as "that woman in the cap" (207), Meridian participates in a reconstitution of the news:

> The wooden steps were broken and the porch sagged. In the front room a thin young man worked silently in a corner. In front of him was a giant pile of newspapers that looked as though they'd been salvaged from the hands of the children who ate dinner over the funnies. Meridian and Truman watched the man carefully smooth out the paper, gather ten sheets, then twenty, and roll them into a log around which he placed a red rubber band. When he finished the"log" he stacked it, like a piece of wood, on top of the long pile of such "logs" that ran across one side of the poorly furnished, rather damp and smelly room. (207)

Much of the novel's closing debate circulates around these slick news discards. The print record and its accounts mean little but potential fuel and income to this struggling man and his dying wife. Because the record must be reconstructed to accommodate the nuance and individuality of news and history, Meridian, in a poignant reconception of the printing process itself, begins by "slowly pressing the papers flat, then rolling them into logs" (209). The abandonment of the press enables an alternative mode of expression and entitlement in which Meridian justifies the voter registration movement. The vote "may be useless. Or maybe it can be the beginning of the use of your voice" (210).

The political extension of voice, voting, seems incidental to Meridian's qualified admonition: to use a local and transient means of expressive participation. Meridian, so often described as "inarticulate," has advanced the cause of originality and purpose in one's own voice. If the revolution will be neither televised nor printed in the daily news, it may nonetheless survive in immediate expressions of will and conviction, leading to a reconstruction of history and genealogy that will inform *The Color Purple*. Imperative to the seeding of this new historical field is the "voiding" or "repressing" of "established meanings."

*   *   *

> Dying for one's country, which usually one does not choose,
> assumes a moral grandeur which dying for the Labour Party,
> the American Medical Association, or perhaps even Amnesty
> International can not rival, for these are all bodies one can
> join or leave at easy will. Dying for the revolution also draws
> its grandeur from the degree to which it is felt to be some-
> thing fundamentally pure.
>
>   – Benedict Anderson (1983: 144)

If there is an authentic subnarrative to this novel that rejects narrativity and closure, it concerns the sequential conceptual advance from
an integrated civil rights movement to black nationalism. The cultural and political revolution of the 1960s resulted in a racial and national formation that was historical, performative, derivative, and
patriarchal. Black Power as a slogan, a strategy, a manifesto, and a
rhetoric fused into what Amiri Baraka declared, in "The Legacy of
Malcolm X, and the Coming of the Black Nation," to be "a form of a
process: movement seen" (1965: 166). Unlike the century's earlier
black nationalisms, Black Power projected an immediate, televisual
posture, indifferent to justification or definition by what Baraka called
"white magic" (1965: 167).[28] As Baraka proclaimed, in "The Need for
a Cultural Base to Civil Rites & Bpower Mooments": "There are wars
going on now to stop black power, whether in Sinai, Vietnam, Angola,
or Newark, New Jersey. The difference is that in Newark, New Jersey,
many colored people do not even *know* they are in this war (tho they
might realize, on whatever level of consciousness, that they are losing)" (1967: 121). Baraka saw the revolution as advancing from "civil-
righter" to "nationalism, nationalization" (1967: 119–20). The
revolution was planned as the nation was imagined.[29]

     Throughout *Meridian*, Walker deliberates upon the tactical and
socioethical consequences of nationalism, allowing it to permeate
and bind the denarratized whole. Anne-Marion's decade-old challenge – "Will you kill for the Revolution?" (14) – provides the novel's
first flashback to that time when the Movement was subsumed by the
Revolution. In its earliest formulation, the question, never rhetorical, forces Meridian to extend the logic of Camus's resigned opinion that "Rational murder runs the risk of finding itself justified by
history" (286). And yet the historical compromise to her seems aesthetic and ethical in nature, one that profoundly influences cultural
inheritance:

> Meridian alone was holding on to something the others had let go. If not completely, then partially – by their words today, their deeds tomorrow. But what none of them seemed to understand was that she felt herself to be, not holding on to something from the past, but *held* by something in the past: by the memory of old black men in the South who, caught by surprise in the eye of a camera, never shifted their position but looked directly back. . . . If they committed murder – and to her even revolutionary murder was murder – *what would the music be like?*
>
> (14–15)

Words and deeds anchored in the past exemplify for Meridian the sense of justice and history. By 1976, the decade's interposition of feminist consciousness-raising and antiwar activities intensifies Walker's commitment to alternative renderings of nationalism and race consciousness, martyrdom and revolution. Christianity confronts mysticism in this struggle to retain the notion of exemplarity and survival. Walker identifies Meridian's need "to flee" as a representation of "her struggle to break with Christianity because Christianity really insists on martyrdom" (Tate 1983: 180).

Although Walker will work her way through to an enlarged sense of Pan-Africanism in *The Color Purple*, she stalls in this midpoint reflection upon substitute national narratives – whether of imagined communities or revolution.[30] Meridian embodies an oppositional force to counter those who, like Ron Karenga, declare: "You can't fight a revolution on a local level. It has to be fought through a national struggle" (1968: 167). Veteran of a protracted and rupturing national struggle, she nonetheless settles into a routine of local engagement, sporadic in nature but preserving the aura of the Movement. In an aestheticization of political activism, Walker turns Meridian's path of resistance into a performative display in which statements sustain life, avoiding degradation into artifact. She achieves what Baraka might term an African subversion of the Euro-American obsession with artifactual treasures.[31] Walker, committed to the process of the Movement and its present-tense history, reaches for an alternative mode of political engagement: one that insists upon the formation and definition of a racialized national narrative.

Walker subverts what she believes to be the inherited script of the dominant black nationalist narrative with an indeterminate script. Suspicious of the narrative whole presented by the mass media, and uncomfortable with narrative's need to cohere,[32] she shuffles Meridian's life into a disjunct field of experience and activity. In what may be seen as one of the more revolutionary Bicentennial gestures, Walker creates a protagonist who embodies the Declaration of Independence: one committed to people not nations, life not death.

In many ways, *Meridian* may be seen as a deliberate disruption of all sequential, successive narratives. Black nationalism in this reading is but another patriarchal myth that falsifies relationships, historical and otherwise, and therefore must be replaced. Its rhetoric permeates the text, generating narrative from brute facts unshared by the protagonist. The administered culture forms an antagonistic narrative community, one that must be questioned and countered by Meridian throughout the text. Nationalisms, of whatever construction, run counter to her intuited, epistemological striving.

Nationalism's ontological deficit resides in what Meridian perceives of as its anachronistic grounding of its argument in patriarchal structures and murder. Black nationalism's ultimately imitative structure concedes creative force to the dominant culture, thereby failing to establish inventive oppositional expectations. Though Walker's longer narrative of a potentially creative and restorative nationalism exceeds the boundaries of *Meridian*, it nonetheless grounds its argument there. The hybridity of the text belies the authority with which Meridian mediates, historically and ideologically, between the Movement and the Revolution. Her unique redemptive status resides in her ability to reconcile the tensions between her self-deconstructing narrative and the consuming subnarrative of black nationalism.

Although nationalism, itself often the result of revolutionary rhetoric, provides a vital counterdiscourse in almost every chapter, it is distilled as Meridian's reformative vision in "Camara." Following the rhetorical exercise of "Questions," in which Truman and Meridian debate the vitality of the very concept of "revolution," this station (positioned "sometime after the spring of '68" [197]) proceeds with sermonic audacity to devolve a progressive rhetoric and ideology for Meridian and her future constituencies. Neither nostalgic nor reactionary, "Camara" commemorates the history and memory of the present, thereby initiating the "return" celebrated in the opening chapter.

The experience seems at first a total immersion in all that Meridian has left behind, discarded, rejected. The details are familiar from earlier descriptions, but here are realigned to resonate with the cumulative power of the text. The timing is indeterminate, with only King's murder as a relative marker of this return to church and its enactments of community and history: "She sensed herself an outsider, as a single eye behind a camera that was aimed from a corner of her youth, attached now only because she watched. If she were not there watching, the scene would be exactly the same, the 'picture' itself never noticing that the camera was missing" (197). The service revisits all that has come before, representing the perpetual community at once obscured and dismissed in televised and textual accounting. Meridian registers this ceremonial depiction as a culturally defined defiance, a preliterate ritual lodged in the timeless and parallel musical culture of black America: "she could not remember the words; they seemed stuck in some pinched-over groove in her memory" (198).

The service is at once antiphonal and univocal, as it shifts from the voice of the father of "a slain martyr in the Civil Rights struggle" (198) to that of the "minister – in his thirties, dressed in a neat black suit and striped tie of an earlier fashion – [who] spoke in a voice so dramatically like that of Martin Luther King's that at first Meridian thought his intention was to dupe or to mock" (199). Obscuring the borders of devotion and politics, this imitative reconfiguration defamiliarizes both survivor and minister, transforming each into an extension of a cultural continuum independent of historical particularities. The preacher becomes but one of "the voice of millions who could no longer speak" (200).

The narrative of the grieving father, "thankful to be alive and to be, for the most part, healthy, and holding together as a community and as families" (198–9), encapsulates Meridian's own struggles of loss and gain – "of bullets, of bombs, of revolution" (201). History and memory enmesh on this anniversary – voicing words "from a throat that seemed stoppered with anxiety, memory, grief, and dope" (202) – recasting Meridian's earlier contemplation of martyrs, murders, and abortions. The immediacy of this survivor's grief anchors her immersion in the aesthetic tangents of music and iconography.

The inarticulate music assuages, as does its aesthetic counterpart: the stained-glass window, "B.B., With Sword," done by one of the church's young artists (203). Meridian recalls her childhood pleasure in stained-glass transformations, but is astonished by this revolutionary projection of an ancient form: "a tall, broad-shouldered black man . . . [with] a guitar . . . and . . . a long shiny object the end of which was dripping with blood" (202–3). The window, when read against the text of the service, reflects the aesthetic, devotional, and political strands of Meridian's quest.

The ceremony becomes a witnessing of the incursion of cultural memory on a subject's grief, which in turn liberates a locating force of common or shared history. The father's grief, conjoined with Meridian's worn despair, enacts an intertextual display of this communal ritual. At last Meridian reasons a cultural imperative to the ceremony as she imagines the congregation's accounting to the father:

> "Look," they were saying, "we are slow to awaken to the notion that we are only as other women and men, and even slower to move in anger, but we are gathering ourselves to fight for and protect what your son fought for on behalf of us. If you will let us weave your story and your son's life and death into what we already know – into the songs, the sermons, the 'brother and sister' – we will soon be so angry we cannot help but move." (204)

The chastening exemplarity of the congregation's "communal spirit, togetherness, righteous convergence" (204) identifies for Meridian a singular and revolutionary aspect of African-American life: "existence extended beyond herself to those around her because, in fact, the years in America had created them One Life" (204). Resolutely freed from the rhetoric of nationalism and revolution in this "church surrounded by the righteous guardians of the people's memories," Meridian admits "the concept of retaliatory murder" into her purview (205). Though even justified murder remains problematic, she succeeds in locating its authority while denying its rhetorical power.[33]

Such competence enables Meridian to forestall future revolutionary promises in favor of cultural performances that are at once devotional and political. She becomes a mediating intertext between the Movement and the Revolution, arrested in momentary relation to her community and its needs. Released from the amnesia of cultural and historical disjunction, Meridian may now articulate her way:

> It was this, Meridian thought, I have not wanted to face, this that has caused me to suffer: I am not to belong to the future. I am to be left, listening to the old music, beside the highway . . . when [the revolutionaries] find their throats too choked with the smell of murdered flesh to sing, I will come forward and sing from memory

songs they will need once more to hear. For it is the song of the people, transformed by the experience of each generation, that holds them together, and if any part of it is lost the people suffer and are without soul. (205–6)

The cooperative agency of history, memory, and culture embedded in the church's devotional practices displaces the inherited, patriarchal script of black nationalism with its deliberative response to a longer cultural narrative.

Meridian's public and private indeterminancy yields a narrative in which neither kin (Camara) nor photojournalism (camera) can successfully mediate the tensions between the self and the historical. Consequently she refuses the interlocutory role of medium (one that Walker herself will assume in *The Color Purple*), becoming instead a moment of actualization. Her cap, once a sentimental signifier in a text that resisted synecdochic potential, now signifies the release from the "conflict in her own soul which she had imposed on herself – and lived through" (228). Habitually a character within a subversive narrative, she turns solitary in the interstitial space within the public and private spheres. Comfortable in this detached state that so troubles Truman, she comforts him: "'But that is my value,' said Meridian. 'Besides, all the people who are as alone as I am will one day gather at the river. We will watch the evening sun go down. And in darkness maybe we will know the truth'" (227). Meridian's progressive and final abandonment of enduring genealogical and social kinship possibilities – family, school, the Movement – registers the historical (and generational) failure of the novel's alternative mythic constructs – the Wild Child, Sojourner, Indians and Ecstasy, motherhood, nationalism. The collapse of exemplary states, whether personal or national, releases Meridian from the immediacy and corruption of a mediated public sphere into an originary consciousness, off the grid, unaccounted for by clock, calendar, or map. Projective and nostalgic in her (resign)nation, she "will come forward and sing from memory . . . the song of the people" (205) – becoming the epistolary consciousness of *The Color Purple*.

8

HISTORY AS STORYTELLING

JAY WRIGHT'S SOOTHSAYERS AND OMENS

The soothsayers who found out from time what it had in store
certainly did not experience time as either homogeneous or
empty. Anyone who keeps this in mind will perhaps get an
idea of how past times were experienced in remembrance – namely, in just the same way.
    – Walter Benjamin, "Theses on the Philosophy of History"
        (1940: 264)

What is happening in the world more and more is that people are attempting to decolonize their spirits. A crucial act of
empowerment, one that might return reverence to the Earth,
thereby saving it, in this fearful-of-Nature, spiritually colonized
age.
        – Alice Walker, "Clear Seeing Inherited Religion and
            Reclaiming the Pagan Self" (1997: 54)

> Young poets sit in their rooms
> like perverted Penelopes,
> unraveling everything,
> kicking the threads
> into the wind . . .
> – Jay Wright, "Death as History" (1967: n.p.)

In 1976, during the national enactments of the Bicentennial, Jay
Wright published *Dimensions of History* (Corinth) and *Soothsayers and
Omens* (Seven Woods Press), two independent sequences of poems
dealing with the cultural and aesthetic imperative to construct an
enlarged historical path into the cultural geographies of the diaspo-

ra. Like Ezra Pound's *Cantos*, these collections are more than poems "containing history"; they are active attempts to reconstruct the very method and modes of the aestheticized historical, the energized field of narrative threads: storytelling and national (de)construction.[1] For Wright, national*isms* serve as oppositional sponsors of an emerging aesthetic of history. Such efforts require more than the invention or discovery of new historical certainties: They necessitate the deconstruction of received history itself. And what better time than the Bicentennial to investigate the problematic boundaries of nationality and modernity and reason in this historically suspect construction: the United States of America.

Wright's poetry, seeking "imaginative dissolution and reconstruction of its material" (Rowell 1983: 4), responds not simply to the miscarried extensions of Enlightenment dicta, historical revolutionary manifestos, and received national identity; it seeks to escape the oppression of reason and national coherence embedded in even more recent countercultural stirrings such as black nationalism.[2] Recalling Frederick Douglass's determination to authenticate the Centennial celebration through an honest appraisal of the promise and fulfillment of life in America, Wright's aestheticized history moves to supplant the temporal, inherited, and brittle constellation of the Founding Fathers with a centering Pan-African patriarchy[3] curiously akin in impulse to Alice Walker's decentering, womanist rift with mediated history in her Bicentennial novel, *Meridian*. Wright, as if responding to Pound's lament that "*le personnel manqué . . .* we have not men for our times" ("Canto 62"), invents a postnational[4] narrative in which his "founding fathers" actually dissolve national corridors, boundaries, and chronology to construct an ephemeral, transactional tale.

Like the Centennial, which followed and apotheosized the Civil War, the Bicentennial was a postwar, mercantile ode to *Pro*gress as well as a subtextual charge to pro*gress* through national cohesion and ambitions.[5] Such epochal celebrations are anathema to Wright, who believes that their sole function is the sheer obliteration of the living consciousness of historical and cultural trace memories. The Bicentennial was an enactment of what Homi Bhabha, in "DissemiNation," defines as "the construction of a discourse on society that *performs* the problem of totalizing the people and unifying the national will" (1994: 160–1) Bhabha further remarks that "this breakdown in the identity of the will is another instance of the supplementary narrative of nationness that 'adds to' without 'adding up'" (1994: 160–1). Inadequate constructions of history serve no one, least of all a poet who seeks authentic and vital commemorative linguistic structures.

Although his aesthetic deliberations are born out of Vietnam-era cynicism and Bicentennial tawdriness, Wright owes much of his anti-historicism to the broader historical tide of the twentieth century.[6] No writer has better captured the elegiac note of humanity's loss of history and the leisure of historical time sounded by Walter Benjamin in his 1936 disquisition on narrative, history, community, and solitude, "Der Erzähler" ("The Storyteller"). Written in the late 1920s, it laments an aesthetic and *historical* concern: "the art of telling stories is coming to an end" (1936a: 83). And with that simple assertion Benjamin displaces the very meanings of "story," "experience," and "history." The essay enacts repeatedly that which began with the First World War:

> a process began to become apparent which has not halted since then. Was it not noticeable at the end of the war that men returned from the battlefield grown silent – not richer, but poorer in communicable experience? . . . A generation that had gone to school on a horse-drawn streetcar now stood under the open sky in a countryside in which nothing remained unchanged but the clouds, and beneath these clouds, in a field of force of destructive torrents and explosions, was the tiny, fragile human body. (1936a: 84)

Unwilling to fetishize the emblematic ruins of the past and unable to presume attachment to the received history of Pound and Eliot, Wright, adapting and extending the tradition of Emerson, makes a commitment to what Wallace Stevens called, in "Notes toward a Supreme Fiction," "this invention, this invented world" (1942: 380). Stevens's "major man," an example of the exemplary figure thought to be essential to historical constructions, will undergo a startling subordination as Wright creates a decentered, counterdiscourse to a national epic. Stridently postnational and aggressively transnational, he posits a new (w)hole: a poetic of history that attempts utter effacement of a mediating force, either in the person of the poet or in the presence of the text. History, stripped of its numbing informational qualities, demographic insistence, and subservience to pastness and nationalisms, will thrive in the fluid immediacy of a story being told.

189

"Mean egotism" will vanish, as Emerson's and Whitman's poet-priests are effaced by an experiential elder, the patriarch-storyteller, who fades into the story being told.

Suggestive of what Bhabha identifies as the "postcolonial passage through modernity . . . in [which] the past [is] projective" (1994: 253), this chronotropic aesthetic underwrites the historiographical intent of *Soothsayers and Omens*. In this collection, Wright will extend Benjamin's insight that stories represent more than the possibility for experience; they are human history. The figure of the storyteller, which assumes constellatory outline in the opening section of Benjamin's essay, will authorize the potential grandeur and spectacular remove of Wright's poetic of history.

Soothsayers and Omens, a poetic sequence that attempts to provide an opening into discontinuous and simultaneous history, rejects received national and linguistic structures in a lyric alternative to the epic. In its sly echo of Wallace Stevens's "The Comedian as the Letter C" (1923/31),[7] *Soothsayers and Omens* circumscribes a field of poetic resonance that is at once canonical, and therefore recognizable, and foreign. A worldly "pleasure of merely circulating" invests the sequence with a simultaneous familiarity and strangeness (see Stevens 1923/31: 149–50). Poems self-reflexively call to mind Eliot, Pound, Stevens, Crane, and Hayden even as they thwart such patterned allusions with echoes of anthropologically summoned texts. Wright enacts Stevens's "Tea at the Palaz of Hoon," creating the very "compass" of these new landscapes in which readers find themselves "more truly and more strange."

Unlike Pound, who trod the accepted path of westerners seeking perceptual extensions through the art and religion of the Orient, Wright investigates the transatlantic prophetic realms of the Western Hemisphere and Africa to emphasize the crux of westernization as well as its expansiveness. Pound's contributions to the aestheticization of history originate in his ability to fracture and assemble the received European historical script. Wright's appropriation of the earlier modernist historical script yields a decentered inversion of European literatures and inscribes a startling dependence upon African and Western Hemispheric literary artifacts. Revoking Pound's summary of the Enlightenment – "rights / diffusing knowledge of principles / maintaining justice, in registering of peace / changed with the times" ("Canto 63") – Wright advances beyond the formal historical landscape to a local, associative geography that relies upon the routine, not the spectacular, for effect. As if to answer Pound's Revolutionary capsule of national assemblage and cooperative cohesion – "not a Virginian / but an American Patrick Henry" ("Canto 65") – he asks "not an American but . . . ?"[8] And in sounding this cultural ambiguity Wright thwarts the nationalist ends of continuous narrative with the possibilities inherent in the open silences of a discontinuous narrative.

A historically informed poetic, retrieved from the stagnation of chronology and fact associated with history and news, necessitated an enlarged aesthetic, one that would embrace the sense of storytelling that Walter Benjamin had associated with "the ability to exchange experiences" (1936a: 83) in the "realm of living speech" (1936a: 87). Benjamin's "The Storyteller" asserts that the evolution of the novel and "information" in modern society are the primary means by which the life of experience, culture, and history is nullified in favor of a stable and isolating product. Recalling Thoreau's hostile ambivalence toward the invention of the telegraph, Benjamin deplores the subversion of narrative by news: "Every morning brings us the news of the globe, and yet we are poor in noteworthy stories. This is because no event any longer comes to us without already being shot through with explanation" (1936a: 89). Such "information," anticipating the mediated and isolating depletion of television news, surrenders to its immediate, mediated context and dies into history. The spiritual and aesthetic lapses in such constructions were rooted, Benjamin thought, in the difference between "the writer of history, the historian, and the teller of it, the chronicler" (1936a: 95). And it is in this conjoined spirit of orality and textuality in the "act of the poem" (Rowell 1983: 4) that Wright locates his progressively unmediated, historically charged aesthetic. Explanation, if it is to come at all, comes through the grander, suggestive history of the shared experience of a poetry (curiously reminiscent of Stevens's) "in the service of a new and capable personality at home and in the transformative and transformed world" (Rowell 1983: 9).

The four-part, architectonic structure of *Soothsayers and Omens* is at once a reconstruction and a resituation of the romantic poet in the landscape. Wright frustrates a pattern of mere imitation by shuttling between the Emersonian and the transcendental conjurers of many cultural traces. Three sequences detail a grounding and departure, historically and socially, before fulfilling their aesthetic and cultural promise in a concluding, bold-titled excursion into simultaneous discontinuity, "Second Conversations with Ogotemmêli."

The untitled opening sequence progresses from a declamatory initiation of birth and its attendant installation of an alternative patriarchy, through a sequence of mythological potential and shifting chronologies (indebted to Hart Crane), and ends with paired portraits of the exemplary and historical. Poetry inverts history into "a livable assertion" (1976b: 11), insisting upon what Wright calls "spiritual resonance" (Rowell 1983: 4).

"The Charge" initiates Wright's subversion of the chronological in history by means of its ritual-centered, rigidly present-tense installation of patriarch and storyteller. The earlier, foreboding structure of "death as history" yields to its cultural inverse, "history as birth," a dying into a new narrative sequence and coherence: "This is the morning. / There is a boy, / riding the shadow of a cradle, / clapping from room to room / as swift as the memory of him" (11). The faint disjunction between the present-tense, gestural insistence of these opening lines – "This is," "There is" – establishes the sequence's attitude toward temporal and spatial ideas of order. Like Benjamin's soothsayers, Wright's personae will not "experience time as either homogeneous or empty." Through the confluence of memory, history, preexistence, and death, "The Charge" begins the work of the sequence: the denial of death as history.

Suffused with a Blakean and Emersonian insistence of "infant sight," the five-part sequence dis*places* English lyrical conventions into a startling and strange reconfiguration. From Vaughan and Milton to Whitman and Thoreau, Wright culls a lexicon that denies the conventional distinctions of life and death. Whitman's "Out of the Cradle" and Vaughan's "world of light" shrug off their shrouds and don the unexpected raiment of life:

> Now,
> I hear you whistle through the house,
> pushing wheels, igniting fires,
> leaving no sound untried,
> no room in which a young boy,
> at sea in a phantom cradle,

> could lurch and scream
> and come and settle in the house.
> You are so volubly alone,
> that I turn,
> reaching into the light for the boy
> your father charged you to deliver.
>
> (11)

The denial of presence and time, reference and sequential continuities, persists throughout the poem. Generational superiority fades into a Wordsworthian simultaneity at the transitional moment of the birth of a child who resembles Moses in his circumstance and presence: "where the women will hold the boy, / plucked from the weeds, / a manchild, discovered" (12). Pronouns, in their seemingly logical array, realign into suspect, logic-thwarting reference, until the "I"s and "we"s and "you"s forge a collective and cross-referential community of ill-determined genealogy. Even what appears to be the familiar punning of "sun" and "son" – "where the sun forever enters this circle. / Fathers and sons sit" – fails to assume its conventional duality, as the poem advances toward a binary-resistant, structural integrity that departs from lyric and semantic convention.[9]

Enlarging the realm of circumspection and locution to include the finite and infinite tasks the poet to "prepare a place" of history-nullifying, timeless continuities, "where the sun forever enters this circle" (12). Wright extends Blakean "particulars" to create a "whole" where "All things here move / with that global rhythm" (13). What began as a descent into birth ritual has concluded as a startling revision of a death-defying, liberation narrative: "This is the moment / when all our unwelcome deaths / charge us to be free" (13).

Such an imperative insinuates itself into Wright's originary "Sources."[10] Evocative of Hart Crane's "Voyages" in *White Buildings*, another six-poem excursion into "time and the elements," "Sources" bridges the immediate and individual world of "The Charge" with the exemplary and historical realms of the concluding Benjamin Banneker poems. Wright embarks upon an epical journey of vast interiority as he plumbs the potential depths of historical narrative. The sequence moves beyond that which Crane found "answered in the vortex of our grave" to a moment of communicative display of communion and grace (1926: 36). A nourishing rain replaces Crane's tempestuous sea, instilling a certainty and cycle in the consecrated ground.

Orphean strains mix with alien modalities to stress the complexities of cultural weave and historical moment in these poems. The familiar is rendered strange, as allusions drift into tangential relation with barely perceived scripts and recombine into an apparent whole. "Sources" offers an elemental reweaving of the received and intuited histories. Ecclesiastical proffering sustains and restores – "I lift these texts, / wanting the words / to enter my mind like pure wind" (16) – even as the sequence evokes poems as distant as Stevens's "To the Roaring Wind."

The revolutionary passage from source to moment, ancestor to poet, necessitates both the "life / and death of all our fathers" if history is to assume what James Baldwin called its "literal presence." The reanimated historical moment for Wright is one in which liberated ancestral moments are praised and carried in the living descendants. Such freedom resides in the ability of the living to fetch history from the dead, the "new and capable imagination" that refuses to fossilize the exemplary dead into memorial history. As Eliot explains in "Little Gidding," "This is the use of memory: / For liberation – not less of love but expanding / Of love beyond desire, and so liberation / From the future as well as the past" (1942: 142).

The incipient cosmology of the first section solidifies around the arrested figures of Benjamin Banneker and Thomas Jefferson to form constellations of apparent national coherence and construction – apt characters for deconstructive poetics in the season of Bicentennial celebration.[11] In these paired poems, storytelling becomes the means by which Wright creates poems out of history, not poems of history. Remote, historical substrata establish Baldwin's present-tense notion of history. Prefiguration and historical spectacle constitute an enactment, not a reenactment, of encounter and speculation. An extension of the birth ritual of "The Charge," "Benjamin Banneker Helps to Build a City" and "Benjamin Banneker Sends His 'Almanac' to Thomas Jefferson" invoke historical motifs to impose structure on the flux of the present.

Constellatory, like the figure of a poem, the city enlarges beyond its vision, its design escapes the logic of reason to enter into an aesthetic realm with its own spatial order.[12] Just like this secular side of Saint Augustine's City of God, Banneker's realm is at once celestial and earthly, thematizing the Enlightenment projection of attainable worldly, "heavenly" cities.[13] The creativity doubles as history, "moving as though it knew its end, against death" (22). History succumbs to a world of consuming plans and "prefigurations." To shed the confines of either inspiration, the poet forces an encounter:

> I call you into this time,
> back to that spot,
> and read these prefigurations
> into your mind,
> and know it could not be strange to you
> to stand in the dark and emptiness
> of a city not your vision alone.
>
> (22)

"This time" and "that spot" form the nexus, "that spot / where the vibration starts" (22–3). As a descendent of Pound and Eliot, Wright must search "the texts / and forms of cities that burned, / that decayed, or gave their children away" (22). Histories and offspring yielded or were lost.

The juxtaposition of an alternate mode of perception, an aestheticized history that accommodates the irrational in speech and actions, requires the displacement of the ideational constructs and informational models of culture by the astrological force of the metaphysical and mythological. Reason, chronology, and national identity must retire in the face of an enhanced cultural logic. A superimposition of a simultaneous, sanctifying presence serves to redeem and transport the reason-stranded poet and astronomer:

> Over the earth,
> in an open space,
> you and I step to the time
> of another ceremony.
> These people, changed,
> but still ours,
> shake another myth
> from that egg.
>
> (23)

Such between-ness epitomizes the hybridity of the black Atlantic cultures in which imposed, culture-severing boundaries stranded lives from their mythic structures and historical context.[14] Alternative theologies sustain competing cosmologies and lead to a potential sanctification upon rebaptism: " A city, like a life, / must be made in purity" (23).

Crane's sonorities and Pound's textualities inspired Wright's reconstruction of the historical path by which personage and place are known. Yet Wright's renewing script cannot make use of Pound's syntactical and historical disruptions. A retraction into the "stillness" before genesis – "Image of shelter, image of man, / pulled back into himself, / into the seed before the movement, / into the silence before the sound / of movement, into stillness" (24) – allows for an *inspired* new story, restorative annals. Skirting the allure of myth, that protean antagonist of history, Wright advances into a stylized recapitulation of call-and-response that will allow the documentary presence of Banneker to thrive within an aestheticized frame: "Recall number. / Recall your calculations, / your sight, at night, / into the secrets of stars" (24).

Banneker's epistle to Jefferson, unorchestrated by Wright, serves as the authentic excursion into the rational and purposeful models of history. Unheeded in his time, Banneker slips within the broader compass of prophetic utterance and invocation, challenging the Promethean and Protestant order of this inherited cosmology and spawning the poem's rhetorical challenge to "the movement, / the absence of movement, the prefiguration of movement" in this place (25). The astronomer becomes the very incarnation of the Enlightenment, a transformative cosmology. The authentication of Enlightenment pledges of liberty resides in a historical inversion: "So they must call you, / knowing you are intimate stars; / so they must call you, / knowing different resolutions" (25).

Instead of the modernist clock that drives the collating impulse of Stevens's "souvenirs and prophecies" impelling time into anterior and posterior space, Banneker posts "calculations and forecasts" by which to realign "the small, / imperceptible act, which itself becomes free." Attuned to celestial harmonies and earthly disjunctions, the astronomer represents the unease with which the ideological legacy of the Rights of Man was received by African Americans:

> Free. Free. How will the lines fall
> into that configuration?
> How will you clear this uneasiness,

> posting your calculations and forecasts
> into a world you yourself cannot enter?
> (25)

The proximate "configuration" of lyric space and transtemporality allow this poem to seek a counterdiscourse, one in which "vision" traverses the boundaries of "the city a star, a body" (26) into that still potential space of aestheticized history, the province of the poem.

When Thomas Jefferson received Benjamin Banneker's Almanac, he responded instantly to its synecdochic force:

> Sir, – I thank you sincerely for your letter of the 19th instant and for the Almanac it contained. No body wishes more than I do to see such proofs as you exhibit, that nature has given to our black brethren, talents equal to those of the other colors of men.
>
> (Jefferson 1791: 982)

"Benjamin Banneker Sends His 'Almanac' to Thomas Jefferson" countermands Jefferson's presidential approbation with its own lyrical reinvestment of speculative reason and prophetic vision. Though it lacks the intense communion of the earlier poem, it nonetheless collaborates in Wright's evolving historical display.[15] For here, the poet visits the astronomer, not in some interstitial space, but rather "in mind," in historical setting. At once a colloquy and a dialogue, the poem necessitates a larger view of "calculation," "language," and "form" – the things that submit to reason and those that do not. Verifications of celestial truths, those of Banneker's purview – "Solid, these calculations / verify your body on God's earth" – give way to mythological extractions, those of Wright's aesthetic – "I, who know so little of stars, / whose only acquaintance with the moon / is to read a myth, or to listen / to the surge / of the songs the women know" (27).

The celestial order posited by Banneker's science is one that conducts a historically sound and metaphysically charged dialogue:

> So you look into what we see
> yet cannot see,
> and shape and take a language
> to give form to one or the other,
> believing no form will escape,
> no movement appear, nor stop,

197

> without explanation,
> believing no reason is only reason,
> nor without reason.
>
> (27)

The prophetic realm of the soothsayer or seer is one that both formalizes and accepts an utter lack of formality in the perceived order of things. The aesthetic gaps or "silences" that Wright requires for his interventions into history are to be found in the "crack of the universe" of the previous poem or the "flaw" of this one. Beyond the compass of the perfect number, the numerical whole forwarded by Banneker, beyond the reach of "the perfect line," the lyrical snare offered by Wright, rest the "omissions" of the historical and the aesthetic. Within this silenced realm lurks the quarrel between "the man and the God," the free and the captive.

Banneker becomes the mediating force between the genealogical and historical imperatives that order the received texts. The challenge of Banneker's Almanac is more than one of cognitive display: It is one of justified existence. To argue with reason in the person of Jefferson is to quarrel with the ordering principle of the nation itself: "Your letter turns on what the man knows, / on what God, you think, would have us know" (28). Wright inverts the cosmological relationship into one where Banneker scrutinizes the order of being itself:

> All stars will forever move under your gaze,
> truthfully, leading you from line to line,
> from number to number, from truth to truth,
> while the man will read your soul's desire,
> searcher, searching yourself,
> losing the relations.
>
> (28)

"Losing the relations" is an encumbered line, resonant with the promise of calculations as well as the frailty of transactions even as it suggests the ultimate sacrifice of a stabilizing genealogy. Like the one "so volubly alone" in "The Charge," Banneker moves beyond the barely perceptible relations to assume the potential charge of a space of silence and imperfection.

The transient arc from the "livable assertion" to "losing the relations" is one that guides both poet and reader to a cunning instability, a moment and place of irrationality and aesthetic crisis. Within part 1, Wright has succeeded in moving in and through history in such a way that even the most mundane occurrence has become one of speculative poise and abiding uncertainty. Part 2 requires an application of this emerging knowledge, an unseating of domestic ordinariness in the light of this newly found celestial turbulence.

Readers of *Soothsayers and Omens* have expressed relief upon reaching the collection's middle sections, mistaking them for familiar, confessional, anecdotal lyrics "grounded in 'personal' experience" (Rowell 1983: 6). The Baedeker surface of familiar detail obscures the restless lines of call-and-response, false seculars and spirituals, Catholic and Protestant rituals – the unsettled logistics of history surging beneath the surface. Ceremonies of possession, rituals of sacrifice fail to quiet the dead of many cultures, lost inhabitants of the once named and noble New Mexican landscape. What Adrienne Rich has called "contraband memories" suffuse the history emergent in this shifting landscape "still untouched by the step and touch / of the sons of slaves, / where no slave could ever go" (1993: 32).[16] One knows not what might be summoned from the depths of local or national histories:

> Call,
> and some pantalooned grandfather may come,
> with the leisure of Virginia still on his tongue,
> and greet you uneasily.
> Here, he holds uneasy land
> from which he pistols out intrusions . . .
> ("Entering New Mexico," 32)

Naming itself assumes unpredictable and prophetic powers as it summons "A history that is none, / that may never be written, / nor conceived again" ("The Master of Names," 34). Within the proper name resides "a power / . . . almost forgotten" (36).

Extending Benjamin's reflection that "Counsel woven into the fabric of real life is wisdom" (1936a: 86), Wright surmounts the difficulty of his predetermined landscape – one in which reason and order have been disabled – by weaving his determinations into local historical and genealogical sites in order to discover the matrix of historical wisdom. "The Albuquerque Graveyard" and "Family Reunion" may be seen as application sites for his evolving aesthetic structures of history.

At once an excursion and an incursion into the borderland of grief and remembrance, "The Albuquerque Graveyard" occasions an aesthetic debate on memory, literacy, and history.[17] The incremental advance into the scene of commemoration – "take three buses, / walk two blocks, / search at the rear / of the cemetery" (38) – echoes grander historical slights, as "buses" and "rear" metonymically realign into "the back of the bus." "The pattern of the place" anticipates a deeper historical disquisition: "I am going back / to the Black limbo, / an unwritten history / of our own tensions" (38). This apparent historical act of recovery is balanced by the tugging immediacy of "our." Steeped in the catholicity of the place, the poem toys with its racial and cultural inversions of Dante as well as its hemispheric soundings. History expresses itself in the silence of the ruins; Wright discovers himself in the volatile "tensions" of the buried "curse[s] and rage."

If history is to be extracted from this fossilized underlayer of neglect,[18] Wright must turn beyond the evidential to correspondence between the exemplary and the collective – "of one who stocked his parlor / with pictures of Robeson, / and would boom down the days, / dreaming of Othello's robes" (38). Dreaming here has a nearly astrological force as it locates the individual within a commemorative historical sweep of potential realized. In reminiscence, the recognition scenes of "small heroes" resonate locally and nationally, as the poet fades into the persona of Frederick Douglass: "Here, I stop by the simple mound / of a woman who taught me / spelling on the sly, / parsing my tongue / to make me fit for her own dreams" (38–9).

The ordered summoning of "unwritten history" produces discontent. The quest yields to an enactment of a modest call-and-response in which the poet "search[es] the names / and simple mounds [he] call[s] [his] own / . . . and turn[s] for home" (39). "Home," having acquired an internal and external voice in Wright's canon, recalls the historical cascade of "The Homecoming Singer": "her voice shifting / and bringing up the Carolina calls, / the waterboy, the railroad cutter, the jailed, / the condemned, all that had been forgotten / on this night of homecomings" (1971: 31). To "turn for home" is to position oneself in direct relation to the genealogical site of history itself. If history is to be rescripted into a living and inclusive form, it must be superimposed upon its recognizable origins: the family. Home is where Wright will reacquaint himself with Benjamin's "source" for storytelling, the place of "the securest among our possessions . . . the ability to exchange experiences" (Benjamin 1936a: 83).

Unlike "the hierarchy of small defeats" populating "The Albuquerque Graveyard," "the elders and saints" of "Family Reunion" confront the traces of that earlier, "unwritten history." Semblance becomes resemblance as "an unfamiliar relative's traces" are confronted (39). Cropped and candid, the snapshots aestheticize lives into glimpsed, historical extensions. Images engender familiar narratives, exchanged experiences, and recognition scenes. Graveyard ruins surrender to the always spontaneous, genealogical accord with the living:

> of hearing a voice, and being able to coax
> the speaker into echoes of himself, his selves,
> his forgotten voices, voices he had never heard:
> of calling your own name, and having it belled
> back in tongues, being changed and harmonized
> until it is one name and all names.
>
> (40)

Historical recognition depends upon individuation, which must then evolve into a harmonious whole, *re*cognition insisting initially upon cognition. Because authentication of his aesthetic demands the restorative sound of a *vox humana* without, as Benjamin Banneker knew, "losing the relations," Wright must open his discontinuous narrative to the hemispheric pulse of historical antecedent.

Readers of *The Homecoming Singer* will recall Wright's initial fascination with Chapultepec: "This is the castle where they lived, / Maximilian and Carlotta, / and here is where Carlotta slept" (1971: 40). What may be seen as the primary historical grounding of that earlier collection has slipped into duplicitous aesthetic service in part 3 of *Soothsayers and Omens,* as the recurrent sounding of Chapultepec recalls the euphonious slopping of Stevens's "November off Tehuantepec" in "Sea Surface Full of Clouds" (1931: 98–102). The preparatory path to Wright's new history lies along abbreviated recapitulations of "The Comedian as the Letter C," in which tone and circuit shift to include "The Sense of Comedy: I" (roman numeral or personal pronoun?) in hope of circumventing Crispin's "faint, memorial gesturings" (1923: 29).

Unlike Stevens's "introspective voyager," Wright's persona prefers "Moore's concrete apples, / Giacometti's daggers" to Crispin's porpoises and apricots ("The Museums in Chapultepec," 49). And yet he, like Crispin, is drawn by "A sunken voice, both of remembering/And of forgetfulness, in alternate strain" (1923: 29). So enmeshed is this section of *Soothsayers and Omens* in the aesthetic web of Stevens that the poetic sequence seems proximate to its ancestor, steadily moving toward Crispin's discovery: "*The Idea of a Colony /* Nota: his soil is man's intelligence" (1923: 36). Wright, like Crispin, writes "his prolegomena, / And, being full of caprice, inscribe[s] / Commingled souvenirs and prophecies" (1923: 37).

The confluence of history and literature occurs in the announcement of "The Birthday." Shuttling between the Emersonian and Blakean contraries of temporal and spatial logic, Wright seeks a fixed and fluid identity for the historical. The speaker is as focused as Benjamin Banneker: "and my eyes kept focussed / at one point in the light, / as though I would fix / the face and name of a friend / absent even from my memory" (52). Caught "between one day and another, / between one age and another," the poet seeks to resolve an apparent conundrum at the center of his debate: "a chosen point to celebrate / the fact of moving still" (52). The definitional instability of "still" has troubled the entire collection, nagging the lines into an uncertain correspondence, but here it offers the promise of reflection and endurance: the promise of history itself.

The prophetic trajectory of desire and reminiscence coalesces in "Jason Visits His Gypsy." This poem of agitated display attempts to define history linguistically. Even as the gypsy's spectacle draws one simultaneously into and away from the unraveling truth, it becomes the very celebration of "the fact of moving still," as she "moves, / raveling the sand into her sleeve, / past your still body, / past your stilled desires" (54). Nomadic, nationless, the gypsy seems the ideal simulacrum for Wright's emerging transhistorical and transnational identity: "The gypsy knows what you have forgotten, / . . . / knows the rhythm of raveling / the sand into the dark and closeness / of a space, where only she can live" (54).

The section comes to a rest with another "Homecoming: *Guadalajara-New York, 1965*," a bifurcated tradition and hemispheric ellipsis that reannunciate as well as terminate the earlier sequential debates of reason, history, identity, and narrative. The disembarkation, to use the language of Gwendolyn Brooks, necessitates a conceptual and linguistic pastiche: Syntax and diction strain to accommodate competing visions, and allusions collide as architect and poet debate the structural integrity of inheritance. Insistent on its lineage, the poem echoes Stevens's "The Worms at Heaven's Gate," noting that "The strange and customary turns / of living may coincide" (58).

In a different city, at a different time, the poet transgresses the boundaries of language, nation, history, and time. The Enlightenment constructions so in favor during the Bicentennial have lost even their oppositional, aesthetic value for Wright:

> From line to line,
> from point to point,
> is an architect's end of cities.
>
> But I lie down
> to a different turbulence
> and a plan of transformation.
>
> (58)

The *dis*ease between "turbulence" and "plan" intensifies the undetermined path to come. Suspension of the defining boundaries of individual and collective identity will enable Wright to proceed into a history tolerant of "the strange and customary turns / of living" (58).

"Second Conversations with Ogotemmêli," the final section, is doubly estranged from the text proper in that it bears the only subtitle and it commits wholeheartedly, and perhaps unexpectedly (to those who neglected the note on the verso of the half-title page), to structures and silences inherent in Marcel Griaule's version of Dogon tribal cosmology. Though previous historical, geographical, and biographical references may have been unfamiliar to the reader, they were inevitably assimilated and accommodated by the overlap of the poems. "Second Conversations," with alienating familiarity, presumes an antecedent, a "first" that signals Wright's dependence upon Griaule; "Ogotemmêli" becomes the *named* initiator, the medium through which disclosure (if it is to come at all) will come. Unlike *Dimensions of History, Soothsayers and Omens* offers neither "cautionary remarks" nor explanation; except for the prefatory notes, it insists upon the aesthetic self-sufficiency of its materials. Wright's cautionary and sly modernist introduction to the notes appended to *Dimensions*, on the other hand, shares his expectations for readers of this collection:

> The notes are offered as an aid in reading the poem, not as the poem itself, nor a substitution for it. The notes could have been more extensive, and more detailed. I have given only so many because I must, ultimately, rely on the good will and intelligence of the reader. If the reader trusts the poem as much as I trust him or her, he or she should have no difficulty with my exploration of these dimensions of history. (105)[19]

The acute intimacy of these extended poetic explorations in *Soothsayers and Omens* transfers responsibility for coherence and vitality to the reader. In this final, elaborate response to Stevens's Western world of "inconstancy," Wright pilots an excursion into the deepest recesses of transatlantic narrative literatures and histories, allusions and mythologies, in the hope of grasping the weave of the design.

Reading initiates this conversation: Wright's reading of a translation of Marcel Griaule's *Conversations with Ogotemmêli: An Introduction to Dogon Religious Ideas* (1962). Poetic invention, the mind creating, closes the silences between poet, who is alienated by successive mediation and remove – stories "heard" through the scrim of translator, text interposed, allusive field (Emerson, Stevens, Pound, Crane, Hayden, Derrida, Bloom) – and experience as well as between the poet and the Dogon storyteller. The anthropological study sponsors the radical subversion of texts inherent in the collection as a whole, extracting poetry in recital. Wright has acceded to Benjamin's situational definition of storytelling – "A man listening to a story is in the company of a storyteller; even a man reading one shares this companionship" (1936a: 100) – and, in doing so, has relinquished poetic authority to the patriarchal storyteller in the act of disclosure. Emblematic discontinuities abound, as conversations, auditorily ephemeral, evade the structures of time and reason and create a momentarily reciprocal aesthetic. Anxious to move beyond the totalizing fields of myth or history, Wright locates coherence and correspondence in that space where poetic and epistemology are one.

Although scholarly attention to the source reveals the imitative array of poems and descriptive language, received diction, and gloss, it does little to disclose the aesthetic of Wright's evolving cosmology. As Hugh Kenner cautions, "It is hard alone to wring song from philology" (1971: 195). Immersion in the contextual source leads to an informational gloss that is counterproductive to the revealed revisionary attitude toward aesthetic form and history. This overlapping series reinscribes as it reanimates the lost voice – and the silences – of Ogotemmêli upon the accreted, Western canonical context of Wright's experience. Polyphony and polyvocality display the syncretic instability of history and biography under erasure.

"Ogotemmêli" originates the concluding sequence through an intimate dialogue between speaker and storytelling mediator, described by Griaule as one with an "eagle mind and considerable shrewdness" (14), that is at once instructive and obfuscating. The three-part poem startles with its patterned and excluding repetitions; it is indeed a series of "second conversations," exchanges with a history at once textual and informal, European and African, "civilized" and "primitive," historical and simultaneous. The stanzas resemble reliquaries, storing barely contained allusions, artifacts, and utterances as they threaten to sound a tide of discontinuous meanings. Even as the image of Ogotemmêli begins to take visual and linguistic form in parallels and transmutations of its textual origin, it shades into a dimly perceived auditory presence – "But your voice comes clearly / only where I found you" (61) – insisting upon the phenomenological instability of the poetic record. If this "you" grows in familiarity – "You tilt your head like a bird, / and wait until my step stops. / You squint and sniff, / as though you would brush away / some offensive smell or movement" (61) – it does so in its tangential and immediate relationship to antecedent visions. Recalling earlier, ambiguously aligned descriptions – "These others stand with you, / squinting the city into place, / yet cannot see what you see" (22) – these actions coalesce to form an enlarged and enlarging series of qualities associated with the historical and eternal in Wright's world.

The second stanza's clustered reduplications of the original force an immediacy and contrariness that spirals into arch parodies of the pastoral – "trace the fat, wet sheep" – and startling inversions of Miltonic atmosphere – "when no light comes, / you will lead me into the darkness" (61), which then resolve into aversions and reversals of Cotton Mather's patriarchal speculations on an invisible world – "Father, your eyes have turned / from the tricks of our visible world" (62). The display of correspondences, far from insisting upon relation and wholeness, advances the poem into a provisional world of displacement and disjunction. Closure of this final history can be achieved only through a tolerance of what Benjamin has termed *Stillstand*, a gap in temporality itself:

> So I arrive,
> at the end of this, my small movement,
> moving with you, in the light you control,
> learning to hear the voice in the silence,
> learning to see in the light
> that runs away from me.
>
> (62)

That moment of static, enduring immediacy of "reaching into the light for the boy" ("The Charge," 11) or "learning to see in the light" is the time of Benjamin's storytelling, the moment of Wright's history.

The figure of the named Dogon elder reinscribes and decenters the collection's originating patriarchal figure, the poet-patriarch of "The Charge," prompting a regenesis and realignment of the phenomenal world. The open yet culminating sequence – from "Beginning" to "The Dead" – articulates the newness of Wright's transcultural diasporic aesthetic. Semantic and linguistic disjunction denies the verifiable and informational qualities of the history embedded in this discontinuous narrative of postnational consciousness. Emerson's poet-priest and Wright's own poet-patriarch dissolve into Benjamin's storyteller as patriarch, one who (as Benjamin concludes) "has borrowed his authority from death" (1936a: 94).

"Beginning" appears to dismantle the raiment and facades of received cultural hierarchy and to establish a modernist tableau relative to the "dung and death" of Eliot's "East Coker" or the dust swirling about Pound's cage at the Detention Training Center north of Pisa:

> Alive again,
> you wait in the broken courtyard.
> Oblivious of its dungheap and ashes,
> you sit once more,
> near the main façade,
> and listen for this unfamiliar footstep.
>
> (63)

The historicity of Maximilian and Carlotta, essential to the poems of *The Homecoming Singer*, fractures into the postmodernist shards of this "broken courtyard," an abandoned system of figuration. The discontinuity of "arrive, / at the end of this, my small movement" extends this celebratory, posited continuum: "Alive again." The return signaled is more complex than being to origins; it cycles through a temporality as yet unannounced, or at least unclear. Movement, life's linear creep or history's expected chronological order, meets with immediate status: the weight of "wait." All of this seems to echo Benjamin's "Ur-history of the 19th Century," in which truth was found in the "garbage heap" of modernity, the "rags, the trash" of commodity production.

And yet readers of the antecedent text will recall more than the atmospheric sponsor of these descriptions: They will recognize clusters of the details themselves. The essential confrontation is not with the prefigured storyteller but with his linguistic trace, fossilized in Griaule's "Conversations." The inspiration of that unmediated, original space will come not from the figure but from the word – "Facing you, / I cannot tell what word, / or form of that word, I shall face" (63) – or soundings of the exchange. The word, the thread that Robert Duncan called "the torn cloth" (1984: 137–9), initiates the "reaving" of Wright's aesthetic.

If the epistemologically charged aesthetic is to redeem history, it must offer an unmediated space of enactment or realization that is at once provisional and whole. Such constructions Nathaniel Mackey, in the light of Griaule, sees as "fabrications":

> What this means is not only that our purchase on the world is a weave but also that the word is a rickety witness, the telltale base on which our sense of the weave sits. *Fabric* echoes *fabrication*, as both go back to a root that has to do with making. The creaking of the word calls attention to the constructedness of the hold on the world fabrication affords. (Mackey 1993: 180)

Such "purchase" affords little if it fails to secure trust. For Wright, trust responds to dependency and cultural reversals as he relinquishes history to conversation, word to silence. "Lurking near the borders of speech" ("The First Word"), he succumbs to "the craft of the first word, / weaving speech into spirit" (64).

The evanescence of form thematizes the perceived cosmography of the Dogon tribe, its "world system associated with constellations" (Griaule 1965: 32) as well as the canonical tide of poems under erasure. "The Third Word" – "this seed / being broken there / on the smithy's anvil / will burst to stars, / design a man" (67) – reduplicates a system of parallels expansive enough to claim both Griaule and the Stevens of "The Auroras of Autumn," Ogotemmêli and Eliot. Decipherings yield analogues that share a global urge for the construction of provisional structures to define and stabilize the existential mysteries of being human.

Ogotemmêli incarnates the problematic of Wright's evolving, historical poetic: the denial of the emblematic, the effacement of the authorial self. Ogotemmêli's ego inheres in the story. From the Poundian personae, "these masks, / with a place at last" (73), Wright posits an essential emancipation: "Living, we free them; / dying, we learn / how we are freed ourselves" (73). No longer is the Emersonian equation of poet as seer applicable: "I come here, / . . . attuned to some animal's / tentative step, / . . . the design / that escapes my eyes" (74). The New World extension of this ancient, received covenant will be "to design / your own prefiguration" (76).

The Dogon supernatural fear of naming, a "marked reluctance, arising from respect and fear, to mention the names or picture the forms of supernatural powers" (Griaule 1965: 113), denies the possibility of narrative or lyric coherence in the Western sense. The simultaneous weaving and unweaving of Ogotemmêli's conversations result in the absence of an aesthetic construction; the story exists only in the telling. The "reluctance" to name refuses linguistic access to the Emersonian poet as "Namer" but not to the poet as "Language-maker" or as "the only teller of news." If, as Benjamin asserts, "a man's knowledge or wisdom, but above all his real life – and this is the stuff that stories are made of – first assumes transmissible form at the moment of his death" (1936a: 94), then the unresisted lines of "The Dead" initiate the transmission of the sequence's discontinuities and disjunctions. Epistemology and poetic come under erasure in this final telling.

Movement subordinates death in a progressive distancing from Western aesthetics and traditions. Silence (and silences) animate the internal path of allusion to the Banneker poems and their attendant histories and cosmologies, as well as to the forlorn and fetishized dead in "The Albuquerque Graveyard." The indeterminate silence of the animistic and ill-defined displaces the beginnings and endings, linearity and logic of the articulate, creating a space where contraries embrace – "moves still," "living dead." Poundian masks and Yeatsian dance fail to unify perceptions and resolve disjunction, so the poems slip "into the rhythm / of emptiness and return, / into the self / moving against itself, / into the self / moving into itself, / the word, and the first design" (78).

"Design," the province of the creator, yields to self-designation as Wright advances into the ultimate, because self-determined, liberation narrative – "Now, / I designate myself your child" (78) – in which covenant and circumstance "will have their place" and the poet, now subservient to the patriarch, will "learn these relations." The transmutation of "design" from nominal to verbal status reduplicates the pattern of this provisional, and often self-negating, collection. The progressive disabling of the textual field intensifies Wright's earlier judgment on Thomas Jefferson, "the man [who] read [Banneker's] soul's desire, / . . . / losing the relations" (28).

The linguistic trace of "The Dead" restlessly echoes from Winthrop of Massachusetts Bay Colony to Ogotemmêli, from religious predestination to aesthetic prefiguration. If Wright's cultural inversions constitute a temporizing, postnational, postmodern aesthetic, they do so with an ironic, solipsistic imperative: Trust the telling, not the tale. The split pairing of death and freedom advances a new "covenant" of admitted contraries: "a sign, / that your world moves still" (78). Wright has invented a simultaneous historical field in which language, culture, and nation are subsumed by the *telling* of the tale of the tribe.

Writing America Black employs a chronological order of representational encounters. While not encyclopedic, this ordering nonetheless results in an eccentric renarrativization of twentieth-century American history. Exploiting the narrative ambitions of black historians, both journalistic and literary, the study has constructed a literary history that is illustrative, authenticating, explanatory, and problematic. Its consideration of textual features relative to their contexts, and its contemplation of circulation and negotiation within rhetorical modes and historical sites, are intended to serve as paradigms for the subsequent and necessary reconfiguration of national historical narratives that situate textuality within what Edward Said has called "the circumstances, the events, the physical senses that made it possible and render it intelligible as the result of human work" (1983: 4).

Each chapter represents a case history in rhetoric, event, and genre that situates the black public sphere within that of an idealized national public. For Hopkins, the site of history was biography; for the journalists covering Chicago's 1919 riot, rhetoric was shaped by their separate linguistic communities; for Tolson, journalism shared the lyrical and historical ambitions of his poetry; for Johnson and Burns, the column "If I Were a Negro," within the blackened editorial context of *Negro Digest*, foregrounded the subversive indifference of white liberalism; for Brooks, competing textualities of Chicago's "official" story inspired the counterdiscourse of her evolving black nationalist aesthetic; for Cornish, fragmented ancestral narratives yielded surrogate historical and lyrical texts; for Walker, dissolving narratives resisted intrusive totalizing media like television; for Wright, cosmology and orality rescripted a simultaneous historical field.

Appropriately, then, *Soothsayers and Omens* culminates this study of nearly a century of black America's definitions of the rhetorical, ideological, and territorial borders of the nation and boundaries of citizenship. With his invention of a historical consciousness independent of nation and narration, Jay Wright evolves beyond the chaotic "carnival of gods, customs, and arts . . . the alien and disconnected" that Nietzsche had most feared (1980: 10, 28) into the uncharted ambivalence of the "cultural space . . . [of] the nation with its transgressive boundaries and its 'interruptive' interiority" (Bhabha 1990: 5). The discrete representational strategies of race rhetoric that once had underwritten the narrative of black America resolve in Wright's poetry into a simultaneous field of textual orality, a site of critical memory in which the postnational and postmodern continue to write America black.

NOTES

Preface

1. See Du Bois 1915 (1166): "Democracy is not a gift of power, but a reservoir of knowledge. Only the soul that suffers knows its suffering. Only the one who needs knows what need means. Ignorance may vitiate the expression of needs and vice may deceive, but it remains true that despotism and aristocracy have displayed far more ignorance of the real needs of the people than the most ignorant of democracies. The people alone are the sources of that real knowledge which enables a State to be ruled for the best good of its inhabitants. And only by putting power in the hands of each inhabitant can we hope to approximate in the ultimate use of that power the greatest good to the greatest number."

2. Jefferson (1787: 880) saw the press as an essential component of democracy. As he explains in his January 16 letter to Edward Carrington, written from Paris: "The basis of our governments being the opinion of the people, the very first object should be to keep that right; and were it left to me to decide whether we should have a government without newspapers or newspapers without a government, I should not hesitate a moment to prefer the latter." For consideration of the influence of the daily press upon American fiction, see Fishkin (1985) and Shi (1994).

3. As Baker (1994: 7) distinguishes the rhetorical structures:

    > Nostalgia does not here mean arrested development, a distraught sentimentality ever pining for "ole, unhappy, far-off things, and battles long ago." Rather it suggests *heimweh* or homesickness. Nostalgia is a purposive construction of a past filled with golden virtues, golden men and sterling events. Nostalgia plays itself out in two acts. First, it writes the revolution as a well-passed aberration. Second, it actively substitutes allegory for history.
    >
    > Critical memory, by contrast, is the very faculty of revolution. Its operation implies a continuous arrival at turning points. Decisive change, usually attended by considerable risk, peril or suspense, always seems imminent. To be critical is never to be safely housed or allegori-

cally free of the illness, transgression and contamination of the past. . . . The essence of critical memory's work is the cumulative, collective maintenance of a record that draws into relationship significant instants of time past and the always uprooted homelessness of now.

4.   See Rukeyser (1994):
I lived in the first century of world wars.
Most mornings I would be more or less insane,
The newspapers would arrive with their careless stories,
The news would pour out of various devices
Interrupted by attempts to sell products to the unseen.

Chapter 1. Race Progress and Exemplary Biography

1.   In a promotional note for Hopkins's *Contending Forces*, a CAM colleague suggests the very intensity of her authorial fervor: "[Her] ambition is to become a writer of fiction, in which the wrongs of her race shall be handled as to enlist the sympathy of all classes of citizens, in this way reaching those who never read history or biography" (CAM 1 [September 1900]: 195–6).

   See Carby (1987: esp. chaps. 6–7), for a historical account of Hopkins at the CAM.

2.   Certainly the work of James Olney, William Andrews, Jean Fagan Yellin, Mary Helen Washington, Elizabeth Fox-Genovese, and others has deepened and expanded our sense of African-American autobiography and history. The richness of this debate prompts my inquiry into the relatively ignored realm of African-American biography. Unlike the relatively commonplace journalistic efforts – e.g., *Twentieth Century Negro Literature*, "written by One Hundred of America's Greatest Negroes" (*CAM* 5 [1902]), Child's sketches in *The Freedmen's Book* (1865), Hine and Thompson's history of black women (1998) – Hopkins's biographies, while suffering from the formulaic repetitiveness of the genre, ask to be treated seriously as literary historical acts of recovery and commemoration that have influenced subsequent scholarly writing. Her exhaustive and compassionate profile of Sojourner Truth – with its insistence that "the details of the life of one who experienced all the horrors of Northern servitude are peculiarly interesting" (Hopkins 1901– : 124) – reads like a précis of Nell Irvin Painter's *Sojourner Truth: A Life, A Symbol* (1996).

   See Andrews (1989: 72) for a discussion of Booker T. Washington's preference for biography; see Bercovitch (1975: esp. chap. 5) for a suggestive account of the early-nineteenth-century culture of American biography and the ways in which it reflects Cotton Mather's attempt to construct history through hagiography in the wake of another great migration; see also Murdock (1977: 26–48).

   In many ways, Hopkins's commitment to biography anticipates what was soon to become a more generalized enthusiasm among American historians. See Kammen (1991: 336–7) for consideration of the ways in which biography helped reverse "long-standing stereotypes concerning our cultural inferiority."

3. Hopkins targeted an audience conversant with those Puritan ancestors of Emerson and Child as well as with Frederick Douglass, Paul Lawrence Dunbar, Charles Chestnutt, and W. E. B. Du Bois. Her readers, acquainted with the literary conventions of *Up from Slavery* (published serially in *Outlook* [November 3, 1900 – February 23, 1902]) as well as Du Bois's articles in the *Atlantic Monthly* and elsewhere (soon to form the core of *The Souls of Black Folk* [1903]), would hear the double-voiced ambition of a cultural history bonded to an authentic national context. But because African-American culture drew on experiences greatly differing from those of the Puritans and other white New Englanders, she appropriately modified her inherited rhetoric, subverting the classical oration and its Puritan and Emersonian embellishments by insinuating strategies drawn from the slave narrative, tailoring them to meet the needs of her audience of partially enfranchised citizens.

   For a compelling continuation of black America "seeing New Englandly," see S. A. Williams, "Letters from a New England Negro" (1982: 11–38).

4. Hopkins, "Edwin Garrison Walker" (*CAM*, March 1901, 358); compare with Emerson (1841: 240; 1982: 219); see also Du Bois (1897: 817). See White (1973: 68-9) for an extended discussion of "the conception of history as the story of heroes . . . as the special achievement of the Romantic age of the early nineteenth century"; West (1989: 138–50) for consideration of Du Bois's debt to Emerson and William James; Bruce, "W. E. B. Du Bois."

5. For a photojournalistic reading of this tradition, see Tolson (1982: 235–6), "Some Flashes from an Old Copy of *Flash*," which celebrates the iconographic in history: "Shall I ever forget my first pictures of Dunbar, Senator Bruce, Booker T. Washington, and Toussaint L'Ouverture? I should not. They were burning stars in my young life"; see Painter (1996), chap. 20.

6. The recurrent generic structure, as well as Hopkins's variations upon it, may be recognized in several ways. Borrowing from rhetorical structures familiar to readers of Mather, Emerson, and Child, these reconstructed exemplary lives of major historical figures typically include most of the following: a classical invocation or exordium followed by narration that supplies the genealogical information characteristic of the slave narrative, information of particular interest to people forcibly deprived of their ancestry; a dramatic narration, evoking the slave narrative in its rhetorical urgency and purpose; relevant historical documentation to authenticate the drama; an exhortation reminiscent of Mather and Emerson; dialogue (a novelist's means of persuasion) – fictional, of course – to bring the subject to life; and a classical epilogue, again in the Emersonian mode, which to effect closure summarizes the postnarrative relevance for a contemporary audience. As Olney notes, readers of slave narratives are apt to be "dazed by the mere repetitiveness of it all" (1990: 148). The generic conventions of the typical exemplary biography share this lack of rhetorical variance.

7. Child appended this editorial instruction to Harriet Jacobs's "The Good Grandmother," noting: "The above account is no fiction. The author, who was thirty years in Slavery, wrote it in an interesting book entitled 'Linda.'

She is an esteemed friend of mine; and I introduce this portion of her story here to illustrate the power of character over circumstances" (1865: 218).

8. See White (1973: 1–42) for definitions of emplotment and argument in history; see Tate (1989: 107) for consideration of the fundamental differences between the racial discourses of black male and female narratives.

9. There is considerable disagreement in the dating of these series. Roses and Randolph, in *Harlem Renaissance*, date "Famous Men" from February 1901; Carby, in *Reconstructing Womanhood*, dates "Famous Men" from December 1900. Internal promotional indexes date the series as follows: *Famous Men of the Negro Race* (November 1900–October 1901); *Famous Women of the Negro Race* (November 1901–October 1902). A complete list of the articles in these series can be found in the references.

10. The advertisements, running heads, and text of this issue employ the less conventional spelling "L'Overture"; subsequent *CAM* articles by Hopkins use the more familiar "L'Ouverture." I accept the currently orthodox "Louverture."

11. Du Bois writes (1897: 817): "This history of the world is the history not of individuals, but of groups, not of nations, but of races, and he who ignores or seeks to override the race idea in human history ignores and overrides the thought of all history. . . . [Race becomes] a vast family of human beings generally of common blood and language, always of common history, traditions, and impulses, who are both voluntarily and involuntarily striving together for the accomplishment of certain more or less vividly conceived ideals of life."

12. See Carby (1987: 141), in which she notes that this generational history informs Hopkins's historical fiction as well: "In Hopkins's fictional representation of the social relations between black and white, she reconstructed a generational history across a century to situate the contemporary reassertion of the doctrine of white supremacy within a framework that demythologized the American story of origins."

13. Though Nell Irvin Painter seems not to have read Hopkins's biographical sketch of Sojourner, she did experience many of the frustrations of Truth's earlier biographer. See "A Note on the Sources" (Painter 1996: 289):

> People like Truth do have a history, of course. But a Truth biographer, like the biographer of any poor person, any person of color, or a woman of any stratum, cannot stick to convention, for conventional sources mostly are lacking. This history demands more or less uncommon research methods, starting with the richest potential resource: newspaper articles published by friends, colleagues, and competitors, principally, in Truth's case, the anti-slavery press and articles reprinted in the *History of Woman Suffrage*.

14, See Bercovitch (1975: esp. chap. 5) for a discussion of the typological significance of Moses in American biography. From John Winthrop to Daniel Boone and Mark Twain, Americans have found Moses to be an archetype for their "errand into the wilderness."

15. See Lerner (1972: 575–6) for Fannie Barrier Williams's account of being

shunned by a white women's club in Chicago: "progress includes a great deal more than what is generally meant by the terms culture, education and contact. The club movement among colored women reaches into the sub-social condition of the entire race . . .the club is only one of the many means for the social uplift of a race. . . .The club movement is well purposed. . . . It is not a fad. . . . It is rather the force of a new intelligence against the old ignorance. The struggle of an enlightened conscience against the whole brood of social miseries, born out of the stress and pain of a hated past."

Chapter 2. Reading Riot

1. For a discussion of Chicago's degeneration into a "biracial society," see Spear, *Black Chicago* (49) and Drake and Cayton, *Black Metropolis* (53, 58–61). Drake and Cayton give a detailed reading of the growing tensions between the immigrant and migrant populations beginning in 1915. See also Philpott, *The Slum and the Ghetto*, regarding the "extraordinary" degree of segregation in Chicago by 1900.

2. For a contemporaneous reading suggestive of the national import of the riot, see "Chicago Rebellion" and "A Report on the Chicago Riot" in the *Messenger* (September 1919); for a detailed reading of the various accounts of the riot, see Tuttle (1970: 3–11).

3. For analysis of the varying reliability of journalistic sources, including the *Chicago Defender*, see Tuttle, *Race Riot*; Grant, *The Black Man Comes to the City*; Grossman, *Land of Hope*; Chicago Commission on Race Relations (CCRR), *The Negro in Chicago*. Grossman provides the most language-sensitive study, pausing to assess diction and syntax in competing accounts of the riot and the broader migration and labor issues. In contrast, Lemann's *The Promised Land* fails to decode the *Defender*'s community-building rhetoric. See, for example, the dismissal of Abbott's "Great Northern Drive" campaign as one of "slogans" and "songs" (1989: 16). If Lemann had met the expectations of his subtitle – "the Great Migration and How It Changed America" – he might have "heard" Abbott's variations on a theme.

4. For a discussion of the larger and vexing issues of such reader-response questions, see Radway, "Interpretive Communities and Variable Literacies" (1984: 49–72). Though Radway focuses on the "romance," she nonetheless offers real insight into the interpretive concerns of audience and reception. In journalism, editors and writers traditionally have presumed that a message sent *is* a message received. For consideration of linguistic codes in general, see Fowler, *Linguistic Criticism* (1986: 27): "[They] do not reflect neutrality; they interpret, organize, and classify the subjects of discourse. They embody theories of how the world is arranged: worldviews or ideology."

5. In *The Dialogic Imagination* (1981: 271), Bakhtin argues that the centripetal force in language attempts to "supplant," "incorporate," and "enslave" other languages. The resonance of these metaphors is deliberate. The attempt to gain hegemony at the expense of competing languages parallels

the journalist's desire to monopolize public discourse on a given issue, to impose both one's reportage and one's point of view (editorialize) at the expense of competing reporters and editors. The other force in language, the centrifugal, rejects this hegemony, unravels linguistic unity, and resists enslavement. In poststructuralist theory, this centrifugal force operates at the level of the signifier; in the rhetoric of journalism it is the pressure of perceived reality. Bakhtin argues that every utterance, written or oral, is crossed by both forces, and therefore participates in "unitary language" while at the same time bearing traces of a "heteroglossia" that is the very embodiment of the marginal.

6. See Spear, *Black Chicago* (1967: 115), for documentation of the changes brought about at the *Defender* by J. Hockley Smiley. Relying primarily on Ottley, *The Lonely Warrior*, Spear claims: "At his most flamboyant, Smiley would not hesitate to invent stories. . . . By the time of Smiley's death in 1915, the *Defender*, now audaciously proclaiming itself the 'World's Greatest Weekly,' was a hard-hitting, flamboyant organ of racial protest well on its way to becoming the first Negro newspaper in history with a mass circulation."

    See also "Public Opinion in Race Relations," in CCRR, *The Negro in Chicago* (436–594) for coverage of the riot in the *Whip* and *Searchlight* compared with that of the *Defender*. Sandburg notes: "The State Street blocks south of 31st street are newspaper row, with the Defender, Broad Axe, the Plaindealer, the Searchlight, the Guide, the Advocate, the Whip, as weekly publications, and there are also illustrated monthly magazines such as the Half Century and the Favorite" (1922: 51).

7. As a newspaper man, James Weldon Johnson was particularly interested in the effects of journalism on race issues. See his "The Negro Press" in *Negro Americans, What Now?* (1938: 26–33). Park takes a larger view in "The Natural History of the Newspaper" (1925: 80–98). He sees journalism as the first front of literacy movements for migrants and immigrants alike.

8. See Strickland, *History of the Chicago Urban League* (1979: 56–82); Waskow, *From Race Riot to Sit-In* (1966: 38-60); and Grossman, *Land of Hope* (1989: 140–50), for a thorough description of the UL's attempts to offset such economic and environmental stresses.

9. See C. S. Johnson, "How the Negro Fits into Northern Industry" (1926: 399–412). Certainly Grossman's *Land of Hope*, with its commanding documentation of family and community kinship networks, would seem to refute Johnson's early, born-of-despair assessment.

10. For consideration of racial politics in the American Federation of Labor, see Tuttle (1970: 142–56); Grossman (1989: 214–16); regarding the Chicago Federation of Labor, see Tuttle (1970: 110, 124, 135, 145, 200); Grossman (1989: 216, 219, 226, 241–2).

11. Regarding Irish rule in the wards, see Drake and Cayton (1945: 62); Tuttle (1970: 102-3, 167); Grossman (1989: 118, 162, 164, 178, 217, 220).

    See also Baldwin, "Introduction: The Price of the Ticket" (xix–xx) for a comparison of the black and Irish "middle passage" experience:

    Later, in the midnight hour, the missing identity aches. One can

216

neither assess nor overcome the storm of the middle passage. One is mysteriously shipwrecked forever, in the Great New World.

The slave is in another condition, as are his heirs: *I told Jesus it would be all right / If He changed my name.* If *He* changed my name.

The Irish middle passage, for but one example, was as foul as my own, and as dishonorable on the part of those responsible for it. But the Irish became white when they got here and began rising in the world, whereas I became black and began sinking.

12. Republished in Ottley, *The Lonely Warrior* (1955: 183). The handbill displayed the Hearst-like banner of the *Defender* with boldface header – "EXTRA!! / To The Citizens of Chicago." Each bit of guidance was keyed at the left margin with the following bold captions [in order]: "Your Duty and Mine"; "Keep Off the Streets"; "Riots Mean an Irreparable Loss to Innocent and Guilty Alike"; "This Is No Time to Solve the Race Question"; "Help the Police Do Their Duty."

See also Waskow, "Appendix B" (1966: 308–14): "Posters in Negro Areas during the 1919 Riot" [NAACP MS], esp. the following one-page broadside issued by the Chicago *Whip* (August 2, 1919):

PEACE ON EARTH, GOOD WILL TOWARD MEN

The riot is over. Let us go back to our work and forget that it ever happened. Your jobs await you; your safety is guaranteed. But Dont forget the State and City Authorities who have labored untiringly to give equal protection to all peaceful citizens both white and black. . . .

Special credit should be given to Chief John J. Garrity, 1st Deputy Alcock, and the entire police force. . . .

On account of labor shortage, we are not able to get out our normal supply of papers this week. Therefore we reprint at the request of several civic organizations our front page editorial of this week's issue:

THE RIOT AND THE HIDDEN HAND

We admit that there has been a laxity on the part of authorities which in all probability served as an incubator for the growth of trouble. But the hand which contrived with criminal cleverness to originate the Ku Klux Klan, Jim Crow car, and other unwholesome organizations and conveyances is ninety per cent responsible for this horrible state of affairs. . . .

The Whips Dont's for avoiding trouble: Dont forget that interests of white and colored people are so intertangled you cannot harm one to any extent without damage to the other. Dont congregate on corners. Dont carry a chip on your shoulder. Dont allow your sentiment to overcome best judgment. . . . Dont forget that the good name of Chicago is at stake.

13. Scholars continue to explore the volatile history of Irish immigrant and African-American community relations. The commerce of such national tensions troubles the twentieth century. As late as the mid-1920s, a trade

card from the Boston Shoe Store, Skowhegan, Maine (Chicago Historical Society) extended stereotypes from the era of the Civil War draft riots: e.g., a pipe-smoking Irish washerwoman gazing out the window at two young street toughs: one black, one white. The caption reads: "Mrs. O'Toole – 'Give it to im Mickey. T'was for de loikes of sich as him, yer fayther got kilt in the war.'" For an incendiary example from the Black Arts Movement, see Baraka, "SOS" (1969: 219): "Assassin poems, Poems that shoot / guns. Poems that wrestle cops into alleys / and take their weapons leaving them dead / with tongues pulled out and sent to Ireland"; for a contemporary scholarly reading, see Ignatiev (1995).

14.   For a more detailed discussion of Harcourt and its founder, Joel Spingarn, see D. L. Lewis (1981).

15.   Richard Wright's Mr. Dalton and Langston Hughes's "Dinner Guest: Me" are fictional constructs of just such assured liberals. Belief in their own supe-riority frees them to care for those they perceive of as "disadvantaged." These liberals, Ralph Ellison claimed, "write as though Negro life only exists in the light of their belated regard." For a crucial interpretation of racial discourse in Sandburg's poetry (specifically "Mammy Hums," "Nigger," and "Singing Nigger"), see Nielsen (1988: 34–7).

16.   As Nielsen notes, "What was really bothering Sandburg was the, to him, unjustifiable increase in the black population of his city" (1988: 35). The stress upon "his city" is perfectly justifiable in light of Sandburg's articles. I would add that his concern was greater than the question of numbers; it circles always about the issue of class. In Sandburg's mind, the "wrong" sort of "folks" were goin' to Chicago.

17.   See Sandburg (1922: 8–11) for an annotated presentation of this "famous negro song" learned from John Lomax. Sandburg's introductory note con-cludes: "I have known this song for eight years . . . and it never loses its strange overtones, with its smiling commentary on the bug that baffles the wit of man, with its whimsical point that while the boll weevil can make a home anywhere the negro, son of man, hath not where to lay his head, and with its intimation, perhaps, that in our mortal life neither the individual human creature, nor the big human family shall ever find a lasting home on the earth" (8). After eleven verses that chart the course of the weevil's migration, the song concludes: "An' if anybody should ax you / Who it was dat make dis song, / Ju' tell 'em 'twas a big buck niggah wid a paih o' / blue duckin's on, / Ain' got no home, ain' got no home"; see Lomax and Lomax (1934: 112–17) for Sandburg's source material: the twenty-two vers-es of "De Ballit of De Boll Weevil"; see A. Lomax (1993: 490–2) for com-parison of Sid Hemphill's with an "early Texas version"; see Henderson (1972: 113) for Eddie "Son" House's "Dry Spell Blues"; see *Blind Willie McTell* (1940), the Library of Congress Folk Song Archive recording by J. Lomax; Lomax, revealing his ethnomusicological stance, urges McTell to sing of "colored people havin' hard times in the south . . . complainin' songs . . . you know, ain't it hard to be a nigger, nigger . . . why is it a mean world to live in." McTell, repeatedly refusing to succumb to Lomax's racist

appeals, sings "Boll Weevil." As Balfour notes, "Suspicions that 'Boll Weevil' and 'Kill It Kid' were sung to order are perhaps borne out by the frequency with which each appears in the repertoire of other Lomax discoveries" (1990). For the most comprehensive discography to date, see J. Place (1997), "Selection 26: 'Mississippi Boweavil Blues.'" The song became a musical bridge between the Mississippi Delta and Chicago, one that (as Sandburg demonstrates) entered the mainstream as shorthand for the migration experience.

18. See Hughes (1954: 81) for a biographical note for young readers: "Because, until very recently, the big national advertisers like the makers of motor cars and breakfast foods, did not advertise in Negro newspapers, these papers had to depend almost entirely on newsstand sales and subscriptions for income. Realizing this, Mr. Abbott instituted colorful and dramatic reporting of news in the *Defender*, the use of big headlines in red ink, and other attention-getting devices. He kept close to the common people so that he might express in his pages their wants and desires."

19. See Meltzer (1967: 31–2), citing *The Crisis* October 1919 article on the Chicago riot. Its writers saw the *Daily News* as the "exception" to the "prominent style [of Chicago papers with their] . . . glaring, prejudice-breeding headlines."

20. See Tuttle (1970: 103–7) for a discussion of racism in Chicago's dailies; R. Wright (1937: 144–5). Wright offers the most damning indictment of such racism: "I told Granny that I planned to make some money by selling papers. . . . For the first time in my life I became aware of the life of the modern world, of vast cities, and I was claimed by it; I loved it. . . . The cheap pulp tales enlarged my knowledge of the world. . . . I was happy and would have continued to sell the newspaper and its magazine supplement indefinitely had it not been for the racial pride of a friend of the family." Confronted with the hateful stereotypes in the very paper he peddled, he could only protest: "'But these papers come from Chicago' . . . feeling unsure of the entire world now, feeling that racial propaganda could not be published in Chicago, the city to which Negroes were fleeing by the thousands."

21. This view of Chicago's new citizens as "human merchandise" was so commonplace that both the police and the white dailies referred to the Illinois Central Railroad Station at Twelfth Street as "Uncle Tom's Cabin." Frank London Brown's *Trumbull Park* (1959) describes the persistence and depth of such custodial views, this time in a formerly white housing project that requires its new black tenants to register upon entry and exit and to be escorted "outa the project" (87).

22. See Meltzer (1967: 31) for an editorial from *The Crisis* (Oct. 1919), substantiating this claim: "With regard to economic competition, the age-long dispute between capital and labor enters. Large numbers of Negroes were brought from the South by the packers and there is little doubt that this was done in part so that the Negro might be used as a club over the heads of the unions."

23. See D. L. Lewis (1981) for a discussion of the evolution of African-American scholarship and journalism. His consideration of Park and Johnson has informed this study throughout.

24. For an in-depth discussion of the Johnson-led, Robert Park research team for the CCRR report, see Waskow (1966: 60–104). Taking advantage of the archives of the NAACP, the Chicago Commission on Race Relations, and the National Archives, Waskow has pieced together the most complete history of the CCRR, its formation, method, and effect.

Chapter 3. Rendezvous with Modernism, Fascism – Democracy

1. See Farnsworth (1982: vi) for his rationale in selection: "From 9 October 1937 to 24 June 1944, assuming that the *Washington Tribune* appeared once a week, there would have been 350 issues. There are 217 'Caviar and Cabbage' columns on microfilm. I have selected 101 for this collection. The microfilm records of the *Tribune* during this period have significant gaps, but there are copies of the *Tribune* in which 'Caviar and Cabbage' did not appear. For two years, 1939 and 1940, there are copies of fifty columns each year, indicating that for at least those two years a column appeared practically every week."

2. For background to *Gallery* (completed in 1935; published posthumously in 1979), see Farnsworth (1984: 42–4), Nielsen (1994: 48–70), Bérubé (1992: 158, 165). See also Tolson's "The Odyssey of a Manuscript," the story of how he came to write his first collection of poems (Farnsworth 1984: 42).

3. The *Tribune*, perhaps because of its limited availability, has been a neglected weekly. Even the standard reference, Wolseley (1990), fails to mention it (though it does note the *Tribune*'s competitor, the *Washington Afro-American*). Regrettably, there is at present no scholarly history of the black press. Wolseley offers an unreliable, because of omissions and errors, though useful reference.

4. Readers familiar with Tolson's interest in the teachings of G. I. Gurdjieff (received by way of Jean Toomer and A. R. Orage) should be alert to the possibilities of encrypted alchemical, numerological, and anagrammatic references throughout his work. As Jon Woodson has suggested to me, even the title of his column succumbs to this method of reading: Lewis Carroll's "The Walrus and the Carpenter" recalling "cabbages and kings" as it mutates from "cabbages and czars" to "cabbages and caviar" to "caviar and cabbage." The intensity of Tolson's linguistically tuned, mathematical playfulness is characteristic of Harlemites who succumbed to Gurdjieffian mysticism. P. D. Ouspensky's *In Search of the Miraculous* (1949) provides an invaluable overview of Gurdjieff's teachings.

    Woodson's "Melvin Tolson and the Art of Being Difficult" and "To Make a New Race: Jean Toomer, G. I. Gurdjieff and the Harlem Renaissance" (unpublished MS) are essential readings of esotericism in the writings of Tolson, Hurston, Schuyler, Larsen, Thurman, and Fisher.

5. Sandburg's aesthetic, class, and national identity postures were often quite

congenial to Tolson. See, for example, Tolson's "The Merry-Go-Round and the Ferris Wheel of History" (October 19, 1940): "I shall never forget Sandburg's poem describing a 'Dago,' the descendant of Aristotle, laying a roadbed for the Anglo-Saxons of today! In Aristotle's time the Anglo-Saxon was a savage, and today we're all wondering what Hitler will do to the Anglo-Saxons in England. The Ferris Wheel of History!" (Farnsworth 1982: 91).

6. Nielsen's discussion of Tolson and the "deterritorialization of modernism" concludes: "Tolson is a decolonizer after Whitman and Toussaint L'Ouverture; he will emphasize and glorify the *African* Americanism of his art, and he does it on the plain of the master's colony, on the site of the colonized master text of modernism" (1994: 53).

7. Whereas Hopkins and Abbott actively cultivated the black middle class, Tolson anticipates the unease found in Alice Walker's attitudes toward the white sponsors and black bourgeois administrators of the fictional Saxon College of *Meridian*. "Hagar," "Sambo," and "Chittling" would remain Tolson's shorthand personifications, infinitely suggestive of empowerment through appropriation of what Lippmann would have labeled "the perfect stereotype" (1922: 88–9) of white derogation. See, for example, "Black Cats – Black Women – and Black Spirits" (March 29, 1941; 93) as well as the "Eta" section of *Harlem Gallery* (1965). For a history of "the rise and demise of an American jester," see Boskin (1986).

8. Such assurance is consistent with Tolson's sense of himself as a Gurdjieffian initiate who, in Woodson's reading, participated in a "consistent literary attack on racialist thought" (unpublished MS, 32).

9. "Candid Camera Shots of Negro Intellectuals" (June 29, 1940), Tolson's recollection of "A Negro Poet and a Taxicab in the Rain—1932," depicts his first encounter with the socially aware Langston Hughes (1982: 255–6).

10. As Tolson echoes in "An Ex-Judge at the Bar," published in the "Woodcuts for Americana" section of *Rendezvous with America* (1944: 19):

> "To make the world safe for Democracy,
> You lost a leg in Flanders fields – *oui, oui?*
> To gain a judge's seat, you twined the noose
> That hung the Negro higher than a goose."

11. See "The Editorial Policy of Negro Newspapers of 1917–18" (1944: 24–31). Though regional in its emphasis, Sullivan's *Days of Hope: Race and Democracy in the New Deal Era* (1996) is a crucial contribution to our understanding of the nationalization of the race issue, especially during the Second New Deal.

12. See Anderson (1983: 149) for a consideration of "Patriotism and Racism": "The fact of the matter is that nationalism thinks in terms of historical destinies, while racism dreams of eternal contaminations, transmitted from the origins of time through an endless sequence of loathsome copulations: outside history. Niggers are, thanks to the invisible tar-brush, forever niggers; Jews, the seed of Abraham, forever Jews, no matter what passports they carry or what languages they speak and read. (Thus for the Nazi, the *Jewish* German was always an imposter.)"

13. See Schomburg (1925: 231): "Though it is orthodox to think of America as

the one country where it is unnecessary to have a past, what is a luxury for the nation as a whole becomes a prime social necessity for the Negro. For him, a group tradition must supply compensation for persecution, and pride of race the antidote for prejudice. History must restore what slavery took away, for it is the social damage of slavery that the present generation must repair and offset. So among the rising democratic millions we find the Negro thinking more collectively, more retrospectively than the rest, and apt out of the very pressure of the present to become the most enthusiastic antiquarian of them all."

14. See "Your History" (1936: sec. 2.2) for an illustrated fact column on the feature page that typically combined "ancient" roots with "modern" American history and contemporary news. "Your History," on this day, displays a historical collage of sketches of Haile Selassie, Civil War black regiments, and Booker T. Washington.

15. Harris discusses Italian-American reactions to the war in chapter 5. For consideration of Roosevelt's 1936 campaign in relation to the Ethiopian war as well as minority issues, see K. S. Davis (1986: 583–95, 627–48); for a suggestive description of Ethiopianism in the United States, which is useful in reading Sandburg's misreading of "Abyssianism" in Chicago, see Asante (1977: 10–11).

16. See, for example, *A Nation of Nations*, Adamic's *Common Ground* essays from the war years. Though published in 1945, the collection fairly represents the "sympathetic" depiction of the necessary Americanization of immigrants. Of particular note in Adamic's volume is the racial isolation imposed by its table of contents. Sandwiched among chapters on "Americans from [national origin]" rests chapter 8, "Negro Americans." It is clear throughout Adamic's many books celebrating "*e pluribus unum*" that race origins perplex him – or at least defy his sense of the composite national identity that is, for him, "America." *Two-Way Passage* (1941), published on the eve of "the next war," offers Adamic's most searching discussion of America's enduring Eurocentricity.

17. See Hughes (1944: 299) on language and citizenship: "Yet many Americans who cannot speak English – so recent is their arrival on our shores – may travel about our country at will securing food, hotel, and rail accommodations wherever they wish to purchase them. *I may not.* These Americans, once naturalized, may vote in Mississippi or Texas, if they live there. *I may not.* They may work at whatever job their skills command. *But I may not.* They may purchase tickets for concerts, theatres, lectures wherever they are sold throughout the United States. *Often I may not.* They may repeat the Oath of Allegiance with its ringing phrase of 'Liberty and justice for all,' with a deep faith in its truth – as compared with the limitations and oppressions they have experienced in the Old World. I repeat the oath, too, but I know that the phrase about 'liberty and justice' does not fully apply to me. I am an American – *but I am a colored American.*"

18. See E. Johnson (1942: 39–41) for a national survey of community weeklies and their editorial responses to the war with the Axis powers.

19. See Steel (1980: sec. 2, chap. 24) for a detailed consideration of Lippmann's public opinion and its effect on the incoming Roosevelt administration; K. S. Davis (1986: chap. 1) for an investigation into the relationship
between public opinion and FDR's conception of executive power.

20. Rainey argues against a reading of fascism as "an anomaly in the rhythm of
history, devoid of authentic connection with the culture that nurtured
it . . . [it was] a diverse and dynamic movement that succeeded because it
could speak to intelligent contemporaries, because its ideological premises coincided with concepts essential to ordinary scholars at work on quotid-
ian problems of their field" (1991: 3).

21. In spite of their shared subjects – the tyranny of capitalism, the failure of
democracy – Tolson and Pound lacked a common language. Tolson's racially inscribed marginal status liberated languages of possibility and redemption (in Bakhtinian terms, "heteroglossia"), enabling him to condemn his
nation's historical and immediate transgressions while projecting an attainable democracy. Pound's marginality ironically depended upon his notion
of an embattled, if not utterly collapsing, Anglo-Saxonism. Though Pound,
like Tolson, was born far from the centers of eastern cultural authority, he
was schooled in a withering cultural myth of whiteness and masculinity that
prohibited an imaginative engagement with the coming postcolonial world.
Mussolini and Jefferson were, for Pound, abstractions of a unitary language
that was perpetually receding into obscurity.

22. See W. C. Williams (1935: 61–2) for an enthusiastic review of *Jefferson and/or
Mussolini* in *New Democracy* that notes the absence of a genuine proletarian
movement in the 1930s but the existence of one of "group power . . . [with-
in which there was] a great emphasis on the newly discovered significance
of economic forces – the most dangerous of which is today credit control";
also (1939: 23) for his review of *Guide to Kulchur*, which concludes: "And
his conclusion from all this is totalitarianism! The failure of the book is that
by its tests Mussolini is a great man; and the failure of Pound, that he thinks
him so. The book should be read for its style, its wide view of learning, its
enlightenment as to the causes of many of our present ills. The rest can be
forgiven as the misfortune of a brave man who took the risk of making a
bloody fool of himself – and lost."
    See Pound (1996: 172) for a postinvasion justification to Williams (Octo-
ber 1935?):
    Muss. is having a war. All right. We got Louisians and a war in Africa
    is better than one in Europe which ALL the buggaring gun makes
    wanted.
        ANYhow. what's italy to you. If you cd. read wop. you might learn
    something from Odon Por's article in Civilta Fascista for May.
        AND it is loony to judge Italy as if Muss. were alone in Europe with
    no international finance. . . .
    For a discussion of Williams, Pound, and the Social Credit Movement, see
Mariani (1981: 382): "Jefferson, then, was like Mussolini: two men of extraordinary leadership abilities attempting to make their respective govern-

ments work. 'Instead of Mussolini it might have been Lenin, Hitler, Roosevelt, Horthy, Mustapha Kemal,' Williams summed up. They were all 'integers of different values.' In 1935 Williams was willing to listen to Pound's view of Mussolini as the good leader with a vision. But by 1937, after Mussolini had invaded Abyssinia and especially Republican Spain, Williams could barely mention *Il Duce* without spitting. The rift with Pound would by then have become deeper than ever." Although Mariani would like to suggest Williams's aversion to Mussolini's invasion, correspondence reveals that his genuine indignation was reserved for the attack on Spain.

23. For Pound's view of the Italo-Ethiopian War, see Meacham (1967: 37, 62, 139, 159); Torrey (1984: esp. chap. 5); Stock (1970: 331–41); Heymann (1976: "Settings," sec. 7–10); Gallup (1969: esp. sec. C).

24. *The Crisis* and the *Pittsburgh Courier* are two of the most detailed (in terms of history and immediate events) and eloquent sources throughout the Italo-Ethiopian war. *Crisis* editorials, letters to the editor, feature articles, and political cartoons make vivid the collapse of Haile Selassie's realm; see in particular Haile (1935) and Padmore (1936). The *Courier* – with front-line dispatches from J. A. Rogers, George Schuyler's editorials, the "Views and Reviews" columns, and even opinion columns by Du Bois – sustain the vitality of this foreign war.

25. See Pound (1950: 283) where he writes to Hemingway on November 28, 1936:

> Banks make 90% of all buggaring money, of all exploding gunrunnin gunselling jawbreaking and eviscerating and . . . amputating moncy that goes into buggarin shells for the bloody, was it a WAR.
>
> And if the . . . chance to kill the sonvabitch that profits by hiring some poor simp to like you first, is all . . . economics and to the bottom of that to bitch the bastids is the job.

And yet he paused to caution "me deah Hembo": "[it] don't lower me respekk for Benito."

Lest this be considered unique to the banter of Pound or the sermons of Tolson, see Sandburg (1936: sec. 82, 569):

> I pledge my allegiance,
> say the munitions makers and the international bankers,
> I pledge my allegiance to this flag, that flag,
> any flag at all, of any country anywhere
> paying its bills and meeting interest on loans,
> one and indivisible,
> coming through with cash in payment as stipulated
> with liberty and justice for all,
> say the munitions makers and the international bankers.

26. Readers surprised by Tolson's exculpation of Roosevelt may locate his generous rationale in the earlier "The King and Queen: Behind the Headlines" (June 17, 1939). Here he explains, with a particular anticolonial flourish, the relationship between J. P. Morgan (favorite of the royal family) and Roosevelt: "Mr. Morgan does not have a deep affection for President Roo-

svelt. Mr. Morgan cannot boss Mr. Roosevelt. Franklin D. kicks off the sixty families too much" (1982: 72). Compare with Pound's contemporary indictments of Roosevelt as part of the international Jewish banking conspiracy. See, in particular, Doob (1978).

27. See Tolson (1982: 81–2), "I Am Thankful for the Great Depression" (September 30, 1939), for elaboration upon his theories of race, class, and community in America:

> As a black citizen in a white democracy, I consider the Great Depression the brightest blessing that my race has experienced since Mr. Lincoln issued the militarily brilliant and economically profitable Emancipation Proclamation. . . .
>
> A Negro middle class emerged, nurtured by the Dale Carnegie philosophy of Dr. Booker T. Washington and the aristocratic titbits of Dr. W. E. Burghardt Du Bois. Negro weeklies flourished, displaying the buxom charms of high-yellow society matrons basking on the jim-crow beach at Atlantic City. . . .
>
> To America's largest minority group, color is a birthmark and poverty a birthright; the Bill of Rights is a book sealed with seven seals; and the quest for a job, in prosperous times, takes on the hazard and ingenuity and sensation of a Homeric episode. The simple prerogatives and opportunities which white citizens take for granted are luscious fruit beyond the reach and grasp of black men. The Negro suffers all the disadvantages of being poor, plus the proscriptions of being black.

28. See Tolson (1953) where he abandons the too static merry-go-round in his "Africa-To-Be."

29. Tolson, inclined to take Jefferson at his word, declares: "There can be no democracy without economic equality. Thomas Jefferson said that when he wrote the Declaration of Independence. There can be no brotherhood of man without a brotherhood of dollars" (1982: 92).

30. See Tolson (1965: 51), the "Eta" section of *Harlem Gallery*: "'Old Probabilities, *what* am I? / Mister, *what* are you? / An eagle or a chicken come home to roost? / I wish I knew!'"

31. See Tolson (1982: 197), "The Word *Freedom* in the Wolf's Dictionary" (Feb. 26, 1944), for Tolson's "little discourse on the Golden Rule versus the Dog-Eat-Dog Rule," in which he concludes:

> Bilbo calls Walter White a traitor and we call him a patriot! Bilbo says the Negro should be free to go to Africa; and I say the Negro should be free to stay in Mississippi. The wolf and the sheep can never agree on the word *freedom!* Well, what should we do? I agree here with Abe Lincoln and the little people. We must repudiate the wolf's dictionary. What does repudiate mean? It means to reject, disown, discard, renounce, cast away! Yes, this is what we must do with the Dog-Eat-Dog Rule which is derived from the wolf's dictionary.
>
> But I, for one, am ready to do more than discard the wolf's dictionary. I am ready to cast out the wolf himself!

32. For consideration of Eleanor Roosevelt's tenant farmer activities, see K. S. Davis (1986: chap. 16, sec. 6); for Tolson's sharecropper organizational work, see Farnsworth (1984).

33. No doubt recalling Eleanor Roosevelt's sponsorship of Marian Anderson's 1939 Easter Sunday concert at the Lincoln Memorial, Tolson notes (1982: 97–8), "Our Good White Friends Get Cold Feet" (January 23, 1943): "In times of peace it was profitable for certain educated white men and women to pose as friends of the Negro. It gave them a special niche in American life. They attracted attention to themselves. They were invited to attend big meetings, where the golden brown chicken sagged the tables. . . . Those good old days of Negro patronage have gone forever. White people have always accepted the Marian Andersons and Richard Wrights."

34. In many columns, black Americans become America's ideal citizens. See Tolson (1982: 249), "I Am an Unprejudiced Negro" (August 26, 1939) – "America is bone of my bone, blood of my blood, and flesh of my flesh. No Negro has ever betrayed the Stars and Stripes. I know of no black Benedict Arnold or Aaron Burr. I was born an American. I shall die an American" and (1982: 99), "Who Said: 'This Is a White Man's Country?'" (July 31, 1943) – "A Negro who thinks this country – the United States – is not his country is a damned fool. My native land! Where is it? It is where my mother gave me birth. My hometown is where I was born. Jesus was a Nazarene, because He was born in Nazareth. I am just as much an American as President Roosevelt. And for the same reason. We both were born in the United States."

35. In the wake of most racially motivated demonstrations, violent or nonviolent, two responses were common: the official report (for example, *The Negro in Chicago*) and the interracial committee. Interracialism took many forms, including publication. One of the richest wartime sources of "Christian Democracy," the espoused philosophy of the Catholic Interracial Program, is the monthly *Interracial Review*. Rejecting "artificial inequalities due to racial myths, material greed or physical violence," the *Review* advanced social and political objectives as well: "Christian Democracy [is] a society in which the God-given dignity and destiny of every human person is fully recognized, in laws, government, institutions, and human conduct" (manifesto printed on contents page of each issue).

36. Croly remains an essential figure in America's twentieth-century debates regarding nationalism, citizenship, and imperialism. Overwhelmed by Theodore Roosevelt's muscular leadership, he severely critiqued Jeffersonian democracy as he grew increasingly less interested in the rights of the individual. Though it is likely that Tolson drew his American debate from the founding documents, it is unlikely that he would have remained untouched by this all-pervasive study. See Croly (1909: chaps. 8–9) for a discussion of "democracy" and "nationality"; (1909: chap. 4) for his reading of "slavery and American nationality" and "slavery as a democratic institution" in which Abolitionists are read as "perverted conceptions of democracy, one of the most perverted and dangerous . . . that . . . identifies . . . exclusively with a system of natural rights" (1909: 80–1). For a con-

temporary response to the impact of Croly's thinking had on twentieth-century discussions of federalism and the individual, see Beer (1993: x): "For Croly, the two governing ideas of American politics have been 'the principle of nationality' and 'the principle of democracy,' given expression at the time of the founding by Alexander Hamilton and Thomas Jefferson, respectively. From that time, according to Croly, the two wings of the American party system have usually been distinguished by their emphasis on one or the other of these principles."

37. The snaking, centered two-syllable lines so sharply recall and diminish Whitman's epic inventions that Tolson would seem to be suggesting that the Whitmanesque epic embrace of our individual and national ambitions may no longer be possible. Tolson's substitution of "for" for Whitman's "of" recasts the national into a personal poem of consolation.

38. Though never mentioned in his poetry or his columns, Huey Long and Father Coughlin helped Tolson (in his reaction against their projections) to formulate his notion of the ideal citizen. The apparent failure of governmental and economic systems spawned a range of realignments, social as well as chronological. As Tolson notes in "Rendezvous with America": "time unhinged the gates!" Pound's calendrical shift to the chronos and topos of Mussolini is but one phase of his complete rejection of the notion of social, economic, and cultural progress.

39. Hughes (1936: 190) appropriates national rhetoric, the homiletics of mythology and anthems, to orchestrate and emphasize America's unfulfilled promises. The parenthetical, endstopped ambivalence of the unspecified narrator ("America was never America to me."), which at first forms a qualifying subtext (*Say, who are you that mumbles in the dark?*") to the increasingly empty recitation of patriotic discourse, soon overtakes the "national" discourse and assumes the dominant subject position of the disfranchised:

> I am the poor white, fooled and pushed apart,
> I am the Negro bearing slavery's scars.
> I am the red man driven from the land,
> I am the immigrant clutching the hope I seek –
> And finding only the same old stupid plan
> Of dog eat dog, of mighty crush the weak.

40. Even when attempting to celebrate the powerless, Sandburg succumbs to buffoonery (1936: sec. 63, 537–8):

> In a winter sunset near Springfield, Illinois
> In the coming on of a winter gloaming,
> A Negro miner with headlamp and dinner bucket,
> A black man explained how it happens
> In some of the mines only white men are hired,
> Only white men can dig out the coal
> Yet he would strike if the strike was right
> And, "For a just cause I'd live in the fields on hard corn."
>
> White man: "You take the crow and I'll take

the turkey or I'll take the turkey and you
take the crow."
Indian: "You don't talk turkey to me once."

In a corn-belt village after a Sunday game
a fan said to a farmhand second baseman:
"You play great ball, boy, a little more time
for practice and you could make the big leagues."
"Sure, I know it, shoveling cow manure, that's
all that holds me back."

41. See Rampersad (1988: 234–6) for consideration of Tolson's ascendancy over Gwendolyn Brooks and Langston Hughes. His dismissal of *Rendezvous with America* ("militant pro-Marxism of his first volume") seems a partisan not a critical gesture. Surely, when read against Sandburg and MacLeish, Tolson seems relentlessly in the American grain. Yet, when read in the Gurdjieffian mode (as Woodson suggests), Tolson's left-leaning politics seems just another of his "false personalities." See Sollors (1994: 113–15) for a discussion of citizenship issues in Tolson.

42. It is interesting to compare Bakhtin's theories of the centrifugal and centripetal forces of discourse with Adamic's perception of American national identity in *Two-Way Passage*: "the *international* derivation of the American people and their great diversity whose centripetal path is outward unity" (Adamic 1941: 253).

Chapter 4. "If I Were a Negro"

1. See *Fortune*: "Special Issue on Business and the Urban Crisis," January 1968, in particular the editorial "The Deeper Shame of the Cities" (2):

   Big business, the city, and the Negro have something in common: all three are victims of the tyranny of the agrarian myth over the American mind. The dominant American social myth is still Thomas Jefferson's set of values and ideals, which assumes a lightly organized society of self-sufficient farmers and abhors the bigness and specialization necessary to modern society. Largely in consequence of this agrarian bias, the subfederal level of our public life has been falling further and further behind the responsibilities thrust upon it by social change. We were taught to despise our cities until they did become despicable.

   The nation will not surmount the racial crisis unless it makes rapid progress toward resolving the broader crisis of the city – the urban complex that includes towns, suburbs, and satellite cities, as well as the core cities themselves. The U.S. cannot be made fit for the black man unless it is also made fit for the white man. And by publicly taking its stand on the side of the city and the Negro, business can at the same time help to restore its own reputation and its own internal morale.

2. See J. H. Johnson (1989: 116) for his recollections of his early "lowly life" of many tedious jobs: "It's fashionable nowadays for employees to talk about what they call the s—— detail, the petty and sometimes menial tasks assigned to low-ranking employees. Well, the s—— detail made me a millionaire. Although I resented some of the little things I was doing, one of them – running the Speedaumat machine – was the key to the *Negro Digest* sweepstakes."

3. See J. H. Johnson (1989: 119) for "every word and comma of the letter [he] wrote":

> Dear Mr. Brown:
>
> A good friend of yours told me about you.
>
> He told me that you are a person who likes to keep abreast of local and national events. He said that you are the kind of person who will be interested in a magazine that will help you become more knowledgeable about your own people and about what they are doing to win greater recognition for you and other members of our race. Because of your position in the community and the recommendation I received, I would like to offer you a reduced rate on the magazine *Negro Digest*, which will be published in the next thirty days.
>
> Magazine subscriptions will sell for $3.00 a year, but in view of the recommendation we are offering a subscription to you for $2.00, if you send your check or money order by September 30.

   Not surprisingly, Burns recalls the effort somewhat differently: "Since he confessed that writing was not his strong suit, I was called upon to help draft solicitation letters, the first of many subscription promotion pieces I created in the early years of *Negro Digest*" (1989: 32).

4. Until the recent publication of Burns's memoir, *Nitty Gritty*, the collaborative nature of Johnson's publishing empire was unsuspected or ignored, with the possible exception of Hoyt Fuller. Followers of Fuller's editing of the second run of *Negro Digest* (after the decade-long hiatus in the 1950s) as well as the aesthetically innovative and politically charged *Black World* are vehement, vocal, and well known (including Henry Louis Gates, Jr., Houston Baker, Arnold Rampersad, Stephen Henderson, and Randall Kennedy). Johnson's less-than-total recall in *Succeeding against the Odds*, more characteristic of the generic rags-to-riches autobiography than of personal slight, is noted by Fuller partisan Randall Kennedy in his *Reconstruction* essay-review "Making It" (1990). Innocent of the larger editorial picture at Johnson Publishing, Kennedy nonetheless questions the contributing threads of the empire. Without benefit of Burns's memoir, he believes Johnson's account of the early years, wary only of the fact that Johnson "devotes distressingly little attention . . . to the editorial substance of his periodicals . . . [and] says virtually nothing about working with writers or planning layouts or determining what issues to focus upon" (66). Most disappointing to this Hoyt Fuller partisan are "omissions with respect to the history of *Negro Digest*," which Kennedy labels "particularly egregious" (66). Although Burns's memoir must be approached with an equally skeptical reading,

Nitty Gritty provides at least a partial corrective to Johnson's memoir and encourages scholars to investigate more fully the rich, collaborative nature of publishing.

5. In the wake of the 1942 relocation of Japanese "aliens" from the West Coast and the 1943 riots in Los Angeles (with its infamous "zoot suit" riot), Detroit, and Harlem, the Chicago Mayor's Committee on Race Relations indexed the "resentment" yet again. Willing to concede the national proportion of the crisis, though unwilling to see beyond the local imperatives, the committee further obfuscated "the problem": "The problem is to give Negroes, as for the most part *we* have given *other immigrant* groups, full rights and free opportunities. Many issues, of course, cannot be settled in any single city. For example, deep resentment is felt by the colored group at segregation and discrimination in an army drafted to fight for democracy" (1945: 3; emphasis added). The innocence with which the mayor's committee assumes its right to broker citizenship, its agency to determine "inalienable" rights, and its consignment of African Americans to simply another "immigrant" group reveals a startling continuity with *The Negro in Chicago*, the 1922 "official" story of the 1919 riot.

6. See Clark (1965: 172) for consideration of the singular difference between the weeklies and the national magazines:

> Some of the more obvious deficiencies of the Negro press seem to be absent in the national magazines which are devoted to Negro news, aspirations, and achievements. The most successful of these magazines are published by John H. Johnson of Chicago. Johnson is a shrewd man, deceptively calm in manner. . . . His magazines are significant not only because of their nationwide circulation, which for the first time demonstrates that Negroes can sustain a national press, but because they show that publications controlled by Negroes can meet the competitive, aesthetic standards of the "larger," i.e., the white, society.

Clark's *Dark Ghetto*, published during the early years of President Johnson's "Great Society," remains an essential discussion of community formation and social power.

7. For a consideration of such discourse communities in Habermasian terms, see Calhoun (1992: 37–8):

> In nearly any imaginable case there will be clusters of relatively greater density of communication within the looser overall field. These clusters may be only more or less biased microcosms of the whole, as cities have their own public discourse within countries, and as neighborhoods within cities. But these clusters may also be organized around issues, categories, persons or basic dynamics of the larger society. . . . For any such cluster we must ask not just on what thematic content it focuses but also how it is internally organized, how it maintains its boundaries and relatively greater internal cohesion in relation to the larger public, and whether its separate existence reflects merely sectional interests, some functional division of labor, or a felt need for bulwarks against the hegemony of a dominant ideology.

8. As with so many features of the magazine, this revenue producer (the celebrity status of many of the columnists, from Eleanor Roosevelt to Edward G. Robinson, boosted sales of many issues) is recalled differently by Johnson and by Burns. Though Johnson in his autobiography retreats from early interview claims that he originated the column, he claims control over its direction. He asserts that, in response to stalled circulation figures, he "studied the situation and decided that the most promising area of development was one of our regular features, 'If I Were a Negro.' We were getting a lot of unsolicited advice in this period from Whites, some well-meaning, some not so well-meaning. I decided to take advantage of this trend by asking Whites to put themselves in our shoes and answer some difficult questions" (1989: 130).

   Burns, however, describes a more complex path to this feature (1996: 37-8):

   > Over the years Johnson came genuinely to believe that he personally had originated many of the new features in *Negro Digest*. A typical instance was the idea for the much publicized "If I Were a Negro" series, which originated under that title as an article in the *Chicago Daily News*, written by its financial editor, Royal F. Munger, and reprinted in the second issue of *Negro Digest*. Thereupon, I drafted a form letter to nationally known individuals requesting similar articles and offering them a token payment. Eventually we were surprised to receive a contribution from Eleanor Roosevelt, which impressively boosted the circulation of our October 1943 issue and proved a turning point in the magazine's profitability. When Johnson later retold the story, however, as he did in a *New York Post* article by Helen Duder in 1962, he claimed, "I got the idea of running a series of articles by prominent people on 'If I Were a Negro.'"

   For Johnson's version of the Eleanor Roosevelt column, chap. 16: "The President's Wife Turns the Tide."

9. See Du Bois (1920: 925-38) for his vision of "these [white] souls undressed and from back and side . . . the working of their entrails" (923) and Hughes (1934: 19) for his tales of "people who went in for Negroes" (19). For a contemporary transracial reading, see June Jordan (1989: 35) "What Would I Do White?" in which she concludes: "I would do nothing / That would be enough."

10. See Mailer (1957: 585), "The White Negro," in which solace for postwar malaise and disjunction is located in "the Negro . . . [who] living on the margin between totalitarianism and democracy for two centuries" became for him the quintessence of "the Hip."

    See also Ellison (1963/4: 178), a critique of Irving Howe's *Dissent* essay, "Black Boys and Native Sons," reflecting anew upon the nature of "collective experience": "More important, perhaps, being a Negro American involves a *willed* (who wills to be a Negro? *I* do!) affirmation of self as against all outside pressures – an identification with the group as extended through the individual self which rejects all possibilities of escape that do not involve a basic resuscitation of the original American ideals of social and political justice. And those white Negroes (and I do not mean Norman Mailer's dream creatures) are Negroes too – if they wish to be."

11. For an overview of the black middle-class reaction to Myrdal, see Banner-Haley (1994: 174-5); for an essential reading of Myrdal's impact upon American race liberalism, see W. A. Jackson (1990).

12. See Ellison (1944: 328-45) for a meditation (in the guise of a review of Myrdal's *An American Dilemma*) upon conscience, liberalism, and the New Deal. Of particular interest is his consideration of the political compromises made regarding the Jim Crow army (334):

> The most striking example of this failure is to be seen in the New Deal administration's perpetuation of a Jim Crow army, and the shamefaced support of it given by the Communists. It would be easy – on the basis of some of the slogans attributed to Negro people by the Communists from time to time, and the New Deal's frequent retreats on Negro issues – to question the sincerity of these two groups. Or, in the case of the New Deal, to attribute its failure to its desire to hold power in a concrete political situation, while the failure of the Communists could be laid to "Red perfidy." But this would be silly. Sincerity is not a quality that one expects of political parties, not even revolutionary ones. To question their sincerity makes room for the old idea of paternalism, and the corny notion that these groups have an obligation to "do something *for* the Negro."

13. See Sandburg (1943: 274-5), "Who does a zoot suit suit?" (June 20, 1943), for a familiarly reductive view of the riot:

> Of course, part of the strong-arm stuff in handling zooters lately is plain old-fashioned gang fighting among boys who don't like each other's looks. Some of it is race riot and lynch-law stuff. Part of it is the scorn of the armed services for boogie-woogie bugs who wear hepcat clothes with a hip drape. As a sign and passing phenomenon it may fade into the mist of yesteryear like hobble skirt, the Tom Thumb golf course, tiddledywinks, yo-yo, or mah-jong.

Of particular note is Sandburg's casual conjunction of "race riot" and "lynch-law stuff."

14. See Johnson (1989: 123) for his response to suggestions that he took simplistic paths to his commercial success, providing readers with a pleasing, safely "digested" product: "*Reader's Digest* tended to be upbeat, but *Negro Digest* spoke to an audience that was angry, disillusioned, and disappointed. You couldn't digest that world without digesting the frustration and anger."

15. See Ellison (1945a: 140) for an application of Edward Bland's theory of "pre-individualism": "The pre-individualistic black community discourages individuality out of self-defense. Having learned through experience that the whole group is punished for the actions of the single member, it has worked out efficient techniques of behavior control."

16. See Roosevelt (1943a: 82), condensed from *New Threshold*, for a declaration of Eleanor's global vision of peace and freedom: "We are fighting a war

today so that individuals all over the world may have freedom. This means an equal chance for every man to have food and shelter and a minimum of such things as spell happiness to that particular human personality." Domestic harmony would come only when four "simple freedoms" had been achieved: "equality before the law . . . equality of education for everyone . . . equality in the economic field . . . equality of expression." The First Lady's embellishment of Jefferson's "inalienable rights" resulted in this extension of "fundamental rights . . . on which the men who fight this war can look forward into the future with real hope to a world organization which may gradually bring about a betterment of human conditions the world over" (83).

17. Lerner's preface to "Discrimination on WPA: Black Women Appeal to FDR" (selection of letters from the "WPA Box, Howard University") notes that these letters "are personal appeals by desperate women who had tried all the regular channels for help and had been turned down. Their faith in the all-powerful benevolence of the President is as pathetic as is their need" (399).

Anxious to highlight the tyrannical indifference of such patriarchal institutions as the presidency, Lerner perhaps inadvertently diminishes the appeal of the Roosevelts to African Americans.

Chapter 5. Reportage as Redemption

1. See Witcover (1997: 171) for a discussion of Martin as the epitome of cautious liberalism: "John Bartlow Martin, the author and Indiana native who was now on the Kennedy staff, specifically counseled the candidate in the wake of the King assassination to condemn violence and rioting, but always to combine the condemnation with the observation that neither could racial injustice be tolerated. Kennedy readily agreed."

2. Brooks had a long association with the Mecca; see Brooks's interview with George Stavros (1969: 162):

> Well, when I was nineteen, and had just gotten out of junior college, I went to the Illinois State Employment Service to get a job. They sent me to the Mecca building to a spiritual adviser, and he had a fantastic practice; lucrative. He had us bottling medicine as well as answering letters. Not real medicine, but love charms and stuff like that he called it, and delivered it through the building; that was my introduction to the Mecca building.

3. Of particular note are the volume's original reviews by Stafford and Rosenthal, essays by Melhem, Taylor, and Jones. Clarke's "The Loss of Lyric Space," were it not so atomistic and unfocused, might have been a genuine contribution to the literature on this complex poem.

4. Brooks must have delighted in publishing with a black-owned press that so boldly declared its journalistic ambitions in its name. Randall, signifying upon the etymologic strands of "broadside" and "press," devoted the press to original collections as well as poetry broadsides. See A. Lomax (1993: 49–51) for a

discussion of "broadsheets" and "broadsides" in the African-American blues community, which like the broadsides of "the British street singers of the six-teenth and seventeenth centuries . . . kept the public informed of the latest news by composing, singing, and publishing ballads" (51).

5. Brooks and Brown had a long and generous relationship, in which, as Brooks's biographer Kent explains, "the sentiment of friendship [turned] into deeds" (1990: 158). Like Brooks, Brown wrote frequently for Chicago publications like *Negro Digest*, the *Defender*, the *Sun-Times*, and the *Tribune*, and was an associate editor at Johnson's *Ebony* magazine. Brown did more than write encouraging reviews of Brooks: he orchestrated parts of her teaching career. See Kent (1990: 159): "Only six days prior to his death, Brown's efforts had succeeded in gaining for Gwendolyn an entrée to teaching. On March 6, 1962, his secretary, Freddy L. Nollet, confirmed that she would be teaching American literature in Brown's Union Leadership Program at the University of Chicago, in seven sessions from April 16 through May 7." Brooks's elegy for Brown, who died of leukemia in March 1962, reads as a tribute to all citizens of places like Trumbull Park and the Mecca Building:

He observed
School and garbage and bright shells,
The molasses stickiness of stupidity,
The ticking of quick Tim,
The tender profiles of children,
Unwieldy

Prophecy, political persons
Gone past the place
And point of grace
To slitheriness and slime.

Always
Love and the pledge of the curtain to fall
Erected such reverence of vagabond View after all.
(quoted in Kent 1990: 158)

In the scant literature on Brown's career, essays by Maryemma Graham and Sterling Stuckey stand out as the best overviews of his career, sharing insights into his influence on Brooks.

6. Confusion exists regarding the date of the Mecca's demise. Martin's article notes the transfer of the property to the Illinois Institute of Technology in 1941 with its accompanying plans to "replace the Mecca with a laboratory" (1950: 96), but explains that, as of December 1950, the tenants had suc-cessfully resisted eviction. Melhem, using Martin as her source, telescopes the process incorrectly, stating that in 1941 the institute "bought the build-ing and, despite opposition, tore it down nine years later to extend facilities on the site" (1987: 158); K. J. Williams, in "The Restricted Chicago of Gwen-dolyn Brooks," claims: "Razed in 1952, the Mecca remains in memory as a symbol of absolute urban blight" (1987: 60); Clarke, in "The Loss of Lyric

Space," accepting Williams, declares: "The 1952 razing of Chicago's once magnificent showplace, the Mecca, was an act of erasure, causing Gwendolyn Brooks, by the late 1960s, to reconsider her own location in the tradition of African-American literature" (1995: 136); Taylor, in "Gwendolyn Brooks: An Essential Sanity," also depending upon Williams, notes "the important fact that the building was razed in 1952" (1991: 127). Although few critics have investigated primary materials to ascertain the exact date of the Mecca's razing, they tend to literalize its importance to Brooks. Little suggests that Brooks required the actuality of a building that she had long ago internalized as part of the narrative of her community. For *Life* magazine's photojournalistic rendering of the Mecca's final days, an essay of enormous importance to Brooks, see "The Mecca" (1951: 133–9).

7. *Life* magazine's photo essay casually relates the South Side's lack of style to the influx of African Americans: "By 1912 the first Negro tenants had moved in. The building's noisy jazz activities gave a name to the *Mecca Flat Blues* and the apartment steadily trumpeted its way downhill" ("The Mecca," 1951: 133). In spite of its condescending text, the article so complemented the spirit of her poem that Brooks wanted to use the photograph of the staircases ("up which," as Kent notes, "she herself had 'trudged . . . delivering Holy Thunderbolts and Liquid Love Charms' for the spiritual advisor" [1990: 213]) on the dust jacket. Struck by the stark isolation of the article's photograph of a little girl dwarfed by the Mecca's cavernous and abandoned interior courtyard, Brooks noted: "That could be my Pepita" (quoted in Kent 1990: 213). *Life*, according to Kent, refused permission to use the photograph, leaving the epigraph from Martin's *Harper* essay the sole periodical trace of Brooks's research.

8. See Buck-Morss (1989: 164) for a discussion of the emblematic significance of ruins in Walter Benjamin's Arcades Project, which concludes: "Throughout the *Passagen-Werk* material, the image of the 'ruin,' as an emblem not only of the transitoriness and fragility of capitalist culture, but also its destructiveness is pronounced."

9. See Algren (1951: 82) for an attempt to explain the circumstance of Chicago's African Americans: "The Negro is not seriously confronted here with a stand-up and head-on hatred, but with something psychologically worse: a soft and protean awareness of white superiority everywhere, in everything, the more infuriating because it is as polite as it is impalpable. Nobody even *thought* such a thing, my dear."

10. See Brooks's interview with Ida Lewis (I. Lewis 1971: 170): "I had a wonderful father who really took time with his children. He read us stories and sang songs. . . . He talked about injustices, too; he told us often about the race riots that he had seen in 1919. He knew that things were not right. But he didn't allow that to make our home an unhappy one."

11. Unlike earlier decades, where prominences are easily surveyed, the 1960s, with its intertextual extremes of civil rights and war narratives, render neat periodization problematic. The rhetoric of riot and war grows indistinguishable in the dailies and weeklies, as calendrical events shade into sea-

sonal demarcations of the perpetual wars within and without the United States. By 1965 – after the Voting Rights Act, the Selma march, the assassination of Malcolm X, and the Watts riot – the language of foreign and social policies was of two societies at war. See Zinn (1990: 252–8) for an incisive discussion of rhetoric and representative government in the wake of civil disturbance. For the effect of the Watts riot on national policy rhetoric, see Cohen and Murphy (1966), Waskow (1966: preface), Fogelson (1971), and Horne (1995). For individual readings of mid-decade Chicago and, in particular, neighborhood (mis)understandings of King's Chicago campaign, see Terkel (1967).

12. See Garrow (1986: chaps. 8–9); precampaign discussions among King, Andrew Young, and Rustin are instructive (455):

> At one Atlanta meeting, Rustin and [Tom] Kahn pressed their concerns upon Andrew Young and an unreceptive King. As Kahn remembered:
>
> > King had this naive faith that he could do in Chicago what he had done in the South, that he could reach down and inspire them, mobilize them, and so forth. And Bayard kept saying, "You don't know what you're talking about. You don't know what Chicago is like. . . . You're going to be wiped out."
>
> However, King's patience with Rustin's insistent argument had run out. He ended the discussion, Kahn recalled, by "saying, 'I have to pray now. I have to consult with the Lord and see what he wants me to do.'" Rustin, long familiar with King's proclivity for invoking God's name to avoid disagreements he did not care to hear, was furious. Seeking refuge in prayer – "This business of King talking to God and God talking to King" – would not resolve serious strategic questions. When they left, Kahn recalled, "Bayard was very distressed and very worried about what would happen to King in Chicago."

13. For oral history excerpts from King's "Chicago 1966" campaign, see Hampton and Fayer (1995: 297–320). Particularly striking in its evocation of Chicago's enduring neighborhood tensions is the account of Dorothy Tillman, SCLC staffer who had worked on voter registration in Alabama prior to joining King's Chicago campaign. After the riots surrounding the Freedom Movement's incursion into the all-white neighborhoods surrounding Gage Park and Marquette Park, Tillman recalled (312):

> I finally understood what we had to confront over at Marquette Park. I'd never seen whites like these in the South. These whites was up in trees like monkeys throwing bricks and bottles and stuff. I mean racism, you could almost cut it, a whole 'nother level of racism from hatred. And the sad thing about it was that most of those neighborhoods we went to was like first- or second-generation Americans. I mean, they had not been here as long as we had been here. They were first-generation or second-generation Americans. Most were fleeing oppression. Down south you were black or white. You wasn't Irish or Polish or all of this. And for me, I learned about the different ethnic groups, Chicago taught me that. The most hostile whites that I

found here in Chicago were those ethnic groups who were first-generation. I kind of felt sorry for them and still do, because somehow they believe something that's not real.

14. See Terkel (1967) for oral histories of Chicago's renewal programs.

15. Published in the *Chicago Sunday Tribune* (August 27, 1961) and reprinted in the December *Negro Digest*, the essay concludes with a class sensitivity that readers associate with Brown's writing (quoted in Kent 1990: 159):

> Love is the rainbow she chases – love in the broadest sense: love of each man and woman, by each man and woman. She wants to show her readers the golden cord of humanity that unites every girl in a tattered dress and every girl in a gown of silk.
>
> She declares it in her precise but passionate poetry, and in the jazzlike experiments of her one short novel, "Maud Martha." She is saying that birth, happiness, sorrow, and toil are much more extraordinary than they usually seem to us. She is saying that life's real magic lies in these things alone, and that we are still strangers to the reality which we have abandoned in our search for some vague higher truth.

16. See Brooks (1972b: 91), "African Fragment," for an articulation of this local vision: "The Third World concept seems to me, at this time, too large for blacks to tackle. There is now-*urgent* business. I want blacks – *right now* – to forge a black synthesis, a black union: so tight that each black may be relied on to protect, enjoy, listen to, and warmly curry his fellows. That, at this time, is business enough."

17. See Simpson's *New York Herald Book Week* review of Brooks's *Selected Poems* for an intricate reading of the aesthetic and journalistic tensions in "Jessie Mitchell's Mother": "where Miss Brooks takes a harder look at a more complex scene – one that could not be represented on television or in the newspapers – the confrontation of a rather intellectual, black-skinned young girl and her lighter-skinned mother. . . . This writing moves beyond jazz and sociology; it is poetry" (reprinted in S. C. Wright 1996: 23).

Jamaican-born Simpson, alert to the complexities of Caribbean cultures, nonetheless continues to vex readers who are troubled by his seeming indifference to race. See Kent (1990: 163): "Ironically, the review that would make its author's name well known among blacks contained the jarring formulaic kind of judgment that often seems prepackaged by the white liberal critical consensus. . . . Simpson . . . began innocently enough . . . but his next statement offended many blacks: 'I am not sure it is possible for a Negro to write well without making us aware he is a Negro; on the other hand, if being a Negro is the only subject, the writing is not important.' Does 'being a Negro' preclude being universal? Or is Negro life deprived of universality?"

18. See Brooks (1987b: 1–2):

> The Forties and Fifties were years of high poet-incense; the language-flowers were thickly sweet. Those flowers whined and begged white folks to pick them, to find them lovable. Then – the Sixties: independent fire!

Well, I don't want us to creep back to the weaker flowers of the
old yesterday. I don't want us to subscribe, again, to Shelley or Pound-
Eliot or Wallace Stevens. I don't want us to forget the Fire. Baldwin's
announced "Next Time" is by no means over. I want us to "advance,"
yes, to experiment, yes, to labor, yes. But I don't want us to forget the
Fire.

19. An unsigned review in the *Virginia Quarterly Review* declared Brooks "more
self-consciously a Negro than ever before" (1968: 20); Rosenthal, in the
New York Times Book Review, griped that the title poem was "overwrought
with effects . . . [that] distract from its horror almost as if to conceal the
wound at its center" (1968: 14); while even William Stafford's perfunctory
yet sympathetic review in *Poetry* protested against the poem's "confusing
local" references (1968: 425).

20. See Benson (1969: 203): "she has sharpened her sensibilities to the tunes
fashioned by young Negro intellectuals"; Randall in "Black Poetry" located
her new aesthetic in her workshop association with "militant young Chicago
South-Side writers" (1969: 114).

21. See Melhem (1987: 157) for a discussion of the crucial nature of this copy:
"Two indications of the breadth, indeed, the poetic breath to which *In the
Mecca* would expand greeted the reader of the 1968 volume. Reprinted in
the omnibus, they constitute the jacket quotation from Brooks and the two
sets of dedications. On May 31, 1968, Young [Brooks's editor] sent the
author a copy of the jacket material which had already gone to the printer,
and assured that changes could still be made. Brooks wrote back immediately, relieved that she could alter her statement, and happily inscribed the
final version on the letter itself in both ink and type: 'I was to be a Watchful
Eye; a Tuned Ear; a Super-Reporter.' She was concerned that the semi-
colons and capitals be maintained."

22. See Sandburg (1922: 66), headnote to "The House Carpenter," for a journalist's reading of ballads: "In the days before there were daily newspapers,
or even weekly 'intelligencers,' schools were few, and people who could
read or write were scarce. Then ballads flourished, and ballad singers were
in every tavern where men drank ale. . . ." Brooks's rejection of the Anglo-
American ballad liberated an aesthetic that nonetheless bears an uncanny
resemblance to Sandburg's historical definition. As she explains: "My aim,
in my next future, is to write poems that will somehow successfully
'call' . . . all black people: black people in taverns, black people in alleys,
black people in gutters, schools, offices, factories, prisons, the consulate; I
wish to reach black people in pulpits, black people in mines, on farms, on
thrones; *not* always to 'teach' – I shall wish often to entertain, to illumine"
(1972a: 183). Her verse journalism, at once retrospective and prophetic,
seeks to return the news in poems to the community.

23. See Taylor (1991: 126). Though his reduction of Brooks's characterizations
seems ill-considered, his understanding of their poetic function is of interest: "Flat portrayal of white characters is more effective in such satirical
poems as 'The Lovers of the Poor' and 'Bronzeville Woman in a Red Hat,'

where the reduction of characters to cartoons serves a dual function: it permits broad sarcasm and indulgence in playful diction, and it invites the white reader to feel excluded from the portrait until it is too late to escape inclusion in it."

24. See Thompson (1983: 222) for a discussion of the use and reuse patterns of the "news": "Nelly Bragg, an old black woman of Warrensville Heights, Ohio, was asked 'Why one red sock and one white sock worn deliberately mismatched?' to which she replied, 'To keep spirits away.' For similar reasons, Afro-American cabins once were wall-papered with deliberately jumbled bits of newsprint and crowded squares of magazine." Essential to Thompson's discussion is the spiritual dimension of a utilitarian gesture. To many white readers, the black press read as "jumbled bits of newsprint."

25. The architectural significance of the building cannot be overemphasized. The Mecca essentialized the impersonal aesthetic of European modernism that Brooks was in the process of relinquishing.

26. The basic coherence and continuity of her collections, from *A Street in Bronzeville* to *In the Mecca*, arises from her intimate relationship with her subjects. Repeated categorizations of Brooks as a poet *of* Negro life may have prompted this reiterative construction of her self *in* the black community. As if to confirm her status *in* the community, *In the Mecca* breaks into two cycles – "In the Mecca" and "After Mecca" – the first opening with the prophetic narrative "In the Mecca."

27. "In the Mecca" anticipates Carolyn (Fowler) Gerald's theoretical discussion in "The Black Writer and His Role" (originally published in *Negro Digest*, January 1969); see Gerald (1969: 349–56), an essay quoted by Fuller, "The New Black Literature" (1971: 328): "The white man has developed a myth of superiority based on images which compare him symbolically to the black man. . . . We realize now that we are involved in a black-white war over the control of image. For to manipulate an image is to control a peoplehood." See D. L. Smith (1994) for a compelling review of the "regionalism" of the Black Arts Movement, including Chicago's OBAC.

28. For overviews of the role of the Blackstone Rangers in neighborhood policing, see Fry (1969: 1–44), Melhem (1987: 154, 181–2), Kent (1990: 203–4, 207–10), Brazier (1969: 68-83), and Sale (1971: esp. 59–79). A critical outside view of the Rangers may be found in Mailer (1968: 87): "To the West of the Lake were factories and Ciceros, Mafia-lands and immigrant lands; to the North, the suburbs, the Evanstons; to the South were Negro ghettos of the South Side – belts of Black men amplifying each of the resonances of the other's cause – the Black belt had the Blackstone Rangers, the largest gang of juvenile delinquents on earth, 2,000 by some counts – one could be certain the gang had leaders as large in potential as Hannibal or Attila the Hun – how else account for the strength and wit of a stud who would try to rise so high in the Blackstone Rangers?" The Rangers, like the Black Panthers, represented an essential counterforce to abuses of The Law.

29. It is instructive to read Brooks's poems of the mid-1960s against the "official" recognition of the hundredth anniversary of the Emancipation Procla-

mation. In November 1961, President Kennedy had instructed the United States Commission on Civil Rights (USCCR) to write "a report on the civil rights progress of the Nation during the past century . . . placing the Nation's recent civil rights progress in its historical context" (USCCR 1963: iii). The report's title, *Freedom to the Free: Century of Emancipation,* reflects the inertial quandary of emacipation even as it reveals the rhetorical paradoxes so associated with the Kennedy presidency. Rather than estimating past accomplishments, the report placed "progress" in "historical context," resulting in a study of stagnation and, in some instances, retrogression in civil rights. It concludes with a deconstruction of national identity and promise in keeping with the verbal tensions of the proclamation itself:

> As a Nation, we have solved Tocqueville's paradox of a free society's dependence upon slavery. . . . We have come a far journey from a distant era in the 100 years since the Emancipation Proclamation. At the beginning, there was slavery. At the end, there is citizenship. Citizenship, however, is a fragile word with an ambivalent meaning. The condition of citizenship is not yet full-blown or fully realized for the American Negro. There is still more ground to cover. (USCCR 1963: 207)

30. Chicago-based Elijah Muhammad, in a pamphlet of teachings entitled *The Supreme Wisdom,* enjoins followers not to read the Bible, noting that it is a "poisoned book . . . [that] is the graveyard of my poor people . . . [that] is dedicated to King James (a white man) rather than to God" (quoted in Lincoln 1961: 78). For a detailed discussion of Christianity and the Black Muslims, see Lincoln (1961: chap. 4).

31. Often Brooks's allusions are as cryptic as the musical epigraphs Du Bois placed before the chapters of *The Souls of Black Folk.* The influence of *The Souls of Black Folk* is pervasive not local, though, as Brooks noted in her interview with Ida Lewis: "I wasn't reading the books I should have read, when I was young. If I'd been reading W. E. B. Du Bois, I would have known more, but I didn't even hear of *The Souls of Black Folk* until I was well grown" (I. Lewis 1972: 175). For a suggestive reading of Du Bois's influence on Brooks's subsequent writing, see Hansell (1989: 106–15).

32. See Dixon (1994: 26), in which he concludes: "Memory, whether acquired (through received images as in Cullen) or lived (recalled or recollected images in Senghor and Walcott) or mythologized (as in Lorde), is the poet's chief means of writing the self into the larger history of the race."

33. See "Emmett Till's Mother Remembers Her Son on His 50th Birthday" (1991: 6, 10), in which Mamie Till Mobley makes a kindred appeal to the victims of racial injustice:

> [Mamie Till Mobley] said she plans to continue to share her son's tragic story so that people's "consciences will be aroused and justice be allowed to prevail."
>
> She pointed out that like the Jews who constantly remember the tragedy of the Holocaust, Blacks must remember the lives lost in the struggle against racism.

"When we let things happen and we just sit and say 'Well, that's one of those things that we can't do anything about it.' This is the wrongest thing in the world," she said.

"All we have to do is take a lesson from the Jewish people," she pointed out. "They did not take the Holocaust and lie down and try to hide it. They are constantly bringing it forth, not only to the attention of their children and their people, but to the entire world. I have learned something from watching this come about from time to time."

34. Algren – colleague, fellow Chicagoan and journalist – introduced his polemic *Chicago: City on the Make* with the assertion that "literature is made upon any occasion that a challenge is put to the legal apparatus by a conscience in touch with humanity" (1951: 9). Friends since Algren had secured for her an essay assignment for *Holiday* magazine that resulted in "They Call It Bronzeville" (October 1951), Brooks ultimately found herself being compared to him in reviews of *In the Mecca*. See Kent (1990: 220) for the *Chicago Daily News* review: "In spinning out in spare, blazingly brilliant lines the tragic tale of the death of Pepita Smith, Miss Brooks creates with deft strokes a mini-portrait gallery of Chicago characters unequaled in imaginative power since the creations of Nelson Algren in 'The Man with the Golden Arm.'"

35. Eliot so embodies literary memory and influence in Brooks's active poetic, becoming an audible intertext throughout *In the Mecca*, that "Gerontion" – "My house is a decayed house, / And the jew squats on the window sill, the owner, / Spawned in some estaminet in Antwerp, / Blistered in Brussels, patched and peeled in London" [1920: 21]) – would seem to be the silenced "master" text for "To a Winter Squirrel." Unlike Eliot's "old man in a dry month," Brooks's "bolted nomad" transforms the depravity of her circumstance and revels in little epiphanies, transforming the squirrel into a "mountain and a star" (1968: 35).

36. Within the Western literariness of Brooks's ode rest its African-American folk origins. See, for example, the folk rhyme "Peep Squirrel" in Henderson (1972: 88).

37. See Baker (1987: 49) for a discussion of Charles Chestnutt's success as a "modern" in these terms.

38. Meditating on art (and news) in the public sphere, "Portrait of a Lady" anticipates many of Brooks's concerns. Eliot pre-frames consideration of the disjunction between public, monumental Art and people, even as he introduces the indigenous determination of rhythmic aesthetics (1920: 9):

Among the windings of the violins
And the ariettes
Of cracked cornets
Inside my brain a dull tom-tom begins
Absurdly hammering a prelude of its own,
Capricious monotone
That is at least one definite 'false note.'
– Let us take the air, in a tobacco trance,

> Admire the monuments,
> Discuss the late events,
> Correct our watches by the public clocks.
> Then sit for half an hour and drink our bocks.

39. See Sale (1971: 59–79) for the origins of the Rangers. Sale, a national magazine reporter, met Joel Hampton, one of the founders of the Blackstone Rangers, while covering the Reverend Abernathy's Resurrection City campaign. Hampton explained the spirit of the Rangers (Sale 1971: 62–3):

> "Look," he said, "we got what the United States ain't got: unity. Why, man, nowhere in the history of this country has there been a group of young black men like us, organized with the kind of discipline we have, the kind of organization. Because you got to remember – that's what we are: an organization. We ain't no gang."

40. The ironies of the year could be summarized by Governor Otto Kerner, soon to head the federal investigation into "socially-directed violence," who named Brooks the successor to Carl Sandburg as the Poet Laureate of Illinois.

Chapter 6. Kinship as History

1. See Tolson (1982: 271), "The City by the Patapsco River" (September 4, 1943), for a discussion of the tense racial climate of Baltimore: "I am a Negro American. I look at Fort McHenry. I look at Flag House. I look at Key Monument. I look at the famous Catholic Cathedral, the Mother Church of all Catholic churches in this country. Then I think of Jesus and the 'Star Spangled Banner.' I am a Negro American in Baltimore. I add 2 and 2; and I get 5!"

2. In many ways, Beacon Press epitomizes the liberal sentiment that Jean-Paul Sartre warns against in his preface to Fanon's *Wretched of the Earth*: "And that super-European monstrosity, North America? Chatter, chatter: liberty, equality, fraternity, love, honor, patriotism, and what have you. All this did not prevent us from making anti-racial speeches about dirty niggers, dirty Jews, and dirty Arabs. High-minded people, liberal or just soft-hearted, protest that they were shocked by such inconsistency; but they were either mistaken or dishonest, for with us there is nothing more consistent than a racist humanism since the European has only been able to become a man through creating slaves and monsters" (1963: 26).

3. This perception has little to do with the authors' radical politics and more to do with the audience for Beacon's publications. For a sense of the class privilege of many Beacon readers, see Mungo (1970: 106), in which America's racial divide is rendered solipsistically: "Martin Luther King was dead and where did that leave *us*? When every other reason for leaving Washington made impeccable sense, we would fall back on the argument that black people, after all, *had* to stay there – as if we had made some inviolable pact with the black people not to desert them. Now it became clearer every day that we were no use at all to the black people in Washington; we had no part in their struggle and no material help to offer."

4.	Conarroe's "Poetry Chronicle" includes reviews of Adrienne Rich's *The Will to Change* and Helen Sorrell's *Seeds As They Fall*. Only once does Conarroe mention "race" in his New Critical review of *Generations*. However laudatory the import, such avoidance of the central issues of Cornish's own aesthetic and the Black Arts Movement diminishes the critical judgment: "As I read the book over and over . . . I sense beneath even the sophisticated simplicity of the early poems a powerful indignation – and I use this word purposely, rather than 'rage,' since it is possible that rage is tempered when it finds a voice. In any case, some of the poems are 'explosive'" (1973:81). Read today, this well-meaning review seems startling in its perhaps unwittingly patronizing attitude toward the poets and poetry of "rage." Conarroe, unable to work within the imagined context of Cornish's poems, perceives an aestheticized civility where he should be hearing an eruptive voice of rage. Heffernan, cited in Woodson, also hears a voice of universal import: "Sam Cornish has managed, by pure artistry, to create a book of human perceptions" (Woodson 1985: 66).

5.	See Redmond (1976: 414):

There are myriad problems and conflicts in the writings and lives of many of the new poets. Some, suffering from the "disfigurement of perceptions," do not always portray a correct sociological picture of Blacks, let alone a correct poetic one. Anxious to "saturate" themselves in a new blackness, they disguise their own confusion in half-baked theories of Afro-American life; this results in a poetry that is often riddled with confusions, inaccuracies, and oversimplifications of the black experience. A further result, and this is ghastly, is that star-makers view the poetry through an inverted lens, so that a popular "latex brand" receives a final stamp of approval while the deeper, searching, and more profound poetry (Dumas, Patterson, Cornish, Cortez, Jordan, Lorde, Rivers) is downplayed.

For recent discussions of the African-American anthology wars, see Gates (1987: 32-5); Baker (1984: 74-88, 101–3). Particularly instructive is the distinction drawn between "literary" and "vernacular" cultures that fuels the debate between these critics.

For an extensive reading of the significance of Henderson's attempt, see Gates (1987: 28-35) and Baker (1984: 74–82); for an eager adoption of Henderson's critical structure, see S. A. Williams (1978: 72–87). Henderson passionately advanced a politicized critical structure within which to define and assess the socially and aesthetically genuine in black poetry. Exhaustively mining the fields of black vernacular expression in speech and music, he codified even as he corrected perceptions about poetic preaching to the black community. Embedded in this pioneering and ambitious attempt to extend the line of critical exegesis to black literary criticism is a reliance upon what Gates has termed "cultural exclusivity" (1987: 33). Whether concerning black themes, structure, or language, Henderson resorted to "blackness" as a logocentric self-defining term: "For the knowledge of Blackness is the knowledge of pain and oppression as well as joy. It

is a knowledge rooted in history and the real world, in all its incomplete-
ness and fragmentation" (1972: 69). Though the poems of *Generations* met
the letter and the spirit of Henderson's overarching vision of blackness in
poetry, Cornish was not included in the anthology.

6. See Madhubuti (1972a: 22): "Gwendolyn Brooks' post 1967 poetry is fatless. Her new work resembles a man getting off meat, turning to a vegetari-
an diet. What one immediately notices is that all the excess weight is quickly
lost."

7. See Greenblatt (1990: 175) for an extended discussion of the ways in which
historical sites or contexts nourish literary works, making possible "resonance . . . forged in the barely acknowledged gaps, the cesurae, between
words."

8. In addition to earlier versions of *Generations*, "My Brother Is Homemade"
appears as the centerpiece to the sequence "1935" in *Songs of Jubilee* (1986)
and as a section of *1935: A Memoir* (1990). Mary Helen Washington included it in her recent anthology, *Memory of Kin* (1991).

9. Major cites an interview in which Cornish claims that "some of the best
modern poetry is to be found in the films of John Ford, Richard Lester,
and Samuel Peckinpah" (1974: 43).

10. The phrase is used throughout the report that bears the name of its chairman, the then-governor of Illinois, Otto Kerner. Like most "official" investigations into the causes of "socially-directed violence," the "Kerner Report"
begins with an expression of national "shock, fear and bewilderment" that
"[o]ur nation is moving toward two societies, one black, one white – separate and unequal" (1). So pervasive is this rhetoric of concern that the thir-
tieth-anniversary evaluation of the Kerner Commission report – *The
Millennium Breach* – funded by the Milton S. Eisenhower Foundation and
co-chaired by Fred Harris, former Democratic senator from Oklahoma and
member of the Kerner Commission, reiterates the language and conclusions of the antecedent report.

11. See Ellison (1964: 205) for a discussion of "relatives" and "literary ancestors" ("whom, unlike a relative, the artist is permitted to choose").

12. See Bakhtin (1981: 176–99).

Chapter 7. Nation-ness as Consciousness

1. See Walker (1975a: 48–49): "'Well,' I say, 'I believe that the truth about
any subject only comes when all the sides of the story are put together, and
all their different meanings make one new one. Each writer writes the missing parts to the other writer's story. And the whole story is what I'm after.'"

2. "Dear God. Dear stars, dear trees, dear sky, dear peoples. Dear Everything.
Dear God. . . . White people busy celebrating they independence from England July 4th. . . . Us can spend the day celebrating each other" (1982: 243).

3. See Cornish (1984: B7), in which he registers kinship as well as distance
from his own historical project and asserts that *The Third Life of Grange
Copeland, Meridian,* and *The Color Purple* "form a trilogy of novels embracing

generations of people living in the South but outside of history." And though Walker might take exception to the extrahistorical and sequential nature that Cornish locates in these early novels, she might concur that they place well outside of the expected or sanctioned realm of received historical record. While the idealization of historical narratives residing within the presumed chronology of genealogical records and individual acts sustains much of the public record in *Grange Copeland* and even *The Color Purple* (though there it is reduced to epistolary form), it does little to account for the dissolving narrative and contested history of *Meridian*.

4. See Tate (1983: 176), where Walker explains the eccentric yet planned world of counterpane that offered a flexible engagement with historiography, mythopoesis, and narratology: "A crazy-quilt story is one that can jump back and forth in time, work on many different levels, and one that can include myth. It is generally more evocative of metaphor and symbolism than a novel that is chronological in structure, or one devoted, more or less to rigorous realism, as is *The Third Life of Grange Copeland*." And yet it enforces a visual field that is complex and competitive, producing a "whole." While the novel's structure may be piecework, it denies totality for the sake of its emblematic deconstruction of history. The quilt metaphor served more than one of Walker's critics. See, for example, M. H. Washington (1979), B. Christian (1980), and Baker and Pierce-Baker (1985).

5. Unlike the various submerged strains of black nationalism, the women's cultural movement, securely grounded in the middle class, surfaced into and dominated the mass media; but often only in caricature, serving to accentuate the unease that developed among the sectors of the sisterhood as the high-minded white feminist grew increasingly incomprehensible to what Walker would call "the black womanist." See Rich (1978: 275–310) for consideration of the early racial tensions in the movement; in particular, note (290-1): "I can easily comprehend that when black women have looked at the present-day feminist movement, particularly as caricatured in the male-dominated press (both black and white), and have seen blindness to, and ignorance of, the experience and needs of black women, they have labeled this 'racism,' undifferentiated from the racism endemic in patriarchy."

6. See Fabre (1994: 72–3): "[I]n contrast to most observances which are devised to fix history, African-American feasts partook of the flux of history, commented upon its direction, and indicated, in subtle ways, paths to follow. Whereas commemorations are often seen as oriented toward the past and as a means of preserving tradition, black feasts were primarily concerned with forcing change and inventing a more viable future. If their purpose was to invent tradition, it was, one must emphasize, a tradition of struggle, jeremiad, and claim-staking. As such, these commemorations should be analyzed as a *political gestus* which contributed to the collective memory – not just memory of past events but the *memory of the future*, in anticipation of action to come. . . ."

7. CBS's most popular shows throughout the decade were: "Andy Griffith"

(1960–8), "Petticoat Junction" (1963–70), "The Beverly Hillbillies" (1962–71), "Green Acres" (1965–71), and "Gomer Pyle, USMC" (1964–70). See Baughman (1992: chaps. 5 and 6) for further consideration of network television during the 1960s.

8. See Butler-Evans (1989) for consideration of the historical in *Meridian*.

9. See Coles (1964: 307). Discussing the clinical symptoms of "weariness" attendant to "social struggle," he explains: "The work of these students is not totally the action caught by cameras or reported in the news. The brunt of it is taking actual residence in towns where their goals are considered illegal at best and often seditious; considered so by local police and judges, by state police and judges, by business and political leaders. Their very presence in these towns, in fact, is regarded as a violation of law and order."

10. See Toomer, "It Is Everywhere" (1988: 85):

    There's a life awaiting on the seaboard,
    In the key of states,
    The Empire town,
    And all along to that city
    Of my birth,
    Washed by the Potomac
    Trapped by Meridian Hill . . .

11. See Berlant (1988: 212-13) for a truncated discussion of *Meridian* as prologue to her discussion of nationalism in *The Color Purple*. I disagree with her conclusion that "*Meridian* exposes the gap between official claims of American democracy . . . and views 'personal' relationships as symptoms of the strained political situation" (213). *Meridian* offers no such easy correlation. See Tate (1983: 179), in which Walker explains: "I became aware that the very brave and amazing people whom I knew in the civil rights movement were often incredibly flawed, and in a way, it was these flaws that both propelled them and 'struck' them . . . ."

12. See, for example, Butler-Evans (1989: 116) for a consideration of the novel's "radical departure . . . in its representations of history"; Nadel (1988: 255) for an investigation of a "chain of maternal history, marginalized and suppressed by white patriarchal history."

13. In many ways, *Meridian* may be seen as an early attempt to *re*present the sequence, trauma, and integrity of the civil rights movement. Henry Hampton's documentary, *Eyes on the Prize*, would continue the project of historicization. By the middle of the 1960s, as the civil rights movement moved steadily north, the twin pressures of urban despair and the Vietnam War inspired a series of "long, hot summers" that threatened rather than inspired voters and television's corporate sponsors. The once musical and televisually "nonviolent" demonstrations in the South (where protestors were battered and police were dissolute) yielded to northern riots that menaced the white liberal superstructure supportive (or so it thought) of earlier demonstrations. Television, once the nationalizing agent of the movement, recoiled into its natural posture of enforcer of the status quo, refusing access to the insurgent subnational constituencies, notably the

Black Panthers and the Black Muslims. This withdrawal of the mainstream press from positive race news sparked a renaissance of independent journalism.

So prevalent during this period is the stereotype of the marauding black that it infects otherwise useful discussions of the media of the period. See in particular Baughman (1992: 91): "When riots erupted every spring and summer in different American cities between 1964 and 1968, participants did not march on city hall or other citadels of political or economic power. If there were attacks on property, the targets were invariably neighborhood supermarkets and appliance stores, with the most coveted objects, TV sets." Baughman attempts to recover objectivity by concluding that, "in their fashion, the looters were demonstrating something more specific: the significance of television to American society in the 1960s."

14. See Walker (1976b: 224); in an essay written during the Bicentennial, she recalls traveling to Mississippi a decade earlier, two years after Mississippi Freedom Summer, in hopes of "tirelessly observ[ing] it" and "kill[ing] the fear it engendered in my imagination as a place where black life was terrifyingly hard, pitifully cheap." Mississippi, for Walker, becomes the mediatized nexus of the American dilemma: at once a personal experience and an audience event.

15. See Tolson (1944: 22):

> Against the statue
> Of Confederate dead
> The Mayor spat
> His snuff and said,
> "We need a slogan!"
> And he palmed his hand.
>
> . . . .
>
> On a neon billboard,
> As high as a steeple,
> The travelers puzzle
> The amazing sequel:
> *The Blackest Land*
> *And The Whitest People.*

16. See Jordan (1994a: 172–3) for a contemporary display of Meridian's courage: "I stared at that lone Chinese man who stood in front of the advancing line of tanks at Tiananmen Square in Beijing. Inside the tank, another man had to stop or run over – and crush – his courageous compatriot. The man inside the tank drove to the right, trying to avoid his challenger. The man in the street moved to the right. The tank swerved to the left. The man in the street moved to the left. They were dancing. The tank resumed its front-and-center position. The man in the street jumped on the tank, and threw his body on top of it. Talk about guts! Talk about news! Talk about exhilaration of the soul!"

17. For alternate mythic strains in *Meridian*, see "The Wild Child," "Sojourner," and "Indians and Ecstasy."

18. See Habermas (1992: 456): "The dedifferentiation and destructuring affecting our lifeworld as a result of the electronically produced omnipresence of events and of the synchronization of heterochronologies certainly have a considerable impact on social self-perception."

19. Ultimately, the televisual revolution ran counter to the Enlightenment conception of participatory democracy and citizenship; for, as Adorno (1951: 14) states, "the objective tendency of the Enlightenment is to wipe out the power of images over man."

20. See R. Fowler (1991) and Barnhurst (1994) for reading "whole page" layouts in newspapers.

21. See Walker (1970b: 28-9): "I wanted to give them in addition a knowledge of what history itself *is*. And in order that they see themselves and their parents and their grandparents as part of a living, working, creating movement in Time and Place, I drew on my experience . . . and asked them to write their autobiographies."

22. See Jameson (1991: 346–7) re: the "gratifications of psychic identity (from nationalism to neoethnicity)": "Since they have become images, groups allow the amnesia of their own bloody pasts, of persecution and untouchability, and can now be consumed: this marks their relationship to the media, which are, as it were, their parliament and the space of their 'representation,' in the political fully as much as the semiotic sense."

23. See Benjamin (1955a: 236): "As compared with painting, filmed behavior lends itself more readily to analysis because of its incomparably more precise statements of the situation. In comparison with a stage scene, the filmed behavior item lends itself more readily to analysis because it can be isolated more easily."

24. The *New York Times* plays a pivotal role as social designator in Spike Lee's feature film *Jungle Fever* (1991). The opening post-title shot traces the arc of a newspaper being thrown onto Flipper Purify's doorstep in Harlem – with a momentary freeze-frame, just before landing, on the *Times* banner. The *Times* signifies more than Flipper's professional status, it foreshadows the evolving class and racial complications of the film, signifying transracial (and transethnic) aspiration. "Community news" becomes the property of the Italian Americans of Bensonhurst, who buy the *Daily News*, the *Post*, or *Newsday* from Carbone's Spa. When daily customer Orin Goode, a black professional woman who works at Brooklyn College, asks Paulie Carbone (grown son of the owner) whether he has asked his father "about carrying the *Times*," Paulie explains, "It don't sell." As Goode leaves, the denizens of the spa heatedly (re)mark the territorial boundaries of the news, insisting that they won't carry *Ebony*, *Jet*, or the *Amsterdam News* either. If she wants those, "she should move to Bed-Sty."

25. See Henderson (1968: 69–70) for a contemporary and local reading of the King funeral as an exercise in survival and revolution:

> And there emerged among us a great and powerful spirit, and he galvanized his people and shook the conscience of the nation. But this nation has a seemingly endless capacity for self-deception; it tires eas-

ily from moral confrontation; and by the time that Dr. King was proposing his Poor People's Campaign the nation which four years earlier had thrilled to his golden voice, which had *dreamt* his dream, was now awake and peevish, and warned this man of peace of violence. And so he went up to the mountain to pray, and he saw his God and he saw the glory and he saw the promised land. And when he came down to tell the good news, the dream was "exploded down his throat." . . .

Wait until the funeral!

We waited.

The terrible tension in Atlanta, fearful for its image. The students trooping through the drizzling rain. The sirens. The five fire-bombed stores. The funeral cortege. The governor hiding in the capitol, cracking jokes about coons. The prurient cameras. The popinjays. My college. The boasting. The funeral has brought us to the mainstream of American life. Yes, the mainstream, choked with the bodies of the dead – the President and the prophet, and Malcolm, and gentle Medgar Evers, and all the bodies of all the dead selves that daily die from compromise and corruption and moral imbecility.

26. Unlike JFK's funeral cortege, MLK's procession (in Walker's depiction) admits the folk intimacy that Sarah Orne Jewett associated with turn-of-the-century "walking funerals" in rural Maine; see Jewett (1896: 7): "The services had taken place at one o'clock, and now, at quarter past two, I stood at the schoolhouse window, looking down at the procession as it went along the lower road close to the shore. It was a walking funeral, and even at that distance I could recognize most of the mourners as they went their solemn way."

See Baldwin (1972: 531–2), a "walking funeral" essay. It is this intimacy of the people that Baldwin, famous amid celebrities, recalls in "No Name in the Street":

At last, we were standing, and filing out, to walk behind Martin, home. I found myself between Marlon and Sammy. I had not been aware of the people when I had been pressing past them to get to the church. But, now, as we came out, and I looked up the road, I saw them. They were all along the road, on either side, they were on all the roofs, on either side. Every inch of ground, as far as the eye could see, was black with black people, and they stood in silence. It was the silence that undid me. I started to cry, and I stumbled, and Sammy grabbed my arm. We started to walk.

27. See Ryan (1989) for consideration of the parade as an American representation of social order.

28. See Baraka (1965: 167): "The various black porters, gigglers, ghostchumps and punkish Indians, etc. that inhabit the public image the whiteman has fashioned to characterize Black Men are references by Black Men to the identity of Black Men in the West, since that's what is run on them each

day by whitemagic, i.e., television, movies, radio, etc. – the Mass Media (the *Daily News* does it with flicks and adjectives)."

29. See Anderson (1983: esp. chap. 9); see also Gilroy (1987: 176): "Strengthened by the brutality which was meted out in response to black protest and by the emerging anti-war movement, Black Power developed into a potent, if not always coherent ideological force with a plurality of meanings covering the whole range of political sentiment."

30. For a white feminist reading of the revolution, see Rich (1978).

31. See Baraka (1963: 16): "Only religion (and magic) and the arts were not completely submerged by Euro-American concepts. Music, dance, religion do not have *artifacts* as their end products, so they were saved. These nonmaterial aspects of the African's culture were almost impossible to eradicate. And these are the most apparent legacies of the African past, even to the contemporary black American."

32. See White (1987b: 173) for a discussion of the metaphysics of narrative which asserts that: "A meaningful life is one that aspires to the coherency of a story with a plot."

33. Meridian concludes that she is "a failure then, as the kind of revolutionary Anne-Marion and her acquaintances were. (Though in fact she had heard of nothing revolutionary this group had done, since she left them ten summers ago. Anne-Marion, she knew, had become a well-known poet whose poems were about her two children, and the quality of the light that fell across a lake she owned)" (1976a: 205).

Chapter 8. History as Storytelling

1. Seeking to foreground Wright's aesthetic confrontation with national narratives, I risk invoking "America" as a received (desig)nation for the United States. See Kutzinski (1987: 49–50) for a rationale for its deemphasis: "Wright's territory is the New World, and I am employing this term very self-consciously to de-emphasize as much as possible the nationalistic connotations the term 'America' has acquired as a result of being used as a shorthand expression for the United States. If 'America' in any way suggests a potentially unified area of study, it does so, as we have already seen, only by subordinating all cultural elements of a non-European origin to the claims of the so-called Anglo-North American cultural establishment."

2. For further discussion of the political field of the Black Arts Movement, see the contemporaneous criticism included in the following anthologies: Redmond (1976); Baraka/Neal (1968); Henderson (1972). For contemporary assessment of the aesthetic consequences of these nationalist stirrings, see C. K. Doreski (1992), Gates (1987), Nielsen (1994), and Mackey (1993).

3. See, for example, Hollander (1981), a review of Wright's *The Double Invention of Komo*, in which he identifies among the book's "subsidiary quests": "mythologies of the manly"; see Mullen (1992) for a terse overview of "threatened black masculinity" in African-American letters, specifically Nathaniel Mackey's *Bedouin Hornbook*.

4. For a justification of this problematic term, see Bhabha (1994: 4): "If the jargon of our times – postmodernity, postcoloniality, postfeminism – has any meaning at all, it does not lie in the popular use of the 'post' to indicate sequentiality – *after*-feminism; or polarity – *anti*-modernism. These terms that insistently gesture to the beyond, only embody its restless and revisionary energy if they transform the present into an expanded and ex-centric site of experience and empowerment."

5. See Benjamin, "The Storyteller," "The Image of Proust," and "Theses on the Philosophy of History" for discussions of Enlightenment notions of progress in historical materialism; see Foner (1976) for documentary evidence of "alternative declarations of independence"; see Bhabha (1994: 142) for the ultimate question of nation-as-narration: "How do we plot the narrative of the nation as narration that must mediate between the teleology of progress tipping over into the 'timeless' discourse of irrationality?"

6. See White (1978: 36): "The First World War did much to destroy what remained of history's prestige among both artists and social scientists, for the war seemed to confirm what Nietzsche had maintained two generations earlier. History, which was supposed to provide some sort of training for life . . . had done little to prepare men for the coming of the war. . . ."

7. Although Wright was obviously responding to Wallace Stevens's "The Comedian as the Letter C," not Holly Stevens's *Souvenirs and Prophecies*, it is interesting to note that her project was also published during the Bicentennial.

8. See Bhabha (1994: 246) regarding: de Certeau's formulation of the "nonplace from which all historiographical operation starts, the lag which all histories must encounter in order to make a beginning."

9. See W. Harris (1967: 10) for an expanded discussion of the "sun" and its "terrible" reality in the West Indian world and its metaphorical weight "in the American world [where] energy is the sun of life."

10. See Griaule (1965) and Turner (1974) for the cosmological ground of this partially shared system that underwrites the ontology of these earlier poems.

11. See Kutzinski (1987: 54–72) for a compelling discussion of the Banneker poems as they serve to foreground her study of myth and history in Wright's *Dimensions of History*. All readers of Wright's poetry should be grateful to this model exercise in philology. Though often I take issue with her insistent readings that facilitate the "history as myth" equation (substituting one fixity for another), I am throughout this chapter indebted to her research.

12. Banneker's urbanity continues to inspire. See, for example, Dove (1983: 36–7) for her curatorial reading of "Banneker":

> At nightfall he took out
> his rifle – a white-maned
> figure stalking the darkened
> breast of the Union – and
> shot at the stars, and by chance
> one went out. Had he killed?
> *I assure thee, my dear Sir!*

> Lowering his eyes to fields
> sweet with the rot of spring, he could see
> a government's domed city
> rising from the morass and spreading
> in a spiral of lights . . .

13. For consideration of Benjamin's "readings" of cities, see Bahti (1992: 183–204); Buck-Morss (1989); Benjamin (1955b: 146–62).

14. See Gilroy (1993) and Bhabha (1994) for postcolonial discussions of transatlantic culture.

15. I strongly disagree with Kutzinski's reading of "Benjamin Banneker Sends His 'Almanac' to Thomas Jefferson," which subordinates the poem to "a shorter version . . . a kind of double which revoices most of the important aspects of the former poem" (1987: 55). Such an interpretation ignores the metaphysical and metaphoric vitality of the thing itself: the almanac.

16. See Rich (1993: 130): "Africans carried poetry in contraband memory across the Middle Passage to create in slavery the 'Sorrow Songs.'"

17. In many ways, Wright's poem extends a genre familiar to readers of Allen Tate's "Ode to the Confederate Dead" and Robert Lowell's "For the Union Dead" (see William Doreski [1990: 24–5, 78-80, 139–45]). Wright's elegiac response addresses, not the failure to commemorate, but the inability to do so.

18. See A. Walker (1975b: 93–118).

19. See Rowell (1983: 4) where Wright defines the collectivity of the poetic enterprise: "The *we* is the corporation of human beings who require and accept poetry's charter within it."

BIBLIOGRAPHY

Adamic, Louis. 1932. *Laughing in the Jungle.* New York: Harper and Brothers.
    1938. *My America.* New York: Harper and Brothers.
    1939. *From Many Lands.* New York: Harper and Brothers.
    1941. *Two-Way Passage.* New York: Harper and Brothers.
    1943. *My Native Land.* New York: Book Find Club.
    1945. *A Nation of Nations.* New York: Harper and Brothers.
    1946. "There Are Whites and Whites." *Negro Digest* 4.5: 47–50.
Adorno, Theodor. 1951. *Minima Moralia: Reflections from Damaged Life.* Trans. E. F. N. Jephcott. London: Verso, 1978.
Ai. 1994. "Riot Act, April 29, 1992." In *Every Shut Eye Ain't Asleep,* ed. Michael S. Harper and Anthony Walton, 246–7. Boston: Little Brown.
Algren, Nelson. 1951. *Chicago: City on the Make.* Oakland, Calif.: Angel Island Publications, 1961.
Alinsky, Saul D. 1946a. "Beware the Liberals." *Negro Digest* 4.12: 33–4.
    1946b. *Reveille for Radicals.* New York: Vintage Books, 1969.
American Civil Liberties Union (ACLU). 1942. *The Bill of Rights in War.* New York: ACLU.
    1943. *Freedom in Wartime.* New York: ACLU.
    1945. *Liberty on the Home Front.* New York: ACLU.
Ammons, Elizabeth. 1991a. *Conflicting Stories: American Women Writers at the Turn into the Twentieth Century.* New York: Oxford University Press.
    Ed. 1991b. *Short Fiction by Black Women, 1900–1920.* New York: Oxford University Press.
Amsterdam News. 1943.
Anderson, Benedict. 1983. *Imagined Communities: Reflections on the Origin and Spread of Nationalism.* London: Verso, 1990.
Andrews, William L. 1986. *To Tell a Free Story: The First Century of Afro-American Autobiography, 1760-1865.* Urbana: University of Illinois Press.
    1989. "The Representation of Slavery and the Rise of Afro-American Literary Realism, 1865-1920." In *Slavery and the Literary Imagination,* ed. Deborah McDowell and Arnold Rampersad, 62–80. Baltimore: Johns Hopkins University Press.

Appel, Benjamin. 1944. "One Man Is Not Enough." *Negro Digest* 2.6: 11–13.

Asante, S. K. B. 1973. "The Afro-American and the Italo-Ethiopian Crisis." *Race* 15.2: 167–84.

———. 1977. *Pan-African Protest: West Africa and the Italo-Ethiopian Crisis, 1934-1941.* London: Longman.

Badoglio, Pietro. 1937. *The War in Abyssinia.* Intro. by Benito Mussolini. London: Methuen.

Bahti, Timothy. 1992. *Allegories of History: Literary Historiography after Hegel.* Baltimore: Johns Hopkins University Press.

Baker, Houston A., Jr. 1974. *Singers of Daybreak: Studies in Black American Literature.* Washington, D.C.: Howard University Press, 1983.

———. 1984. *Blues, Ideology, and Afro-American Literature: A Vernacular Theory.* Chicago: University of Chicago Press.

———. 1987. *Modernism and the Harlem Renaissance.* Chicago: University of Chicago Press.

———. 1994. "The Black Public Sphere: Critical Memory and the Black Public Sphere." In *The Black Public Sphere*, ed. Black Public Sphere Collective, 5–38. Chicago: University of Chicago Press.

Baker, Houston A., Jr., and Charlotte Pierce-Baker. 1985. "Patches: Quilts and Community in Alice Walker's 'Everyday Use.'" In *Alice Walker*, ed. Henry Louis Gates, Jr., and K. A. Appiah, 309-18. New York: Amistad, 1993.

Bakhtin, M. M. 1971. "Discourse Typology in Prose." In *Reading Russian Poetics: Formalist and Structuralist Views*, ed. Ladislas and Krytyna Pomorska Matejka, 176–99. Cambridge: MIT Press.

———. 1981. *The Dialogic Imagination.* Trans. Michael Holquist and Caryl Emerson. Austin: University of Texas Press.

Baldwin, James. 1961. *Nobody Knows My Name: More Notes of a Native Son.* New York: Dial Press.

———. 1965. "White Man's Guilt." *The Price of the Ticket: Collected Nonfiction, 1948–1985*, 401–14. New York: St. Martin's Press.

———. 1972. "No Name in the Street." *The Price of the Ticket*, 449-552. New York: St. Martin's Press

———. 1976. *The Devil Finds Work.* New York: Dial Press.

———. 1985a. *The Evidence of Things Not Seen.* New York: Henry Holt.

———. 1985b. "Introduction: The Price of the Ticket." *The Price of the Ticket*, ix-xx. New York: St. Martin's Press.

Balfour, Alan. 1990. Notes for *Blind Willie McTell* [1940]. Library of Congress Folk Archive. Reissued as RST Records BDCD-6001.

Banneker, Benjamin. 1791. "Letter to Thomas Jefferson, 1791." In *The Black Power Revolt*, ed. Floyd B. Barbour, 17–19. Boston: Porter Sargent Publisher, 1968.

Banner-Haley, Charles T. 1994. *The Fruits of Integration: Black Middle-Class Ideology and Culture, 1960-1990.* Jackson: University Press of Mississippi.

Baraka, Amiri [LeRoi Jones]. 1963. *Blues People.* New York: William Morrow.

———. 1965. "The Legacy of Malcolm X, and the Coming of the Black Nation." In *The LeRoi Jones / Amiri Baraka Reader*, ed. William J. Harris, 161-8. New York: Thunder's Mouth Press.

1966. "Hunting Is Not Those Heads on the Wall." *Home: Social Essays*, 173-8. New York: William Morrow.

1967. "The Need for a Cultural Base to Civilrites and Bpower Mooments." In *The Black Power Revolt*, ed. Floyd B. Barbour, 119–26. Boston: Porter Sargent Publisher, 1968.

1969. *Black Magic. The LeRoi Jones / Amiri Baraka Reader*, 210–24.

1972. "The Changing Same (R&B and New Black Music.)" In *The Black Aesthetic*, ed. Addison Gayle, Jr., 112–25. New York: Doubleday-Anchor.

1984. *The Autobiography of LeRoi Jones*. Chicago: Lawrence Hill Books, 1997.

1991. *The LeRoi Jones / Amiri Baraka Reader*. Ed. William J. Harris. New York: Thunder's Mouth Press.

Baraka, Amiri, and Larry Neal, eds. 1968. *Black Fire: An Anthology of Afro-American Writing*. New York: William Morrow.

Barbour, Floyd B., ed. 1968. *The Black Power Revolt: A Collection of Essays*. Boston: Porter Sargent Publisher.

Barnhurst, Kevin G. 1994. *Seeing the Newspaper*. New York: St. Martin's Press.

Baughman, James. 1992. *The Republic of Mass Culture: Journalism, Filmmaking, and Broadcasting in America since 1941*. Baltimore: Johns Hopkins University Press.

Bedient, Calvin. 1986. *He Do the Police in Different Voices: The Waste Land and Its Protagonist*. Chicago: University of Chicago Press.

Beecher, John. 1945. "Their Blood Cries Out!" *Negro Digest* 3.3: 13–15.

Beer, Samuel H. 1993. *To Make a Nation: The Rediscovery of American Federalism*. Cambridge, Mass.: Harvard University Press.

Beiner, Ronald. 1992. *What's the Matter with Liberalism?* Berkeley and Los Angeles: University of California Press.

Bender, John, and David E. Welbery, eds. 1991. *Chronotypes: The Construction of Time*. Stanford, Calif.: Stanford University Press.

Benedict, Ruth. 1943. "I Wouldn't Forget." *Negro Digest* 1.9: 20–1.

Benét, William Rose, and Norman Cousins. 1945. *The Poetry of Freedom*. New York: The Modern Library–Random House, 1948.

Benjamin, Walter. 1928. *The Origin of German Tragic Drama*. Trans. John Osborne. London: Verso, 1985.

1936a. "The Storyteller: Reflections on the Works of Nikolai Leskov." *Illuminations*, 83–110.

1936b. "The Work of Art in the Age of Mechanical Reproduction." *Illuminations*, 217–52.

1940. "Theses on the Philosophy of History." *Illuminations*, 253–64.

1955a. *Illuminations: Essays and Reflections*. Trans. Harry Zohn. New York: Schocken Books, 1968.

1955b. "Paris, Capital of the Nineteenth Century." *Reflections: Essays, Aphorisms, Autobiographical Writings*, trans. Edmund Jephcott, 146–62. New York: Schocken Books, 1986.

Benson, Brian J. 1969. Review of Gwendolyn Brooks, *In the Mecca. CLA Journal* 13 (December): 203.

Bercovitch, Sacvan. 1975. *The Puritan Origins of the American Self*. New Haven, Conn.: Yale University Press.

1993. *The Rites of Assent: Transformations in the Symbolic Construction of America.* New York: Routledge.

Berlant, Lauren. 1988. "Race, Gender, and Nation in *The Color Purple.*" In *Alice Walker*, ed. Henry Louis Gates, Jr., and K. A. Appiah, 211–38. New York: Amistad, 1993.

Bernstein, Charles. 1992. *A Poetics.* Cambridge, Mass.: Harvard University Press.

Bernstein, Michael. 1980. *The Tale of the Tribe: Ezra Pound and the Modern Verse Epic.* Princeton: Princeton University Press.

Bérubé, Michael. 1992. *Marginal Forces / Cultural Centers: Tolson, Pynchon, and the Politics of the Canon.* Ithaca, N.Y.: Cornell University Press.

Bethune, Mary McLeod. 1944. "'Certain Unalienable Rights.'" In *What the Negro Wants*, ed. Rayford W. Logan, 248–58. Chapel Hill: University of North Carolina Press.

Beyer, William C. 1995. "Creating 'Common Ground' on the Home Front: Race, Class, and Ethnicity in a 1940s Magazine." In *The Home-Front War*, ed. Kenneth Paul O'Brien and Lynn Hudson Parsons, 41–62. Westport, Conn.: Greenwood Press.

Bhabha, Homi K. 1994. *The Location of Culture.* London: Routledge.

Ed. 1990. *Nation and Narration.* New York: Routledge.

Biddle, Francis. 1941. "'The Power of Democracy: It Can Meet All Conditions.'" *Vital Speeches of the Day*, October 15: 5–9.

Black Public Sphere Collective, eds. 1995. *The Black Public Sphere: A Public Culture Book.* Chicago: University of Chicago Press.

Blakely, Nora Brooks. 1987. "Three-Way Mirror." In *Say That the River Turns*, ed. Haki Madhubuti, 7–25. Chicago: Third World Press.

Bloom, Harold. 1989. Introduction. *Alice Walker: Modern Critical Views*, ed. Harold Bloom, 1–4. New York: Chelsea House.

Bluestone, Daniel. 1991. *Constructing Chicago.* New Haven, Conn.: Yale University Press.

Bond, Horace Mann. 1942. "'Should the Negro Care Who Wins the War?'" *Annals of the American Academy of Political and Social Science* 223: 81–4.

Bontemps, Arna. 1969. "Negro Poets Then and Now." In *Black Expression*, ed. Addison Gayle, Jr., 82–9. New York: Weybright and Tally.

Bontemps, Arna, and Langston Hughes. 1980. *Arna Bontemps–Langston Hughes Letters, 1925-1967.* Ed. Charles H. Nichols. New York: Paragon House, 1990.

Borgese, G. A. 1944. "A Bedroom Approach to Racism." *Negro Digest* 3.2: 31–5.

Boskin, Joseph. 1986. *Sambo: The Rise and Demise of an American Jester.* New York: Oxford University Press.

Branch, Taylor. 1988. *Parting the Waters: America in the King Years, 1954–1963.* New York: Simon and Schuster.

Brazier, Arthur M. 1969. *Black Self-Determination: The Story of The Woodlawn Organization.* Grand Rapids, Mich.: Wm. B. Eerdmans Publishing.

Brecht, Bertolt. 1966. *Jungle of Cities and Other Plays.* Trans. Anselm Hollo. New York: Grove Press.

Brinkley, Alan. 1996. "Liberty, Community, and the National Idea." *American Prospect* 29 (November–December): 53–9.

Brooks, Gwendolyn. 1945. *A Street in Bronzeville. Blacks*, 17-96.
    1949. *Annie Allen. Blacks*, 77–140.
    1960. *The Bean Eaters. Blacks*, 323–86.
    1963. "Riders to the Blood-Red Wrath." *Blacks*, 389–92.
    1968. *In the Mecca*. New York: Harper and Row.
    1969. *Riot. Blacks*, 469–80.
    1972a. *Report from Part One*. Detroit: Broadside Press.
    1972b. "African Fragment." *Report from Part One*, 87–130.
    1978. Afterword. In Pauline Hopkins, *Contending Forces*, 403–9.
    1987a. *Blacks*. Chicago: The David Company.
    1987b. "Of Flowers and Fire and Flowers," In *Say That the River Turns*, ed.
        Haki Madhubuti, 1–3. Chicago: Third World Press.
    1990. "A Celebration of Life in a Poet's Own Words." Interview by Glenn
        Collins. *New York Times*, April 30: C11.
    1996. *Report from Part Two*. Chicago: Third World Press.
Brooks, Gwendolyn, Keorapetse Kgositsile, Haki R. Madhubuti, and Dudley Ran-
    dall. 1975. *A Capsule Course in Black Poetry Writing*. Detroit: Broadside Press.
Brown, Francis, ed. 1945. *One America: The History, Contributions, and Present Prob-
    lems of Our Racial and National Minorities*. New York: Prentice Hall.
Brown, Frank London. 1959. *Trumbull Park*. Chicago: Henry Regnery.
    1961. "Chicago's Great Lady of Poetry." *Chicago Sunday Tribune*, August 27:
        n.p.
Brown, Sterling. 1944. "Count Us In." In *What the Negro Wants*, ed. Rayford W.
    Logan, 308–44. Chapel Hill: University of North Carolina Press.
    1989. *The Collected Poems of Sterling A. Brown*. Ed. Michael S. Harper. Chicago:
        Another Chicago Press.
Bruce, Dickson D., Jr. 1989. *Black American Writing from the Nadir: The Evolution of a
    Literary Tradition, 1877–1915*. Baton Rouge: Louisiana State University
    Press.
    1992. "W. E. B. Du Bois and the Idea of Double Consciousness." *American Lit-
        erature* 64: 299–309.
Buchanan, A. Russell. 1977. *Black Americans in World War II*. Santa Barbara, Calif.:
    Clio.
Buck, Pearl. 1943. "Needed: Living Heroes." *Negro Digest* 1.3: 82–3.
Buckmaster, Henrietta. 1944. "Can a White Know?" *Negro Digest* 4.4: 47–9.
Buck-Morss, Susan. 1989. *The Dialectics of Seeing: Walter Benjamin and the Arcades
    Project*. Cambridge, Mass.: MIT Press.
Buni, Andrew. 1974. *Robert L. Vann of the* Pittsburgh Courier. Pittsburgh, Pa.: Uni-
    versity of Pittsburgh Press.
Burma, John H. 1947. "'An Analysis of the Present Negro Press'" *Social Forces* 26:
    172–80.
Burns, Ben. 1996. *Nitty Gritty: A White Editor in Black Journalism*. Jackson: Univer-
    sity Press of Mississippi.
Bush, Ronald. 1976. *The Genesis of Ezra Pound's* Cantos. Princeton, N.J.: Prince-
    ton University Press.
Butler-Evans, Elliot. 1989. "History and Genealogy in Walker's *The Third Life of*

Grange Copeland and *Meridian."* In *Alice Walker,* ed. Henry Louis Gates, Jr., and K. A. Appiah, 105–25. New York: Amistad, 1993.

Calhoun, Craig, ed. 1992. *Habermas and the Public Sphere.* Cambridge, Mass.: MIT Press.

Calkin, Clinch. 1942. "Wartime Attorney General." *Survey Graphic,* October: 420–4.

Calverton, V. F. 1937. *The Making of Society: An Outline of Sociology.* New York: The Modern Library–Random House.

Camus, Albert. 1951. *The Rebel: An Essay on Man in Revolt.* Trans. Anthony Bower. New York: Vintage–Random House, 1956.

Carby, Hazel V. 1987. *Reconstructing Womanhood: The Emergence of the Afro-American Novelist.* New York: Oxford University Press.

1988. Introduction. *The Magazine Novels of Pauline Hopkins,* xxix–l. New York: Oxford University Press.

1990. "The Quicksands of Representation: Rethinking Black Cultural Politics." In *Reading Black, Reading Feminist,* ed. Henry Louis Gates, Jr., 76–90. New York: Meridian.

Carnegie, Dale. 1937. *How to Win Friends and Influence People.* New York: Simon and Schuster.

Cayton, Horace. 1943a. "Exhibitionism." *Pittsburgh Courier,* June 26: 13.

1943b. Series on migration. *Chicago Sun,* October 14–16.

Ceaser, James W. 1990. *Liberal Democracy and Political Science.* Baltimore: Johns Hopkins University Press.

Chafee, Zechariah, Jr. 1941. *Free Speech in the United States.* New York: Atheneum, 1969.

Chapman, Abraham, ed. 1972. *New Black Voices: An Anthology of Contemporary Afro-American Literature.* New York: Mentor.

Chicago Commission on Race Relations (CCRR). 1922. *The Negro in Chicago: A Study in Race Relations and a Race Riot in 1919.* Chicago: University of Chicago Press.

Chicago Daily News. 1919–20.

Chicago Defender. 1919–20.

[Chicago] Mayor's Committee on Race Relations (MCRR). 1945. *Race Relations in Chicago, December 1944.* Chicago: n.p.

Chicago Plan Commission. 1942. *Forty-Four Cities in the City of Chicago.* Chicago: n.p.

"Chicago Rebellion: Free Black Men Fight Free White Men." 1919. *The Messenger,* September: 312.

Chicago Riot Study Committee. 1968. *Report to the Hon. Richard J. Daley: August 1, 1968.* Chicago: n. p.

Chicago Tribune. 1919–20.

Chicago Whip. 1919–20.

Child, Lydia Maria. 1865. *The Freedmen's Book.* New York: Arno, 1968.

Chomsky, Noam. 1993. *Rethinking Camelot: JFK, the Vietnam War, and U.S. Popular Culture.* Boston: South End Press.

Christian, Barbara. 1980. "Novels for Everyday Use." In *Alice Walker,* ed. Henry Louis Gates, Jr., and K. A. Appiah, 50–104. New York: Amistad, 1993.

Clark, Kenneth B. 1965. *Dark Ghetto: Dilemmas of Social Power*. New York: Harper Torchbooks, 1967.

Clarke, Cheryl. 1995. "The Loss of Lyric Space and the Critique of Traditions in Gwendolyn Brooks's *In the Mecca*." *Kenyon Review* 17 (Winter): 136–47.

Cleaver, Eldridge. 1968. *Soul on Ice*. New York: Dell Publishing, 1969.

Cohen, Jean L., and Andrew Arato. 1992. *Civil Society and Political Theory*. Cambridge, Mass.: MIT Press.

Cohen, Jerry, and William S. Murphy. 1966. *Burn, Baby, Burn: The Los Angeles Riot, August 1965*. New York: E. P. Dutton.

Coles, Robert. 1964. "Social Struggle and Weariness." *Psychiatry* 27: 305–15.

Conlin, Joseph R., ed. 1974. *The American Radical Press, 1880–1960*. Westport, Conn.: Greenwood Press.

Connaroe, Joel. 1973. "Poetry Chronicle." *Shenandoah* 1: 81–4.

Conot, Robert. 1967. *Rivers of Blood, Years of Darkness*. New York: Bantam Books.

Cook, Fannie. 1946. "An Atomic Approach to Racism." *Negro Digest* 4.10: 23–4.

Cook, Mercer. 1968. "African Voices of Protest." In Mercer Cook and Stephen Henderson, *The Militant Black Writer*, 3–64.

Cook, Mercer, and Stephen E. Henderson. 1968. *The Militant Black Writer in Africa and the United States*. Madison: University of Wisconsin Press, 1969.

Cooke, Michael G. 1984a. *Afro-American Literature in the Twentieth Century: The Achievement of Intimacy*. New Haven, Conn.: Yale University Press.

    1984b. "Walker: The Centering Self." In *Alice Walker*, ed. Henry Louis Gates, Jr., and K. A. Appiah, 140–54. New York: Amistad, 1993.

Cornish, Sam. 1964. *Generations and Other Poems*. Baltimore: Beanbag Press.

    1966. *Generations*. Baltimore: Beanbag Press.

    1971. *Generations*. Boston: Beacon Press.

    1984. "Alice Walker: Her Own Woman." *Christian Science Monitor*, February 3: B1, B7.

    1986. *Songs of Jubilee: New and Selected Poems, 1963–1983*. Greensboro, N.C.: Unicorn Press.

    1990. *1935: A Memoir*. Boston: Ploughshares.

    1991. Conversation with author.

    1996. *Cross a Parted Sea*. Cambridge, Mass.: Zoland Books.

Cornish, Sam, and Lucian W. Dixon, eds. 1969. *Chicory: Young Voices from the Black Ghetto*. New York: Association Press.

Crane, Hart. 1926. *White Buildings*. *The Complete Poems*, 3–44.

    1966. *The Complete Poems and Selected Letters and Prose of Hart Crane*. New York: Liveright Publishing Corporation.

The Crisis. 1935–6.

Croly, Herbert. 1909. *The Promise of American Life*. Boston: Northeastern University Press, 1989.

"Cut the Comedy." 1942. *Pittsburgh Courier*, January 17: n.p.

Daniels, Jonathan. 1942. "'New Patterns for Old.'" *Survey Graphic*, November: 485–7.

Davis, Angela Y. 1981. *Women, Race, and Class*. New York: Vintage Books.

Davis, Charles T., and Henry Louis Gates, Jr., eds. 1985. *The Slave's Narrative*. New York: Oxford University Press.

Davis, Earle. 1968. *Vision Fugitive: Ezra Pound and Economics.* Lawrence: University Press of Kansas.

Davis, Kenneth S. 1986. *FDR: The New Deal Years, 1933–1937.* New York: Random House.

Davis, Mike. 1990. *City of Quartz: Excavating the Future in Los Angeles.* London: Verso.

Dayan, Daniel, and Elihu Katz. 1992. *Media Events: The Live Broadcasting of History.* Cambridge, Mass.: Harvard University Press.

De Capite, Michael. 1942. "War Comes to Little Italy." *Common Ground,* Fall: 51–2.

Detweiler, Frederick G. 1922. *The Negro Press in the United States.* College Park, Md.: McGrath Publishing Company, 1968.

Deutsch, Albert. 1944. "History Is On Our Side." *Negro Digest* 2.8: 19–20.

Dixon, Melvin. 1994. "The Black Writer's Use of Memory." In *History and Memory in African-American Culture,* ed. Fabre and O'Meally, 18–27. New York: Oxford University Press.

Donovan, Robert J., and Ray Scherer. 1992. *Unsilent Revolution: Television News and Public Life.* Woodrow Wilson Center Series. Cambridge, Mass.: Cambridge University Press.

Doreski, C. K. 1992. "Kinship and History in Sam Cornish's *Generations.*" *Contemporary Literature* 33: 663–86.

Doreski, William. 1990. *The Years of Our Friendship: Robert Lowell and Allen Tate.* Jackson: University Press of Mississippi.

Douglas, Ann. 1995. *Terrible Honesty: Mongrel Manhattan in the 1920s.* New York: Farrar, Straus, and Giroux.

Douglas, Helen Gahagan. 1945. "Racial Progress with a Plan." *Negro Digest* 3.10: 49–50.

Douglass, Frederick. 1845. *Narrative of the Life of Frederick Douglass: An American Slave.* New York: Signet Books.

1852. "What To the Slave Is the Fourth of July?" *The Oxford Frederick Douglass Reader,* 108–30.

1950–75. *The Life and Writing of Frederick Douglass.* 5 vols. Ed. Philip S. Foner. New York: International Publishers.

1996. *The Oxford Frederick Douglass Reader.* Ed. William L. Andrews. New York: Oxford University Press.

Dove, Rita. 1983. *Museum.* Pittsburgh, Pa.: Carnegie-Mellon University Press.

1985. "Telling It Like It I-S IS: Narrative Techniques in Melvin Tolson's *Harlem Gallery.*" *New England Review and Bread Loaf Quarterly* 8 (Autumn): 109–17.

Drake, St. Clair. 1951. "The International Implications of Race and Race Relations." *Journal of Negro Education* 20: 261–78.

Drake, St. Clair, and Horace Cayton. 1945. *Black Metropolis: A Study of Negro Life in a Northern City.* 2 vols. New York: Harper and Row, 1962.

Du Bois, W. E. B. 1897. "The Conservation of the Races." *Writings,* 815–26.

1903a. *The Souls of Black Folk. Writings,* 357–547.

1903b. "The Talented Tenth." *Writings,* 842–61.

1915. "From the Boston 'Globe.'" *Writings,* 1164–7.

1919. "Make Way for Democracy." *The Crisis,* April 1: n.p.

1920. "The Souls of White Folk." *Writings*, 925–38.

1986. *W. E. B. Du Bois: Writings*. Ed. Nathan Huggins. New York: Library of America.

Duncan, Robert. 1984. *Ground Work: Before the War*. New York: New Directions.

1985. "The Truth and Life of Myth." *Fictive Certainties*, 1–59. New York: New Directions.

Durr, Robert. 1947. *The Negro Press: Its Character, Development, and Function*. Jackson: Mississippi Division, Southern Regional Council.

"The Editorial Policy of Negro Newspapers of 1917–1918 as Compared with That of 1941–1942." 1944. *Journal of Negro History* 29: 24–31.

Eliot, T. S. 1917. "Prufrock." *The Complete Poems and Plays*, 3–20.

1920. *Poems. The Complete Poems and Plays*, 21–36.

1922. *The Waste Land. The Complete Poems and Plays*, 37–55.

1934. *After Strange Gods: A Primer of Modern Heresy*. New York: Harcourt, Brace, and Company.

1942. "Little Gidding." *The Complete Poems and Plays*, 138–48.

1951. "Tradition and the Individual Talent." *Selected Essays*, 13–22. London: Faber and Faber.

1971. *The Complete Poems and Plays, 1909-1950*. San Diego, Calif.: Harcourt Brace Jovanovich.

Ellison, Ralph. 1944. "*An American Dilemma*: A Review." *Collected Essays*, 328–40.

1945a. "Richard Wright's Blues." *Collected Essays*, 128–44.

1945b. "Beating That Boy." *Collected Essays*, 145–54.

1958. "Change the Joke and Slip the Yoke." *Collected Essays*, 100–12.

1963/4. "The World and the Jug." *Collected Essays*, 155–88.

1964. "Hidden Name and the Complex Fate: A Writer's Experience in the United States." *Collected Essays*, 189–209.

1995. *The Collected Essays of Ralph Ellison*. Ed. John Callahan. New York: The Modern Library.

Emerson, Ralph Waldo. 1841. "History." *Essays and Lectures*, 236–57.

1850. "Representative Men." *Essays and Lectures*, 615–761.

1982. *Emerson in His Journals*. Cambridge, Mass.: Harvard University Press.

1983. *Essays and Lectures*. Ed. Joel Porte. New York: Library of America.

"Emmett Till's Mother Remembers Her Son on His 50th Birthday." 1991. *Jet*, August 12: 6, 10.

Erenberg, Lewis A., and Susan E. Hirsch, eds. 1996. *The War in American Culture: Society and Consciousness during World War II*. Chicago: University of Chicago Press.

Evans, Mari, ed. 1984. "Gwendolyn Brooks." *Black Women Writers (1950–1980)*, 75–110. New York: Doubleday–Anchor.

Fabre, Geneviève. 1994. "African-American Commemorative Celebrations in the Nineteenth Century." In *History and Memory in African-American Culture*, ed. Fabre and O'Meally, 72–91.

Fabre, Geneviève, and Robert O'Meally, eds. 1994. *History and Memory in African-American Culture*. New York: Oxford University Press.

Fabre, Michel. 1990. *Richard Wright: Books and Writers*. Jackson: University Press of Mississippi.

Fanon, Frantz. 1963. *The Wretched of the Earth.* Trans. Constance Farrington. New York: Grove Press.

Faris, Ellsworth. 1943. "The Role of the Citizen." In *American Society in Wartime,* ed. William Fielding Ogburn, 118–42. Chicago: University of Chicago Press.

Farnsworth, Robert M. 1982. Introduction. *Caviar and Cabbage: Selected Columns by Melvin B. Tolson,* 1–25. Columbia: University of Missouri Press.

——— 1984. *Melvin B. Tolson 1898–1966: Plain Talk and Poetic Prophecy.* Columbia: University of Missouri Press.

Farrell, James T. 1935. *The Young Manhood of Studs Lonigan.* In *Studs Lonigan, A Trilogy,* 155–486. Urbana: University of Illinois Press, 1993.

Fast, Howard. 1945. "Proud To Be Black." *Negro Digest* 3.5: 5–6.

Feather, Leonard. 1945. "Wanted: A White Mammy." *Negro Digest* 4.1: 45–7.

Fendrich, James M. 1977. "Keeping the Faith or Pursuing the Good Life: A Study of the Consequences of Participation in the Civil Rights Movement." *American Sociological Review* 42: 144–57.

Field, Marshall. 1945. "The Color of Injustice." *Negro Digest* 3.8: 31–2.

Fineman, Joel. 1989. "The History of the Anecdote: Fiction and Fiction." In *New Historicism,* ed. H. Aram Veeser, 49–76. New York: Routledge.

Fishkin, Shelley Fisher. 1985. *From Fact to Fiction: Journalism and Imaginative Writing in America.* New York: Oxford University Press.

Fiske, John. 1987. *Television Culture.* New York: Routledge, 1994.

Flasch, Joy. 1972. *Melvin B. Tolson.* New York: Twayne.

Fogelson, Robert M. 1971. *Violence as Protest: A Study of Riots and Ghettos.* Garden City, N.Y.: Doubleday.

Foner, Philip, ed. 1976. *We, the Other People: Alternative Declarations of Independence by Labor Groups, Farmers, Woman's Rights Advocates, Socialists, and Blacks, 1829–1975.* Urbana: University of Illinois Press.

Foner, Philip S., and Daniel Rosenberg, eds. 1993. *Racism, Dissent, and Asian Americans from 1850 to the Present: A Documentary History.* Westport, Conn.: Greenwood Press.

Forcey, Charles. 1961. *The Crossroads of Liberalism: Croly, Weyl, Lippmann, and the Progressive Era, 1900–1925.* New York: Oxford University Press.

Fortune. 1934. Special Issue on Fascism. July.

——— 1935. Special Issue on the League of Nations. December.

——— 1968. Special Issue on Business and the Urban Crisis. January.

Foucault, Michel. 1977. *Language, Counter-Memory, Practice: Selected Essays and Interviews.* Trans. Donald F. Bouchard. Ithaca, N.Y.: Cornell University Press.

——— 1978–88. *The History of Sexuality.* Trans. Robert Hurley. 3 vols. New York: Pantheon Books.

Fowler, Roger. 1986. *Linguistic Criticism.* Oxford: Oxford University Press.

——— 1991. *Language in the News: Discourse and Ideology in the Press.* New York: Routledge.

Fox-Genovese, Elizabeth. 1990. "'My Statue, My Self': Autobiographical Writings of Afro-American Women." In *Reading Black, Reading Feminist,* ed. Henry Louis Gates, Jr., 176–203. New York: Meridian.

Frank, Waldo. 1919. *Our America.* New York: Boni and Liveright.

Franklin, John Hope, and August Meier, eds. 1982. *Black Leaders of the Twentieth Century*. Urbana: University of Illinois Press.

Frazier, E. Franklin. 1957. *Black Bourgeoisie*. Glencoe, Ill.: Falcon's Wing Press.

"'The Front Page of the Negro Press.'" 1947. *Events and Trends in Race Relations–A Monthly Summary* 4: 377.

Fry, John R. 1969. *Fire and Blackstone*. Philadelphia: Lippincott.

Fuller, Hoyt. 1964. "The Negro Writer in the United States." *Ebony*, November: 126–34.

1971. "The New Black Literature: Protest or Affirmation." In *The Black Aesthetic*, ed. Addison Gayle, Jr., 327–48.

1972. "Towards a Black Aesthetic." In *The Black Aesthetic*, ed. Addison Gayle, Jr., 3–11. Garden City, N.Y.: Doubleday–Anchor.

Fussell, Paul. 1989. *Wartime: Understanding and Behavior in the Second World War*. New York: Oxford University Press.

Gallup, Donald. 1969. *A Bibliography of Ezra Pound*. London: Rupert-Hart Davis.

Garland, Phyl. 1968. "Gwendolyn Brooks: Poet Laureate." *Ebony*, July: 48–9.

Garrow, David J. 1986. *Bearing the Cross: Martin Luther King, Jr. and the Southern Christian Leadership Conference*. New York: William Morrow.

Gates, Henry Louis, Jr. 1987. *Figures in Black: Words, Signs, and the "Racial" Self*. New York: Oxford University Press.

1997. "The Chitlin Circuit." *New Yorker*, February 3: 44–55.

Ed. 1984. *Black Literature and Literary Theory*. New York: Methuen.

1990. *Reading Black, Reading Feminist: A Critical Anthology*. New York: Meridian.

Gates, Henry Louis, Jr., and K. A. Appiah, eds. 1993a. *Alice Walker: Critical Perspectives Past and Present*. New York: Amistad.

1993b. *Richard Wright: Critical Perspectives Past and Present*. New York: Amistad.

Gayle, Addison, Jr., ed. 1972a. *The Black Aesthetic*. Garden City, N.Y.: Doubleday–Anchor.

1972b. "The Function of Black Literature at the Present Time." In *The Black Aesthetic*, ed. Addison Gayle, Jr., 383–94.

Geertz, Clifford. 1983a. *Local Knowledge: Further Essays in Interpretive Anthropology*. New York: Basic Books.

1983b. "Blurred Genres: The Refiguration of Social Thought." *Local Knowledge*, 19–35.

Gerald, Carolyn [Fowler]. 1969. "The Black Writer and His Role." In *The Black Aesthetic*, ed. Addison Gayle, Jr., 349–57. Garden City, N.Y.: Doubleday–Anchor.

Giddings, Paula. 1984. *When and Where I Enter: The Impact of Black Women on Race and Sex in America*. New York: William Morrow.

Gilroy, Paul. 1987. *'There Ain't No Black in the Union Jack': The Cultural Politics of Race and Nation*. Chicago: University of Chicago Press.

1993. *The Black Atlantic: Modernity and Double Consciousness*. Cambridge, Mass.: Harvard University Press.

Gitlin, Todd. 1980. *The Whole World is Watching: Mass Media in the Making and Unmaking of the New Left*. Berkeley and Los Angeles: University of California Press.

1987. *The Sixties: Years of Hope, Days of Rage*. New York: Bantam Books.

Goodman, Jack, ed. 1946. *While You Were Gone: A Report on Wartime Life in the United States.* New York: Simon and Schuster.

Goody, Jack. 1991. "The Time of Telling and the Telling of Time in Written and Oral Cultures." In *Chronotypes,* ed. John Bender and David E. Wellbery, 77–98. Stanford, Calif.: Stanford University Press.

Graham, Hugh Davis. 1990. *The Civil Rights Era: Origins and Development of National Policy.* New York: Oxford University Press.

Graham, Maryemma. 1990. "Bearing Witness in Black Chicago: A View of Selected Fiction by Richard Wright, Frank London Brown, and Ronald Fair." *CLA Journal* 33 (March): 280–97.

Grant, Robert B., ed. 1972. *The Black Man Comes to the City: A Documentary Account from the Great Migration to the Great Depression, 1915–1930.* Chicago: Nelson-Hall.

Greenblatt, Stephen J. 1990. "Resonance and Wonder." *Learning to Curse: Essays in Early Modern Culture,* 161–83. New York: Routledge.

Greenfeld, Liah. 1992. *Nationalism: Five Roads to Modernity.* Cambridge, Mass.: Harvard University Press.

Griaule, Marcel. 1965. *Conversations with Ogotemmêli: An Introduction to Dogon Religious Ideas.* Trans. Ralph Butler, Audrey Richards, and Beatrice Hooke. New York: Oxford University Press.

Grossman, James R. 1989. *Land of Hope: Chicago, Black Southerners, and the Great Migration.* Chicago: University of Chicago Press.

Gruesser, John Cullen, ed. 1996. *The Unruly Voice: Rediscovering Pauline Elizabeth Hopkins.* Urbana: University of Illinois Press.

Habermas, Jürgen. 1989. *The Structural Transformations of the Public Sphere.* Trans. Thomas Burger. Cambridge, Mass.: MIT Press.

1992. "Further Reflections on the Public Sphere." In *Habermas and the Public Sphere,* ed. Craig Calhoun, 421–61. Cambridge, Mass.: MIT Press.

Haile, Makonnen. 1935. "Last Gobble of Africa." *The Crisis,* March: 70–1, 90.

Halper, Albert. 1945. "Never Bow Down." *Negro Digest* 3.4: 61–2.

Hampton, Henry, and Steven Fayer, eds. 1995. *Voices of Freedom: An Oral History of the Civil Rights Movement from the 1950s through the 1980s.* London: Vintage Books.

Hansell, William. 1989. "The Poet-Militant and Foreshadowings of a Black Mystique: Poems in the Second Period of Gwendolyn Brooks." In *A Life Distilled: Gwendolyn Brooks, Her Poetry and Fiction,* ed. Maria K. Mootry and Gary Smith, 71–80. Urbana: University of Illinois Press.

Harper, Michael S. 1977. *Images of Kin: New and Selected Poems.* Urbana: University of Illinois Press.

Harper, Michael S., and Robert B. Stepto, eds. 1979. *Chant of Saints: A Gathering of Afro-American Literature, Art, and Scholarship.* Urbana: University of Illinois Press.

Harper, Michael S., and Anthony Walton, eds. 1994. *Every Shut Eye Ain't Asleep: An Anthology of Poetry by African Americans since 1945.* Boston: Little Brown.

Harper, Philip Brian. 1994. "Around 1969: Televisual Representation and the Complication of the Black Subject." In *The Black Columbiad,* ed. Werner Sollors and Maria Diedrich, 265–74. Cambridge, Mass.: Harvard University Press.

Harris, Joseph E. 1994. *African-American Reactions to War in Ethiopia, 1936–1941*. Baton Rouge: Louisiana State University Press.

Harris, Mark. 1946. "Citizens of the World." *Negro Digest* 4.9: 45–6.

Harris, Trudier. 1990. "Native Sons and Foreign Daughters." In *New Essays on Native Son*, ed. Keneth Kinnamon, 63–84. Cambridge: Cambridge University Press.

Harris, Wilson. 1967. *Tradition: The Writer and Society: Critical Essays*. London: New Beacon Publications.

Hartoonunian, Harry D. 1996. "The Benjamin Effect: Modernism, Repetition, and the Path to Different Cultural Imaginaries." In *Walter Benjamin and the Demands of History*, ed. Michael P. Steinberg, 62–87. Ithaca, N.Y.: Cornell University Press.

Hayden, Robert. 1985. *Collected Poems of Robert Hayden*. New York: Liveright, 1996. Ed. 1967. *Kaleidoscope*. New York: Harcourt, Brace, and World.

Hayden, Robert, David Burrows, and Frederick R. Lapides. 1971. *Afro-American Literature: An Introduction*. New York: Harcourt, Brace.

Hemingway, Ernest. 1935. "Notes on the Next War: A Serious Topical Letter." In *By-Line: Ernest Hemingway: Selected Articles and Dispatches of Four Decades*, ed. William White, 205–12. New York: Scribner's, 1967.

Henderson, Stephen E. 1968. "'Survival Motion': A Study of the Black Writer and the Black Revolution." In Mercer Cook and Stephen E. Henderson, *The Militant Black Writer in Africa and the United States*, 65–132. Madison: University of Wisconsin Press, 1969.

1972. *Understanding the New Black Poetry: Black Speech and Black Music as Poetic References*. New York: William Morrow.

Herskovits, Melville J. 1958. *The Myth of the Negro Past*. Boston: Beacon Press.

Heymann, C. David. 1976. *Ezra Pound: The Last Rower: A Political Profile*. New York: Viking Press.

High, Stanley. 1942. "How the Negro Fights for Freedom." *The Reader's Digest*, July: 113–18.

Hinsley, Curtis M. 1996. "Strolling Through the Colonies." In *Walter Benjamin and the Demands of History*, ed. Michael P. Steinberg, 119–40. Ithaca, N.Y.: Cornell University Press.

Hobsbawm, E[ric]. 1983a. "Introduction: Inventing Traditions." In *The Invention of Tradition*, ed. Eric Hobsbawm and Terence Ranger, 1–14. Cambridge: Cambridge University Press.

1983b. "Mass-Producing Traditions: Europe, 1870–1914." In *The Invention of Tradition*, 263–308.

1990. *Nations and Nationalism: Programme, Myth, Reality*. Cambridge: Cambridge University Press.

Hollander, John. 1981. "Tremors of Exactitude." Review of Jay Wright, *The Double Invention of Komo*. *Times Literary Supplement*, January 30: n.p.

Holt, Rackham. 1945. "Vision of the Future." *Negro Digest* 3.12: 83–4.

Homberger, Eric, ed. 1972. *Ezra Pound: The Critical Heritage*. London: Routledge and Kegan Paul.

Hopkins, Pauline E. 1900. *Contending Forces: A Romance Illustrative of Negro Life*

North and South. Carbondale: Southern Illinois University Press, 1978.

1900–1. "Famous Men of the Negro Race." A series published in the *Colored American Magazine*: "Toussaint L'Overture," November 1900, 9–24; "Hon. Frederick Douglass," December 1900, 121–32; "William Wells Brown," January 1901, 232–6; "Robert Brown Elliott," February 1901, 294–301; "Edwin Garrison Walker," March 1901, 358–66; "Lewis Hayden," April 1901, 473–7; "Charles Lenox Redmond," May 1901, 34–9; "Sargeant Wm. H. Carney," June 1901, 177–84; "Senator Blanche K. Bruce," August 1901, 257–61; "Robert Morris," September 1901, 337–42; "Booker T. Washington," October 1901, 436–41.

1901–2. "Famous Women of the Negro Race." A series published in the *Colored American Magazine*: "Phenomenal Vocalists," November 1901, 45–53; "Sojourner Truth," December 1901, 124–32; "Harriet Tubman," January/February 1902, 210–23; "Some Literary Workers," March 1902, 276–80; "Literary Workers," April 1902, 366–71; "Educators," May 1902, 41–6; "Educators (Continued)," June 1902, 125–30; "Educators (Concluded)," July 1902, 206–13; "Club Life Among Colored Women," August 1902, 273–7; "Artists," September 1902, 362–7; "Higher Education of Colored Women in White Schools and Colleges," October 1902, 445–50.

1916a. "Editorial and Publishers Announcements." *New Era Magazine* February, March.

1916b. "Men of Vision." A series published in *New Era Magazine*: "Mark Réné Demortie," February: 35–9; "Rev. Leonard A. Grimes," March: 99–105.

1988. *The Magazine Novels of Pauline Hopkins.* Ed. Hazel Carby. New York: Oxford University Press.

Horne, Gerald. 1995. *Fire This Time: The Watts Uprising and the 1960s.* Charlottesville: University of Virginia Press.

Horowitz, Helen Lefkowitz. 1976. *Culture and the City: Cultural Philanthropy in Chicago from the 1880s to 1917.* Chicago: University of Chicago Press.

Horsman, Reginald. 1981. *Race and Manifest Destiny: The Origins of American Racial Anglo-Saxonism.* Cambridge, Mass.: Harvard University Press.

Hughes, Langston. 1934. *The Ways of White Folks.* New York: Vintage Books, 1990.

1936. "Let America Be America Again." *Collected Poems*, 189–91.

1944. "My America." In *What the Negro Wants*, ed. Rayford W. Logan, 299–307. Chapel Hill: University of North Carolina Press.

1945. "Here to Yonder" [comment on Tolson, *Rendezvous with America*]. *Chicago Defender*, December 15: n.p.

1954. "Robert S. Abbott." *Famous American Negroes*, 79–84. New York: Dodd, Mead.

1958. "The Fun of Being Black." *The Langston Hughes Reader: The Selected Writings of Langston Hughes*, 498–500. New York: George Braziller.

1961. *The Best of Simple.* New York: Farrar, Straus.

1962a. "Name in Print." In *The Angry Black*, ed. John A. Williams, 52–4. New York: Lancer Books.

1962b. *Fight for Freedom: The Story of the NAACP.* New York: W. W. Norton.

1965. *Simple's Uncle Sam*. New York: Hill and Wang.

1992. *Good Morning Revolution: Uncollected Writings of Langston Hughes*. Ed. Faith Berry. New York: Citadel Press.

1994a. *The Collected Poems of Langston Hughes*. Ed. Arnold Rampersad and David Roessel. New York: Alfred A. Knopf.

1994b. *The Return of Simple*. New York: Hill and Wang.

1995. *Langston Hughes and the* Chicago Defender: *Essays on Race, Politics, and Culture 1942–62*. Ed. Christopher C. De Santis. Urbana: University of Illinois Press.

Hurst, Fannie. 1946. "The Sure Way to Equality." *Negro Digest* 4.8: 27–8.

Hurston, Zora Neale. 1942. *Dust Tracks on a Road. Zora Neale Hurston: Folklore, Memoirs, and Other Writings*. New York: Library of America, 1995.

1979. *I Love Myself When I Am Laughing. . . .* Ed. Alice Walker. New York: The Feminist Press.

Hutchinson, George. 1995. *The Harlem Renaissance in Black and White*. Cambridge, Mass.: Harvard University Press.

Ignatiev, Noel. 1995. *How the Irish Became White*. New York: Routledge.

Interracial Review. 1941.

Irons, Peter. 1983. *Justice at War*. New York: Oxford University Press.

Jackson, Walter A. 1990. *Gunnar Myrdal and America's Conscience: Social Engineeering and Racial Liberalism, 1938–1987*. Chapel Hill: University of North Carolina Press.

Jacobs, Harriet. 1861. *Incidents in the Life of a Slave Girl*. Ed. Jean Fagan Yellin. New York: Oxford University Press, 1987.

Jacobs, Paul. 1967. *Prelude to Riot: A View of Urban America from the Bottom*. Center for the Study of Democratic Institutions. New York: Vintage Books, 1968.

Jameson, Frederic. 1991. *Postmodernism Or, the Cultural Logic of Late Capitalism*. Durham, N.C.: Duke University Press.

Janeway, Eliot. 1943. "'Fighting a White Man's War.'" *Racial Digest*, April: 1–3.

Jefferson, Thomas. 1787. "Letter to Edward Carrington." *Writings*, 880.

1791. "Letter to Benjamin Banneker." *Writings: Autobiography, Notes on the State of Virginia, Public and Private Papers, Addresses, Letters*. New York: Library of America, 1984.

Jehlen, Myra. 1986. *American Incarnation: The Individual, the Nation, and the Continent*. Cambridge, Mass.: Harvard University Press.

Jewett, Sarah Orne. 1896. *The Country of the Pointed Firs*. New York: Dover Books, 1994.

Johnson, Abby Arthur, and Ronald Maberry Johnson. 1977. "Away from Accommodation: Radical Editors and Protest Journalism, 1900–1910." *Journal of Negro History* 62 (October): 325–38.

1979. *Propaganda and Aesthetics: The Literary Politics of African-American Magazines in the Twentieth Century*. 2d ed. Amherst: University of Massachusetts Press, 1991.

1994. "Charting a New Course: African American Literary Politics Since 1976." In *The Black Columbiad*, ed. Werner Sollors and Maria Diedrich, 369–84. Cambridge: Harvard University Press.

Johnson, Barbara E. 1990. "The Re(a)d and the Black." In *Reading Black, Reading Feminist: A Critical Anthology*, ed. Henry Louis Gates, Jr., 145–54. New York: Meridian.

267

Johnson, Charles S. 1925. "The New Frontage on American Life." In *The New Negro*, ed. Alain Locke, 278–99. New York: Atheneum, 1968.

    1926. "How the Negro Fits into Northern Industry." *Industrial Psychology* 1: 399–412.

Johnson, Ernest E. 1942. "'The Negro Press Reacts to the War'" *Interracial Review*, March: 39–41.

Johnson, Guy B. 1945. "Whites Are Individuals Too." *Negro Digest* 4.2: 34.

Johnson, James Weldon. 1914. "Do You Read Negro Newspapers?" *New York Age* editorial, October 22. *Selected Writings*, 1: 151.

    1919. "Reaping the Whirlwind." *New York Age* editorial, April 2. *Selected Writings*, 1: 162–3.

    1938. "The Negro Press." *Negro Americans, What Now?* New York: Viking Press.

    1995. *The Selected Writings of James Weldon Johnson*. Ed. Sondra Kathryn Wilson. 2 vols. New York: Oxford University Press.

Johnson, John H. 1943. "Mrs. Roosevelt Says. . . ." *Negro Digest* 1.1: front cover.

    With Lerone Bennett. 1989. *Succeeding against the Odds: The Autobiography of a Great American Businessman*. New York: Amistad, 1992.

Johnson, Walter. 1944. "Building a Brave New World." *Negro Digest* 2.3: 64.

Jones, Gayl. 1987. "Community and Voice: Gwendolyn Brooks's *In the Mecca*." In *A Life Distilled*, ed. Maria K. Mootry and Gary Smith, 193–204. Urbana: University of Illinois Press.

Jones, LeAlan, and Lloyd Newman, with David Isay. 1997. *Our America: Life and Death on the South Side of Chicago*. New York: Scribner.

Jones, LeRoi. *See* Baraka, Amiri.

Jones, Lester M. 1944. "'The Editorial Policy of Negro Newspapers 1917–18 as Compared with That of 1941–42.'" *Journal of Negro History* 29: 24–31.

Jordan, June. 1989. *Naming Our Destiny: New and Selected Poems*. New York: Thunder's Mouth Press.

    1994a. "The Dance of Revolution." *Technical Difficulties: African-American Notes on the State of the Union*, 169–74. New York: Vintage Books.

    1994b. "Where Is the Rage?" *Technical Difficulties*, 175–80.

Jordan, Winthrop D. 1969. *White over Black: American Attitudes toward the Negro, 1550-1812*. Baltimore: Penguin Books.

Kaltenborn, H. V. 1946. "High Hope for the Future." *Negro Digest* 4.6: 13–14.

Kammen, Michael. 1991. *Mystic Chords of Memory: The Transformation of Tradition in American Culture*. New York: Vintage Books.

Karenga, Ron. 1968. "The Quotable Karenga." In *The Black Power Revolt*, ed. Floyd B. Barbour, 162–70. Boston: Porter Sargent Press.

    1972. "Black Cultural Nationalism." In *The Black Aesthetic*, ed. Addison Gayle, Jr., 31–7. Garden City, N.Y.: Doubleday–Anchor.

Kennedy, Randall. 1990. "Making It." Essay review of John Johnson's *Succeeding against the Odds*. *Reconstruction* 1 (Winter): 32–5, 65–8.

    1997. *Race, Crime, and the Law*. New York: Pantheon.

Kenner, Hugh. 1971. *The Pound Era*. Berkeley and Los Angeles: University of California Press.

Kenny, Robert. 1943. "Re-Education for Whites." *Negro Digest* 2.2: 44–5.

Kent, George E. 1990. *A Life of Gwendolyn Brooks*. Lexington: University of Kentucky Press.

Kenyatta, Jomo. 1935. "'Hands Off Abyssinia.'" *Labour Monthly* 9 (September): 532–6.

Kerlin, Robert T. 1920. *The Voice of the Negro, 1919*. New York: Dutton.

Kerner Commission Report. *See* U.S. Riot Commission.

King, Martin Luther, Jr. 1964. *Why We Can't Wait*. New York: New American Library.

    1967. *Where Do We Go from Here: Chaos or Community?* Boston: Beacon Press.

King, Mary. 1987. *Freedom Song: A Personal Story of the 1960s Civil Rights Movement*. New York: William Morrow.

Kinnamon, Keneth, ed. 1990. *New Essays on* Native Son. Cambridge: Cambridge University Press.

Kirby, John. 1982. *Black Americans in the Roosevelt Era: Liberalism and Race*. Knoxville: University of Tennessee Press.

Kutzinski, Vera M. 1987. *Against the American Grain: Myth and History in William Carlos Williams, Jay Wright, and Nicholás Guillén*. Baltimore: Johns Hopkins University Press.

LaCapra, Dominick. 1985. "Rhetoric and History." *History and Criticism*. Ithaca: Cornell University Press.

    Ed. 1991. *The Bounds of Race: Perspectives on Hegemony and Resistance*. Ithaca, N.Y.: Cornell University Press.

LaFarge, Reverend John. 1944. "No Time for Defeatism." *Negro Digest* 2.12: 45–6.

Lane, Rose Wilder. 1944. "No Time for Patience." *Negro Digest* 2.7: 43–5.

LeBerthon, Ted. 1944. "Catholics, Christ and Color." *Negro Digest* 2.11: 19–21.

Lee, Don L. *See* Madhubuti, Haki.

Lee, Spike. 1991. *Jungle Fever* (film). New York: A Spike Lee Joint.

Lemann, Nicholas. 1991. *The Promised Land: The Great Migration and How It Changed America*. New York: Alfred A. Knopf.

Lerner, Gerda, ed. 1972. *Black Women in White America: A Documentary History*. New York: Vintage Books, 1992.

Lester, Julius. 1969a. *Black Folktales*. New York: Grove Press.

    1969b. *Look Out, Whitey! Black Power's Gon' Get Your Mama!* New York: Grove Press.

    1969c. *Search for a New Land: History as Subjective Experience*. New York: Dell, 1970.

"Letter to the Editor." 1942. *Pittsburgh Courier*, January 24: n.p.

Lewis, David L. 1970. *King: A Critical Biography*. Baltimore: Penguin Books.

    1981. *When Harlem Was in Vogue*. New York: Oxford University Press.

    1993. *W. E. B. Du Bois: Biography of a Race, 1868–1919*. New York: Henry Holt.

Lewis, Ida. 1971. "Interview with Gwendolyn Brooks." In Gwendolyn Brooks, *Report from Part One*, 167–82. Detroit: Broadside Press, 1972.

Lewis, John P. 1943. "Not One Alone." *Negro Digest* 1.8: n.p.

Lincoln, C. Eric. 1961. *The Black Muslims in America*. Boston: Beacon Press.

Lippmann, Walter. 1915. *The Stakes of Diplomacy*. New York: Holt.

    1919. Introduction. Carl Sandburg, *The Chicago Race Riots*, ix–xxi. New York: Harcourt, Brace, Howe.

1922. *Public Opinion.* New York: Macmillan.

Lipset, Seymour Martin. 1960. *Political Man: The Social Basis of Politics.* Garden City, N.Y.: Doubleday–Anchor, 1963.

Locke, Alain, ed. 1925. *The New Negro.* New York: Atheneum, 1968.

Logan, Rayford W. 1944. "The Negro Wants First-Class Citizenship." In *What the Negro Wants,* ed. Rayford W. Logan, 1–30.

Ed. 1944. *What the Negro Wants.* Chapel Hill: University of North Carolina Press.

Lomax, Alan. 1993. *The Land Where Blues Began.* New York: Delta Books.

Lomax, John. 1940. *Blind Willie McTell.* Library of Congress Folk Archive. Reissued as RST Records BDCD-6001.

Lomax, John A., and Alan Lomax. 1934. *American Ballads and Folk Songs.* New York: Dover Books, 1994.

Long, Huey. 1933. *Every Man a King: The Autobiography of Huey P. Long.* New Orleans: National Book Company.

Longenbach, James. 1987. *Modernist Poetics of History: Pound, Eliot, and the Sense of the Past.* Princeton: Princeton University Press.

Los Angeles Sentinel. 1942–5.

Lott, Eric. 1993. *Love and Theft: Blackface Minstrelsy and the American Working Class.* New York: Oxford University Press.

Lowenfels, Walter, ed. 1969. *In a Time of Revolution: Poems from Our Third World.* New York: Random House–Vintage Books.

Lyle, Jack, ed. 1968. *The Black American and the Press.* Los Angeles: Ward Ritchie.

McDowell, Deborah E. 1989a. "Negotiating between Tenses: Witnessing Slavery After Freedom – *Dessa Rose.*" *Slavery and the Literary Imagination,* 144–65.

1989b. "Reading Family Matters." In *Changing Our Own Words,* ed. Cheryl Wall, 75–97. New Brunswick, N.J.: Rutgers University Press.

1990. "'The Changing Same': Generational Connections and Black Women Novelists." In *Reading Black, Reading Feminist,* ed. Henry Louis Gates, Jr., 91–115. New York: Meridian.

1993. "The Self in Bloom: Walker's *Meridian.*" In *Alice Walker,* ed. Henry Louis Gates, Jr., and K. A. Appiah, 168–78. New York: Amistad.

1996. *Leaving Pipe Shop: Memories of Kin.* New York: Scribner.

McDowell, Deborah E., and Arnold Rampersad, eds. 1987. *Slavery and the Literary Imagination.* Baltimore: Johns Hopkins University Press.

McGann, Jerome. 1993. *Black Riders: The Visible Language of Modernism.* Princeton, N.J.: Princeton University Press.

McKay, Nellie Y. 1990. "The Souls of Black Women Folks in the Writings of W. E. B. Du Bois." In *Reading Black, Reading Feminist,* ed. Henry Louis Gates, Jr., 227–43. New York: Meridian.

MacLeish, Archibald. 1932. *Conquistador.* Boston: Houghton Mifflin.

1939. *America Was Promises.* New York: Duell, Sloan, and Pearce.

McMahon, Francis E. 1945. "Of Human Dignity." *Negro Digest* 3.7: 89–90.

McTell, Blind Willie. 1940. "Boll Weevil." *Blind Willie McTell.* Library of Congress Folk Archive. Reissued as RST Record BDCD-6001, 1990.

McWilliams, Carey. 1935. *Louis Adamic and Shadow-America.* Los Angeles: n.p.

1943. *Brothers under the Skin*. Rev. ed. Boston: Little, Brown, 1964.

1944a. "The Economic Roots of Race Hate." *Negro Digest* 2.10: 53–5.

1944b. *Prejudice: Japanese-Americans: Symbol of Racial Intolerance*. Boston: Little, Brown.

1945. "Jim Crow Goes West." *Negro Digest* 3.10: 71–4.

1946. "What We Did About Racial Minorities." In *While You Were Gone*, ed. Jack Goodman, 89–112. New York: Simon and Schuster.

1948. *North from Mexico: The Spanish-Speaking People of the United States*. New York: Praeger, 1990.

1979. *The Education of Carey McWilliams*. New York: Simon and Schuster.

Mackey, Nathaniel. 1993. *Discrepant Engagement: Dissonance, Cross-Culturality, and Experimental Writing*. Cambridge: Cambridge University Press.

Madhubuti, Haki. 1968. "A Reply from Don L. Lee." *Negro Digest* 17.6: 96–8.

1972a. "Gwendolyn Brooks: Beyond the Word Maker – The Making of an African Poet." *Report from Part One*, 13–30. Detroit: Broadside Press.

1972b. "Toward a Definition: Black Poetry of the Sixties." In *The Black Aesthetic*, ed. Addison Gayle, Jr., 222–33. Garden City, N.Y.: Doubleday–Anchor.

Ed. 1970. *Dynamite Voices I: Black Poets of the 1960s*. Detroit: Broadside Press.

1987. *Say That the River Turns: The Impact of Gwendolyn Brooks*. Chicago: Third World Press.

Mailer, Norman. 1957. "The White Negro." In *The Portable Beat Reader*, ed. Ann Charters, 582–606. New York: Penguin Books, 1992.

1965. *An American Dream*. New York: Dell.

1968. *Miami and The Siege of Chicago: An Informal History of the Republican and Democratic Conventions of 1968*. New York: New American Library.

Major, Clarence. 1972. "The Explosion of Black Poetry." *The Dark and Feeling*, 33–45.

1974. *The Dark and Feeling: Black American Writers and Their Work*. New York: Third World Publishers.

Ed. 1969. *The New Black Poetry*. New York: International Publishers.

1996. *The Garden Thrives: Twentieth-Century African-American Poetry*. New York: Harper Perennial.

Malcolm X. 1965. *The Autobiography of Malcolm X*. Ed. Alex Haley. New York: Grove Press.

Marcus, Greil. 1976. "Review of Alice Walker's *Meridian*." In *Alice Walker*, ed. Henry Louis Gates, Jr., and K. A. Appiah, 11–15. New York: Amistad, 1993.

Mariani, Paul. 1981. *William Carlos Williams: A New World Naked*. New York: McGraw-Hill.

Markel, Lester. 1946. "The Newspapers." In *While You Were Gone*, ed. Jack Goodman, 335–73. New York: Simon and Schuster.

"Mars in the Nursery." 1935. *Fortune*, December: 28.

Martin, John Bartlow. 1950. "The Mecca: The Strangest Place in Chicago." *Harper's Magazine* 201 (December): 86–97.

Mather, Cotton. 1702. *Magnalia Christi Americana; Or, The Ecclesiastical History of New England, Books I and II*. Ed. Kenneth Murdock. Cambridge, Mass.: Harvard University Press, 1977.

Mayer, Harold M., and Richard C. Wade. 1969. *Chicago: Growth of a Metropolis.* Chicago: University of Chicago Press.

Mayer, Milton. 1944. "I Am a White Negro." *Negro Digest* 2.5: 21–3.

Mayfield, Julian. 1972. "You Touch My Black Aesthetic and I'll Touch Yours." In *The Black Aesthetic*, ed. Addison Gayle, Jr., 23–31. Garden City, N.Y.: Doubleday–Anchor.

Meacham, Harry M. 1967. *The Caged Panther: Ezra Pound at St. Elizabeths.* New York: Twayne.

"The Mecca: Chicago's Showiest Apartment Has Given Up All but the Ghost." 1951. *Life*, November 19: 133–9.

Meier, August. 1988. *Negro Thought in America, 1880–1915.* 2d ed. Ann Arbor: University of Michigan Press.

Meier, August, Elliott Rudwick, and Francis L. Broderick, eds. 1971. *Black Protest Thought in America.* Indianapolis: Bobbs-Merrill.

Melhem, D. H. 1987. *Gwendolyn Brooks: Poetry and the Heroic Voice.* Lexington: University of Kentucky Press.

Meltzer, Milton, ed. 1967. *In Their Own Words: A History of the American Negro, 1916–1966.* New York: Crowell.

The Millennium Breach. 1998. Washington, D.C.: The Milton S. Eisenhower Foundation.

Miller, R. Baxter. 1978. *Langston Hughes and Gwendolyn Brooks: A Reference Guide.* Boston, Mass.: G. K. Hall.

Mitchell, W. J. T., ed. 1981. *On Narrative.* Chicago: University of Chicago Press.

Moon, Bucklin. 1944. "Dixie Bottleneck." *Negro Digest.* 3.9: 59–60.

———. 1945. *Primer for White Folks.* Garden City, N.Y.: Doubleday.

Mootry, Maria K., and Gary Smith, eds. 1987. *A Life Distilled: Gwendolyn Brooks, Her Poetry and Fiction.* Urbana: University of Illinois Press.

Morrison, Toni, ed. 1992. *Race-ing, Justice, En-Gendering Power: Essays on Anita Hill, Clarence Thomas, and the Construction of Social Reality.* New York: Pantheon Books.

Moses, Wilson Jeremiah. 1978. *The Golden Age of Black Nationalism, 1950–1925.* New York: Oxford University Press.

———. 1989. *Alexander Crummell: A Study of Civilization and Discontent.* New York: Oxford University Press.

Mullen, Harryette. 1992. "'Phantom Pain': Nathaniel Mackey's *Bedouin Handbook.*" *Talisman* 9: 37–43.

Munger, Royal. 1942. "If I Were a Negro . . . I Should Be So Proud." *Negro Digest* 1.2: 48.

Mungo, Raymond. 1970. *Famous Long Ago: My Life and Hard Times with the Liberation News Service.* Boston: Beacon Press.

Murdock, Kenneth. 1977. Introduction. Cotton Mather, *Magnalia Christi Americana*, 1–48. Cambridge, Mass.: Harvard University Press.

Murray, Florence. 1945. "'The Negro and Civil Liberties during World War II." *Social Forces* 24: 211–16.

Myrdal, Gunnar, in collaboration with Richard Sterner and Arnold Rose. 1944. *An American Dilemma: The Negro Problem and American Democracy.* New York: Harper and Brothers.

1965. Introduction. Kenneth B. Clark, *Dark Ghetto: Dilemmas of Social Power*, ix–xi. New York: Harper Torchbooks, 1967.

Nadel, Alan. 1988. "Race, Rights, Gender, and Personal Narrative: The Archaeology of Self in *Meridian*." *Containment Culture: American Narratives, Postmodernism, and the Atomic Age*, 245–72. Durham, N.C.: Duke University Press, 1995.

Neal, Larry. 1972. "The Black Arts Movement." In *The Black Aesthetic*, ed. Addison Gayle, Jr., 257–74. Garden City, N.Y.: Doubleday–Anchor.

"The Negro Market: An Appraisal." 1947. *Tide*, March 7: 15–8.

"The Negro Press." 1944. *Tide*, September 1: 84–6.

Neihardt, John G., comp. 1932. *Black Elk Speaks: Being the Life Story of a Holy Man of the Oglala Sioux*. Lincoln: University of Nebraska Press, 1979.

The New Majority. 1919.

Nielsen, Aldon Lynn. 1988. *Reading Race: White American Poets and the Racial Discourse in the Twentieth Century*. Athens: University of Georgia Press.

1994. *Writing between the Lines: Race and Intertextuality*. Athens: University of Georgia Press.

1997. *Black Chant: Languages of African-American Modernism*. Cambridge: Cambridge University Press.

Nietzsche, Friedrich. 1980. *On the Advantage and Disadvantage of History for Life*. Trans. Peter Preuss. Indianapolis: Hackett.

Nora, Pierre. 1989. "Between Memory and History: *Les Lieux de Mémoire*." *Representations* 26 (Spring): 7–25.

North, Michael. 1994. *The Dialectic of Modernism: Race, Language, and Twentieth-Century Literature*. New York: Oxford University Press.

"'Now Is the Time Not to Be Silent.'" 1942. *The Crisis*, January: 7.

Oak, Vishnu V. 1948. *The Negro Newspaper*. Yellow Springs, Ohio: Antioch.

O'Brien, Kenneth Paul, and Lynn Hudson Parsons, eds. 1995. *The Home-Front War: World War II and American Society*. Westport, Conn.: Greenwood Press.

Odum, Howard W. 1943. *Race and Rumors of Race: Challenge to American Crisis*. Chapel Hill: University of North Carolina Press.

Ogburn, William Fielding, ed. 1943. *American Society in Wartime*. Chicago: University of Chicago Press.

Olney, James. 1989. "The Founding Fathers – Frederick Douglass and Booker T. Washington." In *Slavery and the Literary Imagination*, ed. Deborah E. McDowell and Arnold Rampersad, 1–24. Baltimore: Johns Hopkins University Press.

1990. "'I Was Born': Slave Narratives, Their Status as Autobiography and as Literature." In *The Slave's Narrative*, ed. Charles T. Davis and Henry Louis Gates, Jr., 148–75. New York: Oxford University Press.

O'Neill, William L. 1993. *A Democracy at War: America's Fight at Home and Abroad in World War II*. Cambridge, Mass.: Harvard University Press.

Ottley, Roi. 1942. "A White Folks' War?" *Common Ground*, Fall: 29.

1943a. "The Negro Press Today." *Common Ground*, Spring: 11–18.

1943b. *'New World A-Coming': Inside Black America*. Boston: Houghton, Mifflin.

1948. *Black Odyssey: The Story of the Negro in America*. New York: Scribner's.

1955. *The Lonely Warrior: The Life and Times of Robert S. Abbott.* Chicago: Henry Regnery.

Padmore, G. 1935. "Ethiopia and World Politics." *The Crisis*, May: 5.

Painter, Nell Irvin. 1996. *Sojourner Truth: A Life, a Symbol.* New York: W. W. Norton.

Park, Robert E. 1925. "The Natural History of the Newspaper." In *The City*, ed. Ernest W. Burgess, Robert E. Park, and Roderick D. McKenzie, 80–98. Chicago: University of Chicago Press, 1967.

1943. "Racial Ideologies." In *American Society in Wartime*, ed. William Fielding Ogburn, 165–84. Chicago: University of Chicago Press.

1950. *Race and Culture: Essays in the Sociology of Contemporary Man.* New York: Free Press–Macmillan.

Patterson, Orlando. 1982. *Slavery and Social Death: A Comparative Study.* Cambridge, Mass.: Harvard University Press.

Pease, Donald E. 1995. "National Identities, Postmodern Artifacts and Postnational Narratives." In *National Identities and Post Americanist Narratives*, ed. Donald E. Pease, 1–13. Durham, N.C.: Duke University Press.

1997. "National Narratives, Postnational Narration." *Modern Fiction Studies* 43 (Spring): 1–23.

Philpott, Thomas. 1978. *The Slum and the Ghetto: Neighborhood Deterioration and Middle-Class Reform, Chicago, 1880–1930.* New York: Oxford University Press.

Pierce, David H. 1935. "Fascism and the Negro." *The Crisis*, April.: 107, 114.

Pittsburgh Courier. 1935–7.

Place, Jeff. 1997. "Supplemental Notes on the Selections," 38–63. In *A Booklet of Essays, Appreciations, and Annotations Pertaining to the* Anthology of American Folk Music, ed. Harry Smith. Washington, D.C.: Smithsonian Folkways.

Polenberg, Richard. 1995. "World War II and the Bill of Rights." In *The Home-Front War*, ed. Kenneth O'Brien and Lynn Hudson Parsons, 11–24. Westport, Conn.: Greenwood Press.

Pollack, Channing. 1945. "Demonstrate Not Demand." *Negro Digest* 3.6: 55–6.

Pool, Rosey, ed. 1962. *Beyond the Blues: New Poems by American Negroes.* Lympne Hythe, Eng.: Hand and Flower Press.

Pound, Ezra. 1926. *Personae: The Shorter Poems of Ezra Pound*, ed. Lea Baechler and A. Walton Litz. New York: New Directions, 1990.

1933. "Murder by Capital." *Selected Prose 1909–1965*, 227–32.

1935a. *L'Italia Nostra.* December 27: n.p.

1935b. *Jefferson and/or Mussolini.* New York: Liveright, 1936.

1950. *The Letters of Ezra Pound, 1907–1941.* Ed. D. D. Paige. New York: Harcourt, Brace and World.

1960. *Impact: Essays on Ignorance and the Decline of American Civilization.* Ed. Noel Stock. Chicago: Henry Regnery.

1972. *The Cantos of Ezra Pound.* New York: New Directions, 1995.

1973. *Selected Prose, 1909–1965.* Ed. William Cookson. New York: New Directions.

1978. *"Ezra Pound Speaking" Radio Speeches of World War II.* Ed. Leonard W. Doob. Westport, Conn.: Greenwood Press.

1996. *Pound / Williams: Selected Letters of Ezra Pound and William Carlos Williams.*

Ed. Hugh Witemeyer. New York: New Directions.

Prattis, P. L. 1947. "Racial Segregation and Negro Journalism." *Phylon* 8: 305–14.

1950. "The Role of the Negro Press in Race Relations." *Phylon* 7: 273–83.

Pryse, Marjorie, and Hortense J. Spillers, eds. 1985. *Conjuring: Black Women, Fiction, and Literary Tradition.* Bloomington: Indiana University Press.

Race Relations: A Monthly Summary of Events and Trends. 1943–4.

Radway, Janice. 1984. "Interpretive Communities and Variable Literacies: The Functions of Romance Reading." *Daedalus* 113.3: 49–72.

Rainey, Lawrence. 1991. *Ezra Pound and the Monument of Culture: Text, History, and the Malatesta Cantos.* Chicago: University of Chicago Press.

Rampersad, Arnold. 1976. *The Art and Imagination of W. E. B. Du Bois.* New York: Schocken Books, 1990.

1986. *The Life of Langston Hughes.* Vol. 1, *I, Too, Sing America: 1902–1941.* New York: Oxford University Press.

1988. *The Life of Langston Hughes.* Vol. 2, *I Dream a World, 1941–1967.* New York: Oxford University Press.

Randall, Dudley. 1968. "An Answer to Don L. Lee's Review of Robert Hayden's *Kaleidoscope.*" *Negro Digest* 17.6: 94–6.

1969. "Black Poetry." In *Black Expression,* ed. Addison Gayle, Jr., 114. New York: Weybright and Tally.

Ed. 1971. *The Black Poets: A New Anthology.* New York: Bantam Books.

Randolph, A. Philip. 1942. "Pro-Japanese Activities among Negroes." *The Black Worker,* September: 4.

1944. "March on Washington Movement Presents Program for the Negro." In *What the Negro Wants,* ed. Rayford W. Logan, 133–62. Chapel Hill: University of North Carolina Press.

Rawls, John. 1971. *A Theory of Justice.* Cambridge, Mass.: Harvard University Press.

Redfield, Robert. 1943. "The Japanese-Americans." In *American Society in Wartime,* ed. William Fielding Ogburn, 143–64. Chicago: University of Chicago Press.

Redmond, Eugene B. 1976. *Drumvoices: The Mission of Afro-American Poetry: A Critical History.* Garden City, N.Y.: Doubleday–Anchor.

Reichley, A. James. 1968. "How John Johnson Made It." *Fortune,* January: 152–3, 178–80.

Review of Gwendolyn Brooks, *In the Mecca.* 1968. *Virginia Quarterly Review* 45 (Winter): 20.

Rich, Adrienne. 1978. "Disloyal to Civilization: Feminism, Racism, Gynephobia." *On Lies, Secrets, and Silence: Selected Prose, 1966–1978,* 275–310. New York: W. W. Norton, 1979.

1993. "History Stops for No One." *What Is Found There,* 128–44. New York: W. W. Norton.

Riffaterre, Michael. 1990. *Fictional Truth.* Baltimore: Johns Hopkins University Press.

Robinson, Edward G. 1945. "Accentuate the Positive." *Negro Digest* 3.11: 23–4.

Roosevelt, Eleanor. 1943a. "The Four Equalities. *Negro Digest* 1.11: 81–3.

1943b. "Freedom: Promise or Fact." *Negro Digest* 1.12: 8–9.

1945. "If You Ask Me." *Negro Digest* 3.4: 9–10.

Rosenthal, M. L. 1968. Review of Gwendolyn Brooks, *In the Mecca*. In *On Gwendolyn Brooks: Reliant Contemplation*, ed. Stephen Caldwell Wright, 27–8. Ann Arbor: University of Michigan Press, 1996.

Roses, Lorraine Elna, and Ruth Elizabeth Randolph. 1990. *Harlem Renaissance and Beyond: Biographies of 100 Black Women Writers, 1900–1945*. Boston: G. K. Hall.

Rowell, Charles H. 1983. "'The Unravelling of the Egg': An Interview with Jay Wright." *Callaloo* 6.3: 3–15.

Rukeyser, Muriel. 1957. *One Life*. New York: Simon and Schuster.

———. 1994. "Poem." In *A Muriel Rukeyser Reader*, ed. Jan Heller Levi, 211–12. New York: W. W. Norton.

Russell, Mariann. 1980. *Melvin B. Tolson's* Harlem Gallery: *A Literary Analysis*. Columbia: University of Missouri Press.

Ryan, Mary. 1989. "The American Parade: Representations of the Nineteenth-Century Social Order." In *The New Cultural History*, ed. Lynn Hunt, 131–53. Berkeley and Los Angeles: University of California Press.

Said, Edward. 1983. *The World, the Text, and the Critic*. Cambridge, Mass.: Harvard University Press.

———. 1993. *Culture and Imperialism*. New York: Alfred A. Knopf.

Sale, R. T. 1971. *The Blackstone Rangers: A Reporter's Account of Time Spent with Blackstone Rangers in Chicago's South Side*. New York: Random House.

Salwak, Dale. 1988. *Carl Sandburg: A Reference Guide*. Boston: G. K. Hall.

Sancton, Thomas. 1943. "Minority to Majority." *Negro Digest* 1.6: 49–50.

Sandburg, Carl. 1919. *The Chicago Race Riots, July 1919*. New York: Harcourt, Brace, and Howe.

———. 1922. *The American Songbag*. Boston: Schirmer Music.

———. 1936. *The People, Yes. The Complete Poems*, 439–617.

———. 1943. *Home Front Memo*. New York: Harcourt, Brace, and Company.

———. 1968. *The Letters of Carl Sandburg*. Ed. Herbert Mitgang. New York: Harcourt Brace Jovanovich.

———. 1970. *The Complete Poems of Carl Sandburg*. Intro. by Archibald MacLeish. San Diego, Calif.: Harcourt Brace Jovanovich.

Sandel, Michael, ed. 1984. *Liberalism and Its Critics*. New York: New York University Press.

Sartre, Jean-Paul. 1963. Preface. Frantz Fanon, *The Wretched of the Earth*. Trans. Constance Farrington, 7–34. New York: Grove Press.

Scarry, Elaine. 1985. *The Body in Pain: The Making and Unmaking of the World*. New York: Oxford University Press.

Schomburg, Arthur. 1925. "The Negro Digs Up His Past." In *The New Negro*, ed. Alain Locke, 231–7. New York: Atheneum, 1968.

Schuyler, George S. 1944. "The Caucasian Problem." In *What the Negro Wants*, ed. Rayford W. Logan, 281–98. Chapel Hill: University of North Carolina Press.

———. 1994. *Ethiopia Stories*. Boston: Northeastern University Press.

Scott, William R. 1993. *The Sons of Sheba's Race: African-Americans and the Italo-Ethiopian War, 1935–1941*. Bloomington: Indiana University Press.

Scott-Heron, Gil. 1970. "The Revolution Will Not Be Televised." *The Revolution*

Will Not Be Televised. RCA Victor–Bluebird Recording. Reissued as BMG 6994-2-RB, 1988.

Scruggs, Charles. 1993. *Sweet Home: Invisible Cities in the Afro-American Novel.* Baltimore: Johns Hopkins University Press.

Seldes, George. 1943. "Fascism: The First Enemy." *Negro Digest* 2.1: 51.

Sheil, Rt. Reverend Bernard J. 1943. "Eyes on the Future." *Negro Digest* 1.4: n.p.

Sherman, Lt. Col. John H. 1946. "Call for Uncle Tom." *Negro Digest* 4.11: 35–6.

Shi, David E. 1994. *Facing Facts: Realism in American Thought and Culture, 1850–1920.* New York: Oxford University Press.

Simpson, Louis. 1968. Review of Gwendolyn Brooks, *Selected Poems.* In *On Gwendolyn Brooks: Reliant Contemplation,* ed. Stephen Caldwell Wright, 23. Ann Arbor: University of Michigan Press, 1996.

Sitkoff, Harvard. 1978. *A New Deal for Blacks: The Emergence of Civil Rights as a National Issue: The Depression Decade.* New York: Oxford University Press, 1981.

Smith, David Lionel. 1994. "Chicago Poets, OBAC, and the Black Arts Movement." In *The Black Columbiad,* ed. Werner Sollors and Maria Diedrich, 253–64. Cambridge, Mass.: Harvard University Press.

Smith, Harry, ed. 1952. *Anthology of American Folk Music.* Folkways Recording. 6 CDs. Washington, D.C.: Smithsonian Folkways, 1997.

Sollors, Werner. 1986. *Beyond Ethnicity: Consent and Descent in American Culture.* New York: Oxford University Press.

——— 1994. "National Identity and Ethnic Diversity: 'Of Plymouth Rock and Jamestown and Ellis Island'; or, Ethnic Literature and Some Redefinitions of America." In *History and Memory in African-American Culture,* ed. Geneviève Fabre and Robert O'Meally, 92-121. New York: Oxford University Press.

Sollors, Werner, and Maria Diedrich, eds. 1994. *The Black Columbiad: Defining Moments in African American Literature and Culture.* Cambridge: Harvard University Press.

Sommer, Doris. 1991. *Foundational Fictions: The National Romances of Latin America.* Berkeley and Los Angeles: University of California Press.

Spear, Allan H. 1967. *Black Chicago: The Making of a Negro Ghetto, 1890–1920.* Chicago: University of Chicago Press.

Spengler, Oswald. 1926. *The Decline of the West,* ed. Helmut Werner. Trans. Charles Francis Atkinson. New York: Oxford University Press, 1991.

Spillers, Hortense. 1991. "Moving on Down the Line: Variations on the African-American Sermon." In *The Bounds of Race,* ed. Dominick LaCapra, 39–71. Ithaca: Cornell University Press.

Spingarn, Arthur B. 1943. "The Time Is NOW." *Negro Digest* 1.7: 51–2.

Spinner, Jeff. 1994. *The Boundaries of Citizenship: Race, Ethnicity, and Nationality in the Liberal State.* Baltimore: Johns Hopkins University Press.

Stafford, William. 1968. "Books That Look Out, Books That Look In." Review of Gwendolyn Brooks's *In the Mecca.* In *On Gwendolyn Brooks: Reliant Contemplation,* ed. Stephen Caldwell Wright, 26. Ann Arbor: University of Michigan Press, 1996.

Stansell, Christine. 1992. "White Feminists and Black Realities: The Politics of

Authenticity." In *Race-ing, Justice, En-Gendering Power*, ed. Toni Morrison, 251–68. New York: Pantheon Books.

Stavros, George. 1969. "Interview with Gwendolyn Brooks." In Gwendolyn Brooks, *Report from Part One*. 147–66. Detroit: Broadside Press, 1972.

Steel, Ronald. 1980. *Walter Lippmann and the American Century*. Boston: Little, Brown.

Stegner, Wallace. 1946. "The Common Cause of Color." *Negro Digest* 4.7: 59–60.

Stein, Gertrude. 1943. *Wars I Have Seen*. New York: Random House.

　　1945. *Brewsie and Willie*. New York: Random House.

Stein, Karen. 1986. "*Meridian*: Alice Walker's Critique of Revolution." *Black American Literature Forum* 20 (Spring/Summer): 129–41.

Steinberg, Michael P. 1996. "The Collector as Allegorist: Goods, Gods, and the Objects of History." *Walter Benjamin and the Demands of History*, 88–118.

　　Ed. 1996. *Walter Benjamin and the Demands of History*. Ithaca, N.Y.: Cornell University Press.

Stevens, Wallace. 1923/31. *Harmonium. Collected Poems*, 3–116.

　　1942. "Notes toward a Supreme Fiction." *Collected Poems*, 380–410.

　　1954. *The Collected Poems of Wallace Stevens*. New York: Alfred A. Knopf.

　　1966. *Letters of Wallace Stevens*. Ed. Holly Stevens. London: Faber and Faber.

　　1976. *Souvenirs and Prophecies: The Young Wallace Stevens*. Ed. Holly Stevens. New York: Alfred A. Knopf.

Stock, Noel. 1970. *The Life of Ezra Pound*. New York: Random House.

Stone, I. F. 1988. *The War Years, 1939–1945*. Boston: Little, Brown.

Strickland, Arvarh E. 1979. *History of the Chicago Urban League*. Urbana: University of Illinois Press.

Stuckey, Sterling. 1968. "Frank London Brown – A Remembrance." In *Black Voices: An Anthology of Afro-American Literature*, ed. Abraham Chapman, 669–76. New York: New American Library.

Sullivan, Patricia. 1996. *Days of Hope: Race and Democracy in the New Deal Era*. Chapel Hill: University of North Carolina Press.

Sundquist, Eric. J. 1990. Introduction. *Frederick Douglass: New Literary and Historical Essays*. Ed. Eric J. Sundquist. Cambridge: Cambridge University Press.

　　1993. *To Wake the Nations: Race in the Making of American Literature*. Cambridge, Mass.: Harvard University Press.

Takaki, Ronald T. 1972. *Violence in the Black Imaginations: Essays and Documents*. Rev. ed. New York: Oxford University Press.

Tally, Justine. 1994. "History, Fiction, and Community in the Work of Black American Women Writers from the Ends of Two Centuries." In *The Black Columbiad*, ed. Werner Sollors and Maria Diedrich, 357–68. Cambridge, Mass.: Harvard University Press.

Tate, Claudia. 1983. "Alice Walker." *Black Women Writers at Work*, 175–88. Harpenden, Eng.: Oldcastle Books, 1985.

　　1985. "Pauline Hopkins: Our Literary Foremother." In *Conjuring*, ed. Marjorie Pryse and Hortense J. Spillers, 53–66. Bloomington: Indiana University Press.

　　1989. "Allegories of Black Female Desire; Or, Rereading Nineteenth-Century

Sentimental Narratives of Black Female Authority." In *Changing Our Own Words*, ed. Cheryl Wall, 98–126. New Brunswick, N.J.: Rutgers University Press.

1992. *Domestic Allegories of Political Desire: The Black Heroine's Text at the Turn of the Century*. New York: Oxford University Press.

Taylor, Henry. 1991. "Gwendolyn Brooks: An Essential Sanity." *Kenyon Review* 13 (Fall): 115–31.

Terkel, Studs. 1967. *Division Street: America*. New York: Avon Books, 1968.

Thomas, Norman. 1944. "Too Proud for Bitterness." *Negro Digest* 3.1: 5–6.

Thompson, Robert Farris. 1983. *Flash of the Spirit: African and Afro-American Art and Philosophy*. New York: Random House.

Todorov, Tzvetan. 1971. *The Poetics of Prose*. Trans. Richard Howard. Ithaca, N.Y.: Cornell University Press.

Tolson, Melvin B. 1933. "Goodbye Christ." *Pittsburgh Courier*, January 26: 10–11.

1944. *Rendezvous with America*. New York: Dodd, Mead and Company.

1953. *Libretto for the Republic of Liberia*. New York: Twayne.

1965. *Harlem Gallery: Book I, The Curator*. Intro. by Karl Shapiro. New York: Twayne.

1979. *A Gallery of Harlem Portraits*. Ed. Robert M. Farnsworth. Columbia: University of Missouri Press.

1982. *Caviar and Cabbage: Selected Columns by Melvin B. Tolson from the* Washington Tribune, *1937–1944*. Ed. Robert Farnsworth. Columbia: University of Missouri Press.

Toomer, Jean. 1988. *The Collected Poems of Jean Toomer*. Ed. Robert B. Jones and Margery Toomer Latimer. Chapel Hill: University of North Carolina Press.

Torrey, E. Fuller. 1984. *The Roots of Treason: Ezra Pound and the Secrets of St Elizabeths*. London: Sidgwick and Jackson.

Tunis, John R. 1944. "Decalogue For Freedom." *Negro Digest* 2.9: 39–40.

Tupper, Eleanor, and George E. McReynolds. 1937. *Japan in American Public Opinion*. New York: Macmillan.

Turner, Victor. 1974. *Dramas, Fields, and Metaphors: Symbolic Action in Human Society*. Ithaca: Cornell University Press.

Tuttle, William M., Jr. 1970. *Race Riot: Chicago in the Red Summer of 1919*. New York: Atheneum.

United Nations Educational, Scientific, and Cultural Organization. 1952. *What Is Race? Evidence from Scientists*. Paris: UNESCO Paris.

United States Commission on Civil Rights (USCCR). 1963. *Freedom to the Free: Century of Emancipation, 1863–1963*. Washington, D.C.: U.S. Government Printing Office.

United States Riot Commission. 1968. *Report of the National Advisory Committee on Civil Disobedience*. New York: Bantam Books.

Van Deburg, William L. 1992. *New Day in Babylon: The Black Power Movement and American Culture, 1965–1975*. Chicago: University of Chicago Press.

Veeser, H. Aram, ed. 1989. *The New Historicism*. New York: Routledge.

Villard, Oswald Garrison. 1943. "No Time for Pessimism." *Negro Digest* 1.5: 9–11.

Vincent, Theodore G., ed. 1973. *Voices of a Black Nation: Political Journalism in the Harlem Renaissance*. Trenton, N.J.: Africa World Press, n.d.

Wacker, R. Fred. 1976. "An American Dilemma: The Racial Theories of Robert E. Park and Gunnar Myrdal." *Phylon* 37 (Summer): 117–25.

Walker, Alice. 1970a. "The Black Writer and the Southern Experience." *In Search of Our Mothers' Gardens*, 15–21.

　　1970b. "'But Yet and Still the Cotton Gin Kept on Working. . . .'" *In Search of Our Mothers' Gardens*, 22–32.

　　1970c. "The Unglamorous but Worthwhile Duties of the Black Revolutionary Artist, Or of the Black Writer Who Simply Works and Writes." *In Search of Our Mothers' Gardens*, 130–8.

　　1973. *In Love and Trouble: Stories of Black Women*. San Diego, Calif.: Harcourt Brace Jovanovich.

　　1975a. "Beyond the Peacock: The Reconstruction of Flannery O'Connor." *In Search of Our Mother's Gardens*, 42–59.

　　1975b. "Looking for Zora." *In Search of Our Mothers' Gardens*, 93–118.

　　1976a. *Meridian*. San Diego, Calif.: Harcourt Brace Jovanovich.

　　1976b. "Recording the Seasons." *In Search of Our Mothers' Gardens*, 223–30.

　　1981. *You Can't Keep a Good Woman Down*. San Diego, Calif.: Harcourt Brace Jovanovich.

　　1982. *The Color Purple*. San Diego, Calif: Harcourt Brace Jovanovich.

　　1983. *In Search of Our Mothers' Gardens: Womanist Prose*. San Diego, Calif.: Harcourt Brace Jovanovich.

　　1997. "Clear Seeing Inherited Religion and Reclaiming the Pagan Self." *On the Issues* 6 (Spring): 16–23, 54–5.

Walker, Melissa. 1991. *Down from the Mountaintop: Black Women's Novels in the Wake of the Civil Rights Movement*. New Haven, Conn.: Yale University Press.

Wall, Cheryl A., ed. 1989. *Changing Our Own Words: Essays on Criticism, Theory, and Writing by Black Women*. New Brunswick, N.J.: Rutgers University Press.

Wallace, Emily Mitchell. 1968. *A Bibliography of William Carlos Williams*. Middletown, Conn.: Wesleyan University Press.

Washburn, Patrick. 1986. *A Question of Sedition: The Federal Government's Investigation of a Black Press during World War II*. New York: Oxford University Press.

Washington, Booker T. 1900. *The Story of My Life and Work*. New York: Negro Universities, 1969.

　　1901. *Up from Slavery*. New York: Penguin Books, 1986.

Washington, Mary Helen. 1979. "An Essay on Alice Walker." In *Alice Walker*, ed. Henry Louis Gates, Jr., and K. A. Appiah, 37–49. New York: Amistad, 1993.

　　Ed. 1991. *Memory of Kin: Stories about Family by Black Writers*. Garden City, N.Y.: Doubleday–Anchor.

Washington Tribune, 1937–44.

Waskow, Arthur I. 1966. *From Race Riot to Sit-In, 1919 and the 1960s: A Study in the Connections between Conflict and Violence*. Garden City, N.Y.: Doubleday–Anchor.

Watson, Mary Ann. 1990. *The Expanding Vista: American Television in the Kennedy Years*. New York: Oxford University Press.

Ways, Max. 1968. "The Deeper Shame of the Cities." *Fortune*, January: 132–5.

Weisbord, Robert G. 1970. "British West Indian Reaction to the Italo-Ethiopian

War: An Episode in Pan-Africanism." *Caribbean Studies* 10.1: 34–41.

1972. "Black American and the Italian-Ethiopian Crisis: An Episode in Pan-Negroism." *Historian* 34:2: 230–41.

Weiss, M. Lynn. 1994. "Para Usted: Richard Wright's *Pagan Spain.*" In *Black Columbiad*, ed. Werner Sollors and Maria Diedrich, 212–25. Cambridge, Mass.: Harvard University Press.

Wellburn, Ron. 1972. "The Black Aesthetic Imperative." In *The Black Aesthetic*, ed. Addison Gayle, Jr., 126–42. Garden City, N.Y.: Doubleday–Anchor.

Welles, Orson. 1944. "Danger! Race Hate at Large!" *Negro Digest* 2.10: 14.

Wendt, Lloyd. 1979. Chicago Tribune: *The Rise of a Great American Newspaper.* Chicago: Rand McNally.

Wesley, Charles H. 1944. "The Negro Has Always Wanted the Four Freedoms." In *What the Negro Wants*, ed. Rayford W. Logan, 90–112. Chapel Hill: University of North Carolina Press.

West, Cornel. 1989. *The American Evasion of Philosophy: A Genealogy of Pragmatism.* Madison: University of Wisconsin Press.

1992a. "Black Leadership and the Pitfalls of Racial Reasoning." In *Race-ing, Justice, En-Gendering Power*, ed. Toni Morrison, 390–401. New York: Pantheon Books.

1992b. "Learning to Talk of Race." *New York Times Magazine*, August 2: 24ff.

White, Hayden. 1973. *Metahistory: The Historical Imagination in Nineteenth-Century Europe.* Baltimore: Johns Hopkins University Press.

1978. *Tropics of Discourse: Essays in Cultural Criticism.* Baltimore: Johns Hopkins University Press.

1981. "The Value of Narrativity in the Representation of Reality." In *On Narrative*, ed. W. J. T. Mitchell, 1–24. Chicago: University of Chicago Press.

1987a. *The Content of the Form: Narrative Discourse and Historical Representation.* Baltimore: Johns Hopkins University Press.

1987b. "The Metaphysics of Narrativity: Time and Symbol in Ricoeur's Philosophy of History." *The Content of the Form*, 169–84.

Whitman, Ruth. 1971. Preface. In Sam Cornish, *Generations*, ix–x. Boston: Beacon Press.

Wilkerson, Doxey A. 1944. "Freedom – Through Victory in War and Peace." In *What the Negro Wants*, ed. Rayford W. Logan, 193–216. Chapel Hill: University of North Carolina Press.

1947. "The Negro Press." *The Journal of Negro Education* 16: 511–21.

Wilkins, Roy. 1935. "Huey Long Talks on Negroes." *The Crisis*, February: n.p.

1944. "The Negro Wants Full Equality." In *What the Negro Wants*, ed. Rayford W. Logan, 113–32. Chapel Hill: University of North Carolina Press.

Williams, John A., ed. 1962. *The Angry Black.* New York: Lancer Books.

Williams, John A., and Charles F. Harris, eds. 1970. *Amistad 1.* New York: Random House–Vintage.

Williams, Kenny J. 1987. "The World of Satin Legs, Mrs. Sallie, and the Blackstone Rangers: The Restricted Chicago of Gwendolyn Brooks." In *A Life Distilled*, ed. Maria K. Mootry and Gary Smith, 47–70. Urbana: University of Illinois Press.

Williams, Patricia J. 1991. *The Alchemy of Race and Rights: Diary of a Law Professor.*
Cambridge, Mass.: Harvard University Press.

1995. *The Rooster's Egg: On the Persistence of Prejudice.* Cambridge, Mass.: Harvard University Press.

Williams, Sherley Anne. 1978. "The Blues Roots of Contemporary Afro-American Poetry." In *Afro-American Literature: The Reconstruction of Instruction,* ed. Dexter Fisher and Robert B. Stepto, 72–87. New York: MLA, 1979.

1982. "Letters from a New England Negro." *Some One Sweet Angel Chile,* 11–38. New York: William Morrow.

Williams, William Carlos. 1935. Review of Ezra Pound's *Jefferson and/or Mussolini. New Democracy,* October 15: 61–2.

1939. Review Ezra Pound's *Guide to Kulchur. New Republic,* June 28: xcix, 229–30.

1996. *Pound / Williams: Selected Letters of Ezra Pound and William Carlos Williams.* Ed. Hugh Witemeyer. New York: New Directions.

Wilson, Edmund. 1969. *Axel's Castle: A Study in the Imaginative Literature of 1870–1930.* New York: Scribner's.

Witcover, Jules. 1997. *The Year the Dream Died: Revisiting 1968 America.* New York: Warner Books.

Wohlfarth, Irving. 1996. "Smashing the Kaleidoscope: Walter Benjamin's Critique of Cultural History." In *Walter Benjamin and the Demands of History,* ed. Michael P. Steinberg, 190–205. Ithaca, N.Y.: Cornell University Press.

Wolin, Sheldon S. 1989. *The Presence of the Past: Essays on the State and the Constitution.* Baltimore: Johns Hopkins University Press.

Wolseley, Roland E. 1990. *The Black Press, USA.* Foreword by Robert E. Johnson. 2d ed. Ames: Iowa State University Press.

Woodson, Jon. 1985. "Sam Cornish." *Dictionary of Literary Biography: Afro-American Poets since 1955,* 41: 64–9. Detroit: Gale Publishing.

1986. "Melvin Tolson and the Art of Being Difficult." In *Black American Poets between Worlds, 1940–1960,* ed. R. Baxter Miller, 19–42. Knoxville: University of Tennessee Press.

1997. "To Make a New Race: Jean Toomer, G. I. Gurdjieff, and the Harlem Renaissance." Unpublished MS.

Wright, Jay. 1967. "Death as History." In *Death as History,* n.p. New York: Poets Press.

1971. *The Homecoming Singer.* New York: Corinth Books.

1976a. *Dimensions of History.* Santa Cruz, Calif.: Kayak.

1976b. *Soothsayers and Omens.* New York: Seven Woods Press.

1987a. "Desire's Design, Vision's Resonance: Black Poetry's Ritual and Historical Voice." *Callaloo* 10.1: 13–28.

1987b. *Selected Poems.* Ed. Robert Stepto. Princeton, N.J.: Princeton University Press.

1988. *Boleros.* Princeton, N.J.: Princeton University Press.

Wright, Richard. 1937. *Black Boy.* New York: Harper and Brothers.

1941. *Twelve Million Black Voices: A Folk History of the Negro in the United States.* Photo direction Edwin Rosskam. New York: Viking Press.

1957. *Pagan Spain*. New York: Harper and Brothers.

1977. *American Hunger*. New York: Harper and Brothers.

Wright, Stephen Caldwell, ed. 1996. *On Gwendolyn Brooks: Reliant Contemplation*. Ann Arbor: University of Michigan Press.

"Your History." 1936. *Pittsburgh Courier*, May 4, sec. 2: 2.

Zara, Louis. 1946. "Coming Days of Glory." *Negro Digest* 4.3: 37–8.

Zinn, Howard. 1990. *Declarations of Independence: Cross-Examining American Ideology*. New York: Harper Collins, 1991.

INDEX

286

House, Eddie "Son," 218n17
"How Many Times?" (Tolson), 59
Howe, Irving, 231–2n10
Huggins, Willis N., 44
Hughes, Langston, xvi, xviii, 57, 70,
84, 85, 91, 94, 126, 218n15,
219n18, 221n9, 228n41; "Air
Raid Over Harlem," 83; "Call of
Ethiopia," 83; on citizenship,
222n17, 227n39, 231n9; influ-
ence upon Tolson, 59, 61, 63; on
Italo-Ethiopian War, 65, 83; "Let
America Be America Again,"
xviii, 63, 83, 227n39
Hurst, Fanny, 111
Hurston, Zora Neale, 59, 112,
220n4
Hutchinson, George, xviii
Hutton, Bobby, 161

"I Am a White Negro" (ND, Mayer),
106
"I Am the World's Oldest Father"
(ND), 116
"I Looked & Saw History Caught"
(Spellman), 143
"I Should Be So Proud" (Mungar),
97
"I Wouldn't Forget" (ND, Benedict),
104
"Idols of the Tribe, The" (Tolson),
82
"If I Were a Negro" (ND), 81, 94, 95,
97–8, 116, 210; audience for, 96;
design, 96, 99; race politics at,
93, 231n8; solicitation of colum-
nists, 97, 99–100, 231n8; see also
titles of individual columns and
columnists
"If I Were Young Again" (ND), xxi, 96
"If You Ask Me" (E. Roosevelt), 104
Ignatiev, Noel, 217n13
Il Giornale d'Italia, 69
Il Progresso Italo–Americano, 66
Illinois Institute of Technology, 123,
130, 234n6

"In the Mecca" (Brooks), 114, 119,
128–41, 143, 239n26
In Search of the Miraculous (Ouspensky), 220n4
Incidents in the Life of a Slave Girl
(Jacobs), 19
Interracial Review, 226n35
interracialism, 81, 91, 92, 95,
226n35
Irish Americans: and race relations,
34, 41, 42, 51, 216–7n11,
217–18n13, 236–7n13
Isaacs, Reginald, 123
"It Is Everywhere" (Toomer),
246n10
Italo-Ethiopian War, 65, 67, 69,
83–4, 222n15, 224n24

Jackson, George, 174
Jackson, Mahalia, 139
Jackson, Walter, 232n11
Jacobs, Harriet, 19, 213n7
James, William, 213n4
Jameson, Frederic, 128, 248n22
Japanese Americans, 92; and the
wartime relocation, 95, 110,
230n5
"Jason Visits His Gypsy" (J. Wright),
202
Jefferson, Thomas, xiii, 68, 71, 77,
80, 82, 84, 194, 197, 198, 209,
211n2, 225n29, 226–7n36,
228n1
Jet (Chicago), 115, 117, 248n24
Jewett, Sarah Orne, 249n25
Johnson, Barbara, 162
Johnson, Charles S., xvii, 29, 47; on
Chicago, 30; and Chicago Com-
mission on Race Relations, 29,
47, 53–5, 220n24; on Great
Migration, 33, 216n9; and Sandburg, 49
Johnson, James Weldon, xiii, 37,
220n23; on literacy and independence, 31; on newspapers, 31,
216n7

Acknowledgments

Page ix: The epigraph is an excerpt from "White Man's Guilt" by James Baldwin. Excerpted from "White Man's Guilt," orginally published in *Ebony Magazine.* Collected in *The Price of the Ticket*, published by St. Martin's Press. Reprinted by arrangement with the James Baldwin Estate.

Page 1: The second epigraph is an excerpt from *After Strange Gods* by T. S. Eliot. Excerpted from *After Strange Gods: A Primer of Modern Heresy* (The Page–Barbour Lectures at the University of VA, 1933), by T. S. Eliot. Copyright © 1934, published by Harcourt, Brace & Company. Reprinted by permission. This material also appeared in "Tradition and the Individual Talent," *Selected Essays* by T. S. Eliot. Copyright © 1951, published by Faber and Faber. Reprinted by permission.

Page 25: The second epigraph is an excerpt from *The Evidence of Things Not Seen* by James Baldwin, copyright © 1985 by The Estate of James Baldwin. Reprinted by permission of Henry Holt & Co., Inc.

Page 117: "Langston Variations 1955" by Sam Cornish. Copyright © 1996 by Sam Cornish. From *Cross a Parted Sea*, published by Zoland Books, Cambridge, Massachusetts. Reprinted by permission.

Chapter 6: All excerpted material attributed to Sam Cornish is from *Generations* by Sam Cornish. Copyright © 1971, published by Beacon Press. Reprinted by permission of Sam Cornish.

Chapter 8: All excerpted material attributed to Jay Wright is from *Soothsayers and Omens* by Jay Wright. Copyright © 1976, published by Seven Woods Press. Reprinted by permission of Jay Wright.

And finally, I would like to thank John H. Johnson, chairman and CEO of the Johnson Publishing Company and the publisher of *Ebony* magazine, for taking time out of his busy schedule to discuss and ultimately encourage this version of his *Negro Digest.*